DISCRIMINATION IN EMPLOYMENT

IN ONTARIO

DISCRIMINATION
IN
EMPLOYMENT
IN ONTARIO

Brian A. Grosman

AND

John R. Martin

CANADA LAW BOOK INC.
240 Edward Street, Aurora, Ontario

Canadian Cataloguing in Publication Data

Grosman, Brian A., 1935—
    Discrimination in employment in Ontario

Includes index.
ISBN 0-88804-151-9

1. Discrimination in employment — Law and legislation —
Ontario.   I. Martin, John R. (John Richard), 1959—
II. Title.

KEO659.G76 1994   344.713'01133   C94-931560-5
KF3464.G76 1994

Preface

It was not so long ago that employment and discrimination law were discrete areas without frequent interface. That is no longer so. Lawyers cannot advise clients with regard to employment rights and responsibilities without a careful consideration of the legislation relating to discrimination. Similarly, most cases of discrimination arise in the workplace. Lawyers dealing with matters of discrimination must become versed in the principles of employment law. In our law firm of Grosman, Grosman & Gale, we regularly deal with issues of employment that touch upon areas of discrimination. This is happening with increasing frequency as the public is made aware by the media and government of their employment and human rights.

As a result of this growing legal interactivity, we believe that there is a need for this publication. In this one volume, we attempt a comprehensive review of laws relating both to employment and discrimination. As well, the linkages between the two are explored. The legislative underpinning of these areas of the law are set out in some detail including relevant legislative and policy provisions which are contained in the appendices.

It is always difficult to take the time from a busy law practice to prepare a book of this kind. The authors were fortunate to have understanding partners and wives as well as an excellent support staff. In particular, we wish to thank Terry Vandervoort, who typed the manuscript. Ms. Jennifer Wootton Regan provided us with timely and thorough research. We also wish to thank J. Geoffrey Howard, formerly of our law firm, for his contribution to the chapter dealing with employment and pay equity. Mr. Justice Walter Tarnopolsky encouraged us to write this book. His untimely death has saddened all those involved in the pursuit of human rights in Canada.

Introduction

Today, more than ever, we are our work. Employment provides personal identification, status and a sense of worth in a turbulent time when family, church and institutions are less able to sustain a sense of identity. The inability to obtain a job or the loss of a job cannot be adequately compensated financially. The loss of status, security, property or the psychological impact of being unemployed at a time when there are few opportunities for immediate re-employment can only be really understood by those who have suffered the trauma. To be out of work is to be out of pride.

The inability to obtain employment because of discriminatory practices or the loss of employment because of discrimination is doubly difficult. Employment is not a purely contractual relationship in the commercial sense of the word. It is a relationship based on shared responsibilities between employers and employees. It is a dynamic relationship. Today it is character-ized by an ever-changing cultural diversity where employers and employment policies must become more flexible and where North American codes of behaviour and rules of conduct need to adjust to new cultural priorities.

In 1962, Ontario took the lead in Canada by enacting human rights leg-islation which for the first time in the province, and in Canada, attempted to provide a comprehensive code to regulate relations and to sensitize the com-munity to the need to accommodate a diverse and dynamic population. Anti-discrimination laws and their enforcement only became a reality in the 1960s. In any historical context, these laws are in their infancy.

Similarly, employment law was virtually unknown in Canada until the early 60s when a number of cases separated issues of employment from general concepts of labour law. It was not until 1969 that a court in Ontario decided that damages for mental distress could be ordered in a wrongful dismissal lawsuit thereby taking such cases out of the narrow confines of commercial contracts into a new field of tort and contract which continues to define the developing area of employment law.

The coalescence of discrimination law and employment law has not been adequately understood because both are in an evolutionary stage relying heav-ily on recent policy and community criteria rather than on traditional juris-prudence and historical precedent.

Both discrimination and employment law spring from a communal sense that there is a compelling need to protect the interests of individuals who are subject to the unregulated commercial control of others. The courts and human rights tribunals have pursued a liberal and broad approach to the construction of human rights and employment legislation in order to protect the individual's interests over those of the more traditional elements in society. The courts and the legislature, when dealing with employment and discrimination laws, have been pro-active and remedial in their activities quite unlike their application of commercial and corporate law which, for the most part, is restrictive and cautious.

No area of the law is more vital to the preservation of individual rights than the law of discrimination and employment. At the same time, the interplay between these two fundamental legal concepts has not been adequately understood by those who do not specialize in this field. Thus, we felt that a text dealing primarily with legislation, written policy and case law would help to clarify the interrelationship and the evolution of these important and growing areas of legal protection.

Law is a crude instrument aimed at limiting and censuring that which is unacceptable to Canadian society. It is an attempt to draw a line in the shifting sands of political policy and to mobilize the state's instruments of investigation, prosecution and adjudication in order to proclaim and enforce the principles propounded by the legislature that reflect communal priorities. Much of this interpretation takes place outside traditional courts which are to remain dispassionate and above the fray. Implementation of discrimination laws in Ontario is quite often initiated by persons who have a substantial commitment to the area of human rights and by members of tribunals who share that commitment.

Accordingly, decisions are not based so much on continuity and precedent but on the need to remedy a particular situation in light of the policies and regulations which continue to evolve with each new situation. This is an area of law and public policy which is supersensitive to public opinion, often made up of vocal elements of the community, who attempt to shift, on a case-by-case basis, attitudes and priorities of the decision-making tribunals. As a result, it is much more difficult to ascertain trends beyond single instances. A growing number of activities are sanctioned by decision-makers in the ever-expanding concept of discrimination. This is indeed a growth industry aimed at protecting important and changing values that deserve the protection of the law.

Emotions run high in the area of discrimination on both sides of the argument. There are those who feel the laws and their implementors have gone much too far by placing issues of fairness and equity above those of competence. Others feel we have a long way to go before people are treated fairly in the Canadian employment environment. We have attempted to avoid value judgments or editorial comment on the values protected and the manner in which those protections are enforced. Similarly, we do not engage in a social or political critique of the decisions made by tribunals or courts but rather attempt to outline and explain the nature of the process and clarify the rationale for the decisions.

The book is aimed at increasing understanding of the laws that govern conduct considered discriminatory in the employment context. Any book of this nature must be limited to a snapshot of the legal situation at a particular time and place. This is so because the laws in this area are evolving quickly and are taking such interesting directions that any attempt at a comprehensive picture of the legal and legislative situation is bound to be obsolete within a very short time. In any legal process subject to rapid expansion, there will be a certain artificiality as legislative commands and case law do not accurately reflect day-to-day implementation. It is important to remain sensitive to the evolutionary nature of this area of the law which is based, more than any other, on administrative decisions by committed persons about policies and regulations that are deemed appropriate today and yet may be considered inappropriate tomorrow.

Laws on discrimination in employment, like employment law itself, are primarily creatures of recent vintage. Thus, the depth of case law by which to trace its evolution is lacking. There is a plethora of single instances of interpretation of particular sections of the legislation. Accordingly, it is impossible to describe the continuity of thinking and decision-making in many areas since these decisions are so fresh. The ink is hardly dry on some legislation and other important pieces of legislation have yet to be implemented. Thus, a case may be included in the text not because it is the leading case on the particular subject but because it is the only case.

Because of the changing nature of laws, policies and regulations in this area, it is important to obtain competent legal advice before venturing into the field and making decisions which may impact on individuals or business. A book of this kind does not review in detail practical issues of process which may be particular to a local jurisdiction. In this area, day-to-day implementation is based primarily on evolving experience with approaches which cannot be easily reproduced on the pages of this book. We attempt to provide guidelines for action and increased sensitivity to issues which might otherwise go unrecognized and create troublesome and costly situations. To be forewarned is to be forearmed particularly in this complex area of law and human relations. What we do not provide is legal advice, but such advice may become critical if problems are to be avoided or to be dealt with within the law and regulations in a careful and cost-efficient manner. The book, in a sense, provides an early warning system so that the reader is better able to determine when legal advice is appropriate.

Human rights disputes can be lengthy and costly in terms of the process of resolving the dispute, the time taken from work-related roles, the negative impact upon the individual and general employee motivation and morale. Good advice taken at an early stage may save both employers and employees from an adversarial confrontation which may not be in their interest.

The adversarial application of the law is the last resort in a system which is aimed at avoiding confrontation and the limitations of the adversary system. Nonetheless, important directions are the product of legal decisions. These decisions confirm some approaches and deny others. Courts and tribunals, by their careful consideration of fact situations, enhance human rights in the province and limit those who would exercise power over individuals without restraint. There are many more settlements than there are cases heard by tribunals. These settlements set important precedents many of which are reported in the news media. It is beyond the scope of this book to discuss settlements and arrangements entered into by human rights commissions and employers or employees that are not reported either by the commissions themselves, the tribunals or the courts. Many settlements and arrangements are based both on earlier decisions of the tribunals and the approach taken by the courts to controversial issues. The principles enunciated by courts and tribunals act as important beacons to those who might otherwise have greater difficulty applying concepts to new fact situations, and finding their way through the legislative maze.

Legislative mandates, no matter how positive their intent, depend upon individual and institutional commitment for their viability. No other area of the law seems so dependent on legislation, regulations and policy statements as does human rights anti-discrimination law. Law itself, no matter how detailed, does not lead to conformity to principle unless there is a broad acceptance of these principles by those who have to work with them. If employees feel human rights legislation does not serve their purpose or employers feel it is unnecessarily onerous, the legislation itself and even the commitment of its administrators will not lead to high levels of co-operation and conflict resolution. Quite the contrary, legislation that is perceived as over or under-kill inevitably leads to conflict and confrontations. That is why human rights legislation generally has been seen as an educational tool aimed at sensitizing both employers and employees to the important role of human rights in all social, political and work-related settings.

Even today, in Canada, those concerned with human rights continue to struggle against bureaucracy and traditional attitudes in order to bring day-to-day practice into line with legislative pronouncements. As society evolves, so will legislation. Each stage of that evolution will require significant re-education. That is currently the case in the areas of sexual harassment, AIDS-related discrimination and the rights of same sex couples, to name only three high-profile issues commanding significant levels of public concern and media attention. In a modest way, it is hoped *Discrimination In Employment In Ontario* assists in that educational process.

Like much of employment and human rights legislation, the aim of the book is to be pro-active and to educate readers so that they become more aware of the issues and are better able to adjust practices to legislative priorities. The better these issues are understood, the more likely that they will be resolved without difficulty. This comprehensive review of the legislation, regulations and court decisions will better enable those who are impacted by these decisions to take a positive approach to the problems faced by every employer and employee in this rapidly evolving area of the law. Human rights codes provide access to a process to resolve disputes by way of the promotion of policies of non-discrimination and rulings to support such policies when they become necessary.

The chapters in this book, for the most part, begin at the pre-hiring stage and end at the post-hiring stage so that the reader is able to follow the application of employment and discrimination laws from the earliest to the last stages of employment. The goal is to survey all the applicable laws and regulations which impact on the employer/employee relationship from the very early stages until the relationship has ended.

Since legislation is a key element in this area of the law, we begin with a discussion of jurisdiction in order that the reader is aware of whether federal or provincial human rights legislation is applicable in the particular situation. We then outline concepts of discrimination. There are three fundamental types of discrimination: direct discrimination; constructive or adverse effect discrimination; and reverse discrimination or affirmative action. We begin by looking at the application of these concepts in a pre-employment or hiring setting. That takes us to the consideration of the prohibited grounds of discrimination within the employment relationship. We deal separately with sexual harassment and AIDS discrimination because of the current importance of these issues. We also consider at some length the important duty to accommodate on the part of the employer. Such a duty, in certain respects, represents a defence to employers charged with discrimination in the workplace. *Bona fide* occupational qualification becomes an important issue particularly with respect to AIDS discrimination in the overall concept of the duty to accommodate.

Liability of employers for acts of employees and how far that liability extends is considered in the context of the personal liability of directors, officers and co-employees as well as the liability of unions to offences under the provisions of human rights legislation. We review the complaint process of filing, investigating and conciliating a complaint. Procedural differences between Ontario and the *Canadian Human Rights Act* are pointed out. We review the hearing process by examining the composition of the tribunal, procedures utilized before the tribunal including rules of evidence, onus and burden of proof, the appeal process and the concept of judicial review. The chapter on remedies deals with legislative provisions which are wide-ranging and provide for damages, mental anguish, reinstatement, and types of orders made against employers extending beyond the particular complaint of an individual. The subject of costs, penalties and fines that can be imposed by the legislation is reviewed. Whether civil actions are available and whether one can continue with both a human rights complaint and civil action dealing with the same subject matter at the same time is also considered.

Part of the last chapter is a review of recent legislation in the pay equity and employment equity field. This new legislation provides a prime example of the fluid and ever-developing nature of law and policy in this area. Most of this legislation, both federal and provincial, which attempts to address inequities in the employment relationship particularly as it impacts on women and visible minorities, is in its infancy. There are few reported decisions and the impact of this legislation upon employers remains, for the most part, speculative and developing.

We felt it was important to include certain schedules for easy reference. In this respect, the Ontario *Human Rights Code*, the *Canadian Human Rights Act* and various key policy rulings made by the Ontario Human Rights Commission are included as a supplement. Also included is an approved form for an employment interview and a written job application prepared by the Ontario Human Rights Commission.

This book is meant to provide, in one text, access to legislation, regulation and policies as clarified by the interpretation of courts and tribunals in Ontario. *Discrimination in Employment in Ontario* aims at heightening awareness of the parties involved in a difficult situation so that the process is better understood and accordingly made more humane.

Brian A. Grosman, Q.C., B.A., LL.B., LL.M.
May, 1994.

Table of Contents

Table of Cases

CHAPTER 1 | *Jurisdiction*

1. FEDERAL VS. PROVINCIAL JURISDICTION

A. Introduction

The very first step in determining the legal principles or rules which apply to an employment-related issue of discrimination involves the subject of jurisdiction. Does the employer in question fall under federal or provincial jurisdiction with respect to anti-discrimination laws? The answer to this preliminary issue is critical, since it will then determine whether the provisions of the Ontario *Human Rights Code*,[1] alone, will govern or whether the combined provisions of the *Canadian Human Rights Act*[2] and the *Canada Labour Code*[3] represent the applicable anti-discrimination legislation.

Generally speaking, laws prohibiting discrimination within the employment relationship fall within provincial jurisdiction. However, the exceptions to the general rule of provincial jurisdiction are, in many instances, difficult to discern. In addition, it is possible that a corporation engaged in multiple businesses and services, can have different aspects of its operations subject to different governing jurisdictions.

While in many cases the answer to the question of jurisdiction will be obvious, the significance of the issue dictates that it be carefully considered by every employer as a necessary pre-condition in addressing any potential human rights matter.

B. Constitution Act, 1867

The Canadian Constitution is the supreme law of Canada and provides for the distribution of authority, legislative and otherwise, between the provinces and the federal government. Sections 91 and 92 of the Constitution set out the primary division of legislative authority between the provinces and the federal government.

---

[1] R.S.O. 1990, c. H.19, as amended.
[2] R.S.C. 1985, c. H-6, as amended.
[3] R.S.C. 1985, c. L-2, as amended.

The Constitution does not confer jurisdiction on either the provinces or federal parliament in relation to "discrimination" or "anti-discrimination" or "equality of access". Nor does the Constitution expressly confer jurisdiction in employment matters on either the provinces or the federal government. Accordingly, the courts have been required, on a number of occasions from the time of Confederation, to establish the boundaries between federal and provincial jurisdiction in this area.

(i) Division of powers under sections 91 and 92

Sections 91 and 92 of the *Constitution Act, 1867*, set out the primary division of legislative authority between the federal government and the provinces, respectively.

Section 91 of the *Constitution Act, 1867*, confers exclusive legislative jurisdiction upon federal parliament in the following areas:

1. The Public Debt and Property.
2. The Regulation of Trade and Commerce.
2A. Unemployment insurance.
3. The raising of Money by any Mode or System of Taxation.
4. The borrowing of Money on the Public Credit.
5. Postal Service.
6. The Census and Statistics.
7. Militia, Military and Naval Service, and Defence.
8. The fixing of and providing for the Salaries and Allowances of Civil and other Officers of the Government of Canada.
9. Beacons, Buoys, Lighthouses, and Sable Island.
10. Navigation and Shipping.
11. Quarantine and the Establishment and Maintenance of Marine Hospitals.
12. Sea Coast and Inland Fisheries.
13. Ferries between a Province and any British or Foreign Country or between Two Provinces.
14. Currency and Coinage.
15. Banking, Incorporation of Banks, and the Issue of Paper Money.
16. Savings Banks.
17. Weights and Measures.
18. Bills of Exchange and Promissory Notes.
19. Interest.
20. Legal Tender.
21. Bankruptcy and Insolvency.
22. Patents of Invention and Discovery.
23. Copyrights.
24. Indians, and Lands reserved for the Indians.
25. Naturalization and Aliens.
26. Marriage and Divorce.
27. The Criminal Law, except the Constitution of Courts of Criminal Jurisdiction, but including the Procedure in Criminal Matters.
28. The Establishment, Maintenance, and Management of Penitentiaries.
29. Such Classes of Subjects as are expressly excepted in the Enumeration of the Classes of Subjects by this Act assigned exclusively to the Legislatures of the Provinces.

Generally speaking, the provinces have the legislative authority to regulate the employment relationship, including discrimination in employment, with the exception of businesses, works or undertakings whose operations fall within one of the specific heads under s. 91 of the *Constitution Act, 1867*.[4] In addition, under heading 10 of s. 92 of the *Constitution Act, 1867*, the following classes of subjects are expressly excluded from provincial jurisdiction:

a.   Lines of Steam or other Ships, Railways, Canals, Telegraphs, and other Works and Undertakings connecting the Province with any other or others of the Provinces, or extending beyond the Limits of the Province.

b.   Lines of Steam Ships between the Province and any British or Foreign Country.

c.   Such Works as, although wholly situate within the Province, are before or after their Execution declared by the Parliament of Canada to be for the general Advantage of Canada or for the Advantage of Two or more of the Provinces.

Finally, the courts have determined that other businesses or services, in addition to those under s. 91 and head 10 of s. 92 of the *Constitution Act, 1867*, are within federal legislative competence. For example, aeronautics and radio and telecommunications have been held to be matters of federal competency.

The Supreme Court of Canada in *Northern Telecom Ltd. v. Communications Workers of Canada*[5] succinctly summarizes these jurisdictional principles as follows:

(1)   Parliament has no authority over labour relations as such nor over the terms of a contract of employment; exclusive provincial competence is the rule.

(2)   By way of exception, however, Parliament may assert exclusive jurisdiction over these matters if it is shown that such jurisdiction is an integral part of its primary competence over some other single federal subject.

(3)   Primary federal competence over a given subject can prevent the application of provincial law relating to labour relations and the conditions of employment but only if it is demonstrated that federal authority over these matters is an integral element of such federal competence.

(4)   Thus, the regulation of wages to be paid by an undertaking, service or business, and the regulation of its labour relations, being related to an integral part of the operation of the undertaking, service or business, are removed from provincial jurisdiction and immune from the effect of provincial law if the undertaking, service or business is a federal one.

---

[4] See for example, decisions in

  (i) *Re Culley and Canadian Pacific Air Lines* (1976), 72 D.L.R. (3d) 449, [1977] 1 W.W.R. 393 (B.C.S.C.);

  (ii) *Canadian Pacific Ltd. v. Attorney General of Alberta* (1979), 100 D.L.R. (3d) 47, 9 Alta. L.R. (2d) 97 (Q.B.), revd 108 D.L.R. (3d) 738, [1980] 2 W.W.R. 148 (Alta. C.A.);

  (iii) *Forest Industries Flying Tankers Ltd. v. Kellough* (1980), 108 D.L.R. (3d) 686, [1980] 4 W.W.R. 13 (B.C.C.A.)

in which it was held that provincial human rights legislation does not apply to federal works business undertakings.

[5] (1979), 98 D.L.R. (3d) 1 at p. 13, [1980] 1 S.C.R. 115.

(5)   The question whether an undertaking, service or business is a federal one depends on the nature of its operation.

(6)   In order to determine the nature of the operation, one must look at the normal or habitual activities of the business as those of "a going concern", without regard for exceptional or casual factors; otherwise, the Constitution could not be applied with any degree of continuity and regularity.

C. Areas of Federal Jurisdiction[6]

Federal jurisdiction over employer and employee relations is limited to those circumstances in which it can be demonstrated that such jurisdiction is an integral part or necessarily incidental to a business or service over which the federal government has, by exception to the general rule, obtained exclusive jurisdiction.

The most comprehensive definition of the entities that fall within federal jurisdiction can be found within the *Canada Labour Code*. The *Canada Labour Code* is a federal statute which prescribes minimum standards of employment that apply to employees under federal jurisdiction. The phrase "federal work, undertaking or business" is defined in the *Canada Labour Code* as follows:

(*a*)   a work, undertaking or business operated or carried on for or in connection with navigation and shipping, whether inland or maritime, including the operation of ships and transportation by ship anywhere in Canada,

(*b*)   a railway, canal, telegraph or other work or undertaking connecting any province with any other province, or extending beyond the limits of a province,

(*c*)   a line of ships connecting a province with any other province, or extending beyond the limits of a province,

(*d*)   a ferry between any province and any other province or between any province and any country other than Canada,

(*e*)   aerodromes, aircraft or a line of air transportation,

(*f*)   a radio broadcasting station,

(*g*)   a bank,

(*h*)   a work or undertaking that, although wholly situated within a province, is before or after its execution declared by Parliament to be for the general advantage of Canada or for the advantage of two or more of the provinces, and

(*i*)   a work, undertaking or business outside the exclusive legislative authority of the legislatures of the provinces;

The definition represents an accumulation of those areas in which the federal government is competent to legislate in an employment context. The examples enumerated are not intended to be exhaustive and, in fact, are not.

A brief review of some of the more obvious areas of federal jurisdiction provides some insight into the nature and extent of these areas of jurisdiction.

---

[6] Part of this sub-chapter is taken from Brian A. Grosman and John R. Martin, *Employment Law in Ontario* (Aurora, Canada Law Book Inc., 1991), pp. 5-7.

(i) Rail transportation

By virtue of the provisions of s. 2(*b*) of the *Canada Labour Code* and s. 92(10)(*a*) of the *Constitution Act, 1867*, the federal government has jurisdiction over employment matters involving businesses or services integrally related to rail transport. However, rail transport companies typically operate subsidiary businesses which do not necessarily fall within federal employment law jurisdiction. When examining the sub-works or services of a rail transportation company, it must be determined whether or not there is a high degree of operational integration of an ongoing nature with the railway.

In a landmark judicial decision referred to as the *Empress Hotel*[7] case, the court was required to determine whether hours of work legislation passed by the federal government or the province of British Columbia, applied to employees of a hotel owned and operated by the Canadian Pacific Railway Company. Although railways clearly fell within exclusive federal jurisdiction, it was held that the matter was one of provincial regulation. This was determined to be so because the operation of the hotel, which did not cater solely or even principally to CPR travellers, was not a vital or integral part of the operation of the railway.

(ii) Air transport

Air transport is a matter that comes within the exclusive jurisdiction of the federal government. Once again, however, this is restricted to businesses or operations which are integral or necessarily incidental to aeronautics or aeronautic operations.

In *Montcalm Construction Inc. v. Minimum Wage Commission*,[8] the Supreme Court of Canada ruled that the employees of a construction company that was engaged to build Mirabel Airport were too far removed from the field of aeronautics to be the subject of federal employment legislation.

(iii) Radio broadcasting

Parliament has the exclusive jurisdiction to legislate with respect to employment matters relating to radio, television, telegraph and telecommunications. However, it is often difficult to determine whether a local radio or television operation is intra-provincial, in which case it is subject to provincial jurisdiction.

(iv) Inter-provincial road transport

The transport of passengers or goods by motor vehicle which connects a province with any other or extends beyond the boundaries of the province is a

---

[7] *C.P.R. v. Attorney-General of British Columbia*, [1950] 1 D.L.R. 721, [1950] 1 W.W.R. 220 (P.C.).
[8] (1978), 93 D.L.R. (3d) 641, [1979] 1 S.C.R. 754.

matter of federal jurisdiction. Since many road transportation companies operate on both a local and extra-provincial level, the issue becomes which jurisdiction properly regulates matters. It is important to look at the work or undertaking as a whole, without separating its different functions. The federal government has jurisdiction over employment matters of a road transportation company if either the operation provides extra-provincial services on a continuous and regular basis, or provides such services on an unscheduled basis but holds itself out to the public as being ready at any time to provide such services without interruption to its normal customer or service base.

By way of example, the Supreme Court of Canada in *R. v. Cooksville Magistrate's Court Ex P. Liquid Cargo Lines Ltd.*[9] held a truck carrier, sending a mere 1.6% of its loads outside the province, was subject to exclusive federal jurisdiction. The court held that the determining feature in the case was the fact that the inter-provincial aspect of the business was of a continuous and consistent nature.

(v) Banking

Pursuant to s. 91(13) of the *Constitution Act, 1867*, and s. 2(*g*) of the *Canada Labour Code*, banking and those aspects of it which deal with employment relations are a federal matter. However, trust companies and insurance companies are provincially regulated.

With recent significant amendments to the *Bank Act*,[10] which allow the banks to both establish and acquire trust companies, a number of complex jurisdictional issues will undoubtedly result in terms of regulation of the employment relationship.

(vi) Radio, television and telecommunications

Parliament has the exclusive jurisdiction to legislate with respect to employment matters pertaining to radio, television, telegraph and telecommunications.[11] However, local radio and television operations, being intra-provincial operations, fall outside the domain of exclusive federal competence, in much the same manner as intra-provincial road transportation.[12]

D. Incorporating Jurisdiction of Employer

It is a common misconception that the incorporating jurisdiction of the employer will dictate, for all purposes, whether the company is under federal or provincial jurisdiction. The concise reasoning of Justice Pigeon in *Canada*

---

[9] (1964), 46 D.L.R. (2d) 700, [1965] 1 O.R. 84 (H.C.J.).

[10] R.S.C. 1985, c. B-1, as amended.

[11] *Canadian Pioneer Management v. Labour Relations Board of Saskatchewan* (1980), 107 D.L.R.(3d) 1, [1980] 1 S.C.R. 433.

[12] See s. 92(*a*) of the *Constitution Act, 1867*, as well as s. 2(*f*) of the *Canada Labour Code*.

Labour Relations Board v. City of Yellowknife[13] effectively dispels this erroneous proposition: "... jurisdiction over labour matters depends on legislative authority over the operation, not over the person of the employer."[14]

It is significant to note that human rights legislation, generally speaking, does not contain definitions or sections which tend to limit its application to a specific class of employee or employer. Accordingly, the employer will find little, if any, guidance within the four corners of the legislation in relation to whether it is bound by federal or provincial anti-discrimination legislation.

2. EXISTENCE OF AN EMPLOYMENT RELATIONSHIP

Once it has been determined whether the federal or provincial legislation applies to a potential human rights complaint, the next most important issue to be determined relates to the existence of an employment relationship. It may appear trite to say that employers and employees are subject to the equal treatment in employment and other employment-related provisions of the applicable human rights legislation. However, it is not always entirely clear whether a given individual or entity is, in fact and in law, an "employee" or "employer".

Determination of the preliminary issue as to the existence of an employment relationship is further complicated by the fact that neither the Ontario *Human Rights Code* nor the *Canadian Human Rights Act* contains a definition of "employee", "employer" and/or "employment". The issue then becomes whether the restrictive definition of an employee at common law is the governing test or, in the alternative, whether the expanded statutory definition of employee under the applicable employment standards legislation governs. It is submitted that the latter test would ultimately govern for two reasons. First, human rights legislation, in many respects, is a specialized form of employment standards legislation. Secondly, the expanded statutory definition of employee is far more consistent with the purpose, spirit and intent of human rights legislation.

A. Definition of Employee Under Ontario Legislation

Section 1 of the Ontario *Employment Standards Act*[15] provides a very general, non-exhaustive definition of the term "employee":

> 1. "employee" includes a person who,
>   (a) performs any work for or supplies any services to an employer for wages,
>   (b) does homework for an employer, or

---

[13] (1977), 76 D.L.R. (3d) 85, [1977] 2 S.C.R. 729.
[14] *Supra*, at p. 90.
[15] R.S.O. 1990, c. E.14, as amended.

(c) receives any instruction or training in the activity, business, work, trade, occupation or profession of the employer,

and includes a person who was an employee;

It is clear that, in determining whether an individual is an "employee" for the purposes of the *Employment Standards Act*, the existence of formal titles or other trappings of a relationship which make the relationship appear to be something other than that of employer/employee will have little, if any, influence on the issue at the end of the day.

For example, in *Re Becker Milk Co. Ltd. and Director of Employment Standards of the Ontario Ministry of Labour*,[16] the company contracted with individuals to act as "owners/managers" of its convenience stores. Becker Milk argued that as owners/managers, the individuals in question were not "employees" and therefore, not subject to the provisions of the Act. The Ontario Divisional Court disagreed, primarily as a result of the degree of control exercised by Becker Milk over these individuals.

A rather extraordinary example as to the breadth of the employment relationship for human rights purposes, can be found in the recent decision of an Ontario Board of Inquiry in *Roberts v. Chmiel and Club Expose*.[17] The pertinent facts of the *Roberts* case may be summarized as follows:

1. Ms Roberts filed a complaint with the Commission on October 2, 1992, alleging that her right to equal treatment in employment without discrimination because of race or colour was infringed, contrary to ss. 5(1) and 9 of the *Human Rights Code*;

2. Ms Roberts described herself as a "freelance burlesque dancer 'stripper'" and worked under the stage name of Nicole with a partner;

3. she worked for Club Expose for one week in February, 1992, and her partner, who was white, was asked by the personal respondent Mr. Chmiel to return to work the following week alone "as he did not want a black woman working in his club";

4. Ms Roberts alleged that when she confronted Mr. Chmiel on the telephone about the comments he made to her partner "he confirmed that he did not want black women working in his club because they brought in black clientele and further stated that he did not want their business";

5. Ms Roberts had been booked to work at Club Expose for one week in early February, 1992, through a conversation between her partner, Ms Power, and the night manager of the establishment;

6. Ms Roberts testified that she received roughly $200 each night, in addition to her shift pay of $300 to $400, for a total of between $500 and $600 per shift;

---

[16] (1973), 41 D.L.R. (3d) 503, 1 O.R. (2d) 739 (Div. Ct.).
[17] (unreported, July 21, 1993, Ont. Bd. Inq.).

7.   on the basis of the evidence adduced at the hearing, the Board of Inquiry concluded that Ms Roberts was hired by Club Expose as a nude dancer for a one-week period in February, 1992, and was paid a standard shift rate by Club Expose for her services. Ms Roberts and her partner, Ms Power, were sent by IM Productions, which was paid by Club Expose for referral services. The Board characterized this relationship as a ''casual agreement to employ Ms Roberts for a period of one week''.

There can be no doubt that the Board of Inquiry in the *Roberts* case had to adopt a very broad definition of employment in order to establish a sufficient nexus between the owner of Club Expose, Mr. Chmiel, and the ''employer''. Since Mr. Chmiel had no direct link or affiliation with the agency that placed Ms Roberts with Club Expose, the Board of Inquiry, by implication, found that Ms Roberts was a co-employee of both the agency and Club Expose for the week-long engagement in February, 1992. The informal or ''casual'' nature of the agreement to employ Ms Roberts in no way detracted from the Board of Inquiry's finding that there was indeed an employment relationship during the material time period.

While the *Roberts* case is a somewhat extraordinary example of a broad and liberal interpretation of the employment relationship by a board of inquiry, it nonetheless is representative of the purposive approach that is typically taken by a board of inquiry in dealing with procedural and preliminary issues raised in the course of a hearing.

B. Definition of Employee Under Federal Legislation

Section 3 of the *Canada Labour Code* defines an employee as ''any person employed by an employer and includes a dependent contractor and a private constable, but does not include a person who performs management functions or is employed in a confidential capacity in matters relating to industrial relations''. It is reasonable to suggest that a tribunal appointed under the *Canadian Human Rights Act* would reject the restriction placed upon the definition of an employee under the *Canada Labour Code*, thereby removing the ''managment functions'' bar expressly contained within the legislation. A managerial employee is no less an employee, from a human rights standpoint, than a non-managerial employee.

CHAPTER 2 | *Human Rights Legislation*

1. FEDERAL HUMAN RIGHTS LEGISLATION

A. The Canadian Human Rights Act[1]

In 1977, the Parliament of Canada enacted the *Canadian Human Rights Act*.[2] This represented a major step forward in the enshrinement of fundamental freedoms and human rights at a federal level. The Act is set up to deal with complaints received from individuals or groups concerned with discriminatory practices. The Act applies to all federal government departments, agencies, crown corporations, as well as business and industry within the federal jurisdiction.

It is clear from decisions to date under the legislation that the Act has and is likely to continue to receive a broad and remedial interpretation. As one justice of the Federal Court of Canada has commented, in dealing with the interpretation of the Act:

> The statute [*ie* The *Canadian Human Rights Act*] is cast in wide terms and both its subject-matter and its stated purpose suggests that it is not to be interpreted narrowly or restrictively.[3]

Section 2 of the *Canadian Human Rights Act* states the purpose of the legislation as follows:

> 2. The purpose of this *Act* is to extend the laws in Canada to give effect, within the purview of matters coming within the legislative authority of Parliament, to the principle that every individual should have an equal opportunity with other individuals to make for himself or herself the life that he or she is able and wishes to have, consistent with his or her duties and obligations as a member of society, without being hindered in or prevented from doing so by discriminatory practices based on race, national or ethnic origin, colour, religion, age, sex, marital status, family status, disability or conviction for an offence for which a pardon has been granted.

---

[1] This portion of the book contains excerpts from M. Norman Grosman, *Federal Employment Law in Canada* (Scarborough, Carswell, 1990) (chapter 6 of the book was written by Fran Carnerie).

[2] S.C. 1976-77, c. 33 (now R.S.C. 1985, c. H-6).

[3] *Cumming v. Canada (Attorney General)* (1979), 103 D.L.R. (3d) 151 at p. 158, [1980] 2 F.C. 122 (T.D.).

The Federal Court of Appeal in *Air Canada v. Carson*[4] interpreted s. 2 of the *Canadian Human Rights Act* as follows:

> As is evidenced by s. 2 of the *Canadian Human Rights Act*, Parliament has made a fundamental decision to give preference to individual opportunity over competing social values. The preference is not absolute . . . But the courts must be zealous to ensure that Parliament's primary intention that people should for the most part be judged on their own merits rather than on group characteristics is not eroded by overly generous exceptions.[5]

The Act, of course, in large part deals with stamping out discrimination in the employment environment. In fact, complaints arising from the workplace outnumber those arising from the discriminatory provisions of goods and services by a nearly 5 to 1 margin. Accordingly, employers in the 1990s must expand their awareness of human rights issues and become more sensitive to their existence in the workplace.

Equality of the individual is the key concept found within the Act. The principle of unhindered equal opportunity is not a guarantee against discrimination in life, but rather against certain specified forms of discrimination, all of which are based on group membership of some kind, whether a natural group such as race and colour or in freely chosen groups such as marital status.

B. The Canada Labour Code

The *Canada Labour Code* provides that certain employment standards must be adhered to by each and every business entity which falls within federal regulation. Standards regulate the fundamental aspects of the employment relationship and include hours of work, minimum wages, vacations, general holidays, maternity and child care leave, bereavement leave and sick leave. Section 168(1) of the Code provides that the employment standards set forth under the Code are minimum standards and cannot be relinquished by any employee, regardless of whether the attempt to forego such a minimum entitlement is by contract, custom or any other type of arrangement. The Code, however, does permit employers and employees to agree between themselves that rights or benefits superior to those set out in the Code will prevail. The Code also provides that the employment standards referenced do not, in most cases, apply to employees who are managers or superintendents or who exercise management functions or who are members of the professions.[6] Certain specific sections of the *Canada Labour Code* apply to the subject of human rights and, in this limited respect, the Code acts as a corollary or extension to the provisions of the *Canadian Human Rights Act*.

Section 182 of the *Canada Labour Code* contains provisions relating to the right to equal wages:

---

[4] (1985), 18 D.L.R. (4th) 72, [1985] 1 F.C. 209 (C.A.).
[5] *Supra*, at p. 93.
[6] See s. 167(2) of the *Canada Labour Code*, R.S.C. 1985, c. L-2.

182(1) For the purposes of ascertaining whether a discriminatory practice under section 11 of the *Canadian Human Rights Act* is being or has been engaged in, sections 249, 250, 252, 253, 254, 255 and 264 apply, with such modifications as the circumstances require, as if this Part expressly required an employer to refrain from that discriminatory practice.

(2) Where an inspector has reasonable grounds at any time for believing that an employer is engaging or has engaged in a discriminatory practice described in subsection (1), the inspector may notify the Canadian Human Rights Commission or file a complaint with that Commission under section 40 of the *Canadian Human Rights Act*.

The specific sections of the *Canada Labour Code* referred to in s. 182(1) of the *Code* contain the following provisions:

(i)   section 249 contains extensive provisions relating to the powers of an inspector appointed by the Minister for the purpose of investigating a complaint;

(ii)   section 250 merely stipulates that an inspector may administer oaths and receive statements in the form of affidavits and statutory declarations;

(iii) section 252 compels employers to provide information relating to wages paid to their employees, hours of work and general holidays, annual vacations and conditions at work and other such related information as the Minister may require;

(iv)   section 253 stipulates the manner in which the information required in section 252 may be delivered to the Minister;

(v)   in s. 254 of the Code, an employer is required to furnish employees with written pay statements setting out specific information relating to the employee's compensation;

(vi)   in s. 255 of the legislation, the Minister may declare that two or more business entities constitute a single employer for specific purposes under the legislation;

(vii) section 264 confers a broad jurisdiction upon the Minister to enact regulations relating to the enforcement of certain provisions of the *Canada Labour Code*.

The only other portion of the *Canada Labour Code* which impacts directly upon the area of human rights, can be found in ss. 247.1 to 247.4[7] which relate to the subject of sexual harassment:

247.1 In this Division, ''sexual harassment'' means any conduct, comment, gesture or contact of a sexual nature
   (*a*) that is likely to cause offence or humiliation to any employee; or
   (*b*) that might, on reasonable grounds, be perceived by that employee as placing a condition of a sexual nature on employment or on any opportunity for training or promotion.
247.2 Every employee is entitled to employment free of sexual harassment.

---

7 Sections 247.1-247.4 enacted R.S.C. 1985, c. 9 (1st Supp.), s. 1.

247.3   Every employer shall make every reasonable effort to ensure that no employee is subjected to sexual harassment.

247.4(1)   Every employer shall, after consulting with the employees or their representatives, if any, issue a policy statement concerning sexual harassment.

(2)   The policy statement required by subsection (1) may contain any term consistent with the tenor of this Division the employer considers appropriate but must contain the following:

> (a)   a definition of sexual harassment that is substantially the same as the definition in section 247.1;
>
> (b)   a statement to the effect that every employee is entitled to employment free of sexual harassment;
>
> (c)   a statement to the effect that the employer will make every reasonable effort to ensure that no employee is subjected to sexual harassment;
>
> (d)   a statement to the effect that the employer will take such disciplinary measures as the employer deems appropriate against any person under the employer's direction who subjects any employee to sexual harassment;
>
> (e)   a statement explaining how complaints of sexual harassment may be brought to the attention of the employer;
>
> (f)   a statement to the effect that the employer will not disclose the name of a complainant or the circumstances related to the complaint to any person except where disclosure is necessary for the purposes of investigating the complaint or taking disciplinary measures in relation thereto; and
>
> (g)   a statement informing employees of the discriminatory practices provisions of the *Canadian Human Rights Act* that pertain to rights of persons to seek redress under that *Act* in respect of sexual harassment.

(3)   Every employer shall make each person under the employer's direction aware of the policy statement required by subsection (1).

The subject of sexual harassment is reviewed, in greater detail, in Chapter 10 of this book.

2. PROVINCIAL HUMAN RIGHTS LEGISLATION

A. The Ontario Human Rights Code

The province of Ontario has been the leading jurisdiction in Canada with respect to human rights legislation.

In 1944, Ontario enacted the *Racial Discrimination Act*,[8] the first Canadian legislation outlawing certain forms of racial discrimination. The Act prohibited the publication, display or broadcast of anything indicating an intention to discriminate on the basis of ''race or creed''.

---

[8]   S.O. 1944, c. 51.

In the years that followed the enactment of the *Racial Discrimination Act,* the province enacted additional human rights legislation, including the *Fair Employment Practices Act,*[9] and the *Fair Accommodation Practices Act.*[10]

Perhaps the most significant event in the history of human rights protection in Canada occurred in 1962, when Ontario first enacted its initial human rights code, the *Ontario Human Rights Code, 1962.* This Code consolidates various human rights legislation governing discriminatory conduct and is the forerunner of today's comprehensive Ontario *Human Rights Code, 1981,* S.O. 1981, c. 53.[11]

(i) Special legal status

The Ontario *Human Rights Code* is intended to establish a comprehensive procedure for investigating and remedying discrimination in the province. The purpose of the Code is set out in its preamble which reads in part:

> And whereas it is public policy in Ontario to recognize the dignity and worth of every person and to provide for equal rights and opportunities without discrimination that is contrary to law, and having as its aim the creation of a climate of understanding and mutual respect for the dignity and worth of each person so that each person feels a part of the community and able to contribute fully to the development and well-being of the community and the Province;

While there is no formal legal distinction between a code and an Act of the provincial legislature, it is clear that the courts have conferred a special legal status upon human rights codes, including the Ontario *Human Rights Code.*

In *Winnipeg School Division No. 1 v. Craton,*[12] the Supreme Court of Canada ruled certain provisions contained in a collective agreement in the *Manitoba Public Schools Act,* which provided for the complainant's mandatory retirement, void because they contravened the *Human Rights Act of Manitoba.* Mr. Justice MacIntyre, speaking for the majority of the court, said:

> Human rights legislation is of a special nature and declares public policy regarding matters of general concern. It is not constitutional in nature in the sense that it may not be altered, amended, or repealed by the Legislature. It is, however, of such nature that it may not be altered, amended, or repealed, nor may exceptions be created to its provisions, save by clear legislative pronouncement.[13]

The court went on to state that if there is a conflict between human rights legislation and any other legislation, with the exception of the Constitution, the human rights legislation must prevail.

---

[9] S.O. 1951, c. 24.
[10] S.O. 1954, c. 28.
[11] Now R.S.C. 1990, c. H.19.
[12] (1985), 21 D.L.R. (4th) 1, [1985] 2 S.C.R. 150.
[13] *Supra,* at p. 6.

Therefore, on the authority of the Supreme Court of Canada's decision in *Craton*, human rights legislation has been vested with a legal status superior to that of all other legislation, second only to the Constitution. Section 47(2) of the Ontario *Human Rights Code*, which provides that the Act has primacy over all other Acts passed by the legislature of Ontario, is consistent with this philosophy:

> 47(2) Where a provision in an Act or regulation purports to require or authorize conduct that is a contravention of Part I [*ie* the first nine sections of the Code which provide for freedom from discrimination], this Act applies and prevails unless the Act or regulation specifically provides that it is to apply despite this Act.

(ii) Discriminatory practices and activities

Generally speaking, discrimination is any distinction, exclusion or preference based on prohibited grounds, as defined by the Code, which nullifies or impairs equality of opportunity in employment or equality of terms and conditions of employment. Section 5 of the Code is the cornerstone of the prohibition against discrimination in the workplace:

> 5(1) Every person has a right to equal treatment with respect to employment without discrimination because of race, ancestry, place of origin, colour, ethnic origin, citizenship, creed, sex, sexual orientation, age, record of offences, marital status, family status or handicap.
>
> (2) Every person who is an employee has a right to freedom from harassment in the workplace by the employer or agent of the employer or by another employee because of race, ancestry, place of origin, colour, ethnic origin, citizenship, creed, age, record of offences, marital status, family status or handicap.

The Ontario *Human Rights Code* is predicated on the philosophy that employment decisions should be based upon merit rather than extraneous considerations unrelated to job performance. To effect this objective, the Code aims to enforce the principles of equal opportunity with respect to employment.

The Code's protection of equal treatment with respect to employment extends to virtually every facet of the relationship including recruitment, hiring, evaluation, promotion, discipline and dismissal. Terms and conditions of employment such as probation, wage rates, benefits, hours of work and overtime must be implemented and administered in conformity with the Code's rigorous requirements involving equal treatment with respect to employment.

Corporate and other employers who carry on business within the province of Ontario must strictly adhere to the far-reaching provisions of the Ontario *Human Rights Code*. Not only does the Code provide extensive safeguards and protection to employees, it also requires employers to observe certain rules and policies in relation to all applicants and prospective applicants for employment.

B. The Employment Standards Act

The Ontario *Employment Standards Act*, R.S.O. 1990, c. E.14, establishes the minimum rights and entitlements of employees who fall within its jurisdiction.

The Act applies to employers and employees in Ontario, other than those companies and businesses which are under exclusive federal jurisdiction. Both oral and written employment contracts alike are covered by the provisions of the Act. Likewise, both organized and unorganized workplaces are governed by the legislation.

Section 3 of the Act states, in unequivocal terms, that the minimum standards provided for in the Act shall be observed in all cases:

> 3. Subject to section 4, no employer, employee, employers' organization or employees' organization shall contract out of or waive an employment standard, and any such contracting out or waiver is null and void.

The only exception to this ironclad rule is spelled out in s. 4, which provides that an employer and employee may agree upon a benefit, right or entitlement which is greater than that provided for in the Act.

Section 6 of the Act provides that "[n]o civil remedy of an employee against his or her employer is suspended or affected by this Act". Accordingly, it is clear that the Act only represents a statutory remedy in relation to the minimum rights and entitlements set out therein. It provides a statutory alternative to those individuals who wish to accept their minimum entitlement under the Act, without engaging in time-consuming and sometimes expensive civil litigation against their former employer, claiming additional damages for wrongful dismissal.[14]

In the area of human rights, s. 32 of the Act prohibits wage differentials based on gender:

> 32(1) No employer or person acting on behalf of an employer shall differentiate between male and female employees by paying a female employee at a rate of pay less than the rate of pay paid to a male employee, or vice versa, for substantially the same kind of work performed in the same establishment, the performance of which requires substantially the same skill, effort and responsibility and which is performed under similar working conditions, except where such payment is made pursuant to,
>
> (a) a seniority system;
> (b) a merit system;
> (c) a system that measures earnings by quantity or quality of production; or
> (d) a differential based on any factor other than sex.

---

[14] For a review of employment legislation in Ontario see Brian A. Grosman and John R. Martin, *Employment Law in Ontario* (Aurora, Canada Law Book Inc., 1991).

(2) No employer shall reduce the rate of pay of an employee in order to comply with subsection (1).

. . . . .

(4) Where an employment standards officer finds that an employer has failed to comply with subsection (1), the employment standards officer may determine the amount of money owing to an employee because of such non-compliance, and such amounts shall be deemed to be unpaid wages.

The only other provision of the *Employment Standards Act* which touches directly upon the subject of human rights involves a statutory prohibition against benefit plans which differentiate or make any distinction, exclusion or preference based on age, sex or marital status of the employee. Section 33(2) of the Act provides:

33(2) Except as provided in the regulations, no employer or person acting directly on behalf of an employer shall provide, furnish or offer any fund, plan, arrangement or benefit that differentiates or makes any distinction, exclusion or preference between employees or a class or classes of employees or their bene-ficiaries, survivors or dependants because of the age, sex or marital status of the employees.

Contraventions of s. 32 or 33 of the *Employment Standards Act* referred to above, permit an employee the option of filing a complaint with the Employment Standards Branch of the Ministry of Labour, which ultimately results in an employment standards order directing the employer to remedy the contravention. This procedure is an alternative to, and not a substitution for, filing a complaint with the Ontario Human Rights Commission.

3. THE CANADIAN CHARTER OF RIGHTS AND FREEDOMS

In 1982, the *Canadian Charter of Rights and Freedoms* was proclaimed,[15] thereby fundamentally altering the constitutional law of Canada. By virtue of the Charter, the British Government ceased to have the ultimate legal authority over the legislature of Canada.

In its very short history, the impact of the Charter has been felt in virtually all areas of law, including employment law. While the judicial interpretation and application of the Charter to employment-related matters remains in its infancy, certain fundamental principles have already become apparent as a result of a number of leading court decisions in the area of human rights and employment.

A. Inapplicability to Private Employment Relationship

One of the major questions that has confronted Canadian courts in Charter cases, is the scope of the application to protected rights and freedoms. Section 32(1) of the Charter states:

---

[15] *Canadian Charter of Rights and Freedoms* as part of the *Constitution Act, 1982*, c. 11 (U.K.).

32(1) This Charter applies,
   (a) to the Parliament and government of Canada in respect of all matters within the authority of Parliament including all matters relating to the Yukon Territory and Northwest Territories; and
   (b) to the legislature and government of each province in respect of all matters within the authority of the legislation of each province.

Based upon the clear wording of this section, it would appear that the Charter applies only to government action, including legislation passed by government, that has the effect of infringing the fundamental rights and freedoms of the individual that are constitutionally protected within the Charter. The Charter has no direct application to the actions of private individuals and citizens in their day-to-day interactions and relationships, including their contractual relationships.

The inapplicability of the Charter to the private contract of employment was confirmed by the Supreme Court of Canada in *RWDSU, Local 580 v. Dolphin Delivery Ltd.*[16] At issue in that case was whether secondary picketing was a constitutionally protected activity under s. 2(b) of the Charter, the right to free speech. The court rejected the proposition that the Charter applied to private persons, within the context of an employment relationship. Mr. Justice McIntyre, speaking for the majority of the court, quoted from Professor Peter W. Hogg:

"The rights guaranteed by the Charter take effect only as restrictions on the power of government over the persons entitled to the rights. The Charter regulates the relations between government and private persons, but it does not regulate the relations between private persons and private persons. Private action is therefore excluded from the application of the Charter. Such actions as an employer restricting an employee's freedom of speech or assembly, a parent restricting the mobility of a child, or a landlord discriminating on the basis of race in his selection of tenants, cannot be breaches of the Charter, because in no case is there any action by the Parliament or government of Canada or by the Legislature or government of a province."[17]

B. Applicability to Employment-Related Legislation

While the Charter does not have a direct impact on the contract of employment, it may have an indirect impact in the sense that it clearly relates to government action and legislation which regulates the employment relationship. In the *Dolphin Delivery* case the Supreme Court of Canada acknowledged this proposition, but cautioned that:

. . . it is difficult and probably dangerous to attempt to define with narrow precision that element of governmental intervention which will suffice to permit reliance on the Charter by private litigants in private litigation.[18]

---

[16] (1986), 33 D.L.R. (4th) 174, [1986] 2 S.C.R. 573.
[17] *Supra*, at p. 191.
[18] *Supra*, at p. 197.

An additional preliminary issue is the extent to which unnatural persons, such as corporations and trade unions, can claim the protection of the Charter. The determination of this issue may depend upon the specific wording of the Charter right in question. For example, ss. 2, 7, 8, 9, 10 and 12 of the Charter refer to "everyone" while s. 6 confers rights on "every citizen" and s. 15, the equality rights provision, refers to "every individual". In the Supreme Court of Canada decision in *Hunter v. Southam Inc.*[19] the term "everyone" was held to include corporations with respect to the constitutional right to be free from unreasonable search and seizure.

C. Applicability to Human Rights Legislation

When considering the Charter of Rights, it is important to bear in mind that the rights and freedoms contained therein are not absolute rights. Section 1 of the Charter, commonly referred to as the "saving provision", provides:

> 1. The *Canadian Charter of Rights and Freedoms* guarantees the rights and freedoms set out in it subject only to such reasonable limits prescribed by law as can be demonstrably justified in a free and democratic society.

Thus, there may be instances where a Charter right is violated but the violation is saved or excused by s. 1.

An example of s. 1 justifying a Charter violation in the employment context is found is the Supreme Court of Canada decision in *Slaight Communications Inc. v. Davidson.*[20] The court upheld the order of an adjudicator appointed under the unjust dismissal provisions of s. 240 of the *Canada Labour Code* which provided, among other things, that the employer provide the unjustly dismissed complainant with a letter of reference of specified content, coupled with a direction that any inquiries relating to the former employee had to be answered exclusively by this letter of reference. Although the court ruled that this order violated the employer's constitutional right to freedom of expression, the majority of the court held that this violation was saved by s. 1 of the Charter. The other interesting aspect of the *Davidson* case is the court's implicit, if not explicit, recognition of the fact that there is a sufficiently close nexus between an order made by a statutory tribunal and the statutory provision from which the tribunal obtains the alleged jurisdiction to make the order, thereby resulting in the statutory tribunal's order constituting "government action" and falling within the realm of the *Canadian Charter of Rights and Freedoms*.

The contract of employment is governed by a variety of legislation. It is highly regulated in other respects as well. The extent of indirect government intervention in the employment relationship invites a significant application of the Charter.

---

[19] (1984), 11 D.L.R. (4th) 641, 14 C.C.C. (3d) 97 (S.C.C.).
[20] (1989), 59 D.L.R. (4th) 416, [1989] 1 S.C.R. 1038.

D. Equality Rights Provision

From a human rights perspective, the most important section of the *Canadian Charter of Rights and Freedoms* is the equality rights provision that is found in s. 15 and became law on April 17, 1985:

> 15(1) Every individual is equal before and under the law and has the right to the equal protection and equal benefit of the law without discrimination and, in particular, without discrimination based on race, national or ethnic origin, colour, religion, sex, age or mental or physical disability.
>
> (2) Subsection (1) does not preclude any law, program or activity that has as its object the amelioration of conditions of disadvantaged individuals or groups including those that are disadvantaged because of race, national or ethnic origin, colour, religion, sex, age or mental or physical disability.

As Madam Justice Wilson of the Supreme Court of Canada has stated, the "evil which s. 15 was meant to protect against is stereotype and prejudice".[21] In commenting upon the specifically enumerated grounds of discrimination contained in s. 15 of the Charter, the Supreme Court of Canada stated, in *Andrews v. Law Society of British Columbia*[22] that these grounds:

> . . . represent some blatant examples of discrimination which society has at last come to recognize as such. Their common characteristic is political, social and legal disadvantage and vulnerability.

It is clear that the *Canadian Charter of Rights and Freedoms* and, in particular, the equality rights provisions contained in s. 15 therein, have direct application to human rights legislation that is enacted by both the provincial legislatures and the federal parliament. One of the most authoritative decisions in support of this principle is the decision of the Supreme Court of Canada in *McKinney v. University of Guelph.*[23]

The *McKinney* decision involved eight faculty members and a professional librarian who were facing mandatory retirement because they had reached the age of sixty-five or were about to reach that age. These individuals brought court applications against four Ontario universities requesting, amongst other things, declarations that their respective retirements contravene s. 15 of the *Canadian Charter of Rights and Freedoms* and that s. 9(1)(*a*) of the Ontario *Human Rights Code, 1981* contravenes s. 15 of the Charter:

> 9. . . . (*a*) "age" means an age that is eighteen years or more, except in subsection 4(1) where "age" means an age that is eighteen years or more and less than sixty-five years;

---

21 *McKinney v. University of Guelph* (1990), 76 D.L.R. (4th) 545 at p. 608, [1990] 3 S.C.R. 229. (Note that although Madam Justice Wilson was in dissent in this decision, she was in agreement with the majority on the issue of whether s. 15(1) of the Charter had been violated.)

22 (1989), 56 D.L.R. (4th) 1, [1989] 1 S.C.R. 143.

23 *McKinney v. University of Guelph, supra,* footnote 21.

[Renumbered as s. 9(1)(a) 1986, c. 64, s. 18(7).]

The trial judge dismissed the application on two grounds:

1.   the Charter does not apply to universities in the sense that there was not a sufficiently close nexus between universities and the provincial government to support the contention that the actions of a university, in its day-to-day affairs, constituted ''government action'';

2.   although s. 9(1)(a) of the Ontario *Human Rights Code, 1981* violates s. 15 of the Charter, it is a reasonable limit that is demonstrably justified in a free and democratic society and, therefore, caught by the saving provisions found in s. 1 of the Charter.

An appeal to the Ontario Court of Appeal was dismissed, thereby leading to the matter being appealed to the Supreme Court of Canada.

In dismissing the appeal, the Supreme Court of Canada addressed a number of issues that are discussed elsewhere in this book. On the issue of s. 15 of the Charter, Mr. Justice La Forest, speaking on behalf of the majority of the court, stated, in part:

> For s. 15 of the Charter to come into operation, the alleged inequality must be one made by ''law''. The most obvious form of law for this purpose is, of course, a statute or regulation. It is clear, however, that it would be easy for government to circumvent the Charter if the term ''law'' were to be restricted to these formal types of law-making. It seems obvious from what McIntyre J. had to say in the *Dolphin Delivery* case that he intended that exercise by government of a statutory power or discretion would, if exercised in a discriminatory manner prohibited by s. 15, constitute an infringement of that provision.[24]

In the course of its judgment, the court reiterated the test for discrimination under s. 15(1) of the Charter as follows:

> I would say then that discrimination may be described as a distinction, whether intentional or not but based on grounds relating to personal characteristics of the individual or group, which has the effect of imposing burdens, obligations, or disadvantages on such individual or group not imposed upon others, or which withholds or limits access to opportunities, benefits and advantages available to other members of society. Distinctions based on personal characteristics attributed to an individual solely on the basis of association with a group will rarely escape the charge of discrimination, while those based on an individual's merits and capacities will rarely be so classed.[25]

In addressing the issue as to whether s. 9(1)(a) of the Ontario *Human Rights Code, 1981* contravened s. 15(1) of the Charter, the court stated, in a very matter of fact manner, that ''[t]here is no question that, the Code being a law, the Charter applies to it''.[26] In concluding that s. 9(1)(a) of the Ontario

---

24   *Supra*, at p. 644.
25   *Supra*, at p. 646.
26   *Supra*, at p. 654.

Human Rights Code, 1981 violates the equality rights provisions of s. 15 of the Charter, Mr. Justice La Forest stated, in part:

> Nor can there be any doubt since the *Andrews* case, which I have already discussed, that the differential treatment to which the appellants have been subjected constitutes discrimination for the purposes of s. 15(1) of the Charter. It deprives them of a benefit under the Code on the basis of their age, a ground specifically enumerated in the Charter. It must be underlined that s. 15(1) expressly guarantees the right to equality before and under the law; it also guarantees the right to equal protection of the law. The following remarks of McIntyre J. in *Andrews v. Law Society of British Columbia, supra*, at p. 15 are apposite:
>
> > ·"It is clear that the purpose of s. 15 is to ensure equality in the formulation and application of the law. The promotion of equality entails the promotion of a society in which all are secure in the knowledge that they are recognized at law as human beings equally deserving of concern, respect and consideration. It has a large remedial component. Howland C.J.O. and Robins J.A. (dissenting in the result but not with respect to this comment) in *Reference Re an Act to Amend the Education Act* (1986), 25 D.L.R. (4th) 1, attempt to articulate the broad range of values embraced by s. 15. They state at p. 42 D.L.R.:
> >
> > > 'In our view, s. 15(1) read as a whole constitutes a compendious expression of a positive right to equality in both the substance and the administration of the law. It is an all-encompassing right governing all legislative action. Like the ideals of "equal justice" and "equal access to the law", the right to equal protection and equal benefit of the law now enshrined in the Charter rests on the moral and ethical principle fundamental to a truly free and democratic society that all persons should be treated by the law on a footing of equality with equal concern and respect.' "
>
> It is right, however, to indicate with some precision what the discrimination is, and what it is not. The Code does not impose mandatory retirement at any age. Its general effect, in this context, is to prevent the making of a contract providing for mandatory retirement at a fixed age of less than 65 unless the employer is able, under s. 23(1)(*b*) of the Code, to establish on a balance of probabilities that age is a reasonable and *bona fide* qualification because of the nature of the employment. Such protection can, in the government sector, also be obtained under the Charter, without reference to age at all, subject to reasonable limitation under s. 1. The Code, however, extends protection within the age limits prescribed against age discrimination in employment in the private sector which, we saw, is not directly affected by the Charter.[27]

In concluding that s. 9(1)(*a*) of the Ontario *Human Rights Code, 1981* was saved by s. 1 of the Charter, in spite of the fact that it violated s. 15(1) of the Charter, Mr. Justice La Forest stated, in part:

> There remains the question whether there is a proportionality between the effects of s. 9(*a*) of the Code on the guaranteed right and the objectives of the

---

[27] *Supra*, at pp. 655-6.

provision. From the perspective from which the arguments were, for the most part, advanced, I could say, as I did in respect of the universities' policies, that this inquiry really involved the same considerations as were discussed in dealing with the issue of whether the legislation met the test of minimal impairment.

. . . . .

In looking at this type of issue, it is important to remember that a legislature should not be obliged to deal with all aspects of a problem at once. It must surely be permitted to take incremental measures. It must be given reasonable leeway to deal with problems one step at a time, to balance possible inequalities under the law against other inequalities resulting from the adoption of a course of action, and to take account of the difficulties, whether social, economic or budgetary, that would arise if it attempted to deal with social and economic problems in their entirety, assuming such problems can ever be perceived in their entirety.

. . . . .

But, generally, the courts should not lightly use the Charter to second-guess legislative judgment as to just how quickly it should proceed in moving forward towards the ideal of equality. The courts should adopt a stance that encourages legislative advances in the protection of human rights. Some of the steps adopted may well fall short of perfection, but as earlier mentioned, the recognition of human rights emerges slowly out of the human condition, and short or incremental steps may at times be a harbinger of a developing right, a further step in the long journey towards full and ungrudging recognition of the dignity of the human person.[28]

Of all of the provisions of the *Canadian Charter of Human Rights and Freedoms*, the equality rights provisions contained in s. 15 of the Charter is related most directly to both human rights legislation and human rights law in general. This section of the Charter will provide a most fertile ground for potentially significant litigation in decades to come, particularly in relation to various aspects of the employment relationship.

E. Charter Remedies

The Charter contains two sections which specifically provide a remedy for infringement of one's constitutionally protected rights. Where the infringement results from a provision contained within validly enacted legislation, s. 52 of the Charter provides the primary remedy:

52(1) The Constitution of Canada is the supreme law of Canada, and any law that is inconsistent with the provisions of the Constitution is, to the extent of the inconsistency, of no force or effect.

Accordingly, any law that violates the Charter, and cannot be saved under s. 1, is void to the extent of its inconsistency with the Charter. The court may, for example, simply strike out the offending law. In the alternative, the court

_____

[28] *Supra*, at pp. 674-6.

may declare that the provision in question is to be interpreted in a way that does not violate the Charter while, at the same time, preserving the spirit and intent of the legislation itself. In the vernacular of constitutional law, this is referred to as "reading down" the legislation.

The second remedial provision contained within the Charter is set out in s. 24(1):

> 24(1) Anyone whose rights or freedoms, as guaranteed by this Charter, have been infringed or denied may apply to a court of competent jurisdiction to obtain such remedy as the court considers appropriate and just in the circumstances.

For obvious reasons, the courts have held s. 24(1) of the Charter to be of extremely broad application. The wide discretion conferred upon the court under s. 24(1) represents a recognition of the increasing volume and diversity of Charter infringements, which may require the court to craft an imaginative and unprecedented remedy for each applicant. In the employment context, potential remedies may include reading language into or out of a statute, altering or adding a term to a contract of employment, reinstatement, monetary damages, injunctive-type relief and a host of other potential remedies. In fact the scope of potential remedies available under s. 24(1) are limited only by the imagination in creativity of the applicant and the court.

4. THE UNIVERSAL DECLARATION OF HUMAN RIGHTS

On December 10, 1948, the international bill of human rights, most commonly referred to as "a universal declaration of human rights", was proclaimed by the United Nations.[29] From a historical human rights perspective, this Declaration is arguably the most significant human rights document that has been enacted in modern legal history. Canada, being one of the member countries of the United Nations that participated in the enactment of this Declaration, pledged to uphold not only the specific articles of the Declaration itself but, perhaps even more importantly, the spirit and intent of the Declaration.

The purpose of the Universal Declaration of Human Rights is perhaps best expressed in its preamble, which states in part:

> *Whereas* recognition of the inherent dignity and of the equal and inalienable rights of all members of the human family is the foundation of freedom, justice and peace in the world,
>
> . . . . .
>
> *Whereas* the peoples of the United Nations have in the Charter reaffirmed their faith in fundamental human rights, in the dignity and worth of the human person and in the equal rights of men and women and have determined to promote social progress and better standards of life in larger freedom,

---

[29] UN Doc. A/810 (1948).

. . . . .

Proclaims this Universal Declaration of Human Rights as a common standard of achievement for all peoples and all nations, to the end that every individual and every organ of society, keeping this Declaration constantly in mind, shall strive by teaching and education to promote respect for these rights and freedoms and by progressive measures, national and international to secure their universal and effective recognition and observance, both among the peoples of Members States themselves and among the peoples of territories under their jurisdiction.

The Universal Declaration of Human Rights has, in many respects, served as the official blueprint for the structuring and drafting of human rights legislation in Canada, both at the provincial and the federal level. It can be seen from a brief review of some of the specific articles of the Declaration that much of its terminology has been expressly incorporated into both the Ontario *Human Rights Code* and the *Canadian Human Rights Act*:

Article 2

Everyone is entitled to all the rights and freedoms set forth in this Declaration, without distinction of any kind, such as race, colour, sex, language, religion, political or other opinion, national or social origin, property, birth or other status.

. . . . .

Article 7

All are equal before the law and are entitled without any discrimination to equal protection of the law. All are entitled to equal protection against any discrimination in violation of this Declaration and against any incitement to such discrimination.

. . . . .

Article 23

1. Everyone has the right to work, to free choice of employment, to just and favourable conditions of work and to protection against unemployment.
2. Everyone, without any discrimination, has the right to equal pay for equal work.
3. Everyone who works has the right to just and favourable remuneration ensuring for himself and his family an existence worthy of human dignity, and supplemented, if necessary, by other means of social protection.
4. Everyone has the right to form and to join trade unions for the protection of his interests.

All of the member countries, including Canada, pledged to use its best efforts to disseminate among all peoples throughout the world the contents of the Declaration. More specifically, Canada and its fellow member countries undertook to use "every means within their power solemnly to publicize the text of the Declaration and to cause it to be disseminated, displayed, read and expounded principly in schools and other educational institutions, without distinction based on the political status of countries or territories".

Not only has the Universal Declaration of Human Rights had a profound influence upon provincial and federal human rights legislation in Canada, it significantly influenced our federal government in its drafting and construction of the single most important constitutional document in Canada — the *Canadian Charter of Rights and Freedoms.* Although the specific provisions of the Universal Declaration of Human Rights cannot be enforced within our courts, it remains the most significant document for those who wish to gain a true understanding of the development of human rights legislation in Canada.

CHAPTER 3

The Concept of Discrimination

The concept of discrimination is far from static. Human rights law itself, in its infancy from a historical legal perspective, is ever-changing as a result of the numerous decisions of statutory human rights tribunals, the courts and amendments to existing legislation. Discrimination is, by its very nature, incapable of precise definition. Conspicuous by its absence in any of the provincial human rights legislation or the *Canadian Human Rights Act*, is a definition, in whole or in part, of discrimination except for the Quebec Charter.[1]

The Quebec Charter is the only human rights legislation in Canada which attempts to provide a definition of discrimination:

> 10. Every person has a right to full and equal recognition and exercise of his human rights and freedoms, without distinction, exclusion or preference based on race, colour, sex, pregnancy, sexual orientation, civil status, age except as provided by law, religion, political convictions, language, ethnic or national origin, social condition, a handicap or the use of any means to palliate a handicap.
>
> Discrimination exists where such a distinction, exclusion or preference has the effect of nullifying or impairing such right.

As noted in Tarnopolsky and Pentney, *Discrimination and the Law*[2] the above-noted definition is quite similar to the definition of "racial discrimination" in the International Convention on the Elimination of all Forms of Racial Discrimination, adopted by the United Nations in 1965, and ratified by Canada:

> Any distinction, exclusion, restriction or preference based on race, colour, descent or national or ethnic origin which has the purpose or effect of nullifying or impairing the recognition, enjoyment or exercise, on an equal footing of human rights and fundamental freedoms in the political, economic, social, cultural or any other field of public life.

The absence of any definition of discrimination in provincial and federal human rights legislation, with the exception of the Quebec Charter, is very likely attributable, at least in part, to the very fluid and ever-changing notion of discrimination. It is for this reason that, in order to gain an understanding

---

[1] Charter of Human Rights and Freedoms, R.S.Q. 1977, c. C-12, as amended.
[2] Walter Tarnopolsky and William F. Pentney, *Discrimination and the Law*, Rev'd 1st ed. (Toronto, Carswell, 1985).

of the law relating to discrimination in employment, one should focus on gaining an understanding of the fundamental concepts involved in or relating to discrimination, as opposed to endeavouring to craft a precise and exhaustive definition of the concept. The most fundamental notions relating to the subject of discrimination are:

1. direct discrimination;
2. constructive or adverse effect discrimination;
3. affirmative action.

The significance of these three concepts warrants some consideration.

1. DIRECT DISCRIMINATION

A. Under the OHRC

Section 3 of the Ontario *Human Rights Code* provides the basic right to contract on equal terms without discrimination:

> 3. Every person having legal capacity has a right to contract on equal terms without discrimination because of race, ancestry, place of origin, colour, ethnic origin, citizenship, creed, sex, sexual orientation, age, marital status, family status or handicap.

This right to contract on equal terms without discrimination clearly applies to contracts of employment, as well as other types of commercial and non-commercial contracts.

The fundamental right to equal treatment with respect to employment without discrimination is set out in s. 5 of the Code:

> 5(1) Every person has a right to equal treatment with respect to employment without discrimination because of race, ancestry, place of origin, colour, ethnic origin, citizenship, creed, sex, sexual orientation, age, record of offences, marital status, family status or handicap.
>
> (2) Every person who is an employee has a right to freedom from harassment in the workplace by the employer or agent of the employer or by another employee because of race, ancestry, place of origin, colour, ethnic origin, citizenship, creed, age, record of offences, marital status, family status or handicap.

Section 7 contains general prohibitions against harassment in the workplace because of sex, as well as sexual solicitation or advances made by a person in a position to confer, grant or deny a benefit or advancement to the person. Section 10, in turn, confirms that the right to equal treatment without discrimination because of sex includes the right to equal treatment without discrimination because a woman is or may become pregnant. Discrimination because of relationship, association or dealings with a person or persons identified by a prohibited ground of discrimination is precluded by the express provisions of s. 12 of the Ontario *Human Rights Code*. Finally, employers are prohibited from engaging in discriminatory employment advertising and attempting to obtain information from an applicant for employment, during the pre-employment stage, where that information could be used to directly or indirectly classify or indicate qualifications by a prohibited ground of discrimination.

The above-noted sections of the Ontario *Human Rights Code* are the prohibitions against direct discrimination in the employment relationship. These provisions are interpreted in an extremely broad and liberal manner so as to give effect to the purpose, spirit and intent of the legislation.

B. Under the CHRA

Section 3 of the *Canadian Human Rights Act* is the general provision in the legislation which sets out proscribed grounds of discrimination:

> 3(1) For all purposes of this Act, race, national or ethnic origin, colour, religion, age, sex, marital status, family status, disability and conviction for which a pardon has been granted are prohibited grounds of discrimination.
>
> (2) Where the ground of discrimination is pregnancy or child-birth, the discrimination shall be deemed to be on the ground of sex.

Sections 5 through 14 of the legislation involve prohibited discriminatory practices. The proscribed discriminatory practices which pertain to the employment relationship are contained in the following sections of the Act:

> 7. It is a discriminatory practice, directly or indirectly,
>
> (*a*) to refuse to employ or continue to employ any individual, or
>
> (*b*) in the course of employment, to differentiate adversely in relation to an employee,
>
> on a prohibited ground of discrimination.

> 8. It is a discriminatory practice
>
> (*a*) to use or circulate any form of application for employment, or
>
> (*b*) in connection with employment or prospective employment, to publish any advertisement or to make any written or oral inquiry
>
> that expresses or implies any limitation, specification or preference based on a prohibited ground of discrimination.

> 9(1) It is a discriminatory practice for an employee organization on a prohibited ground of discrimination
>
> (*a*) to exclude an individual from full membership in the organization;
>
> (*b*) to expel or suspend a member of the organization; or
>
> (*c*) to limit, segregate, classify or otherwise act in relation to an individual in a way that would deprive the individual of employment opportunities, or limit employment opportunities or otherwise adversely affect the status of the individual, where the individual is a member of the organization or where any of the obligations of the organization pursuant to a collective agreement relate to the individual.
>
> (2) Notwithstanding subsection (1), it is not a discriminatory practice for an employee organization to exclude, expel or suspend an individual from membership in the organization because that individual has reached the normal age of retirement for individuals working in positions similar to the position of that individual.
>
> (3) For the purposes of this section and sections 10 and 60, ''employee organization'' includes a trade union or other organization of employees or local

thereof, the purposes of which include the negotiation, on behalf of employees, of the terms and conditions of employment with employers.

10. It is a discriminatory practice for an employee, employer organization or organization of employers
> (*a*)   to establish or pursue a policy or practice, or
> (*b*)   to enter into an agreement affecting recruitment, referral, hiring, promotion, training, apprenticeship, transfer or any other matter relating to employment or prospective employment,

that deprives or tends to deprive an individual or class of individuals of any employment opportunities on a prohibited ground of discrimination.

11(1)   It is a discriminatory practice for an employer to establish or maintain differences in wages between male and female employees employed in the same establishment who are performing work of equal value.

(2)   In assessing the value of work performed by employees employed in the same establishment, the criterion to be applied is the composite of the skill, effort and responsibility required in the performance of the work and the conditions under which the work is performed.

. . . . .

14(1)   It is a discriminatory practice,

. . . . .

> (*c*)   In matters related to employment,

to harass an individual on a prohibited ground of discrimination.

(2)   Without limiting the generality of subsection (1), sexual harassment shall, for the purposes of that subsection, be deemed to be harassment on a prohibited ground of discrimination.

C. Reprisal

Under s. 8 of the Ontario *Human Rights Code*, every person has a right to claim and enforce his or her rights under the legislation, to institute and participate in proceedings under the Act and to refuse to infringe a right of another person under the legislation, without reprisal or threat of reprisal for so doing. Although stated in somewhat stronger language, the *Canadian Human Rights Act* contains a similar provision prohibiting any form of reprisal being taken against an individual with respect to the enforcement mechanisms of the legislation:

> 59. No person shall threaten, intimidate or discriminate against an individual because that individual has made a complaint or given evidence or assisted in any way in respect of the initiation or prosecution of a complaint or other proceeding under this Part, or because that individual proposes to do so.

The existence of reprisal provisions in human rights legislation places employers in a very difficult situation in cases in which they propose to discipline and/or terminate the employment of an individual in circumstances where they are aware of the fact that the individual has either been in contact with or already filed a complaint with the Human Rights Commission. It is by no means an overstatement to suggest that once an individual has consulted with the Human Rights Commission with a view towards filing a complaint or has in fact filed a complaint, to the knowledge of his or her employer, the individual's status as an employee becomes more secure as a result of the implicit protective status which arises as a result of these broadly worded and far-reaching reprisal provisions. An employer would be ill-advised to deal with any employee in an arbitrary or precipitous manner in circumstances whereby they have direct knowledge or reason to believe that the individual has instituted or is contemplating the initiation of a human rights complaint.

D. Exceptions

(i) Under the OHRC

The specifically defined exceptions to direct discrimination, as it applies to the employment relationship, are found in the following subsections of the legislation:

Section 14: Contains extensive provisions relating to the implementation of special programs or, what are often referred to as affirmative action programs;[3]

Section 15: Non-discrimination because of age is not infringed where an age of 65 years or over is a requirement, qualification or consideration for preferential treatment;

Section 16: Non-discrimination because of citizenship is not infringed where Canadian citizenship is a requirement, qualification or consideration imposed or authorized by law;

Section 17: A right of a person is not infringed for the reason only that the person is incapable of performing or fulfilling the essential duties or requirements attending the exercise of the right because of handicap. The employer does, however, have a duty to accommodate the individual short of undue hardship.[4]

Section 24: The right under section 5 to equal treatment with respect to employment is not infringed in certain situations which are particularized in subsections (a) through (d) of s. 24(1) as follows:

---

[3] See, *infra*, heading "Affirmative Action", in this chapter.
[4] See Chapter 9, Duty to Accommodate.

(a)   a religious, philanthropic, educational, fraternal or social institution or organization that is primarily engaged in serving the interests of persons identified by their race, ancestry, place of origin, colour, ethnic origin, creed, sex, age, marital status or handicap employs only, or gives preference in employment to, persons similarly identified if the qualification is a reasonable and *bona fide* qualification because of the nature of the employment;

(b)   the discrimination in employment is for reasons of age, sex, record of offences or marital status if the age, sex, record of offences or marital status of the applicant is a reasonable and *bona fide* qualification because of the nature of the employment;

(c)   an individual person refuses to employ another for reasons of any prohibited ground of discrimination in section 5, where the primary duty of the employment is attending to the medical or personal needs of the person or of an ill child or an aged, infirm or ill spouse or other relative of the person; or

(d)   an employer grants or withholds employment or advancement in employment to a person who is the spouse, child or parent of the employer or employee.

(ii) Under the CHRA

The *Canadian Human Rights Act* contains a number of exceptions to the direct discrimination provisions of the legislation, as they apply to the employment relationship:

Section 9(2):

. . . it is not a discriminatory practice for an employee organization to exclude, expel or suspend an individual from membership in the organization because that individual has reached the normal age of retirement for individuals working in positions similar to the position of that individual;

Section 15: Sets out the primary exceptions to direct discrimination in subsections (a) through (f):

(a)   any refusal, exclusion, expulsion, suspension, limitation, specification or preference in relation to any employment is established by an employer to be based on a *bona fide* occupational requirement;

(b)   employment of an individual is refused or terminated because that individual has not reached the minimum age, or has reached the maximum age, that applies to that employment by law or under regulations, which may be made by the Governor in Council for the purposes of this paragraph;

(c)   an individual's employment is terminated because that individual has reached the normal age of retirement for employees working in positions similar to the position of that individual;

(d)   the terms and conditions of any pension fund or plan established by an employer provide for the compulsory vesting or locking-in of pension contributions at a fixed or determinable age in accordance with section 10 of the *Pension Benefits Standards Act*;

. . . . .

(f)   an employer grants a female employee special leave for benefits in connection with pregnancy or child-birth or grants employees special leave or benefits to assist them in the care of their children;

Section 16:   Provides for the adoption of a special program, plan or arrangement, commonly referred to as affirmative action programs.

2. CONSTRUCTIVE DISCRIMINATION

A. Statutory Definition

(i) Under the OHRC

The Ontario *Human Rights Code* has been described, on many occasions, as being remedial legislation. In other words, the legislation is aimed first and foremost at remedying the effects of discrimination, as opposed to focusing upon punishment of individuals involved in discriminatory practices or other such related considerations. In other words, the legislature has sought to focus its efforts upon remedying the effects of discrimination, however it is caused and by whomever. Consistent with this very basic philosophy of the legislation is the provision found in s. 11 of the Code relating to constructive discrimination:

> 11(1) A right of a person under Part I is infringed where a requirement, qualification or factor exists that is not discrimination on a prohibited ground but that results in the exclusion, restriction or preference of a group of persons who are identified by a prohibited ground of discrimination and of whom the person is a member, except where,
> (a)   the requirement, qualification or factor is reasonable and *bona fide* in the circumstances; or
> (b)   it is declared in this Act, other than in section 17, that to discriminate because of such ground is not an infringement of a right.

In essence, the above-noted constructive discrimination provision of the Ontario *Human Rights Code* is meant to address a situation in which an employer may engage in or adhere to a practice or policy which on its face appears to be neutral but which has the effect of excluding or otherwise being to the disadvantage of a group or class of individuals who can be identified with a prohibited ground of discrimination. For example, a company may be the subject of allegations of discriminatory hiring practices based solely on the historical cross-section of individuals hired over time. If a reasonably large company was found to have hired 92% males for lower, middle and upper management positions over the last fifteen years, it could be subject to a complaint of discriminatory hiring policies. Even though the company may have had an enlightened and comprehensive hiring policy, which was faithfully adhered to by its agents and employees, it could be found to have violated the constructive discrimination provisions of the legislation and possibly subject to an order which includes an ''affirmative action'' hiring policy component.

(ii) Under the CHRA

The constructive discrimination provisions in the *Canadian Human Rights Act* are more subtle in their express wording, as compared to s. 11 of the Ontario *Human Rights Code*:

> 7. It is a discriminatory practice, *directly or indirectly,*
>> (*a*) to refuse to employ or to continue to employ any individual, or
>> (*b*) in the course of employment, to differentiate adversely in relation to an employee,
>
> on a prohibited ground of discrimination.

. . . . .

> 10. It is a discriminatory practice for an employer, employee organization or organization of employers
>> (*a*) to establish or pursue a policy or practice, or
>> (*b*) to enter into an agreement affecting recruitment, referral, hiring, promotion, training, apprenticeship, transfer or any other matter relating to employment or prospective employment,
>
> *that deprives or tends to deprive* an individual or class of individuals of any employment opportunities on a prohibited ground of discrimination.

(Emphasis added.)

There can be no question that ss. 7 and 10 of the *Canadian Human Rights Act*, noted above, embody the concept of constructive discrimination, thereby making it a prohibition within the four corners of the legislation.

B. No Requirement of Intention

Constructive discrimination, by its very definition, covers discriminatory actions and omissions which are completely unintentional.

An employer who conducts its business in good faith and with the most praiseworthy intentions may, nonetheless, be found liable for discriminatory practices under human rights legislation.

In *Ontario (Human Rights Commission) v. Simpson-Sears Ltd.*[5] the Supreme Court of Canada made it clear that proof of intention is not required in order to find an employer liable for discriminatory conduct.

In the *Simpson-Sears* case, an employee called O'Malley alleged discrimination on the basis of creed, because she was periodically required to work

---

[5] (1985), 23 D.L.R. (4th) 321, [1985] 2 S.C.R. 536.

Friday evenings and Saturdays as a condition of her employment contrary to her religious faith. The evidence at the initial hearing established that:

1. O'Malley became a Seventh-Day Adventist seven years after commencing her employment with Simpson-Sears;
2. Simpson-Sears' policy of Saturday opening was adopted for sound business reasons and applied to all retail sales employees;
3. the company offered O'Malley a part-time position when she could not continue her original employment on the required basis;
4. Simpson-Sears undertook to consider O'Malley for any full-time position for which she might be suitable.

In upholding O'Malley's complaint, the Supreme Court of Canada definitively states that "an intention to discriminate is not a necessary element of the discrimination generally forbidden in Canadian human rights legislation".[6] When an employee is detrimentally affected by such "adverse effect discrimination", it is "incumbent upon the employer to make a reasonable effort to accommodate the religious needs of the employee, short of undue hardship to the employer in the conduct of his business". The Supreme Court of Canada defines constructive discrimination as follows:

> It arises where an employer for genuine business reasons adopts a rule or standard which is on its face neutral, and which will apply equally to all employees, but which has a discriminatory effect upon a prohibited ground on one employee or group of employees in that it imposes, because of some special characteristic of the employee or group, obligations, penalties, or restrictive conditions not imposed on other members of the work force.[7]

The statutory recognition of constructive discrimination significantly increases the burden and liability of the employer. An employment policy may be in place for a significant period of time before a new employee enters the workforce and faces discrimination as a result of the impugned policy. Prior to this employee's arrival, the policy appears neutral in its effect. Nonetheless, the employer has a duty to reasonably accommodate the needs of the new employee.

3. AFFIRMATIVE ACTION

A. Statutory Provisions

(i) Under the OHRC

Section 14 of the Ontario *Human Rights Code* contains provisions relating to the implementation of a "special program" or, what is commonly referred to, as an affirmative action program:

---

6 *Supra*, at p. 329.
7 *Supra*, at p. 332.

14(1) A right under Part I is not infringed by the implementation of a special program designed to relieve hardship or economic disadvantage or to assist disadvantaged persons or groups to achieve or attempt to achieve equal opportunity or that is likely to contribute to the elimination of the infringement of rights under Part I.

(2) The Commission may,

    (a) upon its own initiative;

    (b) upon application by a person seeking to implement a special program under the protection of subsection (1); or

    (c) upon a complaint in respect of which the protection of subsection (1) is claimed,

inquire into the special program and, in the discretion of the Commission, may by order declare,

    (d) that the special program, as defined in the order, does not satisfy the requirements of subsection (1); or

    (e) that the special program as defined in the order, with such modifications, if any, as the Commission considers advisable, satisfies the requirements of subsection (1).

(ii) Under the CHRA

Section 16 of the *Canadian Human Rights Act* is the general provision relating to the adoption or implementation of special programs:

16(1) It is not a discriminatory practice for a person to adopt or carry out a special program, plan or arrangement designed to prevent disadvantages that are likely to be suffered by, or to eliminate or reduce disadvantages that are suffered by, any group of individuals when those disadvantages would be or are based on or related to the race, national or ethnic origin, colour, religion, age, sex, marital status, family status or disability of members of that group, by improving opportunities respecting goods, services, facilities, accommodation or employment in relation to that group.

Subsection (2) of s. 16 goes on to provide that the Canadian Human Rights Commission may make general recommendations concerning "desirable objectives" for special programs, as well as giving advice and assistance with respect to the adoption or implementation of a special program, when requested.

Section 17 of the Act specifically relates to the implementation of a special program to meet the needs of a person arising from a disability:

17(1) A person who proposes to implement a plan for adapting any services, facilities, premises, equipment or operations to meet the needs of persons arising from a disability may apply to the Canadian Human Rights Commission for approval of the plan.

. . . . .

(3) Where any services, facilities, premises, equipment or operations are adapted in accordance with a plan approved under subsection (2), matters for which the plan provides do not constitute any basis for a complaint under Part III

regarding discrimination based on any disability in respect of which the plan was approved.

Accordingly, s. 17 of the Act provides a procedure relating to the approval of a plan to address the needs of persons arising from a disability, whereby the Commission's approval would effectively result in the employer being insulated from any complaint on the grounds of disability which relates directly or indirectly to the plan as implemented by the employer. Sections 18 and 19 of the Act provide that the approval of the plan referred to in s. 17 may be rescinded at any subsequent point in time, based on changing circumstances or for any other sufficient reason, whereby all interested parties have an opportunity to make representations with respect to the proposed recission of the plan.

B. General Principles

The importance of affirmative action programs is effectively summarized by the Ontario Law Reform Commission in its study paper on "Litigating The Relationship Between Equity And Equality":[8]

> ... Preferential treatment policies to expedite the representation, access and retention of individuals from under-represented groups in certain societal institutions, activities, and positions remain important components in most equity programs. In expressly endorsing affirmative action as a means for achieving substantive equality, the Supreme Court of Canada has specifically emphasized that hiring quotas may be an important and integral part of employment equity. In the *Action travail des Femmes* case, the court approved a quota order by a human rights tribunal that one out of every four new employees hired be a woman until 18% of the blue collar jobs at Canadian National Railway were filled by women. One of the court's central justifications for hiring quotas was the importance of ensuring a "critical mass" of individuals from historically excluded groups:
>
>> "The presence of a significant number of individuals from the targeted group eliminates the problem of 'tokenism'; it is no longer the case that one or two women, for example, will be seen to 'represent' all women . . . Moreover, women will not be so easily placed on the periphery of management concern . . . once a 'critical mass' of the previously excluded group has been created in the work force, there is a significant chance for the continuing self-correction of the system."[9]

As stated by Judith Keene in her book, *Human Rights in Ontario*,[10] affirmative action programs aimed at increasing the representation of a target group in a particular sector of the economy generally involve the implementation of one or more of the following strategies:

---

[8] Prepared by Colleen Sheppard, Faculty of Law, McGill University, 1990.

[9] *Ibid.*, at pp. 12-13.

[10] Judith Keene, *Human Rights in Ontario*, 2nd ed. (Scarborough, Carswell, 1992), p. 167.

1.   criteria for the position are reviewed and, where the maintenance of relatively unimportant criterion would bar most members of a specific group, that criterion is dropped or relaxed;
2.   the employer or institution actively recruits within the minority group population through advertisements in ethnic newspapers, appropriately worded general advertisements, etc.;
3.   the employer or institution initiates or supports special training programs designed to "upgrade" the qualifications of a specified group;
4.   "goals and time tables" are imposed so that, through the use of the above four or other strategies, the employer or institution, by a specific date, might achieve the employment or enrolment of a number of minority group people equal to their representation in the population.

As was held by the United States Supreme Court in its landmark decision in *United Steelworkers of America, AFL-CIO-CLC v. Weber*[11] there are three requirements for an affirmative action program:

(a)   it should be designed to remedy past discrimination;
(b)   it should be temporary in duration;
(c)   it should not unnecessarily trammel the interests of employees who are not in the groups designated for affirmative action.

The design and implementation of an affirmative action program involves the most delicate exercise in the balancing of the interests of all employees within the workplace in attempting to specially provide for a disadvantaged group within the employee population.

One of the common criticisms lodged against affirmative action programs are that they are typically unfairly "under inclusive". In other words, they tend to provide relief only for some individuals and groups as opposed to providing assistance to all of those in need. In this sense, it is claimed that the grounds for non-inclusion in the program are, in essence, discriminatory.

One of the fundamental criticisms of the concept of affirmative action is persuasively rebutted by the Ontario Law Reform Commission in its study paper:

> In the context of affirmative action, preferential hiring and admissions programs, designed to expedite entry of historically disadvantaged and excluded social groups, have been at the heart of the controversy about the fairness of affirmative action. It is argued that preferential treatment policies constitute unfair departures from merit-based selection criteria. It is illusory, however to speak of any selection system that is premised solely on objective merit. The assessment of what is meritorious is imbued with the subtle and overt biases, that have created the very group based patterns of exclusion that equity initiatives are aimed at redressing. Nevertheless, overt preferential hiring or admissions programs are often regarded as discriminatory against historically advantaged groups.[12]

---

[11]   443 U.S. 193, 99 S. Ct. 2721 (1979).
[12]   "Litigating The Relationship Between Equity And Equality, *ibid.*, footnote 8, p. 39.

In the final analysis, employers are well-advised to take maximum advantage of the potential input of the Human Rights Commission when designing and implementing any affirmative action program. This serves to minimize the potential for future human rights complaints in relation to affirmative action programs, as well as make available experienced advice at no cost to the company.

CHAPTER 4

Advertising, Application Forms, Interviewing and Hiring Policies

1. DISCRIMINATORY EMPLOYMENT ADVERTISING

A. Under the OHRC

Section 5 of the Ontario *Human Rights Code*, R.S.O. 1990, c. H.19, guarantees the right to "equal treatment with respect to employment". This broad provision has been interpreted both by the Human Rights Commission and the courts to apply to all aspects of employment and prospective employment, including the recruitment and hiring of employees.

One of the most significant hiring activities regulated by the Code relates to employment advertising. Section 23(1) of the Code provides:

> 23(1) The right under section 5 to equal treatment with respect to employment is infringed where an invitation to apply for employment or an advertisement in connection with employment is published or displayed that directly or indirectly classifies or indicates qualifications by a prohibited ground of discrimination.

Section 23(1) of the Code is generally referred to as the prohibition against discriminatory employment advertising.

The grounds of discrimination prohibited by s. 5 of the Code are:

— race
— ancestry
— place of origin
— colour
— ethnic origin
— citizenship
— creed
— sex
— sexual orientation
— age
— record of offences
— marital status
— family status
— handicap

Accordingly, pursuant to the provisions of s. 23(1) of the Code, employers are prohibited from discriminating directly or indirectly, in inviting or advertising employment, based on any of the above-mentioned classifications.

Although the prohibition against discriminatory employment advertising appears to be straightforward, the difficulty lies in determining the practical extent or scope of this prohibition. For example, discriminatory employment advertising would include advertisements which, on their face, appear to be fairly innocent and non-discriminatory, such as:

(1) a request for "waitresses" as opposed to "waiters/waitresses", which would constitute sexual discrimination;
(2) a requirement for "able-bodied persons" would, arguably, offend the prohibition against discriminating on the basis of handicap;
(3) the guidelines published by the Human Rights Commission suggest that a stated request or preference for "Canadian experience" may offend the prohibitions against discrimination based on place of origin or citizenship.

Discriminatory employment advertising includes not only the structure or wording of the advertisement itself, but the manner or medium through which the position is advertised. For example, if an employer was to advertise a position for employment in The Catholic Register, and no other newspaper or publication, it is entirely possible that the employer would be vulnerable to a complaint of discrimination on the basis of religion. In other words, the medium through which the position was advertised would seem to imply a requirement or preference for applicants who are members of the Roman Catholic faith.

While employers must be careful in wording their advertisements and in promoting the position in a non-discriminatory fashion, companies are permitted to categorize employment advertisements according to occupational groupings, such as "clerical", "secretarial" or "automotive". Likewise, employers may also note job-related specifications such as, in the case of warehouse work, "heavy lifting involved".

Even strict compliance with the procedural requirements of s. 23(1) of the Code, will not, necessarily, provide an employer with an absolute defence to any complaint of discriminatory employment advertising. It is one thing to advertise in an entirely neutral and non-discriminatory fashion. It is quite another to then refuse to entertain certain applications for employment for discriminatory reasons.

In *Blanchette v. Marinos Investments (Sault) Ltd.*,[1] the employer placed an advertisement in a newspaper which stated "waitress or waiter needed".

---

[1] (unreported, Ont. Bd. Inq.). See *Ontario Human Rights Commission Annual Report*, 1987-88, p. 32.

The complainant and his female cousin both applied for the position. The cousin was granted an interview, while the complainant was not contacted by the company after submitting his employment application. When Mr. Blanchette telephoned to inquire why he was not granted an interview, he was advised that ''we only hire females here''. A board of inquiry found the employer acted in violation of the Code and awarded the complainant $500 for loss of opportunity, $500 for mental anguish and $195 in interest.

Section 24 of the Code provides an exemption from the strict requirements of the right to ''equal treatment with respect to employment'', contained in s. 5 of the Code, in the following circumstances:

(a) a religious, philanthropic, social or similar organization whose primary work involves providing services for persons identified by race, religion, colour, etc., gives preferential treatment to persons similarly identified where the qualification is reasonable because of the nature of the employment;

(b) the discrimination is a reasonable and *bona fide* qualification having regard to the nature of the employment;

(c) the primary duty of the employment is attending to the medical or personal needs of the employer or an individual requiring special care; or

(d) the employer withholds employment based on an anti-nepotism policy.

However, these exemptions relate to the *offering* of employment as opposed to *advertising* for positions of employment. Prudent employers ought to both provide and elicit information relating to a s. 24(1) exemption at the employment interview itself and not through the advertisement for employment.

B. Under the CHRA

Section 8 of the *Canadian Human Rights Act*, R.S.C. 1985, c. H-6, contains the following prohibition in relation to employment applications and advertisements:

8. It is a discriminatory practice
(*a*) to use or circulate any form of application for employment, or
(*b*) in connection with employment or prospective employment, to publish any advertisement or to make any written or oral inquiry
that expresses or implies any limitation, specification or preference based on a prohibited ground of discrimination.

The prohibited grounds of discrimination are in turn found in s. 3 of the Act and consist of race, national or ethnic origin, colour, religion, age, sex, marital status, family status, disability and conviction for which a pardon has been granted.

Section 10 of the *Canadian Human Rights Act* in turn prohibits discriminatory practices in relation to policies affecting recruitment, hiring and related activities:

> 10. It is a discriminatory practice for an employer, employee organization or organization of employers
>
> (*a*) to establish or pursue a policy or practice, or
>
> (*b*) to enter into an agreement affecting recruitment, referral, hiring, promotion, training, apprenticeship, transfer or any other matter relating to employment or prospective employment,
>
> that deprives or tends to deprive an individual or class of individuals of any employment opportunities on a prohibited ground of discrimination.

2. APPLICATION FOR EMPLOYMENT

In drafting employment application forms which comply with existing human rights legislation, employers must walk a very fine line between requesting information that is pertinent to assessing the individual's qualifications, training and experience for the position without endeavouring to obtain information which falls within the realm of a prohibited ground of discrimination. Extraneous questions which have the effect of eliciting irrelevant, personal information in relation to the applicant are to be avoided.

The central provision of the Ontario *Human Rights Code* which regulates the application for employment, is s. 23(2) which provides:

> 23(2) The right under section 5 to equal treatment with respect to employment is infringed where a form of application for employment is used or a written or oral inquiry is made of an applicant that directly or indirectly classifies or indicates qualifications by a prohibited ground of discrimination.

Section 8(*a*) of the *Canadian Human Rights Act* contains a similar prohibition.

The Human Rights Commission clearly recognizes and, to some extent at least, sympathizes with the practical difficulties encountered by employers in endeavouring to comply with the provisions of s. 23(2) of the Code. The Commission prepares and, upon request, distributes a sample application form which complies with the provisions of the Code. In addition, the Commission will advise employers with regard to specific questions relating to the application for employment.

Furthermore, the Commission encourages employers to submit their application forms in order to be approved in advance by the Commission. Employers who receive such approval from the Commission are entitled to note, at the bottom of the application form, that their application form has been approved by the Ontario Human Rights Commission.

The following application form has been prepared and approved by the Ontario Human Rights Commission as a document which is in compliance with the provisions of the Ontario *Human Rights Code:*

APPLICATION FOR EMPLOYMENT

Position being applied for	Date available to begin work

PERSONAL DATA

Last name	Given name(s)

Address	Street	Apt. No.	Home Telephone Number
City	Province	Postal Code	Business Telephone Number

Are you legally eligible to work in Canada? ☐ Yes   ☐ No

Are you 18 years and more and less than 65 years of age?   ☐ Yes   ☐ No

Are you willing to relocate in Ontario? Preferred Location ☐ Yes ☐ No	

To determine your qualification for employment, please provide below and on the reverse, information related to your academic and other achievements including volunteer work, as well as employment history. Additional information may be attached on a separate sheet.

EDUCATION

SECONDARY SCHOOL ■	BUSINESS, TRADE OR SECONDARY SCHOOL ■	
Highest grade or level completed	Name of course	Lenth of course
Type of certificate or diploma obtained	License, certificate or diploma awarded? ☐ Yes ☐ No	

COMMUNITY COLLEGE ■	UNIVERSITY ■		
Name of Program Length of Program	Length of course	Degree awarded ☐ Yes ☐ No	☐ Pass ☐ Honours
Diploma received ☐ Yes ☐ No	Major subject		
Other courses, workshops, seminars	Licenses, Certificates, Degrees		

Work related skills

Describe any of your work related skills, experience, or training that relate to the position being applied for.

EMPLOYMENT

Name and Address of present/last employer	Present/Last job title	
	Period of employment From To	Present/Last salary
	Name of Supervisor	Telephone
Type of Business	Reason for leaving	

Functions/Responsibilities

Name and Address of former employer	Present/Last job title	
	Period of employment From To	Present/Last salary
	Name of Supervisor	Telephone
Type of Business	Reason for leaving	

Functions/Responsibilities

Name and Address of former employer	Present/Last job title	
	Period of employment From To	Present/Last salary
	Name of Supervisor	Telephone
Type of Business	Reason for leaving	

Functions/Responsibilities

For employment references we may approach:

Your present/last employer?	☐ Yes	☐ No
Your former employer(s)?	☐ Yes	☐ No

List references if different than above on a separate sheet.

Personal interests and activities (civic, athletic etc.)

I hereby declare that the foregoing information is true and complete to my knowledge. I understand that a false statement may disqualify me from employment, or cause my dismissal.	Have you attached an additional sheet? ☐ Yes ☐ No
	_____ _____ Signature Date

The following represents a summary of the major grounds of discrimination as they relate to applications for employment:

Birthplace, ancestry, ethnic origin and place of origin. With the exception of philanthropic, religious and social organizations, all questions related to this category are prohibited.

Sex, sexual orientation, marital status and family status. Overt questions relating to this category are prohibited as are requests for photographs. Similarly, asking the applicant to select how they wish to be addressed (Mr., Mrs., Miss, Ms) is inappropriate. Information about spouses or children is also prohibited. Indirect questions which are prohibited include those relating to weight or height. The applicant may be asked if he or she is willing to relocate or travel if the information is relevant to the job.

Age. The prohibition of discrimination based upon age is limited to individuals between the ages of eighteen and sixty-five. Accordingly, it is permissible to ask if the applicant is between eighteen and sixty-five but it is not permissible to request the applicant's age, date of birth, birth or baptismal certificate.

Race, colour. Any questions regarding these categories are prohibited. Indirect questions would include colour of eyes or hair, height, weight and requests for photographs.

Religion, creed. All questions relating to these categories are prohibited. The prohibition includes questions of churches attended, religious holidays or customs observed or willingness to work on specific religious holidays.

Citizenship. Inquiries as to categories such as "Canadian citizen", "landed immigrant", "permanent resident" and so forth are prohibited. An employer, however, may ask if the applicant is legally entitled to work in Canada.

Education. Job-related inquiries such as grade/level completed or diploma received are permissible, however, questions regarding the name and location of elementary school are prohibited.

Record of offences. Where relevant, an applicant may be asked whether s/he has ever been convicted of a criminal offence for which a pardon has not been granted. Inquiries may also be made, where relevant, to determine if the applicant is bondable. General inquiries whether the applicant has ever been convicted for any offence, has ever been charged or arrested for any offences or ever spent time in jail are prohibited.

Handicap. Questions regarding health, handicaps, physical or mental defects or any similar questions are prohibited.

References and membership in organizations. Inquiries should not be made as to membership in organizations and an applicant should not be required to provide references which would identify his or her religious affiliation. The best reference is from a former employer. When requesting a reference, the prospective employer should protect itself by advising the former employer at the outset of the conversation that it is not interested in any information regarding a prohibited ground of discrimination.

The Ontario Human Rights Commission also advises employers not to request a driver's licence number from job applicants. The following is an excerpt from its "Policy on Requiring a Driver's Licence as a Condition of Employment",[2] in which the rationale for its position on this subject is explained:

> As an individual's licence number contains his or her birth date, requesting such information on an application form would be contrary to subsection 22(2).
> Furthermore, a general requirement of a driver's licence may result in the inadvertent exclusion of applicants with certain disabilities who otherwise qualify for the position, but because of their particular disabilities are unable to obtain a driver's licence. Therefore, the question, "Can you drive?" on an application form, also may be contrary to section 10. This section provides that qualifications or requirements that appear to be neutral but have a disproportionately negative impact on a group covered in the Code must be removed or, if that is not possible, that the needs of the group so affected must be accommodated.
> This duty to provide accommodation is discussed further below.
> For positions where driving is an essential duty of the job, the inclusion of the following statement on an application form or in an advertisement would be an appropriate means for addressing both the respective needs and concerns of the employer and applicant.
> "This position requires a valid driver's licence and proof of it is required after hire."

Even with an appropriate application form, the employer may still obtain extraneous information contained, for example, in an applicant's resumé. In the event of a complaint to the Human Rights Commission, it may be difficult for the employer to argue that the information was not considered in the hiring process. Employers may wish to state, on the face of the application form itself, that the applicant is prohibited from providing any information other than that which is expressly requested within the application form itself.

3. THE EMPLOYMENT INTERVIEW

Generally speaking, employers have a greater degree of latitude in relation to questions that may be asked during the course of the employment interview,

---

[2] "Policy on Requiring a Driver's Licence as a Condition of Employment" (Ontario Human Rights Commission, 1990), p. 1. Reprinted, November, 1991.

than they do with respect to information that may be elicited in the application for employment. However, these questions must be carefully structured and directed primarily to the individual's qualifications and suitability for the prospective position of employment.

For example, inquiries may be made regarding Canadian citizenship if:

(1) citizenship is required by law for the particular position;

(2) citizenship or permanent residency is required for participation in cultural, educational, trade union or athletic activities, or

(3) the position requires the holder to be a Canadian citizen or domiciled in Canada with the intention of becoming a citizen.

Similarly, an applicant may be asked to furnish proof of his or her eligibility to work in Canada.

A request for verification of one's educational background may be made at the employment interview, so long as this request does not extend to an attempt to elicit information which falls within a prohibited ground of discrimination. Likewise, inquiries directly related to an applicant's ability to perform a job are permitted. Medical examinations may be conducted following a conditional offer of employment but must be restricted to determining the applicant's ability to perform essential job requirements.

Finally, information relating to the individual's sex, sexual orientation, marital status, family status and/or age, for purposes of pension, insurance or superannuation plans, may be requested only after the individual is hired.

A prudent employer should give serious consideration to drafting a detailed agenda for every employment interview relating to a specific position of employment. The benefits of adhering to such a procedure would include the following:

(1) it would provide a logical structure to follow in interviewing all candidates for the position, thereby ensuring fairness and uniformity;

(2) if the interviewer made reasonably detailed notes of the answers and information given by the candidate, it would provide an accurate record of the interview;

(3) a copy of the agenda could be provided to each candidate, where the individual would verify that the written agenda accurately sets out all questions asked during the employment interview;

(4) in the event that the individual was ultimately hired, the employer would have a permanent record of what the individual was told about the position, as well as the pertinent information provided by the individual to the company at the pre-hiring stage.

The time expended in implementing and adhering to such a procedure would be more than offset by the potential benefits flowing from this procedure.

4. EMPLOYMENT AGENCIES

Employers cannot absolve themselves of all potential liability for human rights violations in the hiring process, by retaining the services of an employment agency.

Section 23(4) of the Ontario *Human Rights Code* makes it unlawful to place an order with an employment agency which would have the effect of contravening s. 5 of the Code. Likewise, it is unlawful for the employment agency to accept such an order. A similar prohibition can be found in s. 10(*b*) of the *Canadian Human Rights Act*.

Employment agencies have come under careful scrutiny by the Ontario Human Rights Commission in recent years. One of the most extensive investigations in the history of the Commission was initiated at the end of January, 1991, when the Commission filed complaints against two Toronto employment agencies. The Commission, through its Systemic Investigation Unit, took a strategic enforcement approach to the investigation, resulting in a tentative settlement with the two agencies, on terms subject to the formal approval of the Commission.

The time, resources and energy that were devoted to this mammoth investigation is indicative of the Commission's commitment to investigate complaints involving the practices and activities of employment agencies. Employers are well-advised to exercise caution and prudence in their selection of and dealings with employment agencies.

5. EMPLOYER HIRING POLICIES

A. Written vs. Unwritten Policies

A common misconception held by many employers is the notion that, in order for something to constitute a "company policy" it must be:

— in writing
— exhaustive
— non-discretionary (in terms of its day to day application).

Neither the Human Rights Commission, nor the courts for that matter, adopt such a highly restricted view of what amounts to "company policy". This is especially so in relation to employer hiring policies.

In the eyes of the Human Rights Commission, the hiring policy of an employer is determined by the conduct of that employer in relation to its treatment and consideration of a candidate or candidates for a position of employment. It is something that is deduced having regard not only to what is said and done by the company in relation to a candidate, but what is not said and not done as well.

By the same token, the creation and implementation of a comprehensive, enlightened, written hiring policy, which does not offend the extensive provisions of the *Human Rights Code*, will not provide an absolute defence to an allegation of discriminatory hiring. A company must conduct itself, on a day-to-day basis, in a reasonable and non-discriminatory manner in its consideration of prospective candidates for employment, as well as in its ultimate hiring decisions. This duty rests upon each and every individual that is involved in the hiring process, from the time of the placing of the advertisement for employment up to and including finalization of the employment agreement between the parties. The ultimate responsibility for ensuring that all members of the hiring team discharge their respective duties in this regard, lies with the employer.

Employers are encouraged and indeed, well-advised, to keep a detailed record of what is said and done in relation to each prospective candidate for a vacant position within the company.

Although this may appear to be a monumental task in today's economy, where applicants for a given position could easily number in the hundreds, a system can be devised whereby basic information in relation to the employer's dealings with each applicant is recorded. Such records assist the employer to establish not only its dealings with a specific applicant, but, perhaps even more importantly, its general hiring procedure with respect to a specific job vacancy.

B. Constructive Discrimination

A company may become subject to allegations of discriminatory hiring practises based solely on the historical cross-section of individuals hired over time. For example, if a reasonably large company was found to have hired 92% males for lower, middle and upper management positions over the last fifteen years, it could be subject to a complaint of discriminatory hiring policies. Even though the company may have had an enlightened and comprehensive hiring policy, which was faithfully adhered to by its agents and employees, it could be found guilty of discrimination and possibly subject to an order which includes an ''affirmative action'' hiring policy component.

An employer could be absolutely gender neutral in terms of its preference between male and female candidates for prospective employment, yet, if historical hiring data disclosed a significant statistical prevalence of male over female or vice-versa, that company could be found guilty of constructive discrimination in its hiring policies. This same principle would have equal application with respect to a significant statistical bias in relation to any of the other prohibited grounds of discrimination.

Perhaps the most vivid example of a human rights commission-ordered affirmative action program, to correct a gross imbalance reflected in historical hiring data of an employer, is the decision of the Supreme Court of Canada in *Action Travail des Femmes v. C.N.R. Co.*[3]

In the *C.N.R.* case, Action Travail des Femmes, a women's activist group, filed a complaint of discriminatory hiring and promotion practices against the railway, contrary to s. 10 of the *Canadian Human Rights Act*. Section 10 of the CHRA provides:

> 10. It is a discriminatory practice for an employer, employee organization or organization of employers,
>> (*a*) to establish or pursue a policy or practice, or
>> (*b*) to enter into an agreement affecting recruitment, referral, hiring, promotion, training, apprenticeship, transfer or any other matter relating to employment or prospective employment,
>
> that deprives or tends to deprive an individual or class of individuals of any employment opportunities or a prohibited ground of discrimination.

It was alleged that the railway had systematically denied employment opportunities to women in certain unskilled blue-collar positions.

The Human Rights Tribunal found that the recruitment, hiring and promotion policies at C.N. prevented and discouraged women from working in blue-collar jobs. Consequently, C.N. was ordered to undertake a special employment program designed to increase the proportion of women working in "non-traditional" occupations to 13% which represented, at that time, the national average. Until that goal was achieved, C.N. was required to hire at least one woman in every four non-traditional jobs filled.

In the course of the thirty-three days of hearings, the Tribunal heard a great deal of evidence, including the findings of a report that had been prepared in 1974 at the request of the then president of C.N. This report, entitled "Canadian National Action Programs — Women", included an extensive survey of the attitudes of male personnel at C.N. towards women. Examples, included:

1. "Women are generally disruptive to the workforce."
2. "Women aren't tough enough to handle supervisory jobs. They fail miserably under pressure."
3. "The best jobs for women are coach cleaners — that's second nature to them."
4. "One big problem in adding women to train crews would be policing the morals in the cabooses."
5. "Work in the yard is too physically demanding. The weather is too harsh."
6. "Women cannot do the physical aspects of a C.N. Conductor's job. There's too much handling of drunks, transients and undesirables."

---

[3] (1987), 40 D.L.R. (4th) 193, [1987] 1 S.C.R. 1114 *sub nom. Canadian National Railway Co. v. Canada (Canadian Human Rights Commission)*, 87 C.L.L.C. ¶17,022, 76 N.R. 161.

7. "Women have no drive, no ambition, no initiative."
8. 'A woman can't combine a career and family responsibilities."
9. "The 'old boy network' for promotions is very strong at C.N. This naturally inhibits women's advancement."
10. "My department is all male — they don't want a woman snooping around."
11. "Railroading is a man's sport — there's no room for women."

The Supreme Court of Canada upheld the order of the Human Rights Tribunal, primarily on the basis that the affirmative action order was designed to break a continuing cycle of systemic discrimination. In arriving at this conclusion, the court expressly underscored an important point in relation to human rights legislation in general:

> There is no indication that the purpose of the *Canadian Human Rights Act* is to assign or to punish moral blameworthiness. No doubt, some people who discriminate do so out of wilful ignorance or *animus*.
>
> . . . . .
>
> The rejection of a necessity to prove intent and the unequivocal adoption of the idea of ''adverse effect discrimination'' by the courts is the result of a commitment to the purposive interpretation of human rights legislation.[4]

A potential remedy in cases involving discriminatory hiring policies is that the commission monitor the hiring practices of the employer for a specified period of time. A precedent for this type of order can be found in the Ontario Board of Inquiry decision in *Hendry v. Ontario (Liquor Control Board)*.[5] In the *Hendry* case, a complaint was filed alleging that the employer refused to continue her employment because of her sex. In upholding the complaint, the Board of Inquiry ordered, in part:

> The Human Rights Commission has requested the opportunity to assist the LCBO in improving its employment practices [*sic*] so that they comply with the Code. It wishes to help develop a program to rectify the imbalance between men and women employed by the LCBO, and it wishes to monitor the LCBO employment practices for a period of twelve months from the date of this decision.[6]

Both the *C.N.R.* case and the *Hendry* decision, provide graphic illustrations as to the nature and extent of the remedial jurisdiction of human rights tribunals in endeavouring to redress discriminatory hiring practices.

C. Nepotism

Some human rights legislation expressly permits discriminatory hiring policies and practices aimed at nepotism.

---

[4] *Action Travail, supra,* footnote 3, at pp. 206-9.
[5] (1980), 1 C.H.R.R. D/160 (Ont. Bd. Inq.).
[6] *Supra,* at p. D/166.

Section 24(1)(d) of the Ontario Human Rights Code provides:

> 24(1) The right under section 5 to equal treatment with respect to employment is not infringed where,
>
> . . . . .
>
> (d) an employer grants or withholds employment or advancement in employment to a person who is the spouse, child or parent of the employer or an employee.

There is no such comparable provision contained in the *Canadian Human Rights Act*. Accordingly, employers falling under the jurisdiction of the *Canadian Human Rights Act* are precluded from enacting policies and/or practices to exclude nepotism in their hiring procedure.

It is clear that the statutorily permitted nepotism policy under the Ontario *Human Rights Code* applies only to a decision to hire or not hire in the first instance but has no application to a decision to terminate in the course of the employment relationship. For example, where co-workers marry while employed by the same company, the employer cannot rely upon the nepotism exception found in section 24(1)(d) to lawfully terminate the employment relationship. Nor can an employer rely upon this exception where it only learns after the fact that an employee it has hired is the spouse of another employee, as demonstrated by the Ontario Board of Inquiry decision in *Mark v. Porcupine General Hospital.*[7]

In the *Mark* case, Rosemary Mark was dismissed from her employment with the hospital because she was married to another employee, Norman Mark, both of whom worked in the same department. Mrs. Mark commenced her employment as a spare housekeeper on October 17, 1983. She worked approximately 110 hours prior to her employment being terminated on November 6, 1983.

The evidence at the hearing disclosed that:

(1) Mrs. Mark was initially hired by the Maintenance Supervisor, Mr. Philion;

(2) the hospital administrator, Mr. Moyle, would ordinarily do most of the hiring but on this occasion Mr. Philion was given express authority to hire a housekeeper because Mr. Moyle was going to be away;

(3) in giving his authority to Mr. Philion, it simply did not occur to Mr. Moyle that Mr. Philion might hire the spouse of an existing employee in Mr. Philion's department;

(4) Mr. Philion had the general and unqualified authority to hire a spouse housekeeper and exercised that authority by hiring Mrs. Mark;

---

[7] (1984), 85 C.L.L.C. ¶17,001, 6 C.H.R.R. D/2538 (Ont. Bd. Inq.).

(5) on learning that Mrs. Mark had been hired as a housekeeper, Mr. Moyle advised Mr. Philion that her employment should be terminated, because the hospital, as a matter of general policy, did not want a husband and wife working in the same department.

In upholding the complaint, the Board of Inquiry, Peter A. Cumming, stated, in part:

> The exemption afforded by paragraph 23(*d*) clearly enunciates a public policy of non-interference in respect of nepotism by some employers in hiring, and non-interference in respect of the opposite position of some other employers in arbitrarily excluding one spouse from consideration for employment when the other spouse is an existing employee. Preference for a spouse, or arbitrary exclusion of a spouse, for employment or advancement, is left to the unfettered discretion of the employer.

> However, the exemption in paragraph 23(*d*) is limited to granting or withholding employment in the first instance, or granting or withholding advancement once employed . . . The problem from the hospital's standpoint in the instant situation is that Mr. Mark became an employee of the hospital, and thus paragraph 23(*d*) does not apply. But for the innocent error of Mr. Philion, in not hiring on the basis of Mr. Moyle's preferences (unknown to Mr. Philion at the time), Mrs. Mark would never have been hired, and the hospital would enjoy a complete exemption from discrimination by reason of paragraph 23(*d*) . . . However, it must be emphasized, Mrs. Mark was herself entirely an innocent party. Once she became an employee, she is entitled to the full protection of the *Code*.[8]

It appears as though the *Mark* case was decided, in large part, on general principles of the law of agency. Mr. Philion had the actual authority to hire Mrs. Mark, and such authority was not expressly limited in any way. Certainly, from the perspective of Mrs. Mark, Mr. Philion had the ostensible authority to hire her, even though Mr. Moyle, who typically handled the hiring process for the sixty-five bed hospital, never would have hired her "in the first instance". The primary difficulty which arises from the *Mark* case is that a precedent is set whereby a very rigid and technical interpretation is given to s. 23(*d*) of the Ontario *Human Rights Code*, 1981 (now s. 24(1)(d) of the Ontario *Human Rights Code*, R.S.O. 1990, c. H.19) in order to afford a remedy to a complainant in an unique factual situation. If human rights legislation is to be given a purposive interpretation, has this objective been achieved in the *Mark* case?

It is equally clear that the term "employer" in s. 24(1)(d) will be given a strict interpretation by human rights tribunals. In *Szabo v. Atlas Employees Welland Credit Union*,[9] the complainant was not hired for an advertised position of employment, for which he was amply qualified, due to the fact that his father was an employee of the Atlas Steel Company and a member of the supervisory board of the credit union. In upholding the complaint, the Ontario Board of Inquiry, Dr. D.J. Baum, stated, in part:

---

8 *Mark, supra*, footnote 7, at p. 16,006.
9 (1988), 88 C.L.L.C. ¶17,009, 9 C.H.R.R. D/4735 (Ont. Bd. Inq.).

... there simply is no basis in law for concluding that a member of the credit union generally, or William Szabo, as a member of the Supervisory Committee in particular, stands in the position of employer or employee. The employer is the legal entity, the Respondent in this matter, known as the Atlas Employees Welland Credit Union. It is that organization which sought the questioned application for employment. William Szabo was in a position of some influence as a member of the Supervisory Committee. It is clear that he sought to use that influence in favour of his son. But, influence, alone, is not enough to transform Mr. Szabo into an employer.[10]

---

[10] *Supra*, at p. 16,064.

| *Pre-Employment Testing*

In order to determine an applicant's suitability for a job, employers frequently require some form of physical or psychological testing. To the extent that the purpose of the test is to measure the individual's ability to perform job requirements, in certain circumstances such testing is permissible.

However, these tests are often unrelated to job skills and may well violate existing human rights legislation. A thorough review of testing procedures, in terms of both their content and timing, is absolutely critical in order to ensure compliance with the legislation.

1. STATUTORY PROVISIONS

A. The Ontario Human Rights Code

The Ontario *Human Rights Code*, R.S.O. 1990, c. H.19, does not specifically address the issue of pre-employment testing.

Section 23(2) of the Code provides:

> 23(2) The right under section 5 to the equal treatment with respect to employment is infringed where a form of application for employment is used or a written or oral inquiry is made of an applicant that directly or indirectly classifies or indicates qualifications by a prohibited ground of discrimination.

A broad and liberal interpretation of s. 23, combined with the general right to equal treatment in employment under s. 5, would clearly limit the nature and extent of pre-employment testing utilized by employers falling within its jurisdiction.

B. The Canadian Human Rights Act

Section 8 of the *Canadian Human Rights Act*, R.S.C. 1985, c. H-6, states that:

> 8. It is a discriminatory practice,
>> (a) to use or circulate any form of application for employment, or
>> (b) in connection with employment or prospective employment, to publish any advertisement or to make any written or oral inquiry
> that expresses or implies any limitation, specification or preference based on a prohibited ground of discrimination.

Accordingly, any pre-employment enquiry that would have the effect of directly or indirectly excluding an individual or class or individuals, based on a prohibited ground of discrimination, is unlawful under both the federal and Ontario legislation.

2. APTITUDE TESTING

In considering the propriety of any form of aptitude testing, the primary difficulty lies in determining the relevancy of the test for the job at hand. In addition, these tests often result in constructive or adverse effect discrimination, often without any overt intent to discriminate. For example, many of these tests are fairly old and may include sexist language or discriminate against individuals not familiar with Canadian culture.

There has been little Canadian caselaw in which the propriety of aptitude testing has been considered under applicable human rights legislation. The American caselaw and, in particular, the decision of the United States Supreme Court in *Griggs v. Duke Power Co.*[1] is instructive on this subject.

In *Griggs*, a class action suit was initiated by Afro-American employees against the company alleging that its employment practices violated the *Civil Rights Act of 1964*. At issue was the company's requirement of a high school education or the passing of a standardized general intelligence test as a condition of employment in, or transfer to jobs.

In reversing the decision of The Court of Appeals, the Supreme Court held that the employer was prohibited from requiring a high school education or the passing of a standardized general intelligence test as a condition of employment in or transfer to jobs. Neither standard was shown to be significantly related to successful job performance, and both requirements operated to disqualify blacks at a substantially higher rate than white applicants. The jobs in question formerly had been filled only by white employees as part of a long-standing practise of giving preference to whites.

In the course of its reasons, issued by Chief Justice Burger, the court summarized the facts of the case:

— the plant was organized into five operating departments: (1) Labour; (2) Coal Handling; (3) Operations; (4) Maintenance, and (5) Laboratory and Test;

— the company instituted a policy in 1955 requiring a high school education for initial assignments to any department except Labour and for transfer from Coal Handling to any ''inside'' department (*ie* — Operations, Maintenance, or Laboratory);

---

[1] 91 S. Ct. 849 (1971).

— Negroes were employed only in the Labour department where the highest paying jobs paid less than the lowest paying jobs in the other four "operations" departments;

— in 1965, completion of high school was also made a prerequisite to transfer from Labour to any other department;

— on July 2, 1965, a further requirement for new employees became effective: to qualify for placement in any but the Labour department it became necessary to register satisfactory scores on two professionally prepared aptitude tests, as well as to have a high school education;

— in September, 1965, the company began to permit incumbent employees who lacked a high school education to qualify for transfer from Labour or Coal Handling to an "inside job" by passing two tests, Wonderlic Personnel Test, which purports to measure general intelligence, and the Bennett Mechanical Comprehension Test;

— neither of the above-noted tests was directed nor intended to measure the ability to learn to perform a particular job or category of jobs;

— the requisite scores used for both initial hiring and transfer approximated the national median for high school graduates.

In his reasons, Chief Justice Burger stated, in part:

On the record before us, neither the high school completion requirement nor the general intelligence test is shown to bear a demonstrable relationship to successful performance of the jobs for which it was used. Both were adopted, as the Court of Appeal noted, without meaningful study of their relationship to job-performance ability. Rather, a vice-president of the company testified, the requirements were instituted on the company's judgment that they generally would improve the overall quality of the work force . . . The facts of this case demonstrate the inadequacy of broad and general testing devices as well as the infirmity of using diplomas or degrees as fixed measures of capability. History is filled with examples of men and women who rendered highly effective performance without the conventional badges or certificates, diplomas or degrees. Diplomas and tests are useful servants, but Congress has mandated the common sense proposition that they are not to become masters of reality.

. . . . .

Nothing in the Act precludes the use of testing or measuring procedures; obviously they are useful. What Congress has forbidden is giving these devices and mechanisms controlling force unless they are demonstrably a reasonable measure of job performance. Congress has not commanded that the less qualified be preferred over the better qualified simply because of minority origins. Far from disparaging job qualifications as such, Congress has made such qualifications the controlling factor, so that race, religion, nationality and sex became irrelevant. What Congress has commanded is that any tests used must measure the person for the job and not the person in the abstract.[2]

---

[2] *Griggs, supra*, at pp. 853-6.

In the *Griggs* decision, the court was considering the interpretation and application of the specific provisions of s. 703 of the *Civil Rights Act of 1964*, the relevant portions of which provide:

> 703.(a) It shall be an unlawful employment practice for an employer —
>
> . . . . .
>
> (2) to limit, segregate or classify his employees in any way which would deprive or tend to deprive any individual of employment opportunities or otherwise adversely affect his status as an employee, because of such individual's race, colour, religion, sex or national origin.
>
> . . . . .
>
> > (*h*) Notwithstanding any other provision of this title, it shall not be an unlawful employment practice for an employer . . . to give and to act upon the results of any professionally developed ability test provided that such test, its administration or action upon the results is not designed, intended or used to discriminate because of race, colour, religion, sex or national origin.

While it is true that no such analogous statutory provisions apply to Ontario employers, it is suggested that the principles embodied within s. 703 of the *Civil Rights Act*, and their interpretation by the U.S. Supreme Court in *Griggs*, have equal application to pre-employment aptitude testing and requirements in Ontario. Any standardized general intelligence test used by Ontario employers should, first and foremost, "bear a demonstrable relationship to successful performance of the jobs for which it is used". More importantly, such tests cannot have the effect of "depriving or tending to deprive any individual of employment opportunities or otherwise adversely affect his status as an employee" because of any prohibited ground of discrimination.

Employers ought to dispense with the requirement of having employees submit to any such aptitude tests or, at the very least, refrain from making the successful completion of such tests a pre-condition to employment. There are clearly more reliable and meaningful ways of assessing a candidate for employment.

3. PSYCHOLOGICAL TESTING — PRE-EMPLOYMENT HONESTY TESTS

The psychological testing of prospective employees is an area fraught with danger for the unwary employer. At the crux of the matter is the fundamental right of the individual to his or her privacy which is to be weighed against the legitimate interests of the employer to make an informed decision when hiring an unknown and unproven individual. Both law and common sense dictate that the human rights commissions and the courts will view the individual's right to privacy as the overriding consideration.

Not all forms of psychological testing necessarily violate the provisions of the human rights legislation. In order for such tests to be lawful, they must specifically relate to the requirements of the job and not inquire into extraneous, irrelevant and/or discriminatory areas of the individual's psychological make-up. Often this is easier said than done.

One particular area of inquiry which courts have come to recognize as legitimate, from the perspective of the employer, relates to the honesty of the prospective employee. In the United States, pre-employment honesty tests, which are a specialized form of psychological testing, are receiving greater recognition and approval from both the courts and the business community than has been the case in Canada.

In 1979, the American Management Association surveyed a sample of 1,686 managers in a wide spectrum of companies with respect to privacy and related issues. In response to the question; "what do you consider to be the most important social or ethical problem facing the U.S. business community today?", honesty in business ranked first among sixteen problems, with privacy ranking tenth.[3]

Losses, due to employee theft and related acts of dishonesty, are estimated at between $40 billion and $50 billion per year in the United States of America.[4] The incidence of employee theft ranges from less than 30% to more than 70%, depending upon the industry involved and the survey methods used.[5] In a recent paper, Jones and Joy summarized the results of studies involving approximately 130,000 individuals in a diverse group of companies and industries and found that the mean percentage of employees who admitted stealing was 32%.[6]

Jones and Terris provide in the same article, an extensive summary of the prevalence of employee theft. They also review a number of personnel selection programs used by employers, as an alternative to pre-employment polygraph testing, which include:

— selection interviews
— reference checks
— credit checks
— criminal background checks
— paper and pencil honesty tests

The authors conclude that not only are professionally developed honesty tests the most scientifically valid of these selection procedures, but they are also inexpensive, typically inoffensive and non-discriminatory.

---

[3] Employee Relations L.J., Vol. 15, p. 561.
[4] *Ibid.*, citing M. Caprino, In all Honesty (1989).
[5] Hefter, The Crippling Crime, 23 Security World 36, 38 (1986).
[6] Emp. Rel. L.J., *ibid.*, footnote 3.

A distinction has been made between "clear purpose" and "disguised purpose" honesty tests. With clear purpose tests, the intent of the assessment is straightforward and obvious to the examinee. With disguised purpose tests, examinees are unclear as to what the test is trying to measure.

The most valid and reliable clear purpose honesty tests, often called "overt honesty tests" are almost completely transparent. There can be little doubt, in the mind of the examinee, that the questions relate to their attitudes toward honesty and employee theft in the workplace. The general characteristics of such tests are as follows:

— they do not inquire into family life, home ownership, criminal records or finances,
— it is a test booklet in which the examinee marks responses to written, job-related questions, pertaining to the applicant's current attitudes toward, perceptions of, and opinions about theft and other counterproductive behaviour in the workplace.

If an employer is intent upon administering some form of psychological testing in pre-employment interviews, these tests must be specifically related to valid job-performance characteristics of the applicant. It is suggested that "clear purpose" honesty tests, which are carefully devised with the assistance of an industrial psychologist, represent a non-discriminatory method of attempting to discern one of the most vital characteristics of the applicant — his or her honesty.

4. PRE-EMPLOYMENT MEDICAL

The Ontario Human Rights Commission has issued a policy statement on "Employment-Related Medical Information", a subject which is not specifically addressed within the four corners of the legislation itself.

In its policy statement, the OHRC briefly addresses the historical rationale for the policy referring to the Ontario *Human Rights Code, 1981*, S.O. 1981, c. 53:

> In the past employers often screened out applicants with disabilities based on medical information requested on application forms or obtained through pre-employment medical examinations. The Commission believes that such questions, asked as part of the applicant screening process, violate subsection 22.—(2) of the *Code*, which states:
>
>> 22.—(2) The right under section 4 to equal treatment with respect to employment is infringed where a form of application for employment is used or a written or oral inquiry is made of an applicant that directly or indirectly classifies or indicates qualifications by a prohibited ground of discrimination.[7]

---

[7] "Policy on Employment-Related Medical Information" (Ontario Human Rights Commission, 1990), p. 1.

The Commission goes on to state, within its policy statement that "any assessment to verify or decide an individual's ability to do the job, including a medical examination, should only take place after a conditional offer of employment is made, preferably in writing".[8] The purpose for this requirement is obvious — it allows the applicant with a disability the right to be considered exclusively on his or her merits during the selection process.

Section 23(3) (previously s. 22(2) of the 1981 Code) of the Code provides that:

> 23(3) Nothing in subsection (2) precludes the asking of questions at a personal employment interview concerning a prohibited ground of discrimination where discrimination on such ground is permitted under this Act.

This section allows an employer, at a personal interview, to ask whether an applicant has any disability-related needs that would require accommodation in order to enable him or her to perform the essential duties of the job. The duty to provide accommodation extends to all aspects of the employment process: hiring, employment testing, on-the-job training, working conditions, transfer, promotions and related areas.

The reason for the Commission stating that a medical examination should only take place after a conditional offer of employment is made, is as follows:

> It is not unusual for an employer to ask about, or for a worker to volunteer information about, his or her specific medical condition. While not expressly prohibited by the *Code*, an employer or supervisor may be placed in a vulnerable position if he or she directly receives any information about the particular medical condition of an applicant or worker. Any subsequent employment-related decision may be perceived to be based on this information and a human rights complaint may result. It is the view of the Commission that to protect the employer as well as the applicant or worker, such information should remain exclusively with the examining physician and away from a worker's personnel file.[9]

It is suggested that employers falling under federal human rights legislative jurisdiction should also follow the policy statement of the Ontario Human Rights Commission on the subject of pre-employment medicals.

5. TESTING FOR DRUG OR ALCOHOL DEPENDENCY

The matter of mandatory drug testing in the workplace is both a highly significant and bitterly disputed labour relations issue in Canada. The Toronto-based Addiction Research Foundation sees drug testing as "likely the most contentious labour management issue of the '90's".[10]

A study released in 1990 by Toronto consultant William M. Mercer & Co., estimated that the annual cost of substance abuse to the Canadian economy

---

[8] *Ibid.*
[9] *Ibid.*
[10] "Drug Tests Enter Canadian Workplace", Toronto Star, pg. D1, Oct. 21/91.

is \$2.6 billion.[11] This estimated cost is contested by the position taken by Alliance for a Drug-Free Canada which pegs the cost at approximately \$6 billion per annum.[12] Direct costs include absenteeism and higher health care levies for employees, while indirect costs include lower productivity, low employee morale and customer dissatisfaction.

American studies have indicated that workers who use drugs are one-third less productive than those who do not; miss ten times as much work; are three times more likely to injure themselves or others; are late three times as often; and are five times more likely to file workers' compensation claims.[13] Consequently, mandatory testing for drugs in the workplace has increased significantly in the past decade in both the public and private sector in the United States. The American Management Association reported in a 1987 survey of the Fortune 100 list of companies that approximately 45% of the employers surveyed were conducting pre-employment testing.[14]

In Canada, compulsory drug testing in the workplace is not as widespread. In 1991, roughly 2% of Canadian companies, including the Toronto Dominion Bank, CP Rail and Canadian National Railways Co. have some form of mandatory drug testing. That compares with approximately 29% of companies in the United States in the same year.

Sandra Chapnik, currently a Justice of the Ontario Court, General Division and former part-time Vice Chairperson of the Ontario Workers' Compensation Appeal Tribunal, points out that urinalysis drug testing of employees and prospective employees is the most common type of testing in the United States and Canada. Madame Justice Chapnik further notes that there are three major objections to the urinalysis testing procedure:

(1) obtaining the sample — the procedure is clearly, to some degree, embarrassing and intrusive. Furthermore, the sampling process must be vigilantly monitored, otherwise samples may be substituted, diluted or contaminated;

(2) the accuracy of test results — to say a test result is positive conveys little objective information, since there is no standard or accepted definition of what constitutes a positive result. Immunoassays are the most commonly used method for initial screening due to their simplicity and relative inexpense. The Addiction Research Foundation reports 95 to 98 percent accuracy for the EMIT (Enzyme Multiplied Immunoassay Technique), with false positive results 2 to 5 percent of the time. False positive results can result from detection of traces obtained by passive inhalation, as well as mistaken identification of natural body chemicals or cross-actions with other substances such as aspirin;

(3) the relevance of test results — assuming a test result is accurate, what does it reveal about the ability of the employee to perform the essential require-

---

[11] *Ibid.*

[12] *Ibid.*

[13] Bickerston, "Urinalysis: Dilemma of the 80's" (EAP Digest, September, 1986).

[14] "Drug Abuse: The Workplace Issue" (The American Management Association, 1987).

ments of his or her job? Test results are of no predictive value for past or future on the job impairment since certain drugs will register for days and even weeks after the intoxicating effect has worn off.[15]

It is the last of the above-noted objections to drug testing, which is the basis on which the Ontario Human Rights Commission has promulgated its "Policy Statement on Drugs and Alcohol Testing".[16] As the Commission quite rightly points out, there are various ways in which the use of legal and illicit drugs or alcohol may fall within the Code's definition of "handicap":

1. Where an individual's use of drugs or alcohol has reached the stage that it constitutes an addiction or dependency.
2. Where an individual is perceived as having an addiction or dependency due to drug or alcohol use.[17]

Since the testing for alcohol or drug use constitutes a medical examination, the Commission's "Policy on Employment-Related Medical Information" is applicable. The main features of this policy are as follows:

1. Employment-related medical examinations or inquiries, conducted as part of the applicant screening process, are prohibited under subsection 22.—(2) of the Code.
2. Medical examinations should only be administered after a conditional offer of employment has been made, preferably in writing.
3. Any employment-related medical examinations or inquiries are to be limited to determining the individual's ability to perform the essential duties of a job. If the applicant or employee requires accommodation in order to enable him or her to perform the essential duties, the employer is required to provide such accommodation unless to do so would cause undue hardship.[18]

Within its policy statement, the Ontario Human Rights Commission outlines the requirement which must be adhered to in performing drug testing:

It is essential that drug testing, when performed, be done by qualified professionals and the results be analyzed in a competent laboratory. Further, it is the responsibility of the employer to ensure that the samples taken are properly labelled and protected at all times.

In order to protect the confidentiality of testing results, all health assessment information should remain exclusively with the examining physician and away from the worker's personnel file.

Procedures also should be instituted for the physician to review the testing results with the employee concerned.

If workers will be required to undergo drug and alcohol testing during the course of their employment — on the grounds that such testing, at the time that it is administered, would indicate actual impairment of ability to perform or fulfil

---

[15] Sandra Chapnik, "Mandatory Drug Testing in the Workplace", Admin. L.J., Vol. 5, No. 4, p. 67.
[16] "Policy Statement on Drug and Alcohol Testing" (Ontario Human Rights Commission, November, 1990).
[17] *Ibid.*, p. 1.
[18] *Ibid.*

the essential duties or requirements of the job, as opposed to merely detecting the presence of substances in the system — the employer should notify them of this requirement at the beginning of their employment.[19]

The fundamental consideration to be addressed by each and every employer on this subject relates to the necessity for testing both at the pre-employment stage and during the employment relationship proper. As the Commission indicates, the primary questions to be addressed on this issue are as follows:

1. Is there an objective basis for believing that job performance would be adversely affected by the disability of drug or alcohol dependency?
2. In respect of a specific employee, is there an objective basis for believing that unscheduled or recurring absences from work or habitual lateness to work are related to alcoholism or drug addiction/dependency?
3. Is there an objective basis to believe that the degree, nature, scope and probability of risk caused by this addiction or dependency will adversely affect the safety of co-workers or members of the public.[20]

With respect to the majority of the employee population, mandatory drug testing cannot be substantiated on the basis of the above-noted criteria.

---

[19] *Ibid.*, p. 2.
[20] *Ibid.*

CHAPTER 6 | Forms Of Discrimination In The Workplace

The Ontario *Human Rights Code*, R.S.O. 1990, c. H.19, is predicated on the philosophy that employment decisions should be based upon merit rather than extraneous considerations unrelated to job performance. To effect this objective, the Code aims to enforce the principles of equal opportunity with respect to employment.

The Code expressly prohibits discrimination based upon:

(1) sex;
(2) ancestry;
(3) place of origin;
(4) citizenship;
(5) creed;
(6) handicap;
(7) age;
(8) marital status;
(9) family status;
(10) sexual orientation;
(11) colour;
(12) ethnic origin;
(13) record of offences.

These same prohibited grounds of discrimination in the employment relationship can be found in the *Canadian Human Rights Act*, R.S.C. 1985, c. H-6, as well, with the exception of sexual orientation.

Terms and conditions of employment such as probation, wage rates, benefits, hours of work, promotion and overtime must be implemented and administered in conformity with the Code's vigorous requirements involving equal treatment with respect to employment. In addition, every employer has the unconditional obligation to provide a work environment which is free from these prohibited grounds of discrimination. Accordingly, a continuous and objective assessment of the rules and conditions of the workplace is necessary in order that every employer ensure compliance with the Code.

1. RACE AND COLOUR

The Ontario Human Rights Commission Annual Report for 1990-91 indicates that 14% of the total complaints received by the Commission over that period of time pertained to race and colour. Of the employment-related complaints disposed of by the Commission during that period, 25% of those complaints involved an allegation of discrimination on the basis of race and colour.

The Code provides no definition of the term "race" largely because, as Mr. Justice Tarnopolsky points out:

> . . . the real concern is not with the "race" or "colour" or other hereditary origin of the individual who has been discriminated against, but rather with what the respondent perceives the complainant to be. Thus, even if a person is seven-eighths of European origin and one-eighth of African origin, if the respondent perceives that person to be a "Negro" or "black" and characteristic or origin is the ground upon which the person is discriminated against, then the discrimination is on the grounds of "race" or "colour".[1]

Under the *Human Rights Code* an employer is held to a strict duty of providing a work environment free from racial harassment. Professor Peter Cumming, in the case of *Persaud v. Consumers Distributing Ltd.*[2] has defined racial harassment in the workplace as follows:

> Racial harassment is present when one person verbally insults another person on the basis of his race, colour, ancestry and place of origin, irrespective of the underlying events that trigger the outburst. Such harassment is contrary to . . . the *Code* . . . When derogatory racial references are used between employees in the context of a heated argument . . . as an expression of anger and frustration, such racial references constitute racial harassment.[3]

Harassment is defined in s. 10(1) of the Code to mean "engaging in a course of vexatious comment or conduct that is known or ought reasonably to be known to be unwelcome". The Ontario Human Rights Commission has published a policy statement on "Racial Slurs and Harassment and Racial Jokes", a copy of which can be found in Schedule (viii) of this book. Within this policy statement, the Commission states, in part:

> Each situation will be assessed on its own merits. However, racial epithets, comments ridiculing individuals because of race-related physical characteristics, religious dress, etc. or singling an individual out for humiliating or demeaning "teasing" or jokes related to race or to any of the race-related grounds, would in most instances be viewed as conduct or comments which "ought reasonably to be known to be unwelcome".

> Conduct or comments which are motivated by consideration of a person's membership in one of the race-related groups and which may not, on their face, be considered offensive on an objective basis, may still be "unwelcome" from the

---

[1] Walter Tarnopolsky and William F. Pentney, *Discrimination and the Law*, Rev'd 1st ed. (Toronto, Carswell, 1985), p. 5-11.

[2] (1990), 14 C.H.R.R. D/23 (Ont. Bd. Inq.).

[3] *Supra*, at p. D/27.

perspective of a particular individual. If the individual clearly indicates that this is the case, then a repetition of a similar type of activity will, in most instances, constitute a violation of the *Code*.[4]

The Commission specifically cites, within the above-mentioned policy statement, examples of racial slurs or actions which constitute a racial harassment:

- demeaning racial remarks, jokes or innuendos about an employee, client or customer, or tenant told to other employees, tenants, clients or customers

  - may impair the right of those persons who are the subject of the comments to be viewed as equals and create a "them/us" barrier.

- racial remarks, jokes or innuendos made about other racial groups in the presence of an employee, tenant or client

  - may create an apprehension on the part of members of other racial minorities that they are also targeted when they are not present.

- the displaying of racist, derogatory or offensive pictures, graffiti or materials

  - is humiliating and also impairs the right of those persons who are members of the targeted racial group to be viewed as equals.

- racial remarks, jokes or innuendos about an employee, client, or tenant or about the racial group of which they are a member, which are stated to or in the presence of a non-racial minority person

  - may cause discomfort on the part of the non-racial minority person and may have the effect of creating an environment where the opportunity for beneficial inter-racial interaction is lost or impaired.

In the above or similar situations, the conduct at issue must be objectively evaluated. It must be of such a nature and degree so as to amount to a denial of equality through the creation of a poisoned environment.[5]

The Board of Inquiry decision in *Lee v. T.J. Applebee's Food Conglomeration*[6] provides an excellent example of a decision in which it was held that the complainant had been discriminated against in a "racially poisoned atmosphere".

In the *T.J. Applebee* case, Ms Lee, who is of Chinese ancestry, was employed in the kitchen of a restaurant. In the course of her employment she:

(a) applied to become a waitress but was never accepted, although on two occasions she was promised that the move would be effected in time;

(b) worked with other predominantly non-white employees in the kitchen, while the waiting staff was overwhelmingly white;

---

[4] "Policy Statement on Racial Slurs and Harassment and Racial Jokes" (Ontario Human Rights Commission, 1989), p. 2.

[5] *Ibid.*, p. 4.

[6] (1987), 88 C.L.L.C. ¶17,011, 9 C.H.R.R. D/4781 (Ont. Bd. Inq.).

    (c) was subject to racial slurs and stereotypical language in the kitchen which, although not specifically directed at her, came primarily from the kitchen managers, both of whom were white;

    (d) ultimately resigned from her employment and shortly thereafter filed a complaint of discrimination.

In finding for the complainant, the Board of Inquiry stated, in part:

> . . . when discriminatory racial practices are or seem to be at play in a particular environment, non-whites will tend to stay away. This kind of circular development (absence of non-whites leads to a lack of applications by non-whites which leads to a preponderance of whites) is common in many work situations, and the effect is an entrenchment of discriminatory practices, whether or not they are intended.[7]

It was further held that since "an employer has a duty to keep the work environment free of racial insults and must take reasonable steps to stop them",[8] both the company and the company's general manager were jointly and severally responsible to afford Ms Lee adequate compensation.

As stated by the Commission in its policy statement on racial slurs and harassment in the workplace:

> It is very important, therefore, that employers, including those whose business it is to provide accommodation or services, have policies in place making it clear that activity which results in a poisoned environment is prohibited in the context of the workplace, whether directed at employees, clients, customers, or tenants and will be met with strict discipline if it occurs. Similarly, it is important that managers and supervisors be instructed to ensure that all staff are aware of the policy and to deal with any such incidents which come to their attention quickly and effectively.[9]

In spite of the very onerous duties placed upon an employer to provide a work environment free from racial harassment, it is, nonetheless, possible for an employer to successfully defend against such a complaint. In *Persaud v. Consumers Distributing Ltd.*,[10] the Board of Inquiry ruled in favour of the employer because management had demonstrated, by its past practice and disciplinary process, including the mediation of disputes between feuding employees, that it did not "authorize, condone, adopt or ratify . . . actions of harassment".[11] Accordingly, the company was not found liable.

---

[7] *Supra*, at p. 16,088.
[8] *Supra*, at p. 16,090.
[9] "Policy on Racial Slurs", *ibid.*, footnote 4, p. 6.
[10] (1990), 14 C.H.R.R. D/23 (Ont. Bd. Inq.).
[11] See case summary, *supra*, p. D/24.

2. NATIONALITY, CITIZENSHIP, ANCESTRY OR PLACE OF ORIGIN

Although there is, in many cases, an overlap between human rights complaints alleging discrimination on the basis of race or colour, on the one hand, and nationality, citizenship, ancestry or place of origin, on the other nonetheless, the grounds are distinct and, therefore, ought to be addressed separately.

A. Citizenship and Nationality

"Citizenship" is, of course, the status of being a citizen. This specific ground of discrimination was first added as a separate ground of discrimination in Ontario in 1981. It had been considered in pre-1981 decisions as falling under discrimination on the basis of nationality.

In *Shy Ker v. Fort Francis Rainy River Board of Education*[12] the Board of Inquiry defined the terms "citizenship" and "nationality", and distinguished the two concepts:

> The terms "citizenship" and "nationality" refer to the status of the individual in his relationship to the state and are often used synonymously. The word "nationality", however, has a broader meaning than the word "citizenship". Likewise, the terms "citizen" and "national" are frequently used interchangeably. But here again the latter term is broader in its scope than the former. The term "citizen" in its general application is applicable only to a person who is endowed with the full political and civil right in the body politic of the state. The term "national" includes a "citizen" and a person who, though not a citizen, owes permanent allegiance to the state and is entitled to its protection.[13]

The Ontario *Human Rights Code* sets out specific exceptions to discrimination on the basis of citizenship:

(a) section 16(1) provides an exemption for situations in which Canadian citizenship, as a requirement, qualification or consideration is imposed or authorized by law;

(b) section 16(2) provides that trade union activities can be restricted to Canadian citizens and permanent residents;

(c) section 16(3) provides an exception to discrimination on the basis of required Canadian citizenship or domicile with the intention to obtain citizenship, when adopted by an organization or enterprise for the holder of senior executive positions.

B. Ancestry, Place of Origin and Ethnic Origin

The Board of Inquiry in *Cousens v. Canadian Nurses' Assn.*[14] defined ancestry as follows:

---

[12] (unreported, 1979, Ont. Bd. Inq.).
[13] *Supra*, p. 5 of unreported judgment.
[14] (1981), 2 C.H.R.R. D/365 (Ont. Bd. Inq.).

The term "ancestry" is here interpreted to mean family descent. In other words, one's ancestry must be determined through the lineage of one's parents through their parents, and so on.[15]

In the *Cousens* case the complainant alleged that he was dismissed from his employment because he is not a Francophone. In its decision, the Board concluded that discrimination on the basis of ancestry could include the attributes of ancestry, such as language or one's "mother tongue", as well as one's heredity.

Place of origin is not specifically defined in human rights legislation, nor do there appear to be any cases which specifically define the term. Presumably it could include a town, city, province or state, as well as a country.

Mr. Justice Tarnopolsky[16] adopts the following definition of "ethnic group" in defining discrimination on the basis of ethnic origin:

> An ethnic group is a distinct category of the population in a larger society whose culture is usually different from its own. The members of such a group are, or feel themselves, or are thought to be bound together by common ties of race or nationality or colour.

A number of cases have dealt with allegations of constructive or indirect discrimination on the basis of ancestry, place of origin or ethnic origin.

The imposition of height and weight requirements by an employer could amount to discrimination on the basis of ancestry, place of origin, since such standards are, in most instances, based upon the average height and weight of white Anglo-Saxon males. In its "Policy Statement on Height and Weight Requirements",[17] a copy of which is included in Schedule (vii) to this book, the Ontario Human Rights Commission states:

> ... employers cannot impose requirements which have the effect of excluding members of those groups covered by the *Code*, unless it can be shown that the requirements are reasonable and bona fide in the circumstances.

. . . . .

> There also appears to be little evidence to demonstrate that height and weight requirements constitute bona fide occupational requirements. This view is supported by decisions of human rights tribunals in Ontario, other Canadian provinces, and the United States, as well as empirical research which indicates that physical stature alone is not determinative of an individual's ability to perform the essential duties of jobs which require significant physical exertion . . .

---

[15] *Supra*, at p. D/367.

[16] Walker Tarnopolsky and William F. Pentney, *Discrimination and the Law*, Rev'd 1st ed. (Toronto, Carswell, 1985), p. 5-25.

[17] "Policy Statement on Height and Weight Requirements" (Ontario Human Rights Commission, 1989).

In any event, it should be noted that section 10 of the *Code* incorporates a duty to "accommodate" persons adversely affected into the analysis of whether requirements are reasonable and bona fide . . .

The Commission would urge all Ontario employers to abandon the use of uniform height and weight requirements in hiring employees unless they can demonstrate their lack of adverse effect on women or members of minority ethnic or racial groups.[18]

In a recent decision of the Ontario Board of Inquiry, the employer successfully defended a complaint of discrimination on the basis of race, ancestry, place of origin or ethnic origin, in which it was alleged that a large physical stature was a requirement of the position.

In *Gaba v. Lincoln County Humane Society*[19] the complainant, of Filipino ancestry, alleged that he was not selected for the position of Inspector/Assistant Manager because of his small physical stature. Professor Gorsky, in his written decision, stated:

It is essential, in providing evidence to substantiate this instance of alleged constructive discrimination to show that a large physical stature was a requirement for the position, and that such a requirement resulted in the exclusion of a group identified by a prohibited ground, contrary to s. 10 of the *Code*.[20]

In rejecting the complaint of discrimination, in spite of evidence of racial slurs and other derogatory remarks having been made, Professor Gorsky stated:

The Commission, quite properly, emphasized the racial comments which had been heard by several witnesses. While I prefer the evidence of the witnesses, and discount Mr. Hampson's denial, I cannot, on the facts before me, impose a causal link between such thoughtless, insensitive, inappropriate and hurtful expressions and the choice of an inspector/assistant manager.

The pieces of the jigsaw puzzle must be arranged in such a manner that the picture is complete. The evidence, when circumstantial, in cases such as this one, in order to succeed must go further than producing several equally consistent results; the second test, above referred to, which is more favourable to the position of the Commission, still requires that the inference of discrimination be "more probable than the other inferences or hypotheses".[21]

The requirement of verbal and written facility in the English language could form the basis for a complaint of discrimination on the basis of ancestry, place of origin or ethnic origin. In *Romano v. North York (City) Board of Education*,[22] the Ontario Board of Inquiry concluded that the school board's requirements of English proficiency were unreasonable and not justifiably

---

[18] *Ibid.*, p. 1.
[19] (1991), 15 C.H.R.R. D/311 (Ont. Bd. Inq.).
[20] *Supra*, at p. D/312.
[21] *Supra*, at p. D/316.
[22] (1987), 8 C.H.R.R. D/4347 (Ont. Bd. Inq.), affd 10 C.H.R.R. D/5807 (Ont. Div. Ct.).

related to the job requirements of a school bus driver. However, the complaint was ultimately dismissed on the basis that there was insufficient evidence before the Board of a disproportionate effect upon persons of Italian origin. It was held that this requirement had an adverse impact upon persons who are functionally illiterate, a group that is not subject to protection under the *Human Rights Code*. This decision was upheld by the Ontario Divisional Court.

In a recent decision of the Ontario Divisional Court, a finding of discrimination was set aside where the employer's mistaken perception of the interviewee was attributable to the interviewer's failure to appreciate or understand a certain cultural trait of the complainant. In *Toronto (City) Board of Education v. Quereshi*,[23] the evidence adduced at the hearing in the first instance was that Dr. Quereshi's cultural background, being of Pakistani origin, "inhibited his answers during his interviews". The decision of the majority of the court in this case, which was delivered by Mr. Justice O'Leary, is as follows:

> . . . can the failure of the interviewers, to understand this cultural restraint and give it due consideration constitute discrimination based on place of origin or ethnic origin? In my view it cannot, unless there was some avoidable unfairness in the selection method or process used by the Board of Education and none was suggested, let alone found to exist by the board of inquiry.[24]

As the majority of the court so aptly stated in the course of its reasons:

> . . . the ultimate issue before the board of inquiry was not whether the Board of Education chose the best candidate, but whether it failed to choose Dr. Quereshi because it was guilty of adverse effect discrimination against him because of his place of origin and his ethnic origin.[25]

3. RELIGION OR CREED

The *Canadian Human Rights Act*, R.S.C. 1985, c. H-6, s. 2, prohibits discrimination on the basis of "religion". The Ontario *Human Rights Code*, s. 1, prescribes discrimination on the basis of "creed". As Mr. Justice Tarnopolsky points out: "for purposes of Canadian human rights legislation, these terms are essentially synonymous".[26]

The leading decision in Canada on the subject of discrimination on the basis of religion/creed is the decision of the Supreme Court of Canada in *Ontario (Human Rights Commission) v. Simpson-Sears Ltd.*,[27] which has come to be referred to as "the O'Malley decision", in recognition of the name of the complainant. In fact, the *O'Malley* decision is perhaps the most important

---

[23] (1991), 42 O.A.C. 258, 14 C.H.R.R. D/243 (Ont. Ct. (Gen. Div.)).
[24] *Supra*, at p. 262.
[25] *Supra*, at pp. 261-2.
[26] *Discrimination, ibid.*, footnote 16, at p. 6-1.
[27] (1985), 23 D.L.R. (4th) 321, [1985] 2 S.C.R. 536.

and authoritative decision in Canada dealing with general principles pertaining to the interpretation and effect of human rights legislation. For that reason, it requires a comprehensive review and analysis.

In *O'Malley*, the evidence before the Board of Inquiry at the initial hearing may be summarized as follows:

(1) O'Malley became a Seventh Day Adventist seven years after commencing her employment with Simpson-Sears;

(2) Simpson-Sears' policy of Saturday opening was adopted for sound business reasons and applied to all retail sales employees, including O'Malley, who had complied with this policy prior to the conversion of her faith;

(3) Seventh Day Adventists recognize Saturday as being the Sabbath, which runs from sundown on Friday to sundown on Saturday;

(4) the company offered O'Malley a part-time position when she could not continue her original employment on the required basis;

(5) Simpson-Sears undertook to consider O'Malley for any full-time positions for which she might be suitable.

The Supreme Court of Canada was called upon to decide, among other things, whether proof of an intention to discriminate is an essential component to finding an employer guilty of discrimination. Mr. Justice McIntyre, speaking on behalf of a unanimous Supreme Court, held that proof of intention is not a necessary ingredient for a successful human rights complaint.

In overruling the decision of the Ontario Court of Appeal, Mr. Justice McIntyre concisely articulates the practical problems associated with ascertaining the nature and extent of freedom of religion in the workplace:

> The question is not free from difficulty. No problem is found with the proposition that a person should be free to adopt any religion he or she may choose and to observe the tenets of that faith. This general concept of freedom of religion has been well-established in our society and was a recognized and protected right long before the human rights codes of recent appearance were enacted. Difficulty arises when the question is posed of how far the person is entitled to go in the exercise of his religious freedom. At what point in the profession of his faith and the observance of its rules does he go beyond the mere exercise of his rights and seek to enforce upon others conformance with his beliefs? To what extent, if any, in the exercise of his religion is a person entitled to impose a liability upon another to do some act or accept some obligation he would not otherwise have done or accepted . . . To put the question in the individual context of this case: In the honest desire to exercise her religious practices, how far can an employee compel her employer in the conduct of its business to conform with, or to accommodate, such practices? How far, it may be asked, may the same requirement be made of fellow employees and, for that matter, of the general public?

> These questions raise difficult problems. It is not, in my view, either wise or possible to venture an answer that would apply generally. We are, however, faced with the necessity of finding an answer at least for this case and, therefore, in the nature of the judicial process an answer for similar cases. In my view, for

> this case the answer lies in the *Ontario Human Rights Code*, its purpose, and its general provisions. The Code accords the right to be free from discrimination in employment. While no right can be regarded as absolute, a natural corollary to the recognition of a right must be the social acceptance of a general duty to respect and to act within reason to protect it. In any society the rights of one will inevitably come into conflict with the rights of others. It is obvious then that all rights must be limited in the interest of preserving a social structure in which each right may receive protection without undue interference with others. This will be especially important where special relationships exist, in the case at bar the relationship of employer and employee. In this case, consistent with the provisions and intent of the *Ontario Human Rights Code*, the employee's right requires reasonable steps towards an accommodation by the employer.[28]

The Supreme Court then proceeded to decide that there is a duty on employers to ''reasonably accommodate'' an employee's right to freedom of religion or creed, short of ''undue hardship'':

> Accepting the proposition that there is a duty to accommodate imposed on the employer, it becomes necessary to put some realistic limit upon it. The duty in a case of adverse effect discrimination on the basis of religion or creed is to take reasonable steps to accommodate the complainant, short of undue hardship: in other words, to take such steps as may be reasonable to accommodate without undue interference in the operation of the employer's business and without undue expense to the employer. Cases such as this raise a very different issue from those which rest on direct discrimination. Where direct discrimination is shown the employer must justify the rule, if such a step is possible under the enactment in question, or it is struck down. Where there is adverse effect discrimination on account of creed the offending order or rule will not necessarily be struck down. It will survive in most cases because its discriminatory effect is limited to one person or to one group, and it is the effect upon them rather than upon the general work force which must be considered. In such cases there is no question of justification raised because the rule, if rationally connected to the employment, needs no justification; what is required is some measure of accommodation. The employer must take reasonable steps towards that end which may or may not result in full accommodation. Where such reasonable steps, however, do not fully reach the desired end, the complainant, in the absence of some accommodating steps on his own part such as an acceptance in this case of part-time work, must either sacrifice his religious principles or his employment.
>
> To relate the principle of accommodation to the facts at bar, we must begin with the proposition that the employer is lawfully entitled to carry on business and to stay open for business on Saturdays. It is accordingly entitled to engage employees on the condition that they work on Saturdays. The complainant, however, is lawfully entitled to pursue the practices of her religion and to be free from compulsion to work on Saturday, contrary to her religious beliefs.[29]

In the final result, the Supreme Court of Canada allowed the appeal, thereby reversing the decision of the Ontario Court of Appeal and awarded Ms

---

[28] *Ontario, supra*, pp. 334-5.
[29] *Supra*, at pp. 335-6.

O'Malley compensation equal to the difference in her earnings as a full-time employee and a part-time employee over the period of her part-time employment.

The *O'Malley* decision graphically illustrates both the extent of an individual's right to be free from discrimination in the workplace and the concomitant obligations imposed upon an employer to, in certain instances, "reasonably accommodate" an employee short of "undue hardship". Due to the fact that an intention to discriminate is not a necessary element to establish a breach of the Code, the employer's reasonable efforts in attempting to address the problem are immaterial where those efforts fall short of "reasonable accommodation".

A recent decision of the Ontario Divisional Court has many factual and legal parallels to the landmark decision of the Supreme Court of Canada in *O'Malley*. In *OPEIU, Local 267 v. Domtar Inc.*[30] the court was called upon to review a finding of discrimination made against both the company and the union, the particulars of which are as follows:

(1) On August 12, 1981, Gohm commenced her employment with Domtar as a Junior Technician at its facility in Red Rock, Ontario;

(2) Ms Gohm was advised, at the outset of her employment, that she would be required to work one Saturday every six weeks;

(3) subsequent to her commencing her employment with Domtar, Ms Gohm asked her supervisor whether she could work on Sunday instead of the scheduled Saturday in order to allow her to observe the Sabbath day of her religion, which was Seventh Day Adventist;

(4) the company had no objections to this proposal, provided the union agreed;

(5) the executive of the union informed Ms Gohm that they would not agree with management to allow her to work on Sundays;

(6) her employment was subsequently terminated.

The Board of Inquiry found that the company could have reasonably accommodated her request and failed to do so by, among other things, not scheduling her to work on Sundays at an annual additional cost of $160 and failing to specifically offer to take the matter up with the union.

In upholding the decision of the Board of Inquiry, the first time in Ontario that a union has been held liable for adverse effect discrimination under s. 4 of the Code, the majority of the court stated:

> The rights of a complainant cannot be lost in the struggle to assess competing interests of the company and the union.
>
> Discrimination in the work place is everybody's business. There can be no hierarchy of responsibility. There are no primary and secondary obligations to

---

[30] (1990), 12 C.H.R.R. D/161, 90 C.L.L.C. ¶17,027, *sub nom. Gohm v. Domtar Inc.* (Ont. Bd. Inq.), affd 89 D.L.R. (4th) 305, 55 O.A.C. 24 (Div. Ct.).

avoid discrimination and adverse effect discrimination; companies, unions, and persons are all in a primary and equal position in a single line of defence against all types of discrimination. To conclude otherwise would fail to afford to the *Human Rights Code, 1981* the broad purposive intent that is mandated. Any interpretation short of this would, in our view, be inconsistent with the philosophy and policy enunciated by the Supreme Court of Canada in *O'Malley v. Simpsons-Sears*.

The discrimination barrier created in the collective agreement slammed the door on continued employment in the face of a Seventh Day Adventist. The union aided the company in the creation and erection of that barrier. It owed an equal duty with the company to dismantle that roadblock.

We agree with the decision of the Board to apportion the liability equally between the company and the union.[31]

One of the most recent pronouncements of the Supreme Court of Canada on the subject of freedom of religion in the workplace is *Central Alberta Dairy Pool v. Alberta (Human Rights Commission)*.[32] In this case, the complainant, Jim Christie became a prospective member of the worldwide Church of God in February, 1983, some two and one-half years subsequent to the commencement of his employment in the production operations of the dairy. The church recognizes a Saturday Sabbath, a five-day Fall Feast of the Tabernacle and five other holy days during the year. Religious adherents are expected not to work on these days, although the church does not impose sanctions for disobedience.

In 1983, Mr. Christie requested, in accordance with his religion, that he be permitted to take a two-day unpaid leave of absence on Good Friday and Easter Monday, both of which were holy days. He was granted the former but denied the latter day on the basis that plant operating needs required his attendance on Easter Monday. After discussions with his superior, Mr. Christie was told that if he did not attend work on Easter Monday his employment would be terminated. Mr. Christie failed to attend work on Easter Monday and his employment was terminated the following day.

In upholding the complaint, Madam Justice Wilson, speaking on behalf of majority of the court, concluded that the employer had failed to act reasonably in accommodating Mr. Christie:

> Turning to the question of reasonable accommodation, I adopt the observations made by McIntyre J. at pp. 335-6 in *O'Malley* with respect to Mrs. O'Malley and find here too that the complainant was lawfully entitled to pursue the practices of his religion and to be free of the compulsion to work on Monday, April 4, 1983, contrary to his religious beliefs. The onus is upon the respondent employer to show that it made efforts to accommodate the religious beliefs of the complainant up to the point of undue hardship.

---

[31] *Supra*, at p. 312 (Div. Ct.).
[32] (1990), 72 D.L.R. (4th) 417, [1990] 2 S.C.R. 489.

I do not find it necessary to provide a comprehensive definition of what constitutes undue hardship but I believe it may be helpful to list some of the factors that may be relevant to such an appraisal. I begin by adopting those identified by the board of inquiry in the case at bar — financial costs, disruption of a collective agreement, problems of morale of other employees, interchangeability of work force and facilities. The size of the employer's operation may influence the assessment of whether a given financial cost is undue or the ease with which the work force and facilities can be adapted to the circumstances. Where safety is at issue both the magnitude of the risk and the identity of those who bear it are relevant considerations. This list is not intended to be exhaustive and the results which will obtain from a balancing of these factors against the right of the employee to be free from discrimination will necessarily vary from case to case.

In the case at bar the board of inquiry found as a fact that concerns of costs, disruption of a collective agreement, employee morale and interchangeability of work force did not pose serious obstacles to accommodating the complainant's religious needs by permitting him to be absent on Monday, April 4, 1983. Indeed, it would be very difficult to conclude otherwise in light of the existence of a contingency plan for dealing with sporadic Monday absences. If the employer could cope with an employee's being sick or away on vacation on Mondays, it could surely accommodate a similarly isolated absence of an employee due to religious obligation. I emphasize once again that there is nothing in the evidence to suggest that Monday absences of the complainant would have become routine or that the general attendance record of the complainant was a subject of concern. The ability of the respondent to accommodate the complainant on this occasion was, on the evidence, obvious and, to my mind, incontrovertible. I therefore find that the respondent has failed to discharge its burden of proving that it accommodated the complainant up to the point of undue hardship.[33]

In the course of her judgment, Madam Justice Wilson made the extraordinary comment that the Supreme Court of Canada may have erred in one of its earlier decisions, relating to the application of the *bona fide* occupational requirement exception to a complaint of adverse effect discrimination on the basis of religion. Quite simply, Madam Justice Wilson was of the view that where an employer rule or policy does not discriminate directly but, rather, has an adverse discriminatory effect, the appropriate response is to uphold the rule and determine, on a case-by-case basis, whether the employer could have accommodated the employee without undue hardship. Her consideration of this issue came about as a direct result of the argument raised by the dairy that the requirement to work on Monday was a *"bona fide* occupational requirement"*.

In determining whether an objection to complying with a request or policy of an employer is subject to protection under the Code on religious grounds, the test would appear to be as follows:

(1) is the belief sincerely held?

---

[33] *Supra*, at p. 439.

(2) is it religious?
(3) is it the cause of the objection?[34]

This extremely broad and deceptively simple test would appear to focus upon the subjective interpretation and preferences of the individual in practising his or her faith, as opposed to an objective analysis of the rules of the religion or faith in question. In addition, it would appear to afford protection to members of new creeds, and, probably, non-deistic creeds as well.[35]

4. AGE

A. Mandatory Retirement

Mandatory retirement is currently one of the most controversial issues in Canadian employment law. Approximately one half of the work force in Canada have employment with contractual provisions which stipulate a mandatory retirement age.[36] Until this issue is thoroughly and decisively adjudicated upon by the Supreme Court of Canada it will remain a highly contentious issue between employer and employee.

Section 5 of the Ontario *Human Rights Code* provides that every person has a right to equal treatment with respect to employment without discrimination because of, among other things, age. The term "age" is defined within the Code in s. 10(1) as "an age that is eighteen years or more and less than sixty-five". Since many employers in Ontario have policies that provide for mandatory retirement of their employees at age sixty-five, it is clear that these companies are not contravening the provisions of the *Human Rights Code*. The only recourse available to the affected individuals who wish to contest their mandatory retirement, is to challenge the constitutional validity of the provisions of the *Human Rights Code* relating to age discrimination. This is, of course, assuming that the mandatory retirement provision of sixty-five is a contractually enforceable term of the individual's employment contract.

The *Canadian Human Rights Act*, on the other hand, includes no specific limitation whatsoever upon the term "age". However, s. 15(c) of the Act provides as follows:

> 15. It is not a discriminatory practice if
>
> . . . . .
>
> (c) an individual's employment is terminated because that individual has reached the normal age of retirement for employees working in positions similar to the position of that individual;

---

[34] Walter Tarnopolsky and William F. Pentney, *Discrimination and the Law*, Rev'd 1st ed. (Toronto, Carswell, 1985), at p. 6-14.
[35] *Ibid.*
[36] *McKinney v. University of Guelph* (1990), 76 D.L.R. (4th) 545 at p. 658, [1990] 3 S.C.R. 229.

This specific exception may raise more problems and questions than it presumably was intended to answer:

(1) how does one determine the ''normal age of retirement'' in any given situation?

(2) does this include both voluntary and involuntary retirement?

(3) can this ''normal age of retirement'' change over the tenure of an individual's employment?

(4) what criteria does one review and consider in determining when a position or positions are ''similar'' to the position of the individual in question?

The answer to these and many other questions which arise in relation to s. 15 of the *Canadian Human Rights Act* are far from clear.

In 1990, the Supreme Court of Canada decided *McKinney v. University of Guelph*,[37] which considered the constitutional validity of the restriction on age discrimination in the Ontario *Human Rights Code* to an age of between eighteen and sixty-five years.

In considering the constitutionality of mandatory retirement, the Supreme Court was called upon to decide two issues:

(1) is mandatory retirement contrary to the equality right provisions contained in s. 15 of the Charter?

(2) if so, is it nevertheless a ''reasonable limit'' prescribed by law that is demonstrably justified in a free and democratic society, thereby bringing it within the ''saving provision'' contained in s. 1 of the Charter.

In answer to the first question, six of the seven judges concluded that mandatory retirement contravened the equality rights provisions of the Charter. However, five of the seven justices ruled that, on the evidence before the court in this case, mandatory retirement represented a ''reasonable limit'' prescribed by law and, accordingly, was saved by s. 1 of the Charter.

In the course of its reasons, the court provides a brief synopsis of the historical development of mandatory retirement in Canada:

> In Canada, mandatory retirement developed with the introduction of private and public pension plans. It is not based on law. In 1927, public security plans began with the *Old Age Pensions Act, 1927*, S.C. 1927, c. 35, which adopted 70 as the age of entitlement, but this was lowered to 65 in the 1960s. Other programmes, such as the Old Age Security (O.A.S.), Guaranteed Income Supplement and the Canada and Quebec Pension Plans also provided that retirement benefits were to be paid beginning at age 65. By the 1970s, the orientation in respect of the treatment of age had been set. Public social security and pension schemes as well as private pension plans were put in place in order to provide income security to older persons: see M. Elizabeth Atcheson and Lynne Sullivan, ''Passage to

---

[37] *McKinney, supra*, footnote 36 (S.C.C.).

Retirement: Age Discrimination and the Charter'' in Anne F. Bayefsky and Mary Eberts, eds., *Equality Rights and the Canadian Charter of Rights and Freedoms* (Toronto: Carswell, 1985), at p. 231.

Private businesses developed or adapted their plans to complement and integrate with government pensions. About one half of the Canadian work force occupy jobs subject to mandatory retirement, and about two-thirds of collective agreements in Canada contain mandatory retirement provisions at the age of 65, which reflects that it is not a condition imposed on the workers but one which they themselves bargain for through their own organizations. Generally, it seems fair to say that 65 has now become generally accepted as the ''normal'' age of retirement.

. . . . .

Age had not fully emerged as an unacceptable ground of discrimination when the early international human rights documents were adopted. These did not specifically refer to age among impermissible grounds of discrimination although their specific enumerations were never regarded as exhaustive. At all events, in the light of growing concerns about the issue, the United Nations undertook a study on the aged (Question of the Elderly and the Aged (report of the Secretary-General) U.N. Doc. A9126 (1973)), which culminated in a resolution of the General Assembly in which that body, emphasizing the ''respect for the dignity and worth of the human person'', urged member states to ''discourage, whenever and wherever the overall situation allows, discriminatory attitudes, polices and measures in employment practices based exclusively on age'' (G.A. Res. 3137, U.N. Doc. A19030 (1973)).

The evolving right against discrimination on the ground of age is gaining ground in this and other countries. I have mentioned earlier its partial recognition in the Human Rights Codes. In some provinces, as in the British Columbia statute dealt with in *Connell, supra*, it is still only recognized in the form in which it existed in Ontario before 1982. Other provinces, Quebec, New Brunswick and Manitoba, have now gone further and prohibited age discrimination in employment altogether. Similarly, in 1967, the United States enacted the *Age Discrimination in Employment Act*, 29 U.S.C. §§ 621-34 (1976), although it was limited to persons between 40 to 65. In 1977, however, Maine abolished as of 1980 all mandatory retirement in both the public and private sectors (the Act is discussed by Susan Dana Kertzer, ''Perspectives on Older Workers: Maine's Prohibition of Mandatory Retirement'' (1981), 33 Main Law Rev. 156.[38]

At the same time that the Supreme Court released its decision in *McKinney*, it also handed down its judgment in *Harrison v. University of British Columbia*.[39] In *Harrison*, the court rejected a similar attack upon the age discrimination provisions under the British Columbia *Human Rights Act*, S.B.C. 1984, c. 22, which restricted the scope of the general rule prohibiting discrimination in employment on the basis of age to those between the ages of forty-five and sixty-five.

---

[38] *Supra*, at pp. 657-9 (S.C.C.).
[39] (1990), 77 D.L.R. (4th) 55, [1990] 3 S.C.R. 451.

Although the *McKinney* and *Harrison* judgments of the Supreme Court of Canada are landmark decisions on the subject of mandatory retirement, they hardly represent the final word on the subject. The court was extremely careful to point out that these cases are restricted to the evidence that was before the court and to their specific facts.

It is clear that any mandatory retirement policy which provides for retirement at an age less than sixty-five years, is on its face a violation of the Ontario *Human Rights Code*, unless it can be brought within the *bona fide* occupational requirement exception provided for within the legislation. In its 1982 decision in *Etobicoke (Borough) v. Ontario (Human Rights Commission)*[40] the Supreme Court of Canada provides some guidance as to the criteria to be examined in determining whether a mandatory retirement policy falls within this limited statutory exception.

In the *Etobicoke* case, the collective agreement between the municipality and the Fire Fighter's Association provided for mandatory retirement at age sixty. The two complaints, a deputy chief and a captain who were subject to this retirement provision, filed a complaint of age discrimination with the Ontario Human Rights Commission. Their complaint was successful at the initial board hearing but this decision was set aside by the Court of Appeal, resulting in an appeal to the Supreme Court of Canada.

In allowing the appeal, Mr. Justice McIntyre, speaking on behalf of a unanimous court, stated, in part:

> It would be unwise to attempt to lay down any fixed rule covering the nature and sufficiency of the evidence required to justify a mandatory retirement below the age of 65 under the provisions of s. 4(6) of the Code. In the final analysis the board of inquiry, subject always to the rights of appeal under s. 14*d* of the Code, must be the judge of such matters. In dealing with the question of a mandatory retirement age, it would seem that evidence as to the duties to be performed and the relationship between the aging process and the safe, efficient performance of those duties would be imperative. Many factors would be involved and it would seem to be essential that the evidence should cover the detailed nature of the duties to be performed, the conditions existing in the work place, and the effect of such conditions upon employees, particularly upon those at or near the retirement age sought to be supported. The aging process is one which has involved the attention of the medical profession and it has been the subject of substantial and continuing research. Where a limitation upon continued employment must depend for its validity on proof of a danger to public safety by the continuation in employment of people over a certain age, it would appear to be necessary in order to discharge the burden of proof resting upon the employer to adduce evidence upon this subject.
>
> I am by no means entirely certain what may be characterized as "scientific evidence". I am far from saying that in all cases some "scientific evidence" will be necessary. It seems to me, however, that in cases such as this statistical and

---

40 (1982), 132 D.L.R. (3d) 14, [1982] 1 S.C.R. 202.

medical evidence based upon observation and research on the question of aging, if not in all cases absolutely necessary, will certainly be more persuasive than the testimony of persons, albeit with great experience in fire-fighting, to the effect that fire-fighting is a "young man's game". My review of the evidence leads me to agree with the board of inquiry. While the evidence given and the views expressed were, I am sure, honestly advanced, they were, in my view, properly described as "impressionistic" and were of insufficient weight.[41]

It is important to bear in mind that the non-existence of a written mandatory retirement policy does not, of itself, alleviate an employer from a potential human rights complaint on the basis of age discrimination. On the contrary, the historical practice of an employer in terminating employees once they reach a certain age level would represent compelling evidence of an unwritten mandatory retirement policy. Likewise, a decision to terminate an individual which is based, in whole or in part, on the individual's age, constitutes age discrimination.

B. Maximum Hiring Age

There is a general tendency to consider age discrimination in employment as something that involves an involuntary termination of an individual's employment due to the person's age. In some instances, these dismissals are carried out in accordance with a mandatory retirement policy, while in other cases there is no fixed or established policy in this regard.

However, this common misconception overlooks the fact that age discrimination is something which is practised, consciously or subconsciously, by employers in the hiring process as well. In fact, age discrimination in the job interviewing process may be far more prevalent than age discrimination from the standpoint of mandatory retirement.

One of the leading decisions by the United States Supreme Court on the subject of age discrimination involved the consideration of a company's maximum hiring age policy. In *Hodgson v. Greyhound Lines Inc.*,[42] the court upheld the company's established policy of a maximum hiring age of thirty-five for intercity bus drivers. The bus company argued that, in order to guarantee public safety, an age limit was necessary. The practice of the company was that the newer and younger drivers were given the more strenuous and demanding trips, while the more senior drivers were able to choose the less demanding routes. The company maintained that, if a maximum hiring age were not in effect, this would result in older, less experienced drivers, taking the more dangerous trips.

At trial, Greyhound led evidence to establish degenerative physical changes brought about by the aging process when a person reaches his late

---

[41] *Supra*, at pp. 22-3.
[42] 419 U.S. 1112 (1975).

thirties, as well as statistical evidence to demonstrate the direct correlation between accident rates and the more difficult bus routes. In addition, the company put forth medical evidence to establish the proposition that elaborate, regular medical testing would not necessarily detect degenerative disabilities in older employees.

The United States Supreme Court ultimately ruled that the bus company only had to establish that there was a rational basis in fact to believe that the removal of its maximum hiring age would increase the likelihood of risk to its passengers. Once that onus had been satisfied, the company succeeded in defending its hiring policy.

The *Hodgson* case effectively demonstrates that, in the absence of compelling evidence supporting a *bona fide* occupational qualification or requirement, a maximum hiring age policy will simply not withstand judicial scrutiny. A Canadian case in point is the decision of the Ontario Board of Inquiry in *O'Brien v. Ontario Hydro.*[43]

In *O'Brien*, the forty-year-old complainant alleged that he had been denied acceptance into the company's six-year apprenticeship program on the basis of his age. A considerable amount of evidence was led by Ontario Hydro to establish that it had hired a number of individuals in the forty to sixty-five age range. However, none of these individuals had been admitted into the apprenticeship program. The Board of Inquiry concluded that, although not the only factor, age stereotyping by the company was the proximate cause of its decision not to hire Mr. O'Brien.

Although not specifically raised by the employer in the *O'Brien* decision, it would appear that simple economics may have influenced Ontario Hydro in deciding not to hire Mr. O'Brien. From a cost benefit analysis perspective, would the company have been justified in questioning the potential return on investment that it would have received from hiring someone, who was approximately at the mid-point of his employment career, to enroll in a six-year apprenticeship program? More importantly, would sufficiently compelling economic considerations justify the implementation of a maximum hiring age policy or, on a less formal basis, "age stereotyping" as it has been called by some human rights tribunals?

The defence of formal or informal age-related hiring policy on the grounds of business economics, however compelling the financial considerations may be, will likely fail. The Supreme Court of Canada has made it abundantly clear that:

> Where a working rule or condition of employment is found to be discriminatory on a prohibited ground and fails to meet any statutory justification test, it is simply struck down.[44]

---

[43] (1981), 2 C.H.R.R. D/504 (Ont. Bd. Inq.).
[44] *Ontario (Human Rights Commission) v. Simpson-Sears Ltd.* (1985), 23 D.L.R. (4th) 321 at p. 333, [1985] 2 S.C.R. 536.

It is difficult to prove "statutory justification" based on a purely economic argument.

C. Coerced Early Retirement

Efforts by an employer to persuade an employee to accept an early retirement package or, retire at a point in time earlier than that desired by the employee, may constitute age discrimination on the part of the employer. A recent decision of the Ontario Board of Inquiry in *Hayes-Dana Inc. and McKee (Re)*[45] provides a striking example of such an age-related human rights complaint.

In the *McKee* case, Mr. McKee worked for Hayes Dana Inc. for over thirty-two years. He was a production operator for fifteen years and a foreman for seventeen years in the Forge Shop. In 1985, Hayes Dana decided to reduce staff in the Forge Shop. On August 16, 1985, Mr. McKee's employment was terminated, at age fifty-seven, along with another foreman, age fifty-six, while two younger foremen were retained in the employ of the company.

In concluding that the evidence supported a *prima facie* case of age discrimination, the Board of Inquiry was particularly influenced by a handwritten note by the former Vice-President of Human Resources of the company in which the phrase "hoped to keep people with career potential" was made in relation to the decision to terminate the employment of both Mr. McKee and the other fifty-six-year old foreman, while retaining the two younger foremen. With respect to this evidence, Professor Gorsky, the Board of Inquiry, stated in his reasons:

> Although the suggestion was never made that the phrase "hoped to keep people with career potential" was taken verbatim, and the notion inherent in the phrase was denied by Mr. Mossberger, we prefer to accept the notation as an indication that the Company intended to retain employees who were not on the verge of retirement, and who had many years of service left to perform. The phrase may be a euphemism; its meaning concerns age.[46]

Professor Gorsky made it clear within his reasons that the intentions of the employer in the circumstances were completely irrelevant, in the sense that even if the employer were convinced that it was not discriminating against Mr. McKee on the basis of age it would have no bearing whatsoever upon the validity of the complaint:

> It may be that at the time when the decision was made to give Mr. McKee the option of being permanently laid off or accept enhanced early retirement, the Respondents honestly believed that their decision was not based, in any way, on Mr. McKee's age. For the above reasons, I have found, on a balance of proba-

---

[45] (1992), 92 C.L.L.C. ¶17,029, 17 C.H.R.R. D/79 (Ont. Arb. Bd.).
[46] *Supra*, at pp. 16,257-8.

bilities, that part of the motivation for choosing Mr. McKee as one [of] the foremen in the forge shop who would not be retained was his age.[47]

It is also significant to note that Mr. McKee accepted an enhanced pension package from the company subsequent to his termination and that the Board of Inquiry held that his acceptance of this enhanced pension "was not relevant to the issue of discrimination".

The most significant aspect of the *McKee* decision relates to the order that was made by the Board of Inquiry, which included the following:

1. the company was ordered to compensate Mr. McKee for lost wages and benefits over the eight-year period from the date of his termination to the date of his sixty-fifth birthday, which the parties subsequently agreed amounted to $246,362;

2. given the extended period of time during which Mr. McKee was unable to find an equivalent occupation, the humiliation of being rejected in the way he was after so many years of faithful and competent service, the company was ordered to pay Mr. McKee compensation in the amount of $1,500 as a result of injury to dignity;

3. the company was further ordered to conduct a yearly seminar "Planning for Retirement" and that it also conduct an appropriate seminar prior to offering an early retirement program.

The *McKee* case provides an effective illustration of the danger associated with the attempt to pressure or coerce an individual into an early retirement package or retirement at an earlier point in time than desired by the individual. The implications of this decision are substantial.

In a very recent case, which followed on the heals of the *McKee* decision, the Ontario Human Rights Commission announced what it described as the "largest human rights settlement in Canada".[48] Stanton Stevenson, had his eight-year employment with Ontario Hydro's law department terminated in 1988 during a restructuring. Mr. Stevenson alleged that he lost his job as a lawyer for Ontario Hydro as a result of Hydro's alleged policy or practice of dismissing older employees and hiring younger people. Mr. Stevenson also initiated a contemporaneous legal proceeding in the Ontario Supreme Court based on his termination. That case had been stayed by order of the court in December, 1988, pending a final ruling on the discrimination complaint by the Human Rights Commission.

The complaint was settled on the following terms:

---

[47] *Supra*, at p. 16,258.
[48] Article by James Rusk, Queen's Park Bureau, published in the Globe & Mail, Friday, May 13, 1994, entitled "Lawyer Wins $400,000 settlement"; *Stevenson v. Ontario Hydro* (unreported, February 4, 1994, Ont. Bd. Inq.).

1. Ontario Hydro is to pay Mr. Stevenson the sum of $100,000 as general damages for personal injury, pain and suffering;
2. Ontario Hydro is to pay Mr. Stevenson the sum of $50,000 with respect to his legal costs;
3. Ontario Hydro is to pay Mr. Stevenson the sum of $250,000 in accordance with minutes of settlement entered into between the parties;
4. both the human rights complaint and the contemporaneous legal proceeding were dismissed and Mr. Stevenson provided a full and final release in relation to these claims to Ontario Hydro.

In commenting upon the significance of the *Stevenson* settlement, Rosemary Brown, Chief Commissioner of the Ontario Human Rights Commission stated:

> This is an extraordinary settlement, both in its magnitude and message to employers . . . the message to employers is that it can be costly to engage in practices that result in allegations of discrimination.

5. SEX

Discrimination on the basis of sex is a concept which is separate and distinct from sexual harassment in the workplace.

The term "sex" is not specifically defined within the human rights legislation. However, an examination of the caselaw pertaining to this prohibited ground of discrimination makes it clear that it relates primarily to an attempt to eliminate many of the stereotypical assumptions, especially as they relate to women in the workplace. Examples of findings of discrimination on the basis of sex include:

— concern on the part of an employer that a female employee might be alone in the office at night does not justify a refusal to hire;
— generally speaking, a position of employment requiring a minimum degree of physical strength or capacity for endurance should not be reserved exclusively for males;
— work that is dirty or dangerous by nature should not exclude females from consideration;
— concerns about alleged customer preference for a male or female employee do not constitute *bona fide* occupational requirements;
— dress code or uniform requirements that differentiate significantly between male and female employees.

These obvious examples of sex discrimination in the workplace are by no means exhaustive. One of the most prevalent areas of discrimination on the basis of sex involves constructive discrimination or adverse effect discrimination in which the end product or result of an employer's practices or conduct over time indicates a preference of one sex over another. Perhaps the leading

Canadian decision in this area is the Supreme Court of Canada decision in *Action Travail des Femmes v. C.N.R. Co.*[49]

In the *C.N.R.* case, Action Travail des Femmes, a woman's activist group, filed a complaint of discriminatory hiring and promotion practices against the railway, contrary to s. 10 of the *Canadian Human Rights Act*. It was alleged that the railway had systematically denied employment opportunities to women for unskilled blue-collar positions.

The human rights tribunal found that the recruitment, hiring and promotion policies at C.N. prevented and discouraged women from working on blue-collar jobs. Consequently, C.N. was ordered to undertake a special employment program designed to increase the proportion of women working in "non-traditional" occupations, to 13%, which represented, at that time the national average. Until that goal was achieved, C.N. was required to hire at least one woman in every four non-traditional jobs filled.

The Supreme Court of Canada upheld the order of the human rights tribunal on the basis that the affirmative action order was designed to break a continuing cycle of systemic discrimination. In arriving at this conclusion, the court held that human rights legislation is not intended to punish wrongdoing but, rather, prevent discrimination against identifiable protected groups, in which case it ought to receive a fair, large and liberal interpretation to advance and fulfil its purposes.

Leaving aside the significant and far-reaching terms of the order, the *C.N.R.* case graphically illustrates the extent of an employer's liability for adverse effect discrimination on the basis of sex. Accordingly, it is incumbent upon every employer to regularly review its employment policies and procedures, both in terms of content and their ultimate effect, in an effort to provide a work environment free from discrimination.

A. Pregnancy–Related Discrimination

Perhaps one of the most prevalent and controversial grounds of discrimination on the basis of sex involves rules, policies or practices of the workplace which impact upon pregnant or potentially pregnant employees. For example, to what extent is an employer justified in implementing a rule or policy which is designed to protect pregnant employees from health-related hazards in the workplace?

Section 10(2) of the Ontario *Human Rights Code* provides that "[t]he right to equal treatment without discrimination because of sex includes the right to equal treatment without discrimination because a woman is or may become pregnant".

---

[49] (1987), 40 D.L.R. (4th) 193, [1987] 1 S.C.R. 1114 *sub nom. Canadian National Railway Co. v. Canada (Canadian Human Rights Commission).*

One of the leading cases on this issue is the decision of the Ontario Board of Inquiry in *Wiens v. Inco Metals Co.*[50] In the *Wiens* case, it was clear that Inco had a policy of refusing to employ women with child-bearing potential in the Inco Pressure Carboryl processing area of its Sudbury plant, due to the fact that from time to time there were accidental emissions of nickel carboryl gas, and the company believed that exposure to such an emission could harm a fetus. Ms Wiens was excluded from working in positions in the IPC area, even though she was qualified for the training and she was an employee of some seven years seniority.

The Board of Inquiry heard extensive expert evidence relating to the health hazards of accidental emissions of nickel carboryl gas, as well as the nature and frequency of such emissions. In upholding the complaint, the Board of Inquiry held that the risk of harm to a fetus was minimal and that the said policy did not constitute a reasonable and *bona fide* occupational qualification. In the course of its reasons, the Board of Inquiry stated:

> The employer may be acting with two motives; a desire to protect a potential fetus from physical damage and also a desire to protect the company from tort liability to a child born deformed. Balanced against these issues is the principle of equality of opportunity in the workplace. The complainant in the instant situation has been barred from advancing in the company due to an accident of birth, specifically, that she has the potential to bear children. The issue is a particularly difficult one. Apart from sterilization there is not a known method of complete protection against pregnancy. No one method is 100 percent trustworthy and many women cannot take the pill, the most reliable method, for health reasons. Furthermore, the fetus is most susceptible to damage during the first trimester of development. Pregnancy cannot usually be detected until at least five days after a missed period. Thus, no matter how careful the employer is in keeping the work environment hazard free and no matter how careful the employee is in remaining not pregnant there remains the possibility, however slight, that the complainant could be pregnant without knowing and contemporaneously be exposed to a toxic chemical. Should these two events coincide, there may then be serious injury to the fetus.[51]

In spite of an employer's honestly held belief, based upon the advice of medically trained persons, a general policy pertaining to pregnant or potentially pregnant employees, could nonetheless, constitute a violation of human rights legislation.

6. MARITAL AND FAMILY STATUS

Marital status is defined in s. 10(1) of the Ontario *Human Rights Code* as follows:

---

[50] (1988), 9 C.H.R.R. D/4795 (Ont. Bd. Inq.).
[51] *Wiens, supra,* at pp. D/4811-12.

"marital status" means the status of being married, single, widowed, divorced or separated and includes the status of living with a person of the opposite sex in a conjugal relationship outside marriage.

Employer policies and procedures relating to hiring, probation, benefits, promotion, discipline and dismissal cannot have the effect, directly or indirectly, of discriminating on the basis of marriage.

Discrimination based on marital status takes many forms. For example, an employer may prefer to hire a married man over an unmarried man in the belief that the married man may be more stable and less likely to move on to alternate employment in the short term. Alternatively, employers may be reluctant to hire young married women out of concern that such women may become pregnant which could lead to a disruption of the individual's employment. Other employers may prefer to hire single people in the belief that they will have few outside responsibilities and thus more likely to be dedicated to their work. Still other employers may be reluctant to hire the recently divorced fearing these individuals may be emotionally unstable. Regardless of the validity of any of these considerations, all are prohibited by the *Human Rights Code.*

The Board has also considered whether the marital status provisions prohibit discrimination only on the basis of being married or whether they extend to the status of being married to a particular person. For example, in *Mark v. Porcupine General Hospital*[52] the complainant was dismissed when it was discovered that she was married to another employee working in the same department, contrary to the policy of the hospital. The Board held that the marital status provisions should be given a broad interpretation and found that the dismissal amounted to marital status discrimination under the Code.

The *Mark* decision makes it clear that any employer policy or custom relating to hiring, promotions or transfer that is based, in whole or in part, on one's relation by marriage to anyone else in the company or department, is unlawful. The extent of the prohibition against discrimination on the basis of marital status is effectively demonstrated by the decision of the Federal Court of Appeal in *Cashin v. Canadian Broadcasting Corp.*[53]

In *Cashin*, the complainant was denied continuing employment as a journalist with the CBC when her husband was appointed to the board of directors of Petro Canada, another Crown corporation. The CBC argued that identifiable spouses of public figures lacked "perceived objectivity", no matter how objective their reporting was in reality.

In dismissing the arguments raised by the CBC, and upholding the complaint made by Cashin, the court dismissed, as wholly unsubstantiated, the argument of "perceived objectivity" raised by the CBC.

---

[52] (1984), 85 C.L.L.C. ¶17,001, 6 C.H.R.R. D/2538 (Ont. Bd. Inq.).
[53] [1988] 3 F.C. 494, 88 C.L.L.C. ¶17,019 (C.A.), leave to appeal to S.C.C. refused [1988] 2 S.C.R. v, 97 N.R. 396*n.*

It is clear that discrimination on the basis of marital status is not, in any way, restricted to discrimination involving the fact that one is married, single, divorced, separated or living in a common-law relationship. It also encompasses discrimination relating to the identity and/or characteristics of one's spouse or spousal equivalent.

However, the express statutory definition of "marital status" omits certain relationships which would, arguably, amount to discrimination. First, the status of being engaged to be married, which is expressly protected under the *Saskatchewan Human Rights Code*, S.S. 1979, c. S-24.1, is not included within the Ontario *Human Rights Code*. Secondly, the requirement in Ontario, that an individual be living "with a person of the opposite sex in a conjugal relationship outside marriage", would appear to negate various protections, afforded to homosexual couples living in a common-law relationship. However, a recent decision of the Ontario Human Rights Commission seems to suggest that homosexual common-law relationships are protected under the Code.

The recent decision of the Supreme Court of Canada in *Canada (Attorney General) v. Mossop*[54] makes it clear that a claim of discrimination on the basis of sexual orientation which is not a prohibited ground under the *Canadian Human Rights Act*, cannot be remedied indirectly by filing a complaint of discrimination on the basis of family status.

In *Mossop*, the complainant, a homosexual man in a same-sex conjugal relationship, was denied bereavement leave to attend the funeral of his partner's father. The tribunal concluded that Mr. Mossop had been discriminated against on the basis of family status. However, this decision was reversed by the Federal Court of Appeal. In essence, the court held that the discrimination in question was not discrimination on the basis of family status, which is protected under the *Canadian Human Rights Act* but, rather, discrimination on the basis of sexual orientation, which is not specifically protected under the federal human rights legislation. This decision was upheld by a 4 to 3 majority, of the Supreme Court of Canada.

Chief Justice Lamer made it clear that the appeal in *Mossop* was being dealt with strictly on the basis of statutory interpretation, as opposed to considering the more fundamental issue as to whether the exclusion of sexual orientation as a prohibited ground of discrimination under the *Canadian Human Rights Act*, violated the equality rights provisions of s. 15 of the *Canadian Charter of Rights and Freedoms*. In the course of his reasons for judgment, the Chief Justice provides a brief synopsis of the unaccepted invitation that

---

[54] (1990), 71 D.L.R. (4th) 661, [1991] 1 F.C. 18 (C.A.), affd 100 D.L.R. (4th) 658, [1993] 1 S.C.R. 554.

was extended to the appellant to argue the Charter issue relating to the exclusion of sexual orientation under the *Canadian Human Rights Act*:

> It is important to remember that when this case was heard last June [ie June 1992], the only question submitted to this court was whether, by specifically denying homosexual couples access to certain benefits conferred on heterosexual couples, a union and the government had infringed the C.H.R.A. There was no question of determining whether the *government and the unions should* or should not extend these types of benefits to homosexual couples, nor of deciding whether Parliament when enacting the C.H.R.A. should have prohibited discrimination on the basis of sexual orientation. Also of great importance to the dynamics of the analysis in this case is the fact that none of the provisions of the C.H.R.A. were challenged under the Charter. The question before this court was thus strictly one of statutory interpretation.
>
> Since then, as the result of two important decisions of Canadian courts, the situation in this country has evolved with respect to the questions at issue in this appeal . . .
>
> As a result of these developments, the court invited the parties to this appeal to submit new arguments . . .
>
> The appellant chose not to take this approach, however, and insisted that this court dispose of its action solely on the basis of the meaning of ''family status''.[55]

Chief Justice Lamer summarily disposed of the issue of statutory interpretation in the following passage from his reasons:

> It is thus clear that when Parliament added the phrase ''family status'' to the English version of the C.H.R.A. in 1983, it refused at the same time to prohibit discrimination on the basis of sexual orientation in that Act. In my opinion, this fact is determinative. I find it hard to see how Parliament can be deemed to have intended to cover the situation now before the court in the C.H.R.A. when we know that it specifically excluded sexual orientation from the list of prohibited grounds of discrimination contained in the Act. In the case at bar, Mr. Mossop's sexual orientation is so closely connected with the grounds which lead to the refusal of the benefit that this denial could not be condemned as discrimination on the basis of ''family status'' without indirectly introducing into the C.H.R.A. the prohibition which Parliament specifically decided not to include in the Act, namely, the prohibition of discrimination on the basis of sexual orientation.[56]

Family status is defined under s. 10(1) of the Ontario *Human Rights Code* as ''the status of being in a parent and child relationship''. However, this strict statutory definition has been extended, as illustrated in one recent decision of the Board of Inquiry:

> Section 9(1)(d) [now 10(1))] says ''family status'' ''means the status of being in a parent and child relationship''. Obviously this includes both a biological and an adoptive parent . . . In our view, the definition looks to a ''status'' arising from

---

55 *Supra*, at p. 671 (S.C.C.).
56 *Supra*, at p. 672 (S.C.C.).

being in a parent and child type of "relationship". That is, someone acting in the position of parent to a child is, in our view, embraced by this definition; for example, a legal guardian or even an adult functioning in fact as parent. Occasionally, for example, due to death or illness of a relative or friend, someone will step in and act as parent to a child of the deceased or incapacitated adult. Thus, if a nephew were to reside with an aunt for an indefinite period, in our view their relationship would fall within the meaning of "family status" in section 9(1)(d) [now 10(1)].[57]

7. SEXUAL ORIENTATION

As previously noted, the Ontario *Human Rights Code* specifically prohibits discrimination on the basis of sexual orientation while the *Canadian Human Rights Act* does not contain such an express prohibition. However, the Ontario Court of Appeal in *Haig v. Canada*[58] ruled that homosexuals are entitled to equal benefit and protection of the *Canadian Human Rights Act* and are therefore entitled to seek and obtain redress against discrimination on the ground of sexual orientation from the Canadian Human Rights Commission.

In *Haig*, the complainants filed a complaint of discrimination against the Canadian Armed Forces with respect to its policy directive that homosexuals in the forces are not eligible for promotions, postings or further career training. With respect to the absence of sexual orientation as a prohibited ground of discrimination under the *Canadian Human Rights Act*, Mr. Justice Krever, speaking on behalf of the Ontario Court of Appeal, stated:

> Section 15(1) of the Charter does not, in express terms, include sexual orientation as a basis of discrimination against which constitutional protection is guaranteed as integral to equality before and under the law and equal protection and benefit of the law. It is now clear that s. 15(1) of the Charter provides protection not only to the enunciated grounds but also to grounds that are analogous to them . . . Courts in Canada have acted on the premise that sexual orientation is an analogous ground or is a ground covered by s. 15 of the Charter.

. . . . .

> A comparison of the prohibited grounds of discrimination in s. 3(1) of the *Canadian Human Rights Act* with the grounds listed in s. 15(1) of the Charter reveals that all those who have complaints about discrimination on the grounds listed in s. 15(1) of the Charter have the benefit of access to the ameliorating procedures of the *Canadian Human Rights Act*. Homosexual persons, who fall within a ground analogous to the constitutionally protected ground of sex, are, by exclusion, denied access. Because of the omission of that ground of discrimination, the *Canadian Human Rights Act* withholds benefits or advantages available to other persons alleging discrimination on the enumerated grounds from

---

[57] *York Condominium No. 216 v. Dudnik* (1990), 12 C.H.R.R. D/325 at pp. D/348-9, 12 R.P.R. (2d) 1 (Ont. Bd. Inq.), vard 79 D.L.R. (4th) 161, 45 O.A.C. 381 (Ont. Ct. (Gen. Div.)).
[58] (1992), 94 D.L.R. (4th) 1, 57 O.A.C. 272 (C.A.).

persons who are and, on the evidence, have historically been, the object of discrimination on analogous grounds. The distinction created by the legislation alone, however, is not sufficient to justify a conclusion of discrimination within the meaning of s. 15(1) of the Charter and of *Andrews v. Law Society of British Columbia.* The larger context, social, political and legal, must also be considered.

. . . . .

One need not look beyond the evidence before us to find disadvantage that exists apart from and independent of the legal distinction created by the omission of sexual orientation as a prohibited ground of discrimination in s. 3(1) of the *Canadian Human Rights Act.* The social context which must be considered includes the pain and humiliation undergone by homosexuals by reason of prejudice towards them. It also includes the enlightened evolution of human rights social and legislative policy in Canada, since the end of the Second World War, both provincially and federally. The failure to provide an avenue for redress for prejudicial treatment of homosexual members of society, and the possible inference from the omission that such treatment is acceptable, create the effect of discrimination offending s. 15(1) of the Charter.[59]

The Court of Appeal in the *Haig* case concluded its reasons by expressly ordering that the *Canadian Human Rights Act* be interpreted, applied and administered as though it contained "sexual orientation" as a prohibited ground of discrimination in s. 3 of the Act.

The Supreme Court of Canada in *Canada (Attorney General) v. Mossop*[60] specifically invited the appellant to raise a Charter challenge to the *Canadian Human Rights Act* on the same basis on which it was raised in the *Haig* decision. Unfortunately, the appellant declined the invitation and, therefore, the issue has yet to be ultimately decided by the Supreme Court of Canada. The Federal Minister of Justice, Mr. Allan Rock, has publicly stated that amending the *Canadian Human Rights Act* to specifically include sexual orientation as a prohibited ground of discrimination, is one of his legislative priorities as Federal Justice Minister.

In *Leshner v. Ontario*,[61] the Board of Inquiry was called upon to determine whether the benefit coverage provided by the Ministry of the Attorney General to its employees, including Crown counsel Michael Leshner, was in violation of the provisions of the Code. Although the complaint was formally characterized on the basis of discrimination because of sexual orientation, the facts of the case clearly indicate that the "family" or "marital" status of Mr. Leshner was squarely in issue before the Board.

Mr. Leshner has been employed with the Ministry of the Attorney General since 1975, being appointed Crown counsel in 1976. Mr. Leshner first met his

---

[59] *Supra*, at pp. 6-10.
[60] *Mossop, supra*, footnote 54 (S.C.C.).
[61] (1992), 92 C.L.L.C. ¶17,035, 16 C.H.R.R. D/184 (Ont. Bd. Inq.).

partner, Mr. Stark in 1981 and they began to live together in February, 1983. In the words of Mr. Leshner:

> Michael and I clearly lived in a public way as to a same-sex conjugal relationship. We had longevity, we had joint tenancy in our homes. We had financial arrangements, mutual wills. We went everywhere socially together.[62]

As an employee, Mr. Leshner was entitled to coverage under the Ontario Government's group supplementary health and hospital policy, dental care plan and pension plan. At the time of his complaint, being August 25, 1988, the insured benefit policies and pension plan allowed for "family coverage" by which benefits were extended to the "dependents" of an employee defined to mean their (opposite sex) "spouse" and any children. In March, 1988, Mr. Leshner submitted the appropriate application form to his employer seeking to extend coverage to Mr. Stark by amending his health care, dental care and pension plan benefits form "single coverage" to "family coverage". Mr. Leshner's application was denied which, in turn, gave rise to the filing of his complaint.

In upholding Mr. Leshner's complaint, the Board of Inquiry made a number of key findings and statements of principle, including:

(1) while an employer may have no obligation to provide employment benefits, it is clear that once it has undertaken to provide benefits, those benefits must be provided in a non-discriminatory manner;

(2) an employer cannot escape responsibility for discriminatory benefit coverage on the basis that the plan in question is wholly administered by a third party insurer;

(3) the "marital status" definition set out within the Ontario *Human Rights Code* must be "read down" so as to ignore the restriction of common-law, conjugal relationships being *only* those involving members of the opposite sex.

The express finding by the Board of Inquiry that the definition of "marital status" under the Ontario *Human Rights Code* violated the equality rights provisions under s. 15 of the Charter, by discriminating against homosexuals living in a common-law relationship, is a decision of some significance. The Board of Inquiry took the almost unprecedented step of indirectly amending a provision of the Ontario *Human Rights Code*. The Government of Ontario decided not to appeal this decision.

One year after the *Leshner* decision, an Ontario Board of Inquiry released its decision in *Clinton v. Ontario Blue Cross*.[63] Although the result in *Clinton* was essentially the same as that in the *Leshner* case, the Board of Inquiry in

---

[62] *Supra*, at p. 16,331.

[63] (1993), 93 C.L.L.C. ¶17,026, 18 C.H.R.R. D/377 (Ont. Bd. Inq.), revd (unreported, May 3, 1994, Ont. Div. Ct.).

Clinton disagreed with certain principles and rationale as articulated by the Board of Inquiry in *Leshner.*

In the *Clinton* case, Ms Clinton lived in a conjugal relationship with a female friend, Ms Laurie Anne Mercer, since July, 1988. In May, 1989, they purchased a condominium together. They intermingled their financial affairs by way of a joint credit card account, wills which named one another as executrix and major beneficiary and mutual powers of attorney. In 1991, they celebrated a "holy union" ceremony in their church, exchanging vows in the presence of their community, friends and their closest living relatives. At the time of the hearing, they intended to have a child and were hopeful that Ms Mercer was pregnant at that time.

In June, 1990, Ms Clinton applied for family benefits under the Groups Benefit Plan Agreement through her hospital employer. The application indicated that Ms Clinton wished to have Ms Mercer recognized as her common-law spouse. Ms Clinton was advised later the very same day that she submitted the application, that Ontario Blue Cross Insurance coverage held by the hospital did not allow for same-sex partners to receive benefits and therefore the application was refused. Ms Clinton in turn filed a human rights complaint alleging discrimination in employment and services on the basis of sexual orientation. In upholding the complaint of Ms Clinton, the Ontario Board of Inquiry, Mr. Jeffrey A. House, stated in part:

> Section 5 of the Code [*i.e.*, the Ontario *Human Rights Code*] provides that it is an infringement of the Code to discriminate on the basis of *any* of the proscribed grounds set out therein. S. 25(1) then reaffirms that this is the case, in general, with respect to employee benefit plans. An employee benefit plan which discriminates on *any* of the proscribed grounds, violates the Code. However, the breadth of this prohibition is the attenuated by [*sic*] s. 25(2), which sets out instances in which the right to employment without discrimination is not infringed. Those are: the right to equal treatment in employment because of age, the right to equal treatment in employment because of sex, the right to equal treatment in employment because of marital status, and the right to equal treatment in employment because of family status. It is immediately obvious that a defence is not provided for employee benefit plans which discriminate on the basis of handicap, on the basis of creed or on the basis of sexual orientation.
>
> It seems to me that this absence of the words "sexual orientation" from the section listing what is exempted from the strictures of s. 25(1) is important. Furthermore, the Supreme Court of Canada has held, in *Brossard (Town) v. Commission des droits de la personne du Quebec and Laurin* [53 D.L.R. (4th) 609] that while rights articulated in *Human Rights Codes* are to receive a broad interpretation, defence to the exercise of those rights should be read narrowly.[64]

In the course of his reasons in *Clinton*, the Board of Inquiry provided the following distinction between discrimination on the basis of martial status and discrimination on the basis of sexual orientation:

---

[64] *Supra*, at pp. 16,264-5.

Thus, in my view, the marital status ground means that, in general, opposite-sex couples may not be preferred over those who, without further discrimination, are characterized as single, widowed, divorced or separated.

. . . . .

I propose to analyze this case from the point of view of what I believe to be a minimal definition of sexual orientation, namely, the capacity, or perceived capacity, to be sexually attracted to persons of one's own sex.[65]

The Board of Inquiry articulated the essence of the reason for his decision as follows:

The employee benefit plan grants benefits to conjugal partners of the opposite sex, while denying these same benefits to those of the same sex who chose to live together conjugally. Bearing in mind that the core idea of "sexual orientation" as a prohibited ground is the capacity to be attracted, sexually, by members of the same sex, it seems to me an unavoidable conclusion that the sex of one's conjugal mate is a fact strongly "related to" the prohibited ground itself.[66]

Ms Clinton was awarded the sum of $4,000 for loss of the guaranteed right to be free from discrimination in employment. In addition, the hospital was ordered to provide employee benefits to same-sex couples and that they inform their employees of the availability of such benefits. Finally, Ontario Blue Cross was ordered to amend any employee benefit plan presently in effect in Ontario by deleting the words "of the opposite sex" from the definition "dependant", as well as being prohibited from offering in the province of Ontario any employee benefit plan which limits common-law conjugal benefits to persons of the opposite sex.

The Board of Inquiry's decision in *Clinton* was subsequently appealed to the Ontario Divisional Court. In an abbreviated, oral decision from the bench, Mr. Justice Carruthers, speaking on behalf of a unanimous court, allowed the appeal. The court concluded that the Board of Inquiry had erred in its finding that Ontario Blue Cross had violated the provisions of the Ontario *Human Rights Code* in denying certain benefits to Ms Clinton because she had been discriminated against on the basis of sexual orientation as prohibited by the Code. The court stated that the correct interpretation of the relevant provisions of the Ontario *Human Rights Code*, namely s. 5(1), s. 10(1), in so far as it defines "marital status" and "spouse", and s. 25, together with related provisions of the *Employment Standards Act*, R.S.O. 1990, c. E.14, is that found in the majority decision in *Leshner*, previously discussed in this chapter. In addition, the court refused to hear argument under the equality rights provision of the Charter, being s. 15, on the basis that there had been an absence of

---

[65] *Supra*, at pp. 16,265-6.
[66] *Supra*, at p. 16,266.

adequate notice to the Attorney General and, to an apparently lesser extent, the fact that there had been no decision of the Board of Inquiry with respect to the Charter argument.

8. DISABILITY

Discrimination on the basis of physical disability is one of the most specifically defined grounds of discrimination in human right legislation across Canada.

Section 10(1) of the Ontario *Human Rights Code* reads as follows:

> 10(1) "because of handicap" means for the reason that the person has or has had, or is believed to have or have had,
>> (a) any degree of physical disability, infirmity, malformation or disfigurement that is caused by bodily injury, birth defect or illness and, without limiting the generality of the foregoing, including diabetes mellitus, epilepsy, any degree of paralysis, amputation, lack of physical co-ordination, blindness or visual impediment, deafness or hearing impediment, muteness or speech impediment, or physical reliance on a guide dog or on a wheelchair or other remedial appliance or device,
>> (b) a condition of mental retardation or impairment,
>> (c) a learning disability, or a dysfunction in one or more of the processes involved in understanding or using symbols or spoken language,
>> (d) a mental disorder, or,
>> (e) an injury or disability for which benefits were claimed or received under the *Workers' Compensation Act.*

It is beyond question that discrimination on the basis of disability applies to both actual and perceived disability.

A recent decision of a board of inquiry under the *Canadian Human Rights Act* concludes that persons carrying the HIV virus fall within the definition of disability, even though they may yet be without symptoms of Acquired Immune Deficiency Syndrome ("AIDS").[67]

It is unlikely that a temporary disability will constitute a "handicap" for the purposes of prohibited discrimination under existing human rights legislation. In *Ouimette v. Lily Cups Ltd.*,[68] the complainant was terminated as a direct result of the company's unwritten policy that if a probationary employee missed more than two days work for any reason he or she would be terminated. Ms Ouimette was dismissed after having missed two days due to influenza and another day due to an allergic reaction. The Board dismissed her complaint that her dismissal constituted discrimination on the basis of handicap.

---

[67] *Thwaites and Canadian Armed Forces (Re)* (1993), 93 C.L.L.C. ¶17,025 (Can. Trib.), affd (unreported, March 25, 1994, F.C.T.D.).
[68] (1990), 12 C.H.R.R. D/19 (Ont. Bd. Inq.).

It is important to bear in mind that not all instances of employment discrimination based on disability are prohibited under human rights legislation. There are two very important exceptions which are discussed in greater detail in a separate chapter in this book:

(1) the *bona fide* occupational qualification exception essentially provides that an employer requirement or policy that has the effect of discriminating against certain individuals who are handicapped, will not be a violation of the Act if the rule in question is a "reasonable and *bona fide* qualification because of the nature of the employment";

(2) the reasonable accommodation exception provides that if the human rights commission "is satisfied that the circumstances of the complainant cannot be accommodated without undue hardship on the person responsible for accommodating those circumstances", then the employer has an absolute defence to the discriminatory act in question.

9. CRIMINAL RECORD

The Ontario *Human Rights Code* prohibits employers from discriminating against employees and prospective employees, based on the individual's "record of offences". This term is defined in s. 10(1), in a very limited way, as follows:

> 10(1) "record of offences" means a conviction for,
> (a) an offence in respect of which a pardon has been granted under the *Criminal Records Act* (Canada) and has not been revoked, or
> (b) an offence in respect of any provincial enactment.

In a similar vein, the *Canadian Human Rights Act* simply prohibits discrimination on the basis of a "conviction for which a pardon has been granted".

It is clear that employers will not be in breach of existing human rights legislation by taking into consideration an individual's conviction for an offence under the *Criminal Code*, R.S.C. 1985, c. C-46, which is the primary piece of legislation in Canada which, among other things, both defines and provides penalties in relation to various criminal acts.

A number of British Columbia cases have considered whether an employer may discriminate on the ground of a person having been charged with an offence. In one of the most recent decisions, *Dore v. Crown Tire Service Ltd.*,[69] the Board of Inquiry ruled that the termination of an employee two days after he was charged with a criminal offence contravened the British Columbia *Human Rights Code*, R.S.B.C. 1979, c. 186. Although s. 8 of that

---

[69] (1988), 10 C.H.R.R. D/5433 (B.C.H.R.C.).

Code refers to "criminal conviction", the Board ruled that to refuse to extend protection against discrimination to a person charged but not yet convicted would be "an absurdity and unintended by the legislation", as well as being contrary to the presumption of innocence which is a hallmark of our legal system.

CHAPTER 7 | *Sexual Harassment*

Introduction

Until 1978, the term "sexual harassment" was not in use and such behaviour was referred to as "sexual misconduct", "sexual advances", or "sexual molestation".[1] In fact, the first Canadian decision of a human rights tribunal involving alleged sexual harassment was in 1980, when an Ontario board of inquiry released its decision in *Bell v. Korczak*[2] (the "Cherie Bell case").

Since 1978, there has been a significant expansion in both legislation and case law in the area of sexual harassment. This is attributable, in large part, to the changing attitudes relating to the existence, prevalence and offensiveness of sexual harassment, particularly in the workplace. The televised United States Senate Committee proceedings in relation to the appointment of Clarence Thomas to the United States Supreme Court is the single event which has had the most profound effect upon public opinion in relation to sexual harassment in the workplace.

Every employer in Ontario, irrespective of the size of the company or the nature of the industry in which it conducts its business, has both an ethical and legal obligation to provide a workplace that is free from discrimination. Without question, the elimination of sexual harassment in the workplace provides the single most difficult challenge to virtually every employer. Zero tolerance is an objective which all employers ought to strive for in dealing with sexual harassment in the workplace.

A comprehensive review of the subject of sexual harassment, both from a legal and sociological standpoint, is well beyond the scope of this text. Rather, a concise review and summary is provided of the important legal principles and considerations which ought to be addressed by employers in Ontario.

For reasons discussed later in this chapter, employers are often placed in a "Catch 22" situation in dealing with an allegation of sexual harassment. No matter the way in which a complaint of sexual harassment is dealt with, the

---

[1] A.P. Aggarwal, *Sexual Harassment in the Workplace*, 2nd ed. (Markham, Butterworths, 1992), p. 8.
[2] (1980), 1 C.H.R.R. D/155 *sub nom. Bell v. Ladas*, 27 L.A.C. (2d) 227 (Ont. Bd. Inq.).

employer is almost inevitably faced with the possibility of either a formal human rights complaint being filed or legal proceedings being taken against it by the individual accused of the improper act who may have suffered a wrongful dismissal as a result of an unsubstantiated allegation. In addition, the emotional impact upon the parties involved in any investigation of an allegation of sexual harassment, may be traumatic. The inherent sensitivity and potential ramifications of any allegation of sexual harassment make it mandatory that it be fully and properly investigated in a timely manner, with appropriate consideration being given to the rights and interests of both the complainant and the alleged wrongdoer. It is for these and many other reasons that considerable care must be taken by all employers in addressing any issue pertaining to the subject of sexual harassment.

1. STATUTORY PROVISIONS

A. Ontario Human Rights Code

Section 7(2) of the Ontario *Human Rights Code*, R.S.O. 1990, c. H.19, provides that:

> 7(2) Every person who is an employee has a right to freedom from harassment in the workplace because of sex by his or her employer or agent of the employer or by another employee.

Section 7(3) of the Code specifically addresses the subject of sexual solicitation:

> 7(3) Every person has a right to be free from,
>   (a) a sexual solicitation or advance made by a person in a position to confer, grant or deny a benefit or advancement to the person where the person making the solicitation or advance knows or ought reasonably to know that it is unwelcome; or
>   (b) a reprisal or a threat of reprisal for the rejection of a sexual solicitation or advance where the reprisal is made or threatened by a person in a position to confer, grant or deny a benefit or advancement to the person.

Although the Ontario *Human Rights Code* does not specifically deem sexual harassment to be discrimination, the Supreme Court of Canada in its landmark decision in *Janzen v. Platy Enterprises Ltd.*[3] unanimously held that sexual harassment of female employees by a male co-worker constituted discrimination on the basis of sex contrary to s. 6(1) of the Manitoba *Human Rights Act* (then S.M. 1974, c. 65; R.S.M. 1987, c. H175, rep. & sub. Manitoba *Human Rights Code*, S.M. 1987-88, c. 45, s. 64) which is similar in wording to the above-noted provisions of the Ontario *Human Rights Code*.

---

[3] (1989), 59 D.L.R. (4th) 352, [1989] 1 S.C.R. 1252.

The term "harassment" is specifically defined within the Ontario *Human Rights Code*, s. 10(1) to mean "engaging in a course of vexatious comment or conduct that is known or ought reasonably to be known to be unwelcome".

By specifically incorporating the term "course of vexatious comment or conduct", the clear inference to be drawn is that harassment will typically require more than a single event. In other words, this definition, on its face, seems to suggest a degree of repetition of the "vexatious comment or conduct" in order to constitute harassment under the Code. This interpretation of the definition of harassment is consistent with the decision of the Ontario Board of Inquiry in *Cuff v. Gypsy Restaurant*.[4] In that decision, the Board held that the test of whether or not there is a course of vexatious comment generally requires a recurring event rather than a single incident.

B. Canadian Human Rights Act

The *Canadian Human Rights Act*, R.S.C. 1985, c. H-6, as distinct from the Ontario *Human Rights Code*, specifically prohibits sexual harassment in s. 14.2:

> 14(2) Without limiting the generality of subsection (1), sexual harassment shall, for the purposes of that subsection, be deemed to be harassment on a prohibited ground of discrimination.

Section 14(1) in turn provides as follows:

> 14(1) It is a discriminatory practice,
>
> . . . . .
>
> (*c*) in matters related to employment,
> to harass an individual on a prohibited ground of discrimination.

The above-noted provisions of the *Canadian Human Rights Act* were included within the statute by legislative amendment in 1983.

C. Canada Labour Code

In the *Canada Labour Code*, R.S.C. 1985, c. L-2, the term "sexual harassment" is specifically defined in section 247.1:[5]

> 247.1 In this Division, "sexual harassment" means any conduct, comment, gesture or contact of a sexual nature
>
> (*a*) that is likely to cause offence or humiliation to any employee; or
> (*b*) that might, on reasonable grounds, be perceived by that employee as placing a condition of a sexual nature on employment or on any opportunity for training or promotion.

---

4 (1987), 8 C.H.R.R. D/3972, 87 C.L.L.C. ¶17,015 (Ont. Bd. Inq.).
5 Sections 247.1-247.4 enacted R.S.C. 1985, c. 9 (1st Supp.), s. 1.

Section 247.2 of the Code further expressly provides that ''[e]very employee is entitled to employment free of sexual harassment''.

A further novel provision of the *Canada Labour Code* is the requirement, in s. 247.4, that every employer shall issue a policy statement concerning sexual harassment:

> 247.4(1) Every employer shall, after consulting with the employees or their representatives, if any, issue a policy statement concerning sexual harassment.
>
> (2) The policy statement required by subsection (1) may contain any term consistent with the tenor of this Division the employer considers appropriate but must contain the following:
>
> (*a*) a definition of sexual harassment that is substantially the same as the definition in section 247.1;
>
> (*b*) a statement to the effect that every employee is entitled to employment free of sexual harassment;
>
> (*c*) a statement to the effect that the employer will make every reasonable effort to ensure that no employee is subjected to sexual harassment;
>
> (*d*) a statement to the effect that the employer will take such disciplinary measures as the employer deems appropriate against any person under the employer's direction who subjects any employee to sexual harassment;
>
> (*e*) a statement explaining how complaints of sexual harassment may be brought to the attention of the employer;
>
> (*f*) a statement to the effect that the employer will not disclose the name of the complainant or the circumstances related to the complaint to any person except where disclosure is necessary for the purposes of investigating the complaint or taking disciplinary measures in relation thereto; and
>
> (*g*) a statement informing employees of the discriminatory practices provisions of the *Canadian Human Rights Act* that pertain to rights of persons to seek redress under that Act in respect of sexual harassment.
>
> (3) Every employer shall make each person under the employer's direction aware of the policy statement required by subsection (1).

It is unclear as to why these extensive provisions relating to sexual harassment were incorporated in the *Canada Labour Code*, as opposed to direct amendment of the *Canadian Human Rights Act*. In any event, it is submitted that the provisions of the *Canada Labour Code* in relation to the subject of sexual harassment are to be given the same force and effect as the provisions of the *Canadian Human Rights Act*.

2. CONDUCT WHICH CONSTITUTES SEXUAL HARASSMENT

Chief Justice Dickson of the Supreme Court of Canada in its landmark decision in *Janzen v. Platy Enterprises Ltd.*, defined sexual harassment in the workplace as follows:

Without seeking to provide an exhaustive definition of the term, I am of the view that sexual harassment in the workplace may be broadly defined as unwelcome conduct of a sexual nature that detrimentally affects the work environment or leads to adverse job-related consequences for the victims of the harassment. It is, as Adjudicator Shime observed in *Bell v. Ladas*, and as has been widely accepted by other adjudicators and academic commentators, an abuse of power. When sexual harassment occurs in the workplace, it is an abuse of both economic and sexual power. Sexual harassment is a demeaning practice, one that constitutes a profound affront to the dignity of the employees forced to endure it. By requiring an employee to contend with unwelcome sexual actions or explicit sexual demands, sexual harassment in the workplace attacks the dignity and self-respect of the victim both as an employee and as a human being.

. . . . .

"The forms of prohibited conduct that, in my view, are discriminatory run the gamut from overt gender based activity, such as coerced intercourse to unsolicited physical contact to persistent propositions to more subtle conduct such as gender based insults and taunting, which may reasonably be perceived to create a negative psychological and emotional work environment."

. . . . .

"Sexual harassment is any sexually-oriented practice that endangers an individual's continued employment, negatively affects his/her work performance, or undermines his/her sense of personal dignity. Harassment behaviour may manifest itself blatantly in forms such as leering, grabbing, and even sexual assault. More subtle forms of sexual harassment may include sexual innuendos, and propositions for dates or sexual favours."

. . . . .

"Sexual harassment can manifest itself both physically and psychologically. In its milder forms it can involve verbal innuendo and inappropriate affectionate gestures. It can, however, escalate to extreme behaviour amounting to attempted rape and rape. Physically, the recipient may be the victim of pinching, grabbing, hugging, patting, leering, brushing against, and touching. Psychological harassment can involve a relentless proposal of physical intimacy, beginning with subtle hints which may lead to overt requests for dates and sexual favours."[6]

Chief Justice Dickson went on to articulate the essence of what amounts to sexual harassment:

The main point in allegations of sexual harassment is that unwelcome sexual conduct has invaded the workplace, irrespective of whether the consequences of

---

[6] *Janzen, supra,* footnote 3, at pp. 375, 370, 372, 373.

the harassment included a denial of concrete employment rewards for refusing to participate in sexual activity.[7]

As the Supreme Court of Canada graphically illustrates in the above-noted passages from the *Janzen* decision, sexual harassment is a phenomenon that is incapable of precise or exhaustive definition. More importantly, it covers a potential spectrum of actions and conduct, from somewhat low key verbal innuendo to attempted rape and rape. It becomes necessary for employers to understand the wide scope of potential actions and conduct which may constitute sexual harassment in the eyes of a human rights tribunal.

The Supreme Court of Canada has made it abundantly clear that human rights legislation is to be given a large, liberal interpretation for the purpose of effecting the legitimate objectives of this legislation. Accordingly, a review of the appropriate provisions of the human rights legislation in relation to sexual harassment is but a starting point in attempting to gain an understanding as to the nature and extent of the prohibition against sexual harassment in the workplace. A review of the caselaw is critical if one is to understand the scope of conduct which falls within the realm of sexual harassment.

Guidelines issued by the Canadian Human Rights Commission[8] describe sexual harassment as including:

(1) verbal abuse or threats;

(2) unwelcome remarks, jokes, innuendos or taunting;

(3) displaying pornographic or otherwise offensive or derogatory pictures;

(4) practical jokes which cause awkwardness or embarrassment;

(5) unwelcome invitations or requests, whether indirect or explicit, or intimidation;

(6) leering or other gestures;

(7) unnecessary physical contact such as touching, patting, pinching, punching;

(8) physical assault.

Although the above-noted list of actions and activities which constitute sexual harassment are by no means exhaustive, it has been suggested that behaviour which constitutes sexual harassment can be divided into two categories: sexual coercion and sexual annoyance.[9] Sexual coercion is the traditional notion of sexual harassment, and usually involves an element of reward or potential consequences flowing from the recipient's rejection of the invitation or advance. It would be akin to the concept of sexual solicitation specifically addressed within s. 7(3) of the Ontario *Human Rights Code*.

---

[7] *Supra*, at p. 375.

[8] Issued on February 1, 1983.

[9] J.W. Waks and M.G. Starr, "The Sexual Shakedown in Perspective: Sexual Harassment in its Social and Legal Contexts", (1982) 7 Employee Relations L.J. 567 at p. 572.

Sexual annoyance, on the other hand, includes conduct which is offensive, insulting, annoying or intimidating but lacking in any suggestion or element of a potential benefit or consequence flowing to the recipient. It is this latter category which poses greater difficulties for the employer.

A. Verbal Abuse or Threats

In his excellent text, *Sexual Harassment in the Workplace*,[10] Arjun P. Aggarwal provides a very helpful list of examples of verbal behaviour which have been held to constitute sexual harassment, and include:

- continuous idle chatter of a sexual nature and graphic sexual descriptions;
- offensive and persistent risqué jokes or jesting and kidding about sex or gender – specific traits;
- suggestive and insulting sounds such as whistling, wolf calls or kissing sounds;
- comments of a sexual nature about weight, body shape, size or figure;
- pseudo-medical advice such as "you might be feeling bad because you didn't get enough" or "a little tender loving care (TLC) will cure your ailments";
- staged whispers or mimicking of a sexual nature about the way a person walks, talks, sits, etc.
- derogatory or patronizing name calling;
- gender-based insults or sexist remarks;
- comments about person's looks, dress, appearance or sexual habits;
- inquiries or comments about an individual's sex life and/or relationship with sex partner;
- remarks about a woman's breasts, buttocks, vagina and her overall figure;
- speculations about a woman's virginity, her choice of sexual partner or practices;
- telephone calls with sexual overtones.

It is important to bear in mind that the abuse or threats do not have to be of a positive nature, in the sense that an individual is commenting favourably upon the victim or indicating a desire or willingness to engage in some form of sexual activity. In *Shaw v. Levac Supply Ltd.*[11] a co-worker made a number of derogatory comments to the complainant, including referring to her as a "fridge sister" and a "fat cow". On occasion, as she walked around the office, the respondent would say "waddle, waddle, waddle" and "swish, swish, swish", apparently in an attempt to imitate the sound nylons make when they rub together. These derogatory comments were made to the complainant over a period of approximately fourteen years. On occasion, the complainant registered complaints with management, to no avail. She ultimately resigned from

---

[10] A.P. Aggarwal, *Sexual Harassment in the Workplace*, 2nd ed. (Markham, Butterworths, 1992), p. 11.

[11] (1990), 91 C.L.L.C. ¶17,007, 14 C.H.R.R. D/36 (Ont. Bd. Inq.).

her position of employment when she reached the point at which she could no longer tolerate such abuse.

The Ontario Board of Inquiry concluded that the conduct in question amounted to harassment. In its reasons for decision, the Board stated, in part:

> It seems to me incontestable that to express or imply sexual unattractiveness is to make a comment of a sexual nature. Whether the harasser says "you are attractive and I want to have sex with you", or says, "you are unattractive and no one is likely to want to have sex with you", the reference is sexual. It is verbal conduct of a sexual nature, and it is sexual harassment in the workplace if it is repetitive and has the effect of creating an offensive work environment; it is sexual harassment in the form of an inappropriate comment of a sexual nature.[12]

The *Shaw* decision is further significant for the Board's finding that, "even though many other aspects of his conduct may not have been" sexual harassment, the course of conduct that caused Ms Shaw mental anguish and drove her from her job was sexual harassment and, therefore, harassment because of sex. In other words, the fact that some, even a large part, of the verbal abuse was not technically sexual harassment, the complaint may, none the less, be upheld.

B. Unwelcome Remarks, Jokes, Innuendos or Taunting

One of the primary difficulties in addressing potential sexual harassment in relation to remarks, jokes, innuendos and taunting is, perhaps, best expressed by the Ontario Board of Inquiry in the *Torres v. Royalty Kitchenware Ltd.*[13] decision:

> There are some employers (and employees) who simply are very crude and who speak in bad taste and discussing in the workplace their relationships with the opposite sex, or in telling sex "jokes". It is not the intent, or effect, of the Human Rights Code, or the function of a Board of Inquiry, to pass judgment upon such persons. It is only "sexual harassment" that is unlawful conduct.

How does one go about determining the type of remark, joke, innuendo and/or taunting that is considered to be "normal" in the workplace, as distinct from that which undermines the employee's sexual dignity as a man or woman? Some of the cases take into consideration what may be referred to as the "willing participants" test. A case in point is the Ontario Board of Inquiry decision in *Aragona v. Elegant Lamp Co.*,[14] in which the Board stated, in part, in its reasons:

> There is no doubt that considerable "banter" and "teasing" occurred. There is also no doubt that there are many comments with sexual connotations. However,

---

[12] *Supra*, at p. 16,181.
[13] (1982), 3 C.H.R.R. D/858 (Ont. Bd. Inq.), at p. D/861.
[14] (1982), 3 C.H.R.R. D/1109 (Ont. Bd. Inq.), at p. D/1112.

the evidence indicates that the employees were willing participants who enjoyed the atmosphere and who "gave" as much as they "took".

Perhaps the classic illustration of the "willing participants" phenomena is the decision of the B.C. Humans Rights Council in *Rack v. C. and J. Enterprises Ltd.*[15] In the *Rack* case, the tribunal was required to consider the working environment of certain nightclubs in determining whether to uphold the complaint of sexual harassment. In rejecting the complaint, Chairperson Verburgge stated, in part:

> In this case, overwhelming evidence was presented to show that Vandenoord's language was accepted and, if not exactly enjoyed, certainly reciprocated by the other employees. There was no evidence whatsoever that the complainant expressed disapproval of the language used . . . The fact that we are dealing with three nightclubs where the audience is predominantly male, of a rather rowdy nature, and that the entertainment consists of rock-and-roll bands, exotic dancers and strippers, must also be borne in mind when determining what would constitute "ordinary banter". I therefore find that the language used by Vandenoord during staff meetings and afterwards constitutes ordinary banter in the circumstances, especially in light of the fact that the employees reciprocated.[16]

However, it cannot be said that a woman will forfeit her right to be free from sexual harassment by choosing to work in an environment that is traditionally replete with crude, vulgar, sexist language. Where the complainant either expressly or by implication evinces an unwillingness to be subjected to such conduct, a complaint of sexual harassment may be upheld in such circumstances. In fact, it has been held that even where the complainant was prepared to stay on the job in such a work environment for economic reasons, and circumstances in which the complainant voiced little if any express disagreement with the unwelcome conduct, it nonetheless may constitute sexual harassment that is actionable under existing human rights legislation.[17]

C. Unwelcome Invitation or Requests

It is essential to any successful complaint of sexual harassment that the act in question be both unwelcome and unsolicited by the complainant. Where the alleged sexual harassment in question pertains to an invitation or request by the accused person, this requirement is imperative. Whether an invitation or request is unwelcome and unsolicited will be a question of fact to be determined in each and every case. The fact that a complainant may have complied with an invitation or request will not, necessarily, be fatal to a

---

[15] (1985), 6 C.H.R.R. D/2857 (B.C.H.R.C.).

[16] *Supra*, at p. D/2860.

[17] See, for example, *Haight v. W.W.G. Management Inc.* (1990), 11 C.H.R.R. D/124 (B.C.H.R.C.).

complaint of sexual harassment unless it is established on the evidence that the complainant's conduct was voluntary in the circumstances.

The landmark decision of the United States Supreme Court in *Meritor Savings Bank v. Vinson*[18] provides a classic illustration of the concept of voluntariness in a sexual harassment claim. In *Vinson*, the complainant maintained that her supervisor had persistently subjected her to sexual harassment both during and after business hours, both at the office and away from the office, the particulars of which included:

— he forced her to have sexual intercourse with him on numerous occasions
— he fondled her in front of other employees
— he exposed himself to her
— he raped her on several occasions

It was the evidence of the complainant that she submitted to the above-noted actions for fear of jeopardizing her employment. Both her supervisor and the company denied all of her allegations and claimed that they were contrived by way of response to an employment dispute between the parties.

The U.S. Supreme Court held that the case ought to be remitted to the trial court for consideration under the "hostile environment" theory of employer liability and further held that the proper inquiry focuses on the "unwelcomeness" of the conduct rather than the "voluntariness" of the victim's participation. In other words, the court was of the view that the essence of a sexual harassment claim is that the alleged sexual advances were "unwelcome". Accordingly, the fact that sex-related conduct was voluntary, in the sense that the complainant was not forced to participate against her will, is not a defence to a sexual harassment claim. Although the *Vinson* case was a matter decided under the *Civil Rights Act 1964*, Title VII, of the United States, it is submitted that the concept of unwelcomeness has equal application in sexual harassment claims filed pursuant to Canadian human rights legislation.

In a more recent decision of the United States Supreme Court, it was held that an "abusive work environment", can constitute actionable harassment on the basis of gender, even when the abuse "does not seriously affect employees' psychological well-being". In *Harris v. Forklift Systems Inc.*[19] the court was required to clarify certain unanswered questions from its earlier decision in the *Vinson* case. The facts of the *Harris* case may be summarized as follows:

1. Teresa Harris worked as a manager at Forklift Systems Inc., an equipment rental company, from April, 1985 until October, 1987;
2. Charles Hardy was Forklift's president over the period of Ms Harris' employment;

---

[18] 106 S. Ct. 2399 (1986).
[19] 62 L.W. 4004 (1993).

3.   throughout the course of Harris' employment with Forklift, Hardy often insulted her because of her gender and often made her the target of unwanted sexual innuendos which included comments such as:

   (i)   stating on several occasions, in the presence of other employees, "you're a woman, what do you know" and "we need a man as the rental manager",

  (ii)   telling her that she was a "dumb ass woman",

 (iii)   suggesting to Ms Harris that the two of them "go to the Holiday Inn to negotiate [Harris'] raise",

 (iv)   asking Harris and other female employees from time to time to get coins from his front pants pocket,

  (v)   throwing objects on the ground in front of Harris and other women and asking them to pick the objects up,

4.   Harris ultimately quit her employment on October 1, 1987, and proceeded to sue Forklift, claiming that Mr. Hardy's conduct had created an abusive work environment for her because of her gender.

The primary issue to be determined by the U.S. Supreme Court in the *Harris* case was whether conduct, to be actionable as "abusive work environment" harassment, must "seriously affect an employee's psychological well-being" or lead the plaintiff to "suffer injury". In answering that issue in the negative, Justice O'Connor, who delivered the opinion of the court, stated in part:

> A discriminatorily abusive work environment, even one that does not "seriously affect employees' psychological well-being" can and often will detract from employees' job performance, discourage employees from remaining on the job, or keep them from advancing in their careers. Moreover, even without regard to these tangible effects, the very fact that the discriminatory conduct was so severe or pervasive that it created a work environment abusive to employees because of their race, gender, religion, or national origin offends title VII's broad rule of work place equality . . . we therefore believe that the District Court erred in relying on whether the conduct "seriously affected plaintiff's psychological well-being" or led her to "suffer injury".[20]

The B.C. Human Rights Council in *Dyson v. Louis Pasin Plaster & Stucco Ltd.*[21] stands as authority for the proposition that mere acquiescence in sexual conduct at the workplace is not determinative of the fact as to whether the conduct in question is welcome to the individual. In *Dyson*, the victim's evidence was that she neither welcomed nor voluntarily consented to sexual activities with Mr. Pasin, the respondent, which included masturbating him. Ms Dyson testified, in part, that she was of the view that Mr. Pasin "wasn't

---

[20] *Supra*, at p. 4005.
[21] (1990), 11 C.H.R.R. D/495 (B.C.H.R.C.).

going to stop until he ejaculated'' and that she believed that it was ''the only way to stop it''.

In determining whether certain invitations or requests are unwelcome, Canadian human rights tribunals have adopted certain propositions in dealing with these complaints of sexual harassment:

— it is not necessary to establish that the complainant specifically protested or verbally rejected the invitation or request in question;

— in determining whether the alleged harasser was cognisant of the fact that his or her actions were unwelcome, tribunals have made it clear that the test is an objective test, based upon whether a ''reasonable person'' should have known that the behaviour in question was unwelcome, as opposed to being satisfied on the evidence that the specific alleged harasser in question knew or ought to have known that his or her actions were unwelcome;

— the complainant's past conduct, in terms of his or her sexual behaviour and/or propensities, is, generally speaking, irrelevant unless it relates specifically to the alleged harasser;

— the period of time over which the alleged activities of sexual harassment took place, as well as the delay of the complainant in filing a complainant, are largely irrelevant to the complaint of sexual harassment.

D. Leering or Other Gestures

Arjun P. Aggarwal, in his text *Sexual Harassment in the Workplace*, lists examples of unacceptable gestures and non-verbal behaviours that may constitute sexual harassment:

— sexual looks such as leering and ogling with suggestive overtones;
— licking lips or teeth;
— holding or eating food provocatively;
— lewd gestures, such as hand or sign language to denote sexual activity;
— persistent and unwelcome flirting.[22]

In essence, these forms of sexual harassment involve behaviour that is not directly communicative either verbally or in writing. Body language or other non-verbal gestures may amount to sexual harassment if they have a sexual element to them and are unsolicited and unwelcome by the complainer.

3. INVESTIGATING A COMPLAINT OF SEXUAL HARASSMENT

The Ontario Human Rights Commission has issued a policy statement entitled ''Guidelines for Internal Human Rights Complaint Resolution Pro-

---

[22] *Sexual Harassment, ibid.*, footnote 10, at p. 12.

cedures".[23] In these guidelines, the Commission states that the following standards should be reflected in any internal complaint resolution procedure irrespective of the size or complexity of the company:

— there should be in place a clear written policy stating that discrimination, harassment, and other types of unwelcome comments or conduct are contrary to the policy of the organization, as well as against the law, and that actions or behaviour contrary to the *Human Rights Code* will be dealt with seriously, including by the use of disciplinary measures where appropriate. It is recommended that the actual ground cited in the Code be quoted in the policy. All employees should be made aware of the employer's internal policy and complaint procedures. This should be done when the policy is introduced, with new employees at the point of hire, and when any employee assumes management responsibilities;

— any complaint procedure should be part of an overall human rights program which includes an educational component available to everyone;

— the human rights program should be agreed to by a union where one exists. If there is no union, then a human rights committee or similar group of employee representatives should be struck for this purpose;

— any person wishing to make an internal complaint should be able to contact someone able to assist them without going through their own manager or involving members of their own branch or division;

— a person making a complaint should always be advised of all other options available, especially the option to file a complaint with the Ontario Human Rights Commission and, where it exists, the option to file a grievance under a collective agreement. The person should be told how to contact the human rights commission, union or the agency. (Some employers have found it helpful to incorporate an "advisor" into their system. With the role of the advisor, who maintains strict confidentiality, is not to take action but to provide information to explain options to people with complaints or concerns.)

— a person making a complaint should be advised of the time limits that apply to these other options. Complaints under the *Human Rights Code* should be filed as soon as possible and in any case within six months. With a grievance under a collective agreement, much further time limits (days or weeks) may apply;

— a person making a complaint should be advised to make written notes of occurrences upon which the complaint is based including times, dates, locations, names of witnesses, etc. and to collect any relevant documentation;

— a person making a complaint should be aware of how the internal procedure works, including time frame, the type of information they will receive at the end of the investigation, who will investigate, who will be responsible for making a decision as to what action the employer will take, and what remedies are possible;

— it should be part of the policy that there will be protection from reprisals against those participating in the process, including complainants, witnesses, advisors, representatives, investigators and decision makers;

— the parties to a complaint should be entitled to representation if they wish — a union steward for example, or other representative;

---

[23] "Guidelines for Internal Human Rights Complaint Resolution Procedures" (Ontario Human Rights Commission, 1991).

— those responsible for investigating complaints must be as independent and as far removed from the parties involved as possible. They should report to someone with the authority to make decisions and ensure a settlement is carried out;

— investigation of complaints must not be carried out by those who, in other circumstances, play an advocacy or adversarial role on behalf of the employer vis-a-vis employees, e.g. in labour relations. Similarly, the investigation should not be conducted by anyone who has any direct influence in the career advancement of either of the parties;

— investigators must be sensitive and knowledgeable about human rights in general, and the provisions of the *Human Rights Code* in particular;

— confidentiality must be maintained wherever possible;

— there should be reasonable time limits in the resolution of a complaint by an internal procedure. In all but exceptional circumstances, investigation should be initiated immediately and concluded within 90 days. This time guideline is based on the average resolution time currently experienced by those with internal mechanisms in place;

— where a resolution has not been achieved through the internal procedure, the employee should be advised that they may still exercise their right to have their concerns addressed by the Ontario Human Rights Commission.[24]

Although the above-noted policy statement has general application to all complaints of discrimination and harassment that are prohibited under human rights legislation, many of its constituent elements may be specifically incorporated by employers for the purpose of formalizing an investigation procedure to be followed in relation to complaints of sexual harassment. All investigations of complaints of sexual harassment must be carried out in a timely, confidential, sensitive and reasonable manner whereby the rights and interests of both the complainant and the alleged harasser are balanced and equally protected.

Any investigative process must be, in some respects, certain and defined so as to ensure consistency while at the same time maintaining some element of flexibility so that it may be applied to the specific facts of a given situation. The following model investigative process takes into account many of the factors important to an impartial investigation of a complaint of alleged sexual harassment:

---

[24] *Ibid.*, pp. 3-4.

MODEL INVESTIGATION OF A COMPLAINT

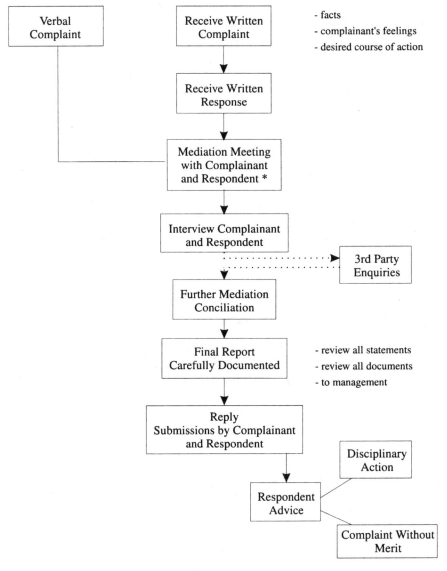

* Mediation can occur at any stage where appropriate to reach resolution
* Investigator should be viewed as independent and bound by confidentiality[25]

---

[25] Excerpt from paper prepared by Sharon M. Lax and J. Geoffrey Howard entitled "Coping with Workplace Discrimination and Harassment" for Grosman, Grosman & Gale in-house conference.

4. DEVELOPING A SEXUAL HARASSMENT POLICY

It is in the interest of employers and employees alike to constantly strive to eliminate sexual harassment in the workplace. In order to achieve this goal a carefully considered and drafted sexual harassment policy is mandatory.

The benefits of an explicit sexual harassment policy, from the employer's perspective, include the following:

— to provide an internal resolution mechanism, thereby reducing recourse to the human rights commissions;

— to reduce the economic costs to the employer of sexual harassment such as high rates of absenteeism, employee turnover, low morale and low productivity. Indirect costs associated with sexual harassment includes backpay for constructive dismissal, as well as consequential damages for loss of self-respect and punitive damages. A study conducted in the United States, from 1978 to 1980, found that sexual harassment of employees costs the federal government an estimated 190 million dollars. This same study was conducted with respect to the 1985 to 1987 time period, with an estimated cost during that period of 267 million dollars;

— to establish due diligence for the purpose of excusing the employer from employer's liability on the basis that it exercised due diligence and fulfilled its obligations to employees to prevent sexual harassment as specifically set out in s. 65(2) of the *Canadian Human Rights Act*. As evidence of due diligence, it is important that a sexual harassment policy be implemented in the workplace.[26]

A. The Essential Elements of a Sexual Harassment Policy

A comprehensive sexual harassment policy should include:

— a strong statement of the employer's philosophy concerning sexual harassment,

— a clearly articulated definition of sexual harassment,

— identification of persons covered by the policy,

— procedures to be followed in response to sexual harassment complaints,

— provisions relating to disciplinary consequences,

— a statement regarding confidentiality,

— a concluding policy statement.

Each one of these sections is dealt with below.

B. The Policy Statement

The employer should state, simply and explicitly, that it will not tolerate any form of sexual harassment whatsoever. In this regard, it is advisable to include examples of conduct which individuals may not realize constitute

---

[26] *Ibid.*

sexual harassment, such as non-verbal gestures and actions of a sexual nature, as well as jokes, innuendos and the like.

C. The Definition of Sexual Harassment

The definition of sexual harassment should reflect the requirements of law both in terms of specific prohibited acts involving unwelcome sexual attention, comments or conduct and as well in terms of the poisoned or hostile work environment concepts. It is advisable to make it clear within the policy that sexual harassment, by its very nature, is incapable of precise, exhaustive definition. Rather, the policy should emphasize the proposition that sexual harassment includes any form of comment, action, gesture or other body language that is of a sexual nature, unwelcome and unsolicited by the recipient. In this regard, it is advisable to endeavour to define or explain the concept of sexual harassment in a positive as opposed to prohibitive way. For example, it ought to be made abundantly clear that one of the primary purposes of the sexual harassment policy is an attempt to uphold the dignity and respect of all employees in the workplace in matters of a sexual nature. Furthermore, the definition of sexual harassment ought not be sexist or stereotypical in nature. Avoid the suggestion that sexual harassment typically involves a female being subjected to unwelcomed comments or actions of a male in the workplace.

D. Identified Persons Covered

It is critical when implementing a policy against sexual harassment to identify who is covered. The policy should be inclusive. It should cover women and men as both harassed parties and harassers. It should cover all employees, including support staff and secretaries as well as members of senior management.

E. Procedures to be Followed in Response to Sexual Harassment Complaints

The policy should contain both a formal and informal complaints procedure. The policy may also outline alternative routes available to an employee in addition to the internal resolution mechanisms.

Informal Procedure

An informal procedure may include the following elements:
— confronting the alleged harasser personally or in writing pointing out the unwelcome behaviour and requesting that it stop,
— discussing the situation with the alleged harasser's supervisor or any supervisor other than the complainant's own manager or members of their own departments,

— discussing the situation with a designated sexual harassment advisor, if one exists. The advisor provides information and explains options to complainants and is not the investigator.

Formal Procedure

The formal procedure may include the following:
— the complainant is to file a formal written complaint with someone outside his/her department,
— a thorough and prompt investigation will be conducted by an investigative team which is specially trained and equipped to deal with this matter. The investigator must be independent, report to someone with authority to implement corrective action, be sensitive and knowledgeable. The investigation should include the following steps:
— inform the harasser of the complaint,
— interview all parties concerned separately,
— at such interviews, the parties have the right to be represented if they so desire,
— interview all witnesses,
— collect all relevant evidence,
— prepare a timely report.

The policy must outline all other options available to an employee including:
— filing a formal complaint with the Human Rights Commission,
— filing a grievance, if applicable,
— laying information under the *Criminal Code*, R.S.C. 1985, c. C-46, if applicable.

F. Statement of Disciplinary Consequences

A sexual harassment policy should specify the range of potential sanctions in the event that the investigation reveals that sexual harassment has indeed occurred. Appropriate disciplinary actions against the harasser include:
— reprimand,
— referral for appropriate counselling,
— withholding of promotion,
— re-assignment,
— temporary suspension,
— termination of employment.

The policy should also recognize that significant damage may result from unfounded charges and allegations. The employer should consider including a provision dealing with the repercussions that flow from false accusations of sexual harassment.

G. Confidentiality

A sexual harassment policy must contain a statement that all reports regarding sexual harassment will be kept in strict confidence, except as is necessary to investigate the complaint and to respond to any legal or administrative proceedings arising out of or relating to the sexual harassment report.

H. Concluding Policy Statement

A strong, effective sexual harassment policy concludes with a re-affirmation of each individual's right to work in an environment free of sexual harassment.

As with any policy or guidelines, the implementation and administration of the policy is critical to its ultimate success. In this regard, the following steps should be taken by the employer to ensure that the sexual harassment policy is effectively implemented:

— a comprehensive education program to sensitize the employees responsible for enforcing the policy. They should be educated not only about the terms of the policy but also in relation to the applicable human rights legislation,

— provide sessions for all employees to explain the problem of harassment and discrimination,

— communicate the written sexual harassment policy to employees on introduction and on hiring in a variety of ways such as:

— include the policy in an employee handbook,

— distribute the policy directly to each employee,

— post the policy in common areas,

— conduct mandatory workshops on the subject of sexual harassment,

— be pro-active in dealing with people who are "known" to engage in harassment. The employer should not wait for a complaint to be made before taking action against these individuals,

— communicate the policy to all agents used by the employer to ensure their compliance.

The true test of any policy will lie in its day-to-day application. Employers should monitor employee recognition of and adherence to its sexual harassment policy on a regular basis. In addition, employers are well advised to amend and revise their harassment policy over time, for the purpose of clarifying its contents, addressing matters that had not been contemplated in the initial draft and to recognize the important principles and propositions laid down from time to time by human rights tribunals and the legislature in relation to the subject of sexual harassment in the workplace. A truly effective sexual harassment policy will only work where there is a genuine commitment by both employer and employee to its success.

CHAPTER 8

HIV-AIDS Discrimination In The Workplace

Preventing the spread of the human immunodeficiency virus (HIV) is one of the great public health challenges of the 1990s.[1] As James D. Watkins, Chair of the United States Presidential Committee on the Human Immunodeficiency Virus Epidemic stated within his report dated June 24, 1988:

> A society is judged by how it responds to those in greatest need. A tragedy such as the HIV epidemic brings a society face to face with the core of its established values and offers an opportunity for the reaffirmation of compassion, justice and dignity.[2]

The Ontario Law Reform Commission, in its 1992 Report on Testing for AIDS, succinctly summarizes society's initial reaction to the disease:

> When AIDS was first identified as a blood-borne infectious disease in 1981, little was known about its etiology. In the relative absence of medical knowledge, a social picture emerged of AIDS as a disease that afflicted only certain groups. In 1983 the causative agent of the disease — the human immunodeficiency virus — was identified, and in 1985 the HIV antibody test was developed. Researchers learned that the disease is not transmitted through casual contact, and that it can be prevented by avoiding specific high-risk behaviour. Nonetheless, the individuals most affected in North America are still homosexual and bisexual men and injection drug users, and HIV infection is still widely perceived as a disease unique to those groups.[3]

Notwithstanding a barrage of information about the disease, many members of the public remain fearful of contracting the disease and suspicious of information that indicates that, in most situations they have little to fear from individuals who are infected. As Professor Philip Bryden has aptly stated: "it should come as no surprise to discover that people who have AIDS find themselves suffering not only from the disease itself, but from a social stigma that, in the minds of some, is attached to the disease".[4]

---

[1] Canada, Health and Welfare, "HIV and AIDS: Canada's Blueprint" (1990), at p. 6.
[2] James D. Watkins, "Human Immunodeficiency Virus Epidemic" (Report dated June 24, 1988).
[3] Report on Testing for AIDS (Ontario Law Reform Commission, 1992), p. ix.
[4] Philip Bryden, "AIDS, Employment Discrimination and the B.C. Human Rights Act" (1988), 9 C.H.R.R. C/88-7.

1. HIV/AIDS: MEDICAL AND SCIENTIFIC CONSIDERATIONS

Before examining the subject of HIV/AIDS discrimination in the workplace, it is important to have some understanding of the disease, from a medical and scientific standpoint. In this regard, a tribunal under the Canadian Human Rights Commission in its recent decision in *Thwaites and Canadian Armed Forces (Re)*,[5] provides a scholarly summary of HIV/AIDS, based upon extensive medical evidence that was called in the course of the twenty-one day hearing. This case is essential reading for anyone who wishes to gain insight into the subject of HIV/AIDS discrimination in the workplace. The tribunal, chaired by Sidney Lederman, Q.C., who was subsequently appointed a Justice of the Ontario Court, General Division provides an excellent and comprehensive overview of the medical, scientific and legal implications of HIV/AIDS discrimination in the workplace. Because of the significance of this decision, lengthy excerpts from the ruling of a human rights tribunal are included.

A. Background Facts of the Thwaites Case

Simon Thwaites enlisted with the Canadian Armed Forces ("CAF") on June 19, 1980, progressing from the rank of Private to Master Corporal at the time of his discharge on October 23, 1989. Thwaites was, at all times material to the complaint, in the trade of Naval Electronics Senior Operator ("NESOP"), which is described in the evidence of the CAF witnesses as a "hand sea trade". Thwaites was stationed at Canadian Forces Base Halifax from May 1, 1987 until his medical discharge.

The chronological sequence of events in the *Thwaites* case can be summarized as follows:

    (i) on March 26, 1986, Thwaites learned that he was HIV positive;

    (ii) by April 10, 1986, Thwaites' commanding officer, aware of his HIV positive status, ultimately promoted him to the rank of Acting / Lacking Leading Seaman;

    (iii) during the period of July 2 through August 22, 1986, Thwaites was, unbeknownst to him, being investigated by the military police as a result of being reported by another CAF member as a homosexual;

    (iv) by October 13, 1986, Thwaites' commanding officer had completed a Change of Circumstances Report, having the effect of downgrading Thwaites' security clearance on the basis of sexual deviation;

---

[5] (1993), 93 C.L.L.C. ¶17,025 (Can. Trib.), affd (unreported, March 25, 1994, F.C.T.D.) (This decision was upheld on the application for judicial review pursuant to s. 18.1 of the *Federal Court Act*, R.S.C. 1985, c. F-7.)

(v) on November 7, 1986, Thwaites was advised that his security clearance had been downgraded to "restricted" and very shortly thereafter he was assigned to the position of doorman at the petty officer's quarters;

(vi) by January 7, 1987, Thwaites learned that he was being recommended for release on the basis of homosexuality;

(vii) between March 6 and June 2, 1987, Thwaites' commanding officer's request that he be discharged had received the support of the Base Commander and the Lieutenant Commander at Maritime Command Headquarters of National Defence;

(viii) on January 14, 1988, Thwaites started AZT therapy, an anti-viral agent that was being used on an experimental basis on HIV positive patients;

(ix) in March, 1988, following a two-stage full medical with the base surgeon, Thwaites' medical category was downgraded from a G-2 to a G-5, on the basis that he required specialist services and treatment. In this regard, he was classified as being unfit for "isolation, sea, field duties";

(x) on August 4, 1988, the Career Medical Review Board, ("CMRB") comprised of one member from each of the Navy, Army and Air Force together with a member of the Career Management Directorate and a consulting Canadian Forces doctor, determined that there was no option other than to release Thwaites on medical grounds, as he was considered disabled and unfit to perform his duties in his present trade or employment and not otherwise advantageously employable under existing service policy;

(xi) Thwaites was advised of the CMRB decision on November 10, 1988 and his release became effective on October 23, 1989.

B. Nature of HIV/AIDS

In the course of its sixty-eight page decision, the tribunal in the *Thwaites* case provided the following summary as to the nature of HIV/AIDS, based upon the medical evidence adduced at the hearing:

HIV/AIDS is one of the most complex and deadly diseases ever encountered by mankind. In addition, HIV/AIDS is not a static disease, in the sense that it evolves quite quickly in its nature and form.

HIV/AIDS is also a relatively young disease, having been identified in the early 80's. Medical knowledge and expertise regarding HIV/AIDS and its treatment have evolved, and continue to do so, since it was first identified. In terms of the medical profession's knowledge of HIV and AIDS, the relevant period for consideration by this Tribunal is January 1986 to and including October 1989 and indeed within this time frame, the period October 1987 to August 4, 1988 becomes critical.

AIDS (Acquired Immune Deficiency Syndrome) is caused by HIV, which in its most basic form is a human retrovirus. The time span between an individual becoming infected with HIV until he or she develops AIDS can be anywhere from a few months to approximately ten years. Although many individuals can live for some years without manifestation of illness, the probability is that ultimately they will develop AIDS. Once the disease reaches that stage, life expectancy depends on the nature of the final illness, the average survival being 18-24 months.

Although individuals with HIV may go for years without any outward sign of illness, most and probably all will eventually develop symptoms. There is no known cure for this disease; treatment can retard but not reverse its progression.

HIV replicates principally, but not exclusively, in CD4 positive lymphocytes, also known as T helper lymphocytes (T-cells) which are essential cells in the various human body functions. During the course of an HIV infection, the numbers of such T-cells diminish in a significant way, thus contributing to a major weakening of the body's immune system.

The evidence has shown that the weakening of the immune system is the most crucial aspect of this disease and of its characterization in patients who are HIV positive.

In fact, the HIV infection is diagnosed and treated in large part on the basis of a patient's T-cell count. This count is also used to assess a patient in terms of his or her position on the HIV infection scale.

As a result of a low T-cell count, a person who has acquired HIV becomes susceptible to a variety of opportunistic diseases which would not normally appear in an otherwise healthy person. One of the most frequent and common opportunistic diseases is pneumocystis pneumonia (PCP). This disease was of great concern to clinicians during the period in question, although by today's standards, physicians are more relaxed about the patient's risk of developing PCP.[6]

C. Classification Systems Used in Respect of HIV/AIDS Patients

It is important for employers to understand the classification systems used in respect of HIV/AIDS patients, in order to gain a greater appreciation as to the stage at which an individual is in the overall progression of the disease. Once again, the tribunal in the *Thwaites* decision provides an excellent explanation of the classification systems used in respect of HIV/AIDS patients:

> Individuals with HIV were formerly described as falling within one of three stages:
>
>   (i) Asymptomatic;
>   (ii) AIDS Related Complex (ARC); and
>   (iii) Full Blown AIDS.
>
> That rudimentary classification system was replaced by the four stage CDC (Center for Disease Control) classification which is based on the signs and symptoms of the infection. There are other recognized classification systems but CDC was the primary one referred to in the evidence in respect of Thwaites' condition.
>
> The CDC system has identified the following groups for the purpose of characterizing HIV /AIDS patients:

---

6 *Thwaites, supra,* at pp. 16,238-9 (Can. Trib.).

GROUP 1: acute infection;
GROUP 2: asymptomatic infection
GROUP 3: symptomatic infection, for example, persistent generalized lymphadenopathy; and
GROUP 4: development of symptoms consistent with impairment of immune function and development of opportunistic disease.

Group 1 includes people who show signs of recent infection and who have antibodies to the HIV virus. Within a month after exposure, many individuals experience acute flu-like symptoms which usually resolve themselves.

Group 2 includes those who have been infected with the virus for some time but who are asymptomatic. Those within Group 1 and Group 2 appear healthy and can maintain a normal lifestyle.

Group 3 includes those who have a persistent generalized lymph node enlargement that lasts more than three months but who evidence no other outward signs or symptoms.

Group 4 includes those with varying outward symptoms of the disease and they are described as having AIDS. Symptoms include wasting syndrome, dementia and other neurologic diseases; opportunistic infections such as PCP; or certain forms of cancer such as Kaposi's Sarcoma, a skin cancer.

There would appear to be at least three main reasons for a classification systems:

(i)   epidemiological, which is the charting of the disease and its study on an overall basis in terms of its impact in the human community;

(ii) biological, in terms of situating an HIV patient on a medical scale which determines the severity of the HIV infection;

(iii) for medical trials, in the sense of a decision by a doctor to prescribe an investigational drug in the fight against HIV. In other words, the point at which a patient has arrived in terms of HIV progression will determine the possibility of prescribing an investigational drug to the patient.

Whatever classification system is used, its primary purpose is epidemiological and thus the decision of placing an HIV patient in a particular group is somewhat arbitrary as the categories do not necessarily reflect disease progression precisely in the individual patient. The disease does not necessarily proceed through each of the four stages. Some individuals never experience the acute infection of Group 1. Some go directly from being outwardly asymptomatic to having a life threatening opportunistic infection without going through any intermediate stages. Some manifestations of Group 4 may be early manifestations of HIV infection unrelated to its subsequent course. The classification system has proved useful for surveillance and administrative purposes and recognizes the concept that an individual with HIV infection can be considered to have AIDS related illness without manifesting life-threatening opportunistic diseases.

In any event, most patients can be classified into broad categories which are independent of the classification systems *per se*, namely that they are either:

(i)   asymptomatic;
(ii) somewhat symptomatic;
(iii) fully symptomatic; and

(iv) at the AIDS stage, which includes any one of several possible opportunistic infections.

These broad categories reflect the fact that there is generally speaking a downward progression in the status of HIV infected persons.

There is an emerging consensus within the medical community that the best indicator of how HIV patients are likely to do is that of their overall T-cell count. This factor is increasingly relied upon by doctors in terms of how they classify and treat HIV patients. Under the new proposed definition of AIDS, as of 1992, those individuals whose T-cell count had fallen below 200 would be described as having AIDS.[7]

D. The Primary Form of Medication Given to HIV/AIDS Patients: AZT

The primary form of medication given to HIV/AIDS patients is the drug AZT. The history and nature of AZT is set out in the tribunal's reasons in the *Thwaites* decision:

In itself, the drug AZT is not new and has apparently been used in the past to combat some forms of cancer. It is only since approximately 1987 that it has been offered to HIV/AIDS patients as an important drug in helping to slow, if not to stop, the progression of HIV in a patient's body.

The Tribunal heard evidence that the drug was first offered on a trial basis, both in the United States and in Canada, to see if it would be effective in the fight against HIV/AIDS. In Canada, AZT became available on such a basis sometime in 1987.

In the face of such a complex and deadly enemy as HIV/AIDS, the medical community involved in the treatment of HIV/AIDS was quite excited with the prospect of being able to prescribe a drug against a killer which had up to that point gone completely unchecked. This enthusiasm for the drug AZT (albeit investigational) can surely not be faulted.

During the entire period at issue in this case, AZT was an experimental or investigational drug as it did not receive the Canadian government's full approval until October 1990. As an investigational drug, AZT was only made available to HIV/AIDS patients through the open trials of the long term safety of the drug conducted by Burroughs Wellcome Inc. Canada and the drug was only available through a provincial co-ordinator who was charged with the administration and distribution of the drug.

In this particular case, Dr. Walter Schlech was appointed the co-ordinator for the Maritime provinces. He occupied that role until the drug's full accreditation in October 1990, at which time it ceased to be an investigational drug and could be prescribed by way of regular channels.

Through the evidence of Dr. William Cameron, Dr. Walter Schlech and Dr. Lynn Johnston, it became evident that in late 1987 and throughout 1988, clinicians did not know very much about AZT and the medical standards of the day required vigilance in following patients who had consented to enroll on the compassionate program which made this otherwise unapproved drug available to HIV positive individuals.

---

[7] *Supra*, at pp. 16,239-40.

As is most likely the case with any investigational drug, there were many unknown factors regarding its use and distribution to HIV/AIDS patients. For example, there was some uncertainty over the required dosage and there was most likely greater uncertainty regarding possible side effects, namely nausea, anaemia and neutropenia, to name but a few.

. . . . .

Due to the investigational nature of this drug, the drug company which was producing it also issued a Protocol which was to be closely followed by all doctors prescribing the drug to their patients. Of most importance to this case is the fact that this Protocol required that the patient be seen by the administering doctor once every two weeks during the first two months and thereafter on a monthly basis. Also, the patient had to go undergo extensive laboratory tests (haematology and chemistry) on a regular basis to ensure that anaemia or other such manifestations would not result from the use of AZT.

As indicated previously, AZT did receive full government accreditation in October 1990 and could thereafter be prescribed through regular channels. The testing period had shown that it could safely be administered to HIV/AIDS patients and that in addition, it did produce beneficial results in most, if not all patients who took the drug.

At the same time, it was also decided that the recommended dosage should be reduced to approximately 500 milligrams a day and that such amount would be sufficient for the purposes of combatting the HIV virus.

In summary, AZT was rightfully seen as a drug which could mean the difference between life and death for many, if not all, HIV/AIDS patients. In the context of this particular case, the evidence suggests that Thwaites has most likely benefitted from the use of AZT.[8]

In spite of the many benefits of AZT, there still is no effective treatment to halt the progression of HIV infection or render the infected person non-infectious.[9]

E. Effect of HIV/AIDS on the Individual's Ability to Work

One of the most important principles articulated by the tribunal in the *Thwaites* case is that employees with HIV/AIDS should be considered and dealt with by employers on an individualized, case-by-case basis, as opposed to being subject to generalized policies and procedures. However, the tribunal did make certain general statements with respect to the effect of HIV/AIDS upon the individual, in terms of his or her ability to continue to discharge their employment duties and responsibilities:

In general terms, patients who have been diagnosed as HIV positive and who show no symptoms are not required to make any drastic changes to their lifestyle and habits. However, the Tribunal did hear evidence that such patients should closely watch their daily eating and sleeping habits. Generally, they should maintain a very healthy lifestyle to assist their body in its struggle to maintain a

---

[8] *Supra*, at pp. 16,241-2.
[9] Report on Testing for AIDS (Ontario Law Reform Commission, 1992), p. 14.

healthy immune system in the face of HIV. There was no evidence that physical exertion would increase an HIV positive patient's susceptibility to opportunistic diseases.

. . . . .

Professor Mark Wainberg testified that he agreed in a general sense with the recommendation of a Royal Society of Canada Report, prepared in 1988, that patients with HIV infections should not be discriminated against in terms of their status in the workplace. Professor Wainberg also agreed with that Report's recommendation that people who are HIV positive and asymptomatic are competent to perform virtually any task in Canadian society. In his opinion, there was nothing to prevent an HIV positive patient from continuing to be a productive member of society.[10]

F. Transmission of HIV Infection

HIV is transmitted primarily through blood and semen. More specifically, the known routes of HIV transmission are as follows:[11]

— by anal intercourse with an infected person;
— by vaginal intercourse with an infected person;
— by use of needles and other skin-piercing equipment contaminated with infected blood;
— from an infected mother to her fetus (perinatal transmission), and through breast feeding;
— by transfusion of infected blood or blood products;
— by tissue, semen, ova, or organ donations from infected donors.

HIV has not been transmitted through air, water, or food, or by the touching of an object handled, touched or breathed upon by a person with AIDS.[12] As the Surgeon General of the United States has said:[13]

Everyday living does not present any risk of infection. You cannot get AIDS from casual social contact. Casual social contact should not be confused with casual sexual contact which is a major cause of the spread of the AIDS virus. Casual social contact such as shaking hands, hugging, social kissing, crying, coughing or sneezing, will not transmit the AIDS virus. Nor had AIDS been contracted from swimming in pools or bathing in hot tubs or from eating in restaurants (even if a restaurant worker has AIDS or carries the AIDS virus). AIDS is not contracted from sharing bed linens, towels, cups, straws, dishes, or any other eating utensils. You cannot get AIDS from toilets, doorknobs, telephones, office machinery, or household furniture. You cannot get AIDS from body massages, masturbation or any non-sexual contact.

---

[10] *Thwaites and Canadian Armed Forces (Re)* (1993), 93 C.L.L.C. ¶17,025 at p. 16,242 (Can. Trib.), affd (unreported, March 25, 1994, F.C.T.D.).

[11] Report on Testing, *ibid.*, footnote 9, at pp. 4-5.

[12] "AIDS and the Workplace" prepared by Ont. Pub. Ed. Panel in AIDS (OPEPA) (Ontario Ministry of Health, January, 1987).

[13] As quoted in *Pacific Western Airlines Ltd. and Canadian Air Line Flight Attendants Ass'n (Re)* (1987), 28 L.A.C. (3d) 291 (Can. L.R.B.), at p. 309.

2. PROHIBITED DISCRIMINATION OR HARASSMENT

An individual cannot be discriminated against or harassed for any one of the following reasons:
— testing HIV positive
— having AIDS
— associating with persons testing HIV positive or those with AIDS
— being a partner or other family member of someone who tests HIV positive or who has AIDS[14]

In terms of potential discrimination or harassment in the workplace, the following issues must be considered from the employer's perspective:
(a) testing for HIV, either at the pre-employment stage or during the employment relationship itself;
(b) accommodating an employee who tests HIV positive or who has AIDS;
(c) HIV negative status as a *bona fide* occupational qualification or requirement of employment;
(d) addressing the rights and interests of individuals who are required to work with the employee who tests HIV positive or who has AIDS.

A. Testing for HIV

(i) Medical considerations

In its thorough Report on Testing for AIDS, The Ontario Law Reform Commission provides the following definitions of voluntary, mandatory and compulsory testing for HIV antibody:
(1) *Voluntary testing* — Testing is done only with the informed consent of the person to be tested (or if the person is incompetent, of his or her parent, legal guardian or next-of-kin, as required by law), and the testing does not fall within the definitions of mandatory or compulsory testing.
(2) *Mandatory testing* — Testing is either a necessary prerequisite for a person to obtain a specified status, benefit, service or access to a given situation, or is a necessary consequence of being provided with one or more of these.
(3) *Compulsory testing* — Testing is required by law, or policy, and the person has no choice to refuse testing and cannot legally avoid it.[15]

As for the methods of testing, evidence of HIV can be obtained by culturing the virus from blood, tissues, or body fluids.[16] However, the most frequently used medical tests focus upon the detection of antibodies specific for HIV in serum rather than on the detection of the virus itself.[17] Antibodies are proteins

---

[14] "HIV/AIDS Discrimination: It's Against the Law", CHRC pamphlet cat. no. HR 21-37 (1991), p. 2.
[15] Report on Testing for Aids (Ontario Law Reform Commission, 1992), p. 8.
[16] *Ibid.*, p. 9.
[17] *Ibid.*

produced by the body in response to foreign substances such as viruses, bacteria or even pollen grains.[18]

HIV antibody testing has been defined by the World Health Organization as a serologic procedure for HIV antibody (or antigen) in an individual, whether recommended by a health care provider or requested by the individual. At present, there are several types of serological tests, a discussion of which is beyond the scope of this text,[19] which include:

(a) the enzyme-linked immuno-sorbet assay (ELISA);
(b) the Western Blot;
(c) the radio immuno precipitation assay (RIPA); and
(d) the immunofluorescent assay.[20]

The Ontario Law Reform Commission in its report provides a general summary of antibody test findings and how they are to be interpreted:

> When an ELISA result is reactive, but its confirmatory test is negative, the person being tested is considered HIV seronegative. In low-risk populations the ELISA may yield an increased proportion of false positive results. If the results of the confirmatory test are inconclusive, the blood sample may be subjected to further testing, or the patient may be asked to undergo testing periodically until a definite result is obtained. Such testing is usually done at three to six month intervals. Until a conclusive result is obtained, the patient is counselled to take precautions to prevent possible transmission of the virus.

> Despite some of the problems associated with the current HIV antibody tests, a finding of seropositivity generally means that a person has developed antibodies to HIV and is infected. The condition is irreversible, and high-risk activity can transmit the virus to others. A negative test result indicates only that HIV antibodies were not found at the time of testing. This does not necessarily mean that the person is seronegative; it may be that he or she has not yet developed detectable antibodies. If a false negative test is suspected, the individual should be counselled about risk-producing activities that transmit HIV to others. Further testing may be indicated.[21]

However, there are numerous potential problems associated with HIV testing, which can be attributable to a number of factors, including:

— the "latency" or "window period" of the disease, being the period between infection with HIV and the presence of detectable HIV antibodies, can result in a false negative test because a recently infected person has not yet developed detectable antibodies (the latency period source of false negative test results is considered an important source of test error);

— the proportion of infected persons in any population who fail to produce antibodies is not known, but has been estimated to be as high as 5%.[22]

---

[18] *Ibid.*
[19] See Report on Testing for Aids, *ibid.*
[20] *Ibid.*, at p. 10.
[21] *Ibid.*, at p. 11.
[22] *Ibid.*, at p. 12.

— there is an unknown portion of HIV-infected persons who are sero-negative;

— false negatives occur if the test was improperly administered;

— although considered to be rare, some persons appear to lose antibodies during the course of their infection.

(ii) Legal considerations

The Ontario Human Rights Commission in its "Policy Statement on HIV/AIDS – Related Discrimination",[23] confirms that since 1985, the Commission has recognized that AIDS, as an illness, falls within the definition of "handi-cap" as set out in the Ontario *Human Rights Code*. Accordingly, all persons infected with HIV or with HIV-related illness, including those that are asymp-tomatic, are entitled to the full protection of the guarantees of equal treatment in respect of employment. Section 17 of the Code sets out a broad duty to accommodate the needs of persons with handicaps and, as expressly stipulated in the OHRC's policy statement, "may be of particular value to persons with HIV or with HIV-related illness".

Testing for HIV infection comes within the Commission's "Policy on Employment-Related Medical Examinations."[24] The policy provides, amongst other things, that employers are prohibited from subjecting job appli-cants to any type of medical examination prior to the offer of employment. Following employment, medical tests designed to identify employees with disabilities may constitute a breach of the Code if the disability being tested for is not a reasonable and *bona fide* concern with regard to the job performed.[25]

As for the Commission's view on the propriety of HIV testing in the workplace, it states:

> In the vast majority of work settings, it is unlikely that testing or other protective measures would be permitted as persons with HIV infection or HIV-related illness pose virtually no risk to those with whom they interact . . . However, in the event that the need for special measures is alleged, the Commission will make a deter-mination based on the particular circumstances.[26]

This view is consistent with the provisions of s. 23 of the Code, which prohibits inquiries, which, directly or indirectly differentiate adversely, based on a pro-hibited ground of discrimination.

Accordingly, an employer that tests applicants for HIV as a condition of employment will, subject to its ability to establish that being HIV negative is a *bona fide* occupational qualification, be in violation of the Code.[27]

---

23 "Policy Statement on HIV/AIDS-Related Discrimination" (Ontario Human Rights Commis-sion, 1989, Reprinted 1991), at p. 2.

24 "Policy on Employment-Related Medical Examinations" (Ontario Human Rights Commis-sion), see Policy Statement on HIV/AIDS, *ibid.*, p. 3.

25 Policy, *ibid.*, footnote 23, at p. 4.

26 *Ibid.*

27 *Ibid.*

Raj Anand, a former head of the Ontario Human Rights Commission, explains why both general testing and selective testing is likely a violation of the Code unless the employer can establish that the tests are a *bona fide* occupational qualification (B.F.O.Q.):

> An employer who adopts a generalized testing policy requiring all workers to be tested for HIV will also violate the Code. Section 11 of the Code prohibits constructive discrimination. A finding of constructive discrimination does not require proof that the employer intended to discriminate against workers adversely affected by a generally applied rule. Accordingly, a neutral testing requirement which has an adverse impact upon some workers based on their protected status would amount to a *prima facie* case of discrimination. The adverse impact would arise as a result of the testing policy producing different reactions and anxieties in those who are or may be HIV positive. These workers may be forced to decide whether to disclose their HIV status or continue in their employment. It is possible that some would prefer to resign or withdraw their application for employment rather than submit to a test. This differential impact based on a person's handicap would thus violate the Code. Section 11 is also subject to the employer establishing a BFOQ.

> Where testing is based on an employer's perception that a worker falls within a so-called high risk group, other grounds of discrimination may also be violated — such as sexual orientation, race, or country of origin.

> Based on the above, irrespective of whether an employer adopts a general or selective testing policy, the results will be *prima facie*, discriminatory. Accordingly, any requirement that workers submit to HIV tests is likely a violation of the Code, unless the employer can establish that the tests are a BFOQ.[28]

B. Duty to Accommodate HIV Positive Employee

In considering the employer's duty to accommodate the HIV positive employee, the recent decision of the Canadian Human Rights Tribunal in *Thwaites*, referred to earlier in this chapter, provides an authoritative articulation of the general legal principles:

> The importance of searching for reasonable alternatives or accommodating the individual to permit him or her to do the job or to lessen any risk (if risk is a factor) is now the bedrock of human rights law in this country. Indeed, without such accommodation, the protection given by the CHRA to certain groups, the disabled in particular, would be quite illusory. Anne M. Molloy, in ''Disability and the Duty to Accommodate'' (1992) 1 *Can Lab. Law Journal* 23 put it well at p. 26:

>> ''For persons with disabilities, the right to accommodation goes to the very heart of equality. To appreciate the importance of this right, one must understand the reality of discrimination. Much of the problem is attitudinal. The barriers to people with disabilities in employment are rarely rooted in loathing or malevolence. On the contrary, the discrimination is quite often

---

28 Raj Anand, "HIV Testing in the Unionized Workplace: The Accommodation Challenges Posed by AIDS", Canadian Labour Law Journal, Vol. 1, at pp. 105-6.

perpetrated with the best of intentions — a genuine concern about the capabilities of persons with disabilities, a desire to protect the disabled person from harm or injury or to shield him or her from the embarrassment of what is seen as the inevitability of his failure to measure up. While this may explain the discrimination, it does not, of course, excuse it nor does it make the ugliness of its result any more acceptable. The accommodation of differences for persons with disabilities therefore requires overcoming the ignorance, stereotypical attitudes and paternalism that are the source of much of the overt disability discrimination.''

Accordingly, the pendulum has swung such that a BFOR can rarely be established if the rule or practice makes generalizations about people solely on the basis of disability without regard to the particular circumstances of the specific class of individuals affected. Moreover, in order for there to be true individualization, a close assessment should be made of the individual in question since even persons with the same disability vary markedly in how they personally function and cope with their affliction or vary in the degree of impairment because of the different stages of their infirmity. This was emphasized by Ms Molloy in her article at p. 26:

"It is of critical importance that the accommodation of persons with disabilities be approached on an individual basis. Disabilities differ dramatically, one from another. There are also great individual variations within the same disability group. The effect of a particular disability on a particular person is very individualized and the accommodation of that disability must therefore also be individualized. In some cases, all that will be required is a little flexibility and creativity. In others, advances in technology will provide a means for a person with a disability to perform a job that years ago would have been utterly impossible. The key in all cases is to consider the individual needs and to provide the individualized accommodation required to meet those needs in a manner consistent with the employee's dignity and self-worth.''

It should be acknowledged that this may add some risks and make matters somewhat more burdensome for employers but this is a small price to pay for the higher value that society has placed on equal opportunity . . . An employer cannot rely on undue hardship unless it would be forced to take action requiring *significant* difficulty or expense which would clearly place upon the business enterprise an undue economic or administrative burden. Professor Cumming in *Mahon v. Canadian Pacific* (1986) 7 CHRR D/3278 stated at p. D/3305:

"It would be less costly in the immediate, narrow economic sense simply to allow employers who act with honesty of motive . . . to preclude the disabled from being employed. Difficult evaluations, with attendant time-consuming uncertainty and expense, would be avoided. However, our society has chosen the course of ensuring 'equality of opportunity' for the disabled in respect of employment, because the immediate cost and difficulty in employment decision-making is far outweighed by the protection and enhancement of core values for the disabled, and hence indirectly, for all members of society. It is only through the extension of equality of opportunity to the disabled as with other so-called minority groups, that a society can say it is truly free and just.''[29]

In rejecting the Canadian Armed Forces' primary position in *Thwaites*, that his ultimate expulsion was based on a *bona fide* occupational requirement (B.F.O.R.), the tribunal further held that the CAF failed to reasonably accommodate Mr. Thwaites, short of undue hardship:

... the law certainly places an obligation upon an employer to accommodate a disabled person to the extent that it can reasonably do so. Concomitant with that obligation is the necessity by the employer to make the appropriate inquiry to ensure that a realistic assessment of the individual has taken place.

. . . . .

In our view no real assessment was made by the CAF as to whether the theoretical risk of sending to sea an HIV member in Thwaites' condition had any basis in fact.[30]

It is significant to note the tribunal's resounding rejection of the proposition that it would be unreasonable to expect an employer to grant certain concessions to an individual employee that would have a potentially inequitable impact upon other employees:

The CAF argued that in view of the principle of universality of service of the CAF, there was no way to accommodate Thwaites in that trade by changing the nature of his duties so as to avoid either his going to sea altogether or to excuse his going to sea for long periods of time. His retention would result in an inequitable proportion of postings to bases and static positions; others in the same occupation would have to serve greater shifts at sea to make up for this accommodation. Nor could his position in the CAF be salvaged by permitting him to remuster to some other occupation. However, it is difficult to believe that the CAF's sea/shore ratio was not sufficiently flexible to accommodate Thwaites' needs. Certain exceptions have traditionally been made from the sea/shore rotation policy and there was no evidence that so accommodating Thwaites would cause the CAF undue hardship in this instance.[31]

Perhaps the most damning piece of evidence which effectively demonstrated an inflexible or unreasonable position by CAF in accommodating Mr. Thwaites' HIV/AIDS illness, was its own general policies relating to HIV infected persons:

What is curious is that the CAF policies on HIV positive members have moved from one of individualistic assessment to a rather generalized approach to all members who fit within a particular stage of the disease regardless of the individual differences that may exist among those members in regard to the type of medical care that is required. The November 8, 1985 interim guidelines for dealing with HTLV-III infection in the CAF emphasized individuality and the

---

[29] *Thwaites and Canadian Armed Forces (Re)* (1993), 93 C.L.L.C. ¶17,025 at p. 16,248 (Can. Trib.), affd (unreported, March 25, 1994, F.C.T.D.).

[30] *Supra*, at pp. 16,253-4 (Can. Trib.).

[31] *Supra*, at p. 16,256.

need for case by case assessment. It did not provide for the automatic regrading of a member.

Paragraph 20 of the guideline stated:

> "20. HTLV-III infected persons will require individualized medical follow-up and, if symptomatic, will likely require some medical restrictions that could involve a change in medical category. Of particular note is that these persons are likely at increased risk for infection and adverse reactions to the administration of live vaccines. Some advice for symptomatic HTLV-III infected persons is contained in Annex D. *It is inappropriate to specify an across-the-board medical category for infected persons; the category will result from restrictions which, in turn, will depend upon the clinical status and trade or classification.*" (Emphasis added.)

On February 2, 1988 the CAF issued a directive for discussion purposes (NDHQ 6635-2-2 DPM 2) which suggested a G3 category (Fit for sea, field, isolated and UN duties) for HIV infected but non-symptomatic members. However, several field comments urged a more restrictive category mainly based on the fact that clinical deterioration was a real possibility, could be sudden, and may need urgent diagnosis and therapy of an advanced type to provide the optimum result. Therefore, a more restrictive category than G3 was recommended and in fact incorporated into the directive. The medical directive which was issued on May 9, 1988 specifically directed that members who had clinically expressed HIV disease requiring fairly frequent medical follow-up of a specialist nature would get a geographic category no better than G5. Those HIV infected members who were asymptomatic would be issued a G4 category (unfit sea, field, medically isolated and UN duties; physician services required). Thus, the CAF had moved from a truly individualized approach to the problem to a more category driven designation depending on the particular stage of the disease in which the afflicted member found himself or herself.[32]

Consistent with the Canadian Human Rights Tribunal decision in *Thwaites*, the Ontario Human Rights Commission in its policy statement states that:

> . . . the spirit of the *Code* requires persons infected with HIV and those with HIV-related illness be given the opportunity to remain an integral member of society and to maintain their social, employment and other relationships. This implies that any assessment of a person's illness must be based on his or her current abilities and on the situation's current risks, rather than on abilities or risks which may arise in the future. The *Code*'s accommodation requirements are designed to ensure integration and sensitivity to the specific needs of persons with disabilities as they may change over time.[33]

The Code prescribes only three factors, which will be considered in assessing the employer's claim of undue hardship: cost, outside sources of funding, if any, and applicable health and safety requirements.[34]

---

[32] *Supra*, at p. 16,254.
[33] "Policy Statement on HIV/AIDS-Related Discrimination" (Ontario Human Rights Commission, 1989), at p. 3.
[34] Ontario *Human Rights Code*, ss. 11(2), 17(2) and 24(2).

The OHRC guidelines for assessing accommodation requirements for persons with disabilities, state that:

> Undue hardship will be shown to exist if the financial costs that are demonstrably attributable to the accommodation of the needs of the individual with a disability, and/or the group of which the person with a disability is a member, would alter the essential nature or would substantially affect the viability of the enterprise responsible for accommodation.[35]

It is clear that the onus on the employer to establish undue hardship, based upon the costs associated with accommodation, is extremely high. The guidelines further provide that the employer's ability to recover its costs of accommodation, through tax deduction, government benefits and related areas of potential relief, will be taken into consideration in assessing the costs of accommodation to the employer. In other words, proof of actual cost is but one factor for the Commission to take into consideration on this subject.

The guidelines further provide that undue hardship will be established where an employer has established and/or is subject to a *bona fide* health or safety requirement and, in spite of efforts to comply with those requirements, the degree of risk that remains after accommodation outweighs the benefits of enhancing equality for the disabled employee. In this regard, one of the most significant sources of health or safety requirements would be the employer's obligations under other employment-related legislation, such as the *Occupational Health and Safety Act*, R.S.O. 1990, c. O.1. With respect to HIV positive employees, employers could argue that the risk of HIV transmission or the potential safety dangers that are posed to other employees and/or the HIV infected employee results in an unreasonably or unacceptably high level of risk. As the *Thwaites* and other decisions amply demonstrate, the onus on the employer to establish undue hardship on these grounds is a very heavy one.

In seeking a remedy to a complaint of HIV/AIDS discrimination, the Commission may, in addition to monetary compensation, order the following:

— implementation of a formal institutional policy expressing a commitment to the equal treatment of persons that have or have tested positive for HIV infection;
— educational programs for others in the environment;
— other accommodation required by the person with HIV infection.[36]

E. (S.T.) v. Bertelsen[37] is one of the first reported human rights decisions in Canada in which it was held that termination of employment due to HIV infection constitutes discrimination. In the *Bertelsen* case the facts can be summarized as follows:

---

[35] "Guidelines for Assessing Accommodation Requirements for Persons with Disabilities" (Ontario Human Rights Commission), p. 8. See Schedule (ix).
[36] "Policy Statement on HIV/AIDS", *ibid.*, footnote 33, at p. 5.
[37] (1989), 89 C.L.L.C. ¶17,017, 10 C.H.R.R. D/6294 (Alta. Bd. Inq.).

(1) S.T.E. was employed by Peter Bertelsen to play in a musical trio at Chateau Lake Louise for the summer;

(2) the trio, with the same members, had played there during previous summers, and S.T.E. expected to be employed from mid-May to mid-September;

(3) the members of the trio shared a two bedroom apartment which was provided to them free of charge by the hotel;

(4) in mid-June S.T.E. contracted pneumocystis pneumonia, one of the infections which AIDS sufferers are prone to contracting and had to be rushed to a hospital in Calgary;

(5) by early July, S.T.E. was completely recovered and ready to return to work;

(6) on July 1, the trio's leader, Peter Bertelsen, terminated S.T.E.'s employment with the trio because he was afraid of contracting AIDS himself through contact with S.T.E. and he believed that S.T.E. had put other members of the trio at risk by not informing them that he had AIDS.

In concluding that Mr. Bertelsen had discriminated against S.T.E., contrary to the provisions of the Alberta *Individual's Rights Protection Act*,[38] the Board accepted expert scientific evidence on AIDS which indicates that there is no risk of infection from ordinary household or workplace contact.

The Board further concluded that, based on the evidence before it, ''the complainant had no obligation to advise others of his infection''. Finally, the Board unequivocally rejected the argument that Mr. Bertelsen's concerns and beliefs were both real and genuine:

> The Respondent's subjective belief that the risks were real does not provide justification for his conduct. The standard must be an objective one or else the purpose of the Act could be thwarted at every turn by ignorance and misinformation. The standard must be established on the basis of the best available scientific research. Ignorance, even widespread ignorance, cannot justify discriminatory conduct where there exists an established body of credible scientific knowledge which is available to anyone who cares to inquire about it. Unfounded concern over the risks of infection cannot justify discriminatory conduct just as unfounded prejudice as to the inferiority of any group cannot justify discriminatory practices. Although proof of intent may be relevant to prove discrimination, its presence is not essential and discrimination can occur without any intention at all.[39]

In its award, the Board refrained from issuing a cease discrimination order and reinstatement, due to the temporary nature of the employment relationship. S.T.E. was awarded compensation equivalent to what he would have earned over the balance of the trio's engagement at the hotel, less what he actually

---

[38] R.S.A. 1980, c. I-2, as amended.
[39] *E. (S.T.) v. Bertelsen, supra*, footnote 37, at p. 16,141.

earned from alternative employment over that same period. In addition, he was compensated for the lost value of free accommodation and meals, as well as interest on these monies.

In addition to the *Bertelsen* decision, there have been additional recent decisions from Canadian human rights tribunals which confirm earlier rulings that an employer had failed to accommodate an HIV infected employee.[40]

C. Bona Fide Occupational Qualification or Requirement

General principles and caselaw pertaining to the *bona fide* occupational qualification or requirement exception to discriminatory conduct has already been discussed elsewhere within this text. This sub-chapter will address principles of the *bona fide* occupational qualification exception as they relate specifically to HIV/AIDS-related discrimination.

As a logical starting point, it has been noted that the Supreme Court of Canada has decided that the B.F.O.R. exception must be interpreted restrictively so that the larger objects of human rights legislation are not frustrated.[41]

An excellent legal analysis of fundamental individual rights and the B.F.O.R. defence, in the context of a complaint of HIV/AIDS-related discrimination, can be found in the recent decision of the human rights tribunal in the *Thwaites* case already referred to in other issues earlier in this chapter:

> ... there is very little, if any, meaningful distinction between what an employer must establish by way of a defence to an allegation of direct discrimination and a defence to an allegation of adverse effect discrimination. The only difference may be semantic. In both cases, the employer must have regard to the particular individual in question. In the case of direct discrimination, the employer must justify its rule or practice by demonstrating that there are no reasonable alternatives and that the rule or practice is proportional to the end being sought. In the case of adverse effect discrimination, the neutral rule is not attacked but the employer must still show that it could not otherwise reasonably accommodate the individual disparately affected by that rule. In both cases, whether the operative words are "reasonable alternative" or "proportionality" or "accommodation", the inquiry is essentially the same: the employer must show that it could not have done anything else reasonable or practical to avoid the negative impact on the individual.
>
> It was once thought that, an employer, relying on safety reasons, as in the present case, could establish a BFOR by merely showing that the employment of such individuals would result in a marginal increase of risk to public safety . . . It is now clear that the standard that the employer must meet is that the group of persons in question excluded by the employment practice will present a "sufficient risk of employee failure" . . .

[40] *Pacific Western Airlines Ltd. and Canadian Air Line Flight Attendants Ass'n (Re)* (1987), 28 L.A.C. (3d) 291 (Can. Lab.); *Fontaine v. Canadian Pacific Ltd.* (1989), 89 C.L.L.C. ¶17,024 (Can. Trib.).

[41] For example, see *Zurich Insurance Co. v. Ontario (Human Rights Commission)* (1992), 93 D.L.R. (4th) 346 at p. 374, [1992] 2 S.C.R. 321.

. . . . .

The significant risk standard recognizes that some risk is tolerable in that human endeavours are not totally risk free. While this standard protects genuine concerns about workplace safety, it does not guarantee the highest degree of safety which would be the elimination of any added risk. What it does, is ensure that the objectives of the CHRA are met by seeking to integrate people with disabilities into the workplace even though such persons may create some heightened risk but within acceptable limits.

The thorny question is determining when some increased risk amounts to significant risk. What must be evaluated, in each case, is whether the risk to safety is sufficiently high to be described as unacceptable in relation to a particular job . . .

The dividing line between insufficient and sufficient risk is ultimately judgmental and turns on the circumstances of each case. In particular, a careful assessment would have to be made of the actual health and safety risks posed by such employees and how they compare with other risks that the employer is willing to accept. If such risks were determined to be significantly higher, then it would have to be asked whether there are any reasonable measures that can be put in place to minimize such risks to an acceptable level — a level that makes them comparable with other tolerated risks.

The determination of significant risk requires a Tribunal to balance the disabled individual's interest in working and participating in society against the need to protect that individual and others from harm. In an attempt to strike the appropriate balance, it is appealing to rely upon percentages of increased risk. High percentages of say 80% or even 50% can be quite compelling. However, this is a less useful tool when the percentages are low. A raw percentage figure of say 2% or 3% or even 12% might seem appreciable to one person and yet quite small or insignificant to another. Since reasonable people can reach very different conclusions based upon an abstract percentage, it may not provide the appropriate or sole bench mark for drawing the necessary conclusion . . .

Significant risk can best be measured in a context of the particular job and then only in comparison with other risks posed by that workplace. In this way, other tolerable risks arising from the employment establish risk thresholds. If risks of comparable magnitude are acceptable in a particular work environment then risks posed by a person who is HIV positive cannot be considered significant.[42]

In applying the evidence adduced at the hearing to the applicable legal principles, the tribunal in *Thwaites* made the following findings in relation to the B.F.O.R. defence advanced by the employer:

(1) it found that, on balance, "The CAF held the honest belief that Thwaites' medical condition had proceeded to the point where he required ongoing specialist care which could not be made available to him at sea". Accordingly, it was held that the subjective elements of the B.F.O.R. test had been satisfied;

---

[42] *Thwaites and Canadian Armed Forces (Re)* (1993), 93 C.L.L.C. ¶17,025 at pp. 16,246-7 (Can. Trib.), affd (unreported, March 25, 1994, F.C.T.D.).

(2) CAF had failed to establish the objective element of the B.F.O.R. test, which was premised upon:
   (i) the need for specialist care,
   (ii) the requirement for AZT therapy and its resulting side-effects,
   (iii) the possibility and/or inevitability of opportunistic disease,
   (iv) the lack of communication between the parties in relation to Mr. Thwaites' medical condition and his required treatment,

(3) "the law certainly places an obligation upon an employer to accommodate a disabled person to the extent that it can reasonably do so. Concomitant with that obligation is the necessity by the employer to make the appropriate inquiry to ensure that a realistic assessment of the individual has taken place";

(4) the Board concluded that "no real assessment was made by the CAF as to whether the theoretical risk of sending to sea an HIV member in Thwaites' condition had any basis in fact. No attempt was made to determine the actual state of Thwaites' condition and the nature of the risks that such condition posed in comparison with the usual risks that seamen face, and what, if necessary, could be done to work around the condition to reduce the risk to an acceptable level."[43]

The Canadian Human Rights Commission in its policy statement on AIDS has suggested one class of employees in which HIV-negative status may constitute a B.F.O.R.: those involved in health care where an individual assessment has determined that no other arrangement of duties is possible and it is an essential requirement of the position that, amongst other things, the employee perform invasive procedures. However, it is important to note that there has been no documented cases of health care workers transmitting the virus to patients and co-workers during their contracts at work.[44]

In the final analysis, establishing HIV-free status as a B.F.O.R. for any individual employee or class of employees will require an extraordinary fact situation which is supported by compelling medical and scientific evidence. Very few employers in the private sector could hope to realistically advance a viable defence to an HIV/AIDS-related discrimination complaint on this ground.

D. Rights and Interests of Co-Workers

The limited rulings to date involving the adjudication of HIV/AIDS-related discrimination complaints, have rejected the argument that the honestly held and genuine concerns of co-workers with respect to working with, or in close proximity to, an HIV infected person is a defence to such a human rights

---

[43] See, *Thwaites, supra,* at pp. 16,249-54 (Can. Trib.).
[44] Raj Anand, "HIV Testing in the Unionized Workplace: The Accommodation Challenges Posed by AIDS", Canadian Labour Law Journal, Vol. 1, at p. 111.

complaint. In other words, the employer's duty to accommodate the HIV infected employee, in the absence of HIV-free status being a B.F.O.R. of employment, will take precedence over the concerns of co-workers in virtually every case.

Raj Anand, in his article "HIV Testing In the Unionized Workplace", states concisely the rationale for rejecting the concerns of co-workers as a defence to a complaint of HIV/AIDS-related discrimination. Although his comments are made specifically in relation to the subject of HIV testing, his analysis has equal application to HIV/AIDS-related discrimination in general:

> With respect to HIV-positive workers, employers could conceivably argue that the risk of HIV transmission or other safety concerns associated with AIDS results in an unacceptably high level of risk, thus justifying testing workers. Moreover, an employer may seek to use its obligation to provide a safe working environment under occupational health and safety legislation as a justification for testing workers. The employer may also be concerned with potential liability if one of its workers infects another with HIV. Its position would be that, absent the ability to test workers, it could not effectively protect those who might be at risk of transmission. While the validity of this rationale may vary depending upon the nature of the particular work environment, in the overwhelming majority of cases, the risk of transmission could best be described as theoretical, and, for practical purposes, non-existent. Occupational health and safety legislation confers a right on a worker to refuse to work if he or she considers the work environment to be unsafe. The following test has been adopted by arbitration tribunals:
>
> 1. Did the worker honestly believe his or her health or well-being was endangered?
> 2. Did he or she communicate this belief to the employer in a reasonable and adequate manner?
> 3. Was his or her belief reasonable in the circumstances?
> 4. Was the danger sufficiently serious to justify the action taken?
>
> The third and fourth factors in the above test are determined objectively, based on an average employee exercising normal and honest judgment. Based on available medical information, it is quite likely that the co-worker's belief would not be considered reasonable and would therefore not justify a refusal to work alongside a worker living with AIDS.[45]

Since the primary mischief that is sought to be addressed in HIV/AIDS-related discrimination cases is the stigma associated with testing HIV positive, it logically follows that the opinions and actions of often times uninformed and/or unenlightened co-workers are irrelevant in considering any such complaints.

---

[45] *Ibid.*, at pp. 110-111.

| *The Duty To Accommodate*

Introduction

The duty to accommodate is one of the most fundamental yet often misunderstood notions in human rights law. There are many reasons for this misunderstanding:

1. only three provincial jurisdictions, Ontario, Manitoba and the Yukon, have enacted express provisions in their respective human rights statutes that recognize a duty to accommodate in the employment context;

2. even in those provincial jurisdictions which have enacted express provisions relating to the duty to accommodate, these provisions are in most instances interpreted so that a duty to accommodate applies only in limited or restricted situations;

3. much of the jurisprudence dealing with the duty to accommodate, creates an enormous amount of confusion particularly with respect to the application of the duty to accommodate in cases of direct discrimination as opposed to "constructive" or "adverse effect" discrimination;

4. the notion of "undue hardship", whereby an employer is required to accommodate an employee short of "undue hardship", has created significant difficulties both in terms of its interpretation and its practical application.

In the context of the employment relationship, the duty to accommodate is perhaps best defined by M. David Lepofsky in his paper: "The Duty to Accommodate: A Purposive Approach":

> At the core of any accommodation is the tailoring of a work rule, practice, condition or requirement to the specific needs of an individual or group. The need may be associated with their religion, gender, disability or other human attribute enumerated in Human Rights Codes. An accommodation can include such steps as an exemption of the worker from an existing work requirement or condition applicable to others, the provision to the worker of a benefit ordinarily or routinely provided to others, and the provision of some kind of job support or assistance which is ordinarily or not routinely provided to others. At its core, it involves some degree of differential treatment. The litmus test of the accommodation's

necessity is whether such a measure is needed to ensure that the worker can fully and equally participate in the workplace.''[1]

In its most general or basic sense, the duty to accommodate involves the requirement that an employer do whatever is necessary, short of ''undue hardship'', for the purpose of ensuring that employees who possess attributes which fall within one of the prohibited grounds of discrimination are able to discharge their duties and responsibilities in the employment relationship in a manner which both recognizes and respects their special status. The duty to accommodate can include such things as physically altering the work premises, purchasing specialized equipment, amending an individual's job description, revising an individual's work schedule and a host of other possible actions and reactions by an employer depending upon the specific circumstances of the individual in question.

For reasons that will be discussed at greater length in another chapter, it is clear that the duty to accommodate is not limited exclusively to the employer. Rather, recent decisions of both the courts and human rights tribunals have recognized that unions as well are subject to the duty to accommodate in certain situations. In addition, by virtue of the general requirement that all persons do their part to respect and uphold the provisions of existing human rights legislation, it can be legitimately argued that co-workers are subject to the duty to accommodate in the employment relationship. It is not suggested that the duty to accommodate in the case of the employer, the union and the co-worker will be identical but that in many instances the duty to accommodate will not be the exclusive responsibility of the employer.

1. STATUTORY PROVISIONS

A. Ontario Human Rights Code

As previously noted, Ontario is one of only three provincial jurisdictions in which there are express provisions contained within its human rights legislation relating to the duty to accommodate.

Section 5 of the Ontario *Human Rights Code*, R.S.O. 1990, c. H.19, confirms the right of every person to equal treatment in the employment relationship:

> 5(1) Every person has a right to equal treatment with respect to employment without discrimination because of race, ancestry, place of origin, colour, ethnic origin, citizenship, creed, sex, sexual orientation, age, record of offences, marital status, family status or handicap.
>
> (2) Every person who is an employee has a right to freedom from harassment in the workplace by the employer or agent of the employer or by another employee because of race, ancestry, place of origin, colour, ethnic origin, citizenship, creed,

---

[1] M. David Lepofsky, ''The Duty to Accommodate: A Purposive Approach'' (1992), Canadian Labour Law Journal, Vol. 1, p. 1.

sex, sexual orientation, age, record of offences, marital status, family status or handicap.

Section 11 of the Ontario *Human Rights Code* confirms the basic rule that "constructive" or "adverse effect" discrimination constitutes a violation of the Code subject to two exceptions, one is where the "requirement, qualification or factor is reasonable and *bona fide* in the circumstances".

Section 11(2) in turn expands upon the reasonable and *bona fide* requirement, qualification or factor exception to adverse effect discrimination:

> 11(2) The Commission, a board of inquiry or a court shall not find that a requirement, qualification or factor is reasonable and *bona fide* in the circumstances unless it is satisfied that the needs of the group of which the person is a member cannot be accommodated without undue hardship on the person responsible for accommodating those needs, considering the cost, outside sources of funding, if any, and health and safety requirements, if any.

Accordingly, the duty to accommodate expressly limits the exception to adverse effect discrimination prescribed in section 11(1)(a) of the Ontario *Human Rights Code*.

Section 17 of the Ontario *Human Rights Code* deals specifically with the duty to accommodate in the case of individuals who are disabled:

> 17(1) A right of a person under this Act is not infringed for the reason only that the person is incapable of performing or fulfilling the essential duties or requirements attending the exercise of the right because of handicap.
>
> (2) The Commission, a board of inquiry or a court shall not find a person incapable unless it is satisfied that the needs of the person cannot be accommodated without undue hardship on the person responsible for accommodating those needs, considering the cost, outside sources of funding, if any, and health and safety requirements, if any.

Finally, s. 24 of the Ontario *Human Rights Code* specifically provides that the *bona fide* occupational qualification exception to discrimination in employment on the basis of age, sex, record of offences or marital status is limited by the employer's duty to accommodate:

> 24(1) The right under section 5 to equal treatment with respect to employment is not infringed where,
>
> . . . . .
>
> (b) The discrimination in employment is for reasons of age, sex, record of offences or marital status if the age, sex, record of offences or marital status of the applicant is a reasonable and *bona fide* qualification because of the nature of the employment;
>
> . . . . .
>
> (2) The Commission, a board of inquiry or a court shall not find that a qualification under clause (1)(b) is reasonable and *bona fide* unless it is satisfied that the circumstances of the person cannot be accommodated without undue hardship on the person responsible for accommodating those circumstances con-

sidering the cost, outside sources of funding, if any, and health and safety requirements, if any.

B. Canadian Human Rights Act

The *Canadian Human Rights Act*, R.S.C. 1985, c. H-6, does not contain any express provisions relating to the duty to accommodate in the employment relationship. The Act does, however, set out the basic prohibition against discrimination in employment in s. 7, subject to the common exemption from the enumerated prohibited grounds based on a "*bona fide* occupational requirement" found in s. 15 of the Act:

> 7. It is a discriminatory practice, directly or indirectly,
>
> . . . . .
>
> (*b*) in the course of employment, to differentiate adversely in relation to an employee,
> on a prohibited ground of discrimination.
>
> . . . . .
>
> 15. It is not a discriminatory practice if
> (*a*) any refusal, exclusion, expulsion, suspension, limitation, specification or preference in relation to any employment is established by an employer to be based on a *bona fide* occupational requirement;

Although the federal human rights legislation is silent on the duty to accommodate, it is clearly based on the jurisprudence to date that employers falling under the jurisdiction of the *Canadian Human Rights Act* are subject to a duty to accommodate that is, for all intents and purposes, the same as those employers who fall within the jurisdiction of the Ontario *Human Rights Code*.

2. NATURE AND EXTENT OF THE DUTY

A. Individualization

Necessarily inherent within the duty to accommodate is the proposition that equality, in the sense of identical treatment, may in fact produce inequality or work to the disadvantage of an individual or group of individuals. The Supreme Court of Canada in its decision in *Andrews v. Law Society of British Columbia*[2] held that "the accommodation of differences" is the "essence of true equality". At one point in its reasons for judgment in the *Andrews* case, the court stated:

> It must be recognized at once ... that every difference in treatment between individuals under the law will not necessarily result in inequality and, as well, that identical treatment may frequently produce serious inequality.[3]

---

[2] (1989), 56 D.L.R. (4th) 1, [1989] 1 S.C.R. 143.
[3] *Supra*, at p. 10.

The concept of individualization is fundamental to the duty to accommodate. In its "Guidelines for Assessing Accommodation Requirements for Persons With Disabilities", the Ontario Human Rights Commission advocates the notion of individualization as central to the duty to accommodate:

> The essence of accommodating people who have disabilities is individualization. That is, each person with a disability must be considered individually in order to determine what changes can be made to a situation, including the physical environment, to accommodate his or her needs. There is no formula for accommodation to alleviate the barriers which confront people with disabilities. Each person's needs are unique and must be considered afresh when a barrier is encountered. A technical solution may meet one person's requirements but not another's. It is also the case that many accommodations will benefit large numbers of persons with disabilities.[4]

Although these comments were contained within guidelines that specifically related to the accommodation of persons with disabilities, the concept of individualization applies equally to the duty to accommodate in all respects and is not specifically restricted to the accommodation of individuals with disabilities.

B. Essential vs. Non-essential Duties

In considering an employer's duty to accommodate, it is necessary to first differentiate between essential and non-essential duties of the position. This is especially important in cases of individuals who are disabled. In its "Guidelines for Assessing Accommodation Requirements for Persons With Disabilities", the Ontario Human Rights Commission provides the following rationale for the purpose of distinguishing between essential and non-essential duties associated with the position of employment:

> For persons with disabilities, the *Code* guarantees equal treatment if the person is capable of performing or fulfilling the essential duties that accompany the exercise of his or her rights. This requirement recognizes that, in some circumstances, the nature or degree of a person's disability may preclude him or her from being able to perform the essential duties. However, a person cannot be found incapable of performing those essential duties unless an effort has been made to accommodate his or her needs. Accommodation of a person's individual needs is required by the *Code* unless such accommodation would cause undue hardship for the person (or organization or company) responsible for making it.
>
> The first step in the accommodation is to determine what is "essential" and what is not. The person must be accommodated with respect to non-essential duties if necessary by having those duties reassigned or by the person responsible for accommodation using an alternate method for having those duties fulfilled. Then, if the person cannot perform the essential duties, accommodation is to be explored that will enable the person to perform those essential duties.[5]

---

[4] "Guidelines for Assessing Accommodation Requirements for Persons With Disabilities" (Ontario Human Rights Commission), p. 3. See Schedule (ix).

[5] *Ibid.*, at pp. 2-3.

In the performance of any job, there will always be certain activities that are critical or key to the essence of the job, while other duties are somewhat less important or tangential to the position in question. Examples of essential duties include the following:

— in the case of a receptionist or switchboard operator, verbal communication would clearly be an essential duty;

— in the case of a police officer, physical mobility would be an essential duty;

— in the case of a warehouse labourer, the physical lifting of heavy objects may be an essential duty to the job.

In a very general sense, non-essential aspects of work must be accommodated while accommodation of essential duties must be considered and undertaken short of undue hardship. However, the duty to accommodate is not by any means a guarantee of employment to an individual who is incapable of performing the job. For obvious reasons, distinguishing between essential and non-essential duties and the corresponding nature and extent of the duty to accommodate will be a question of fact in each specific situation.

C. Employee's Responsibility

It is clear that the employee or potential employee must participate in assisting the employer, union and/or co-worker in discharging the duty to accommodate. The primary responsibility of the employee or potential employee in this regard is to provide timely notice as to both the existence and nature of their needs for an accommodation.

This duty recognizes the precarious position of an employer who must identify and elicit information relating to the individual's need to be accommodated without violating the provisions of the *Human Rights Code* or otherwise infringing upon the individual's right to privacy.

An employer's responsibility in this respect is recognized by the Ontario Human Rights Board of Inquiry in *Ontario (Ministry of Health, Insurance Systems Branch) and Bonner (Re)*,[6] in which it was decided that an employee with a disability ''has a responsibility to inform the employer . . . if special accommodation or treatment is desired''.

A more important issue arises in relation to the nature and extent of an employee's obligations in relation to the duty to accommodate. To what extent, if any, is the employee obliged to accommodate the employer?

In its landmark decision in *Central Alberta Dairy Pool v. Alberta (Human Rights Commission)*,[7] the Supreme Court of Canada reversed the decision of the Alberta Court of Appeal and ordered that the award of the Board of Inquiry should be restored. In that case, an individual who worked in a milk production

---

[6] (1992), 92 C.L.L.C. ¶17,019, 16 C.H.R.R. D/485 (Ont. Arb. Bd.).
[7] (1990), 72 D.L.R. (4th) 417, [1990] 2 S.C.R. 489.

plant requested time off to observe two holy days, Good Friday and Easter Monday. The employer consented to his absence on one of the days but refused the other day off, Easter Monday, because of production requirements. When the individual did not report to work on Easter Monday, his employment was terminated. A board of inquiry held that the employer had violated s. 7(1) of the *Individual's Rights Protection Act*, R.S.A. 1980, c. I-2, and awarded partial compensation.

In her Reasons for Judgment, Madame Justice Wilson, in whose decision three other judges of the court concurred considered, amongst other things, the finding by the Board of Inquiry that in order to establish a *prima facie* case of discrimination, the complainant had to prove:

1. the existence of a *bona fide* religion with a genuine commitment to it;
2. adequate notice of the employee's religious requirements to the employer; and
3. an effort on the part of the employee to accommodate the employer as far as possible without being required to compromise his belief.

While the first two points were not in dispute on the appeal, the respondent contested the third point and the Supreme Court of Canada rejected its submissions relating to the efforts of the employee in question to accommodate, as well as the sincerity of the employee's religious convictions. Although the Supreme Court of Canada did not expressly adopt the principle that the employee had a duty to accommodate the employer as far as possible without being required to compromise his beliefs, it appears implicit within the reasons of the court that this proposition was accepted even in the absence of a detailed discussion on the point. Accordingly, in some instances, an employee may be obliged to make efforts to accommodate an employer, particularly in circumstances where the employee is adhering to or abiding by an existing policy or rule of the organization.

3. UNDUE HARDSHIP

The duty to accommodate is subject only to the qualification that the employer or organization does not have to suffer "undue hardship". Any inconvenience or hardship short of "undue hardship" will not relieve an employer of its obligation to accommodate an employee. The test or criteria for determining "undue hardship" is, difficult to discern from the decisions on the subject.

In the *Central Alberta Dairy Pool* decision, the Supreme Court made the following comments in relation to the issue of undue hardship:

> I do not find it necessary to provide a comprehensive definition of what constitutes undue hardship but I believe it may be helpful to list some of the factors that may be relevant to such an appraisal. I begin by adopting those identified by the board of inquiry in the case at bar — financial cost, disruption

of a collective agreement, problems of morale of other employees, interchange-ability of work force and facilities. The size of the employer's operation may influence the assessment of whether a given financial cost is undue or the ease with which the work force and facilities can be adapted to the circumstances. Where safety is at issue both the magnitude of the risk and the identity of those who bear it are relevant considerations. This list is not intended to be exhaustive and the results which will obtain from a balancing of these factors against the right of the employee to be free from discrimination will necessarily vary from case to case.[8]

In its "Guidelines for Assessing Accommodation Requirements for Persons With Disabilities" under the *Human Rights Code*, the Ontario Human Rights Commission sets out a number of paragraphs which summarize various factors and other information to be taken into account under the heading "Standards for Assessing Undue Hardship". Important excerpts from these guidelines dealing with the assessment of undue hardship are as follows:

A. The *Code* prescribes three factors which are to be considered in assessing whether a requested accommodation would cause undue hardship. These are cost, outside sources of funding, if any, and health and safety requirements, if any . . .

B. The person responsible for accommodation will want to know whose needs must be accommodated in order to determine the extent of its obligation. The cost standard states that it is the needs of the individual person with a disability and/or group of which that person is a member. This recognizes that there are two types of situations in which the requirement to accommodate may arise. One situation is where a person with a disability is a member of a group against which discrimination is alleged and that person requests an accommodation which would also accommodate the needs of the whole group. The other situation is where an individual requires accommodation for his or her own needs. In instances where accommodation of the needs of the group would cause undue hardship, but the needs of an individual with a disability could still be accommodated without undue hardship, the individual accommodation must be made.

C. The standard requires that the current abilities of a person with a disability and the situation's current risks are to be taken into account, rather than abilities or risks which may arise in the future. Where the person has a condition which may cause deterioration of ability over time, the unpredictable nature and extent of future disability cannot be used as a basis for assessing needs in the present. For example, a person who has multiple sclerosis may experience increased fatigue as a symptom of his or her condition, but it will not be possible to predict with accuracy when, for how long, or in what ways the fatigue will affect a person. Or a person may not have that symptom at all, but may show other effects of the illness. These unpredictable future possibilities cannot be used to assess needs for accommodation in the present.

D. The *Code* and the guidelines notably exclude other factors from consideration by specifically designating cost and health or safety factors as determinants of undue hardship. For example, there is no provision for "business inconvenience" or "undue interference" with the enterprise responsible for accommodation in determining undue hardship. The term "business inconvenience" was removed

---

[8] *Supra*, at p. 439.

from the *Code* during the legislative debates on amendments to the *Code*. If there are demonstrable costs attributable to decreased productivity, efficiency or effectiveness, they can be taken into account in assessing undue hardship under the cost standard, providing that they are quantifiable and demonstrably related to the proposed accommodation.

E. Another element which cannot be considered in assessing undue hardship is customer preference, or other third party preferences. It is well established in human rights case law that third party preferences do not constitute a justification for discriminatory acts, and the same rule applies here.

F. A term of a collective agreement or other contractual arrangement cannot act as a bar to providing the kinds of accommodation an employee with a disability might require . . . It is a joint responsibility of the employer and the union to work out a solution with respect to any accommodation involving a conflict with the collective agreement, but if a solution cannot be reached, the employer must make the accommodation in spite of the agreement. If the union takes the position that the collective agreement prevails, and attempts to thwart efforts to accommodate the employee, then the union may be added as a respondent to a complaint filed with the Commission.

G. These standards reflect the expectation that significant changes will be required in employment situations (including collective agreements) . . . The *Code* requires these changes in order to give meaning to the rights to equality and freedom from discrimination guaranteed to persons with disabilities in Part 1 of the *Code*.[9]

In specifically addressing the subject of costs, as an element to be considered in assessing undue hardship, the Ontario Human Rights Commission in its "Guidelines", state, in part:

3. Cost

(1) Standard

Undue hardship will be shown to exist if the financial costs that are demonstrably attributable to the accommodation of the needs of the individual with a disability, and/or the group of which the person with a disability is a member, would alter the essential nature or would substantially affect the viability of the enterprise responsible for accommodation.

Commentary

A. Costs will amount to undue hardship if they are:
1. quantifiable;
2. shown to be related to the accommodation; and
3.(a) so substantial that they would alter the essential nature of the enterprise, or
   (b) so significant that they would substantially affect the viability of the enterprise.
B. There are circumstances under which the undue hardship provisions of the *Code* could require a person responsible for accommodation to undertake significant expenditures to accommodate persons with disabilities. This applies whether one person would benefit from the accommodation, or large numbers of people would benefit. The test of altering the essential nature of

---

[9] "Guidelines", *ibid.*, footnote 4, at pp. 7-8.

the enterprise or substantially affecting its viability will apply whether the benefit is to an individual or to a group.

. . . . .

(2) Types of Financial Costs

Financial costs of the accommodation include:
(A) capital and operating costs;
(B) the cost of additional staff time, beyond what can be accomplished through restructuring existing resources and job descriptions, in order to provide appropriate assistance to the person with a disability; and
(C) any other quantifiable and demonstrably related costs.[10]

It is clear that the Ontario Human Rights Commission will carefully scrutinize the alleged financial costs associated with the proposed accommodation. This is made abundantly clear when the various paragraphs of commentary set out within its guidelines on the subject of financial costs are reviewed:

D. All projected costs which can be quantified and shown to be related to the proposed accommodation will be taken into account. However, mere speculation, for example, about monetary losses which may follow the accommodation of the person with a disability will not generally be persuasive.
E. Where substantial capital expenditures are anticipated, for example, in making physical alterations to a building, work site, vehicle or equipment, it is advisable for the person responsible for accommodation to obtain a proposal and estimate from experts in barrier-free design and construction. This is one step that might be followed by the Commission when investigating a complaint.
F. Creative design solutions can often avoid expensive capital outlays. This may involve very specifically tailoring the design to the individual's functional capabilities rather than installing a device or feature which may not even be appropriate. Where undue hardship is claimed, cost estimates will be carefully examined to ensure that they are not excessive in relation to the stated objective, and to determine whether a less expensive alternative exists which could accomplish the accommodation while still fully respecting the dignity of the person with a disability.[11]

In order to determine whether the financial cost would alter the essential nature or substantially affect the viability of the enterprise, the Ontario Human Rights Commission expressly states within its guidelines that consideration will be given to:

(A) the ability of the person responsible for accommodation to recover the costs of accommodation in the normal course of business;
(B) the availability of any grants, subsidies or loans from the federal, provincial or municipal government or from non-government sources which could offset the costs of accommodation;
(C) the ability of the person responsible for accommodation to distribute the costs of accommodation throughout the whole operation;

---

[10] *Ibid.*, at pp. 8-9.
[11] *Ibid.*, at p. 9.

(D) the ability of the person responsible for accommodation to amortize or depreciate capital costs associated with the accommodation according to generally accepted accounting principles;

(E) the ability of the person responsible for accommodation to deduct from the costs of accommodation any savings that may be available as a result of the accommodation, including:

    (i) tax deductions and other government benefits;

    (ii) an improvement in productivity, efficiency or effectiveness;

    (iii) any increase in the resale value of property, where it is reasonably foreseeable that the property might be sold;

    (iv) any increase in clientele, potential labour pool, or tenants; and

(F) the availability of the Workers' Compensation Board's "Second Injury and Enhancement Fund".[12]

In addressing the health or safety risk considerations to be taken into account in considering undue hardship, the Ontario Human Rights Commission states within its guidelines:

> Undue hardship will be shown to exist where a person responsible for accommodation is subject to or has established a bona fide health or safety requirement and the person has attempted to maximize the health and safety protection through alternate means which are consistent with the accommodation required, but the degree of risk which remains after the accommodation has been made outweighs the benefits of enhancing equality for disabled persons. The health or safety requirement may be informal or it may be a requirement established by law.

. . . . .

> C. An example of such a situation would be where all individuals on a construction site are required to wear safety boots but an individual's disability necessitates his or her use of special orthopaedic shoes or assistive devices which preclude that individual from wearing safety boots. The obligation of the person responsible for accommodation is first to attempt to provide appropriate safety footwear for the person. If that is not possible, there should be an enquiry into whether some other method of achieving adequate safety for the person's feet can be used. If that, too, fails, then the standard would have to be modified or waived if the individual is willing to accept the risk.[13]

In determining whether an obligation to modify or waive the health or safety requirement, whether established by law or not, creates a significant risk to any person, consideration will be given to:

(a) the willingness of a person with a disability to assume the risk in circumstances where the risk is to his or her own health or safety;

(b) whether the modification or waiving of the requirement is reasonably likely to result in a serious risk to the health or safety of individuals other than the person with a disability;

(c) the other types of risks which the person responsible for accommodation is assuming within its enterprise; and

---

[12] *Ibid.*, at pp. 9-10.

[13] *Ibid.*, at p. 12.

(d) the types of risks tolerated within society as a whole, reflected in legislated standards such as licencing standards, or in similar types of enterprises.[14]

Once again, it is abundantly clear from the commentary of the Ontario Human Rights Commission in its ''Guidelines'', that it will carefully scrutinize alleged health and safety risks in addressing the issue of undue hardship:

J. when assessing the seriousness of the risk posed by the obligation to modify or waive a health or safety requirement, consideration must be given to the other types of risks which are assumed within an enterprise. For example, some jobs require considerable physical exertion or stamina, e.g., driving buses, fighting fires, or doing police work. The fitness levels of persons doing these jobs may not be monitored very closely, or at all, after a person has been hired, even though the lack of fitness results in greatly reduced abilities to perform the strenuous tasks involved in the job. Potential employees may be denied employment on the basis of existing disabilities and conditions, yet these same or similar limitations are often developed by existing employees with little or no effect on their ability to satisfactorily perform their duties, and with no impact on their careers.

K. Many sources of risk exist in the workplace, aside from those risks that may result from accommodating an employee with a disability. All employees assume everyday risks that may be inherent in a work site, or in working conditions, or which may be caused by a co-worker's fatigue, temporary inattentiveness, hangover, or stress. Employers have recognized that not all employees are 100% productive everyday by providing counselling programs or other means of coping with financial problems, emotional difficulties, or addiction to alcohol or other substances. Risks from these situations are factored into the level of safety that we all accept in our lives every day.

L. A potential risk that is created by accommodation should be assessed in the light of those other, more common, sources of risk in the workplace. An example of this is an employee who has a condition which makes him or her especially susceptible to respiratory illnesses. This employee requests a promotion to a different section of the plant. The employer refuses the promotion on the grounds that the processes involved in that section pose an increased risk to this employee because of his or her disability. Yet the employer permits smoking everywhere on its premises, including that area where the employee is now working.[15]

In determining the seriousness of risk, a number of factors will be considered, including the following:

(A) the nature of the risk: what could happen that would be harmful?
(B) the severity of the risk: how serious would the harm be if it occurred?
(C) the probability of the risk: how likely is it that the potential harm will actually occur? Is it a real risk, or merely hypothetical or speculative? Could it occur frequently?
(D) the scope of the risk: who will be affected by the event if it occurs?[16]

---

[14] *Ibid.*, at p. 13.
[15] *Ibid.*, at p. 14.
[16] *Ibid.*, at p. 15.

Although it is difficult to specify the tests or criteria that must be satisfied in order to constitute "undue hardship" in the context of a duty to accommodate, there can be no question that the concept of undue hardship by its very nature requires very significant and compelling evidence which will be very thoroughly and carefully reviewed by a human rights commission in the process of investigating a complaint. Employers are well advised to seek out expertise and professional advice when addressing the potential need to raise the issue of undue hardship so that its viability may be objectively and professionally assessed.

4. BONA FIDE OCCUPATIONAL QUALIFICATION

Human rights legislation recognizes that there may indeed be legitimate reasons for employment discrimination on prohibited grounds. For example, an individual's record of criminal offences may be relevant where a person is applying for work as a security officer. Accordingly, the Ontario *Human Rights Code* provides an exemption for discrimination based upon age, sex, record of offences or marital status where it is reasonable and a *bona fide* qualification because of the nature of the employment.

In the Supreme Court of Canada decision in the *Central Alberta Dairy Pool* case, Madame Justice Wilson provides an authoritative review and summary of leading decisions by the Supreme Court of Canada in which the court considered the statutory concept of a *bona fide* occupational qualification ("B.F.O.Q.") or *bona fide* occupational requirement ("B.F.O.R."). In her reasons, Madame Justice Wilson began her review of the leading cases on this subject by determining that these terms are "equivalent and co-extensive": "[m]ost of the jurisprudence treats them as interchangeable and I agree that they are intended to give expression to the same concept."[17]

The first statement made by the Supreme Court of Canada regarding a statutory B.F.O.Q. was made in *Etobicoke (Borough) v. Ontario (Human Rights Commission)*.[18] In that case, the court was required to decide whether the fire department policy requiring mandatory retirement at age sixty constituted a *bona fide* occupational requirement. The employer submitted the policy was a B.F.O.Q. within the meaning of the Ontario *Human Rights Code* and thus did not constitute discrimination on the basis of age. Mr. Justice McIntyre, speaking on behalf of the majority of the Supreme Court of Canada, summarized the procedure for dealing with a B.F.O.Q. provision:

> Once a complainant has established before a board of inquiry a *prima facie* case of discrimination, in this case proof of a mandatory retirement at age 60 as

---

17 *Central Alberta Dairy Pool v. Alberta (Human Rights Commission)* (1990), 72 D.L.R. (4th) 417 at p. 425, [1990] 2 S.C.R. 489.
18 (1982), 132 D.L.R. (3d) 14, [1982] 1 S.C.R. 202.

a condition of employment, he is entitled to relief in the absence of justification by the employer. The only justification which can avail the employer in the case at bar, is the proof, the burden of which lies upon him, that such compulsory retirement is a *bona fide* occupational qualification and requirement for the employment concerned. The proof, in my view, must be made according to the ordinary civil standard of proof, that is upon a balance of probabilities.[19]

In order to constitute a B.F.O.Q., Mr. Justice McIntyre succinctly summarized the criteria that must be met:

To be a *bona fide* occupational qualification and requirement a limitation, such as mandatory retirement at a fixed age, must be imposed honestly, in good faith, and in the sincerely held belief that such limitation is imposed in the interests of the adequate performance of the work involved with all reasonable dispatch, safety and economy, and not for ulterior or extraneous reasons aimed at objectives which could defeat the purpose of the Code. In addition it must be related in an objective sense to the performance of the employment concerned, in that it is reasonably necessary to assure the efficient and economical performance of the job without endangering the employee, his fellow employees and the general public.[20]

As was made abundantly clear by Mr. Justice McIntyre in the *Etobicoke* case, "impressionistic" evidence adduced by the employer in defence of its mandatory retirement policy, on the basis of public safety, is "inadequate to discharge the burden of proof lying upon the employer":

Faced with the uncertainty of the aging process an employer has, it seems to me, two alternatives. He may establish a retirement age at 65 or over, in which case he would escape the charge of discrimination on the basis of age under the Code. On the other hand, he may, in certain types of employment, particularly in those affecting public safety such as that of airline pilots, train and bus drivers, police and firemen, consider that the risk of unpredictable individual human failure involved in continuing all employees to age 65 may be such that an arbitrary retirement age may be justified for application to all employees. In the case at bar it may be said that the employment falls into that category. While it is no doubt true that some below the age of 60 may become unfit for fire-fighting and many above that age may remain fit, recognition of this proposition affords no assistance in resolving the second question. In an occupation where, as in the case at bar, the employer seeks to justify the retirement in the interests of public safety, to decide whether a *bona fide* occupational qualification and requirement has been shown the board of inquiry and the Court must consider whether the evidence adduced justifies the conclusion that there is sufficient risk of employee failure in those over the mandatory retirement age to warrant the early retirement in the interests of safety of the employee, his fellow employees and the public at large.[21]

In *Ontario (Human Rights Commission) v. Simpson-Sears Ltd.*,[22] the Supreme Court of Canada held that intent is not a necessary element of dis-

---

[19] *Supra*, at p. 19.
[20] *Supra*, at pp. 19-20.
[21] *Supra*, at pp. 20-1.
[22] (1985), 23 D.L.R. (4th) 321, [1985] 2 S.C.R. 536.

crimination under the Ontario *Human Rights Code*. In addition, the court drew the following distinction between direct discrimination and adverse effect discrimination:

> A distinction must be made between what I would describe as direct discrimination and the concept already referred to as adverse effect discrimination in connection with employment. Direct discrimination occurs in this connection where an employer adopts a practice or rule which on its face discriminates on a prohibited ground. For example, "No Catholics or no women or no blacks employed here." There is, of course, no disagreement in the case at bar that direct discrimination of that nature would contravene the Act. On the other hand, there is the concept of adverse effect discrimination. It arises where an employer for genuine business reasons adopts a rule or standard which is on its face neutral, and which will apply equally to all employees, but which has a discriminatory effect upon a prohibited ground on one employee or group of employees in that it imposes, because of some special characteristic of the employee or group, obligations, penalties, or restrictive conditions not imposed on other members of the work force . . . An employment rule honestly made for sound economic or business reasons, equally applicable to all to whom it is intended to apply, may yet be discriminatory if it affects a person or group of persons differently from others to whom it may apply.[23]

The distinction between direct discrimination and adverse effect discrimination is significant with respect to the B.F.O.Q. statutory exception, as stated by Mr. Justice McIntyre speaking on behalf of the majority of the Supreme Court of Canada in the *Simpson-Sears* case:

> No question arises in a case involving direct discrimination. Where a working rule or condition of employment is found to be discriminatory on a prohibited ground and fails to meet any statutory justification test, it is simply struck down . . . In the case of discrimination on the basis of creed resulting from the effect of a condition or rule rationally related to the performance of the job and not on its face discriminatory, a different result follows. The working rule or condition is not struck down, but its effect on the complainant must be considered, and if the purpose of the Ontario *Human Rights Code* is to be given effect some accommodation must be required from the employer for the benefit of the complainant.[24]

In *Bhinder v. Canadian National Railway Co.*,[25] the employee, a religious Sikh refused to wear a hard hat because his religion prohibited him from using any headwear other than his turban. The Supreme Court of Canada held that the hard hat requirement was a reasonable and *bona fide* requirement aimed at protecting the health of the worker. The hard hat rule was therefore a reasonable and justified working requirement even though it infringed upon the worker's religious rights. In the *Central Alberta Dairy Pool* case Madame Justice Wilson suggested that the majority of the Supreme Court of Canada may have erred in its decision in *Bhinder*:

---

[23] *Supra*, at p. 332.
[24] *Supra*, at p. 333.
[25] (1985), 23 D.L.R. (4th) 481, [1985] 2 S.C.R. 561.

It seems to me in retrospect that the majority of this court may indeed have erred in concluding that the hard hat rule was a BFOR. I say that not because I disagree with the test set out in *Etobicoke*, nor because I accept the proposition advanced by those in dissent that accommodation is a necessary component of a BFOR, but for two other reasons.

First, the rule was not, to use the terminology of *Etobicoke*, "reasonably necessary to assure the efficient and economical performance of the job without endangering the employee, his fellow employees and the general public". The tribunal found as a fact that the failure of Mr. Bhinder to wear a hard hat would not affect his ability to work as a maintenance electrician or pose any threat to the safety of his co-workers or to the public at large. The tribunal did find that not wearing a hard hat would increase the risk to Mr. Bhinder himself, but only marginally. In light of the findings of fact by the tribunal, I think it is difficult to support the conclusion of the majority of the court that the hard hat rule was reasonably necessary for the safety of Mr. Bhinder, his fellow employees and the general public.

My second reason for questioning the correctness of *Bhinder* concerns the assumption that underlies both the majority and minority judgments, namely that if BFOR defence applies to cases of adverse effect discrimination. Upon reflection, I think we may have erred in failing to critically examine this assumption. As McIntyre J. notes in *O'Malley*, the BFOQ test in *Etobicoke* was formulated in the context of a case of direct discrimination on the basis of age. The essence of direct discrimination in employment is the making of a rule that generalizes about a person's ability to perform a job based on membership in a group sharing a common personal attribute such as age, sex, religion, etc. The ideal of human rights legislation is that each person be accorded equal treatment as an individual taking into account those attributes. Thus, justification of a rule manifesting a group stereotype depends on the validity of the generalization and/or the impossibility of making individualized assessments

. . . . .

I am of the view that *Bhinder* is correct in so far as it states that accommodation is not a component of the BFOR test and that once a BFOR is proven the employer has no duty to accommodate. It is incorrect, however, in so far as it applied that principle to a case of adverse effect discrimination. The end result is that where a rule discriminates directly it can only be justified by a statutory equivalent of a BFOQ, *i.e.*, a defence that considers the rule in its totality. (I note in passing that all human rights codes in Canada contain some form of BFOQ provision). However, where a rule has an adverse discriminatory effect, the appropriate response is to uphold the rule in its general application and consider whether the employer could have accommodated the employee adversely affected without undue hardship.[26]

In *Caldwell v. Stuart*,[27] the Supreme Court of Canada held that adherence to the tenets of the Roman Catholic faith constituted a B.F.O.Q. for a Roman Catholic teacher in a Roman Catholic school. In effect, the Supreme Court of Canada validated the generalization that the creation of an appropriate spiritual

---

[26] *Central Alberta Dairy*, *supra*, footnote 17, at pp. 433-6.
[27] (1984), 15 D.L.R. (4th) 1, [1984] 2 S.C.R. 603.

atmosphere in a Roman Catholic school required of all Catholic teachers that they demonstrate religious commitment themselves.

In *Saskatchewan Human Rights Commission v. Saskatoon (City)*,[28] the Supreme Court of Canada upheld the decision of the human rights tribunal in which the mandatory retirement policy of the city constituted a B.F.O.Q. in the circumstances, having regard to the persuasive evidence before the tribunal as to the relationship between advancing age and declining ability. In addition, the tribunal was satisfied that there was no reliable method of individualized testing, the availability of which would have obviated the need for a uniform age-based rule. As asserted by Madame Justice Wilson in *Central Alberta Dairy Pool*, the Supreme Court of Canada, in the *Saskatoon (City)* case "accepted that the evidence adduced by the employer supported both the generalization about the effect of age on ability and the inadequacy of individualized assessments".[29]

In *Brossard (Ville) v. Quebec (Commission des Droits de la Personne)*,[30] the Supreme Court of Canada was called upon to consider the Quebec equivalent of a B.F.O.Q. provision. At issue in the case was a municipality's anti-nepotism hiring policy which disqualified spouses and relatives of full-time municipal employees and town counsellors for employment with the town.

Section 10 of the Quebec *Charter of Human Rights and Freedoms*, R.S.Q. 1977, C-12, prohibits discrimination on the basis of "civil status". Section 20, in turn, deems non-discriminatory: "[a] distinction, exclusion or preference based on the aptitudes or qualifications required for an employment . . .". Mr. Justice Beetz, speaking on behalf of the majority of the Supreme Court in the *Brossard* case, summarized certain criteria for establishing the existence of an aptitude or qualification required for employment:

(1) Is the aptitude or qualification rationally connected to the employment concerned? This allows us to determine whether the employer's purpose in establishing the requirement is appropriate in an objective sense to the job in question . . .

(2) Is the rule properly designed to ensure that the aptitude or qualification is met without placing an undue burden on those to whom the rule applies? This allows us to inquire as to the reasonableness of the means the employer chooses to test for the presence of the requirement for the employment in question.[31]

As Madame Justice Wilson confirmed in *Central Alberta Dairy Pool*, the principles articulated by the Supreme Court of Canada in the *Brossard* case would have equal application to the B.F.O.Q. provisions of the common-law

---

[28] (1989), 65 D.L.R. (4th) 481, [1989] 2 S.C.R. 1297.
[29] *Central Alberta Dairy Pool v. Alberta (Human Rights Commission)* (1990), 72 D.L.R. (4th) 417 at p. 434, [1990] 2 S.C.R. 489.
[30] (1988), 53 D.L.R. (4th) 609, [1988] 2 S.C.R. 279.
[31] *Supra*, at p. 631.

provinces of Canada, including Ontario, in spite of the fact that the case dealt with specific provisions under the Quebec *Charter of Human Rights and Freedoms.* The court held in *Brossard* that the rule was not a B.F.O.Q. because of the availability of reasonable alternatives:

> It seems to me that, having regard to the nature of the right which is violated by an anti-nepotism policy, *i.e.*, the right under s. 10 not to be discriminated against, the adoption of a total ban is not "reasonably necessary" in order to avoid a threat to the integrity of the town's administration. The town can avoid the threat by the less drastic means I have suggested.[32]

As stated within its guidelines entitled "Exceptions to the Equality Rights Provisions of the Ontario Human Rights Code in the Workplace",[33] dated April 25, 1989, the Ontario Human Rights Commission cites examples of employment practices that are unlikely to be based on B.F.O.Q.'s, and include those which:

(a)   rely upon the ability of members of the excluded groups to perform incidental duties rather than essential components of the job in question;

(b)   impose a requirement based on co-worker or customer preference unrelated to capacity to perform the job;

(c)   are discriminatory even though they are in a collective agreement;

(d)   rely upon stereotypical assumptions in order to determine an individual's capacity to perform the job duties, i.e., no position should be exempted based on physical characteristics attributed to one sex or another, such as relative physical strength or capacity for endurance;

(e)   require that the job be performed only in a certain way where reasonable alternative ways may exist;

(f)   involve the types of role-modelling where the particular application of role-modelling theory is based on traditional or stereotypical conceptions of the appropriate roles of males and females, and where the role-modelling has the effect of reinforcing such stereotypes among the clientele.[34]

In the same guidelines, noted above, the Ontario Human Rights Commission makes reference to examples of *bona fide* occupational requirements that may comply with the provisions of the Ontario *Human Rights Code*:

(a)   *Age*
It may be legitimate to recruit young persons for the position of counsellor in a facility serving a clientele of homeless youths.

(b)   *Sex*
There may be instances in which the demands of public decency or the need for sex-role identification will be sufficiently compelling to warrant an exception. Examples are nurses' aides or orderlies providing intimate personal care for chronically ill persons who request same-sex care and female counsellors in shelters for battered women.

---

[32] *Supra*, at p. 655.

[33] "Exceptions to the Equality Rights Provisions of the Ontario Human Rights Code in the Workplace" (Ontario Human Rights Commission, 1989). See Schedule (x).

[34] *Ibid.*, at pp. 4-5.

(c) *Record of Offences*

Public safety considerations may allow an employer to exclude individuals with a serious record of offences under the *Highway Traffic Act* from employment as bus drivers.

Whether ''record of offences'' is a bona fide occupational qualification will depend on a variety of factors including job duties; the length of time since the individual's conviction; the nature of the offence; what he or she has been doing since the offence was committed; and whether rehabilitation was undertaken and was successful.[35]

While the *bona fide* occupational requirement exception to employment-related discrimination is expressly provided for in all provincial and federal human rights legislation, it is clear that courts and human rights tribunals will require compelling, objective evidence to satisfy them that the rule or policy in question falls within this limited exception. Impressionistic evidence and/or good intentions on the part of the employer will simply not suffice.

---

[35] *Ibid.*, at p. 6.

CHAPTER 10 | *Liability*

1. LIABILITY OF EMPLOYERS

A. Provisions Under the Ontario Human Rights Code

Generally speaking, a corporate employer is held vicariously liable for the discriminatory acts and conduct of its officers, agents and employees under the Ontario *Human Rights Code*, R.S.O. 1990, c. H.19.

Section 45(1) of the Code specifies this basic principle:

> 45(1) For the purposes of this Act, except subsection 2(2), subsection 5(2), section 7 and subsection 44(1), any act or thing done or omitted to be done in the course of his or her employment by an officer, official, employee or agent of a corporation, trade union, trade or occupational association, unincorporated association or employers' organization shall be deemed to be an act or thing done or omitted to be done by the corporation, trade union, trade or occupational association, unincorporated association or employers' organization.

However, the express exceptions to this general rule, within the context of the employment relationship, are as follows:

(1) harassment in the workplace by an agent of the employer or another employee because of race, ancestry, place of origin, colour, ethnic origin, citizenship, creed, age, record of offences, marital status, family status or handicap;[1]

(2) harassment in the workplace because of sex by an agent of the employer or another employee;[2]

(3) a sexual solicitation or advance made by a person in a position to confer, grant or deny a benefit or advancement to the person where the person making the solicitation or advancement knows or ought reasonably to know that it is unwelcome;[3]

(4) a reprisal or threat of reprisal for the rejection of a sexual solicitation or advance where the reprisal is made or threatened by a person in a position to confer, grant or deny a benefit or advancement to the person.[4]

---

[1] See s. 5(2) of the Ontario *Human Rights Code*, R.S.O. 1990, c. H.19, as amended.

[2] See s. 7(2) of the Code.

[3] See s. 7(3)(a) of the Code.

[4] See s. 7(3)(b) of the Code.

The legislature of the province of Ontario has seen fit to specifically exempt employers from liability for the discriminatory conduct of its employees and agents in the above-mentioned circumstances. This is in general recognition of the fact that sexual harassment and sexual solicitation in the workplace is not only morally offensive, but virtually impossible for any employer to effectively monitor and control.

Even in situations where the corporate employer is deemed to be singularly liable, in those cases of discriminatory conduct for which an employee cannot be held personally liable, the company may request a ruling, pursuant to s. 45(2) of the Code, as to whether the corporation authorized or acquiesced in the discriminatory conduct:

> 45(2) At the request of a corporation, trade union, trade or occupational association, unincorporated association or employers' organization, a board of inquiry in its decision shall make known whether or not, in its opinion, an act or thing done or omitted to be done by an officer, official, employee or agent was done or omitted to be done with or without the authority or acquiescence of the corporation, trade union, trade or occupational association, unincorporated association or employers' organization, and the opinion does not affect the application of subsection (1).

The potential significance of a favourable ruling under s. 45(2) is twofold:

(1) first, it provides a moral victory, if nothing else, in that the tribunal is satisfied that the discriminatory conduct in question was not officially sanctioned, or even known by corporate management;

(2) secondly, it could provide a reasonable foundation for terminating the employment of the guilty employee for justifiable cause.

B. Provisions Under the Canadian Human Rights Act[5]

An employer may be held liable under the *Canadian Human Rights Act*, R.S.C. 1985, c. H-6, for discriminatory acts or omissions by its employees. Section 65(1) of the Act provides:

> 65(1) Subject to subsection (2), any act or omission committed by an officer, a director, an employee or an agent of any person, association or organization in the course of the employment of the officer, director, employee or agent shall, for the purposes of this Act, be deemed to be an act or omission committed by that person, association or organization.

For this reason alone, in circumstances where a company is concerned that an employee may have been on a frolic of his or her own when the alleged discriminatory act or omission occurred, it may be useful to consider whether the company and the individual alleged to have caused the act or omission should be jointly or separately represented at a hearing.

---

[5] This subsection is an excerpt from the book by M. Norman Grosman, *Federal Employment Law in Canada* (Scarborough, Carswell, 1990), ch. 8, pp. 258-9.
(Note: chapter 8 was prepared by Fran Carnerie).

Section 65(2) of the Act provides some relief to employers. It states that if it can be established that (a) the employer did not consent to the commission of the act or omission, and (b) exercised all due diligence to prevent the act or omission from being committed and (c) subsequent to the commission of the discriminatory act or omission exercised all due diligence to mitigate or avoid the effect of the discrimination, the employer can avoid this vicarious liability being imposed. What steps then should the prudent employer take to avoid being tarred with the same brush as an employee acting on his or her own? The employer should be certain to avoid explicitly, or more likely tacitly, consenting to an environment which breeds or encourages or perhaps fails to discourage discriminatory acts. For example, a work environment which involves a "rough and tumble, macho" atmosphere may represent a prime breeding ground for racial or ethnic slurs as an accepted part of daily routine. The failure of an employer to act on such matters may represent condonation, a form of implied consent. Employers are well advised to develop a written human rights policy based on expert legal advice and to distribute the policy to all employees. Some employers may go further and provide seminars in conjunction with the implementation of such a policy. The development and dissemination of such a policy may ultimately be viewed by a tribunal as an act of prevention pursuant to s. 65(2), sufficient to exclude the employer from liability. Finally, when an act or possible act of discrimination has taken place and comes to the employer's attention, it is critical that the employer react so as to minimize the effects upon the individual who was the target of the act. These steps and others will assist an employer in avoiding liability. The first two steps, however, are proactive ones and require the employer to address human rights issues now, rather than waiting until it has been served by the Commission with notice of a complaint.

C. General Principles

One of the leading decisions on the topic of employer liability, is the Ontario Board of Inquiry decision in *Commodore Business Machines Ltd. v. Olarte.*[6] Professor P.A. Cumming was appointed as the Board of Inquiry.

The relevant facts of the *Commodore Business Machines* case may be summarized as follows:

1. Mr. DeFilippis was the foreman on the afternoon shift at one of the Commodore plants located in the City of Toronto from 1973 until 1981;

2. the six complainants were factory workers with the company at that plant at the times that they allege sexual harassment on the part of

---

[6] (1983), 83 C.L.L.C. ¶17,028, 4 C.H.R.R. D/1705 (Ont. Bd. Inq.) and (1983), 83 C.L.L.C. ¶17,016, 4 C.H.R.R. D/1399 (Ont. Bd. Inq.), affd 14 D.L.R. (4th) 118, 49 O.R. (2d) 17, *sub nom. Commodore Business Machines Ltd. v. Minister of Labour* (Div. Ct.).

Mr. DeFilippis with the alleged knowledge and acquiescence of the company;

3. Mr. DeFilippis in his position as foreman repeatedly touched and kissed the complainants, asked for invitations to their homes and requested that they engage in sexual intercourse with him. When his advances were refused, Mr. DeFilippis penalized the complainants by shouting at them, finding fault with their work and transferring them to heavier duties with the result that some of the complainants quit and one was fired;

4. the hearing lasted some 36 days, including 9 days of argument, with 56 witnesses giving evidence, 117 exhibits and 37 volumes of evidence and argument being presented to the Board of Inquiry;

5. Mr. DeFilippis completely denied that he sexually harassed any of the female employees and the company in turn denied any sexual harassment by Mr. DeFilippis and, by implication, any knowledge of harassment if such existed.

The Board of Inquiry found that Mr. DeFilippis had engaged in a practice of sexual harassment against the complainants and, accordingly, was held personally liable for the sexual harassment. In addition, the Board found Commodore Business Machines Ltd. liable on the basis that Mr. DeFilippis was held to be part of the "directing mind of the corporation" since he had the general power to hire and fire and discipline employees. The Board was of the view that where an employee is part of the "directing mind" of the corporation, the employer corporation is itself personally liable for contraventions of the Code engaged in by that employee. In his reasons for decision, Professor Cumming held the company liable on the organic theory of corporate responsibility, a subject which he reviewed at some length in the course of his reasons. Professor Cumming summarizes the essence or gist of the organic theory of corporate responsibility:

> In my opinion, the organic theory of corporate responsibility applies in respect of breaches of the *Ontario Human Rights Code*. If an individual is in breach of the Code, and the breach arises in the course of the individual acting as agent for the corporation in the carrying on of its business, and the individual is also the (or at least part of the) "directing mind" of the corporation, then the corporation itself is in breach of the Code.[7]

In the course of his decision in the *Commodore Business Machines Ltd.* case, Professor Cumming provided the following statements of principle in dealing with the important issue of employer liability under the Ontario *Human Rights Code*:

> From my review of the law, it seems to me that an employer would be *personally* in breach of either the new Code or the old Code in the following types of situations.

---

[7] *Supra*, at p. 16,281 (83 C.L.L.C. ¶17,028).

1. Where the employer himself, by his own personal action, directly or indirectly, intentionally infringes a protected right, then he has, of course, contravened section 8 of the new Code.

. . . . .

2. Where the employer does not intend to discriminate, but there is a constructive discrimination, then the employer is in contravention of sections 10 and 8 of the new Code. That is, the employer has personally breached the new Code.

. . . . .

3. Where the employer himself takes no direct action of discrimination, but authorizes, condones, adopts or ratifies an employee's discrimination, then the employer is himself *personally* liable for contravening the Code (whether on a basis of contravening section 8, or section 10 coupled with section 8 of the new Code) as it is the employer himself who has infringed or done, directly or indirectly, an act, "that infringes a right under this Part" (section 8 of the new Code).

. . . . .

4. Where the employer is a corporate entity, and an employee is in contravention of either the new or the old Code, and that employee is part of the "directing mind" of the corporation, then the employer corporation is itself *personally* in contravention. The act of the employee becomes the act of the corporate entity itself, in accordance with the organic theory of corporate responsibility.

. . . . .

5. The difficulty in applying the organic theory of corporate responsibility . . . comes in the factual determination as to whether the employee in question is part of the "directing mind" . . . It seems to me that, generally speaking, whether an employee provides some function of management, that he is then part of the "directing mind" . . . Thus, I would take a broad view of the range of factual situations which are embraced within the concept of "directing mind". Once an employee is part of the directing mind, and the contravention of the Code comes in his performing his corporate function, the corporation is itself also *personally* in breach of the Code.

6. Where an employee unlawfully (i.e. in contravention of the Code) causes the breach of a *contract* between his employer (the employee-agent's principal) and a complainant, then the employer is liable for a contravention of the Code under the common law in respect of agency, for the act of the employee-agent is the act of the employer principal so far as the third party complainant is concerned.

7. The most difficult area then arises when none of the factors in #1 to #6 above are present. To return to Professor Atiyah's quoted statement on "vicarious liability", if the employee is a mere servant (not part of the "directing mind", and there is not a contract between the employer and third party that the servant-agent is causing a breach of) then is the employer liable for a contravention of either the new Code or the old Code by the employee in the course of his employment, even though there is no *personal* contravention of the Code by the employer?[8] (Emphasis in original.)

---

[8] *Supra*, at pp. 16,284-5.

After specifically enumerating the types of situations in which an employer would be personally in breach of the Ontario *Human Rights Code*, referred to above, Professor Cumming then provides the following concluding remarks in the reasons for his decision:

> — the dividing line between situations of "personal liability" (situations #1 to #6) and the situation of vicarious liability (#7) remains important. It is only in the #7 situation that an employer is not liable for the "harassment" by an employee. If it is a situation of sexual harassment by a mere employee (i.e. not someone who is part of the directing mind) of the corporate employer, then it is clear by virtue of the excepting provision in subsection 44(1) that vicarious liability does not attach to the employer. However, if the employee sexually harassing is part of the directing mind of the employer, then while subsection 44(1) does not apply (i.e., there is no deeming of the discriminatory act of the employee to be the act of the employer) there can still be *personal liability* on the part of the employer on the theory as advanced in situations #4 and #5.[9]

The principles articulated by Professor Cumming in the *Commodore Business Machines* case are key to understanding employer liability in the area of human rights. As is clear from the scholarly analysis of Professor Cumming in the *Commodore Business Machines* case, an employer, company or business entity can be held liable for discrimination, even in situations falling within apparent exceptions stipulated within the human rights legislation, where the tribunal is satisfied that the individual or individuals responsible for the discriminatory action represented all or part of the "directing mind" of the employer. Furthermore, as is amply demonstrated by the dicta of Professor Cumming in the *Commodore Business Machines* case, the notion or concept of "directing mind" of the company is interpreted very broadly. Whenever an employee provides "some function of management" then there is a distinct possibility that the corporate employer will be held liable for the discriminatory actions of that individual, in addition to the individual him or herself being held personally liable for their actions. This would appear to be the case even if the individual in question, such as Mr. DeFilippis himself, is quite clearly on a frolic of his or her own, in terms of engaging in conduct which clearly forms no part of his duties and responsibilities as an employee of the company. To say that corporate employers have far-reaching potential liability under existing Canadian human rights legislation, is an understatement. These principles of liability are consistent with one of the primary philosophies of human rights legislation — it is meant to be remedial in nature, as opposed to being designed specifically or primarily to punish individuals or entities who are guilty of discriminatory conduct.

A classic example of the potentially far-reaching impact of the organic theory of corporate responsibility can be found in the Ontario Board of Inquiry

---

[9] *Supra*, at pp. 16,286-7.

decision in *Boehm v. National System of Baking Limited.*[10] In the *Boehm* case, the complainant alleged harassment in employment because of handicap or disability. The Board of Inquiry found that Mr. Boehm had a "condition of mental impairment" and was a "slow learner". He was employed with the company for almost four years, enjoyed his work and was a very good employee. Mr. Boehm experienced no significant problems with his job until a new supervisor, Mr. Woods was hired. Mr. Woods was the company's production manager. The Board concluded on the evidence that Mr. Woods had referred to Mr. Boehm as a "dummy" and a "retard", gave him extra supervision and was much tougher on Mr. Boehm then on other employees under his supervision.

The Board of Inquiry concluded in the *Boehm* case that Mr. Woods was personally liable for having harassed Mr. Boehm on the basis of his mental handicap. In spite of the fact that the respondent company had hired many handicapped people, which was amply supported by the evidence adduced at the hearing, Mr. Woods was found to have been part of the "directing mind" of the company and, accordingly, the corporation was also held to be in violation of the Ontario *Human Rights Code*. The Board of Inquiry stated, quite simply, that since the respondent, Mr. Woods, was part of "management", therefore his acts were held to be the acts of the corporation, thereby resulting in the company being held liable in addition to Mr. Woods.

The principle of strict vicarious employer liability under human rights legislation has been confirmed by the Supreme Court of Canada in *R. v. Robichaud.*[11] In the *Robichaud* case, which involved a complaint filed under the *Canadian Human Rights Act*, the Supreme Court of Canada heard an appeal from the Federal Court of Appeal on the issue of whether or not an employer is responsible for the unauthorized discriminatory actions of its employees in the workplace. In answering this question in the affirmative, the court held that the "statute contemplates the imposition of liability on employers for all acts of their employees". Mr. Justice Le Dain, speaking for the majority of the Supreme Court in the *Robichaud* decision, stated:

> Indeed, if the Act is concerned with the *effects* of discrimination rather than its *causes* (or motivations), it must be admitted that only an employer can remedy undesirable effects; only an employer can provide the most important remedy — a healthy work environment.[12]

In its policy statement entitled "The Liability of Principals for the Actions of Their Agents" the Ontario Human Rights Commission makes the following statement in relation to employer liability for acts of harassment of its employees:

---

[10] (1987), 87 C.L.L.C. ¶17,013, 8 C.H.R.R. D/4110 (Ont. Bd. Inq.).
[11] (1987), 40 D.L.R. (4th) 577, [1987] 2 S.C.R. 84.
[12] *Supra*, at p. 584.

An employer may be liable for acts of harassment carried out by its employees through the "organic theory of corporate responsibility". This theory provides that where an employee is in a position of authority (i.e., part of the "directing mind") in the organization, the employer will be held responsible for the actions of that employee. To put it in more direct terms, the acts of supervisors, managers, etc. are considered to be acts of the employer.[13]

In summary, it appears that human rights tribunals will not hesitate to find a corporate employer liable when an employee harasses another employee if the harassing employee is part of the "directing mind" of the corporation. The jurisprudence on this subject clearly suggests that the employee need only be part of "management", irrespective of the formal title, if any, which the individual in question holds. The employee must have some authority over the direction of the workforce in order to be considered part of "management". In addition, it is important to bear in mind that a corporation may be found liable even if the harasser was not part of the "directing mind" of the corporation, but if a member of the "directing mind" of the company became aware of the harassment but did not take any reasonable steps to in any way eliminate or address the conduct in question. In other words, where the "directing mind" is held to have condoned, ratified, acquiesced in and/or authorized the harassment in question, the corporate employer may be held liable.

2. PERSONAL LIABILITY OF EMPLOYERS, OFFICERS AND DIRECTORS

A. Provisions Under the Ontario Human Rights Code

Section 9 of the Ontario *Human Rights Code* simply provides:

> 9. No person shall infringe or do, directly or indirectly, anything that infringes a right under this Part.

The "Part" referred to in s. 9 is Part 1 of the Ontario *Human Rights Code* which contains various sections relating to "freedom from discrimination" including the fundamental provision contained in s. 5 of the Code being the right to equal treatment with respect to employment. It is submitted that the very basic provision prescribed in s. 9 of the Ontario *Human Rights Code* has equal application to all other provisions within the Ontario *Human Rights Code* itself and, indeed, all Canadian human rights legislation. In other words, it is entirely consistent with the fundamental principles and philosophies that have been articulated by both human rights tribunals and courts in relation to the importance of human rights legislation, that any individual who has engaged and/or assisted in a violation of human rights legislation, can and will be held accountable for their actions.

---

[13] "The Liability of Principals for the Actions of Their Agents" (Ontario Human Rights Commission). See Canadian Employment Law Guide, p. 63,722.

Sections of the Ontario *Human Rights Code* which specifically refer to personal liability of employees and agents of the employer, which would include both officers and directors, are as follows:

1. Section 5(2) of the Ontario *Human Rights Code* which provides that "Every person who is an employee has a right to freedom from harassment in the workplace by the employer *or agent of the employer or by another employee* because of race, ancestry, place of origin, colour, ethnic origin, citizenship, creed, age, record of offences, marital status, family status or handicap";
   (Emphasis added.)

2. Section 7(2) of the Ontario *Human Rights Code* specifically provides that "every person who is an employee has a right to freedom from harassment in the workplace because of sex by his or her employer *or by another employee*";
   (Emphasis added.)

3. Section 7(3) of the Ontario *Human Rights Code* specifically addresses sexual solicitations advanced by individuals who are in a position to confer, grant or deny a benefit or advancement:

   (3) Every person has a right to be free from,
   - (a) a sexual solicitation or advance made by a person in a position to confer, grant or deny a benefit or advancement to the person where the person making the solicitation or advance knows or ought reasonably to know that it is unwelcome; or
   - (b) a reprisal or a threat of reprisal for the rejection of a sexual solicitation or advance where the reprisal is made or threatened by a person in a position to confer, grant or deny a benefit or advancement to the person.

It is clear, having regard to the above-noted specific provisions of the Ontario *Human Rights Code*, that personal liability may attach in instances where any employee, officer or director is involved in a human rights violation but, in particular, in instances relating to sexual harassment and/or solicitation in the workplace.

B. Provisions Under the Canadian Human Rights Act

The primary provision under the *Canadian Human Rights Act* relating to personal liability of employees, officers and directors of a company is found in s. 65 of the Act:

65(1) Subject to subsection (2), any act or omission committed by an officer, a director, an employee or an agent of any person, association or organization *in the course of the employment of the officer, director, employee or agent shall, for the purposes of this Act, be deemed to be an act or omission committed by that person, association or organization.*

(2) An act or omission shall not, by virtue of subsection (1), be deemed to be an act or omission committed by a person, association or organization if it is established that the person, association or organization did not consent to the

commission of the act or omission and exercised all due diligence to prevent the act or omission from being committed and, subsequently, to mitigate or avoid the effect thereof.

(Emphasis added.)

Accordingly, it could be argued that an employee, officer or director may be relieved of liability under the *Canadian Human Rights Act* if it is established that the discriminatory act or omission in question fell "within the course of their employment". The single exception to this general principle is where, as prescribed in s. 65(2) of the Act, the employer can satisfy the tribunal that it did not consent to the conduct in question and it took reasonable steps to prevent the discriminatory act or omission from being committed.

The phrase or concept of "in the course of employment" can be found in ss. 7 and 14 of the *Canadian Human Rights Act*, both of which are the primary provisions of the Act relating to discriminatory practices in employment:

> 7. It is a discriminatory practice, directly or indirectly,
>   (*a*) to refuse to employ or continue to employ any individual, or
>   (*b*) *in the course of employment*, to differentiate adversely in relation to an employee,
> on a prohibited ground of discrimination.
>
> . . . . .
>
> 14.(1) It is a discriminatory practice,
>
> . . . . .
>
>   (*c*) *in matters related to employment*,
> to harass an individual on a prohibited ground of discrimination.
>   (2) without limiting the generality of subsection (1), sexual harassment shall, for the purposes of that subsection, be deemed to be harassment on a prohibited ground of discrimination.

(Emphasis added.)

It is significant to note that there is no general provision comparable to s. 9 of the Ontario *Human Rights Code* to be found within the four corners of the *Canadian Human Rights Act*. Accordingly, there is a very real issue as to whether an employee, officer or director of a company can be held to be personally liable for discriminatory conduct, separate and aside from whatever liability may attach to the corporate employer, in circumstances where the individual's act or omission is found to be "within the course of their employment". The very recent decision of the Federal Court of Canada in *Cluff v. Canada (Department of Agriculture)*[14] graphically illustrates the difficulties associated with interpreting and applying the phrase "in the course of employment" to a given fact situation.

---

[14] (unreported, November 12, 1992, Can. Trib., affd December 21, 1993, F.C.T.D.).

The pertinent facts of the *Cluff* case may be summarized as follows:

1. Ms Cluff was, at all relevant times, an information officer in the Communications Branch of the Department of Agriculture of the Government of Canada;

2. Mr. Michael Sage was also an employee in the Communications Branch of Agriculture Canada, being a permanent employee and therefore significantly senior to the complainant, Ms Cluff;

3. Ms Cluff's specific area of work was the preparation of radio programs;

4. with the approval and support of her immediate supervisor, being the acting Chief of Media Relations for Agriculture Canada, and others in the Communications Branch, Ms Cluff became active on the executive of the Eastern Canada Farm Writers Association (E.C.F.W.A.);

5. Ms Cluff was responsible for the organization of the E.C.F.W.A. 1986 Annual Conference and was authorized by her supervisors to carry out the organization responsibilities during her normal working hours at Agriculture Canada so long as that work did not interfere with her normal assigned responsibilities;

6. Ms Cluff chaired the conference which commenced on Friday, December 5, 1986. On the evening of that day, there was a buffet dinner in conjunction with the conference;

7. following the buffet dinner which was held in the hotel where the conference was taking place, the E.C.F.W.A. had provided for a hospitality suite in the hotel. Part of Ms Cluff's responsibilities as organizer and chairperson of the conference involved hosting in the hospitality suite;

8. since it was anticipated that Ms Cluff's duties would keep her at the hotel until late the night of December 5, 1986 and her activities for the next day would start early in the morning, it was arranged that Ms Cluff would stay overnight at the hotel in the bedroom portion of the hospitality suite which was separated from the rest of the suite only by an archway, not by a locking door;

9. activities in the hospitality suite got underway at approximately 9:00 p.m. on December 5, 1986. By some time not long after midnight, most people had left;

10. at approximately 2:00 a.m. on the Saturday morning, being the morning of December 6, 1986, Ms Cluff found herself alone in the suite with the respondent Sage and another male person who was a delegate at the conference from outside the Government of Canada;

11. between 2:00 a.m. and shortly after 3:00 a.m. Ms Cluff alleges that certain acts of harassment on prohibited grounds of sex allegedly took place in the hospitality suite, which were allegedly initiated by the respondent Mr. Sage.

At the commencement of the hearing before the Canadian Human Rights Tribunal, counsel for both the Department of Agriculture and Mr. Sage made a preliminary motion, on the basis that the Tribunal lacked jurisdiction over the subject matter of the complaint. In essence, the respondents argued that if the alleged sexual harassment did not occur "in the course of employment" and/or "in matters related to employment", as required under ss. 7 and 14 of the *Canadian Human Rights Act*, the Tribunal lacked jurisdiction to hear the complaints because any remedy for violation of ss. 7 and 14 that is available under ss. 53 and 65 of the Act applied only to the employer. In granting the motion of the respondents and ordering the adjournment of the proceedings, on the basis that the actions in question did not take place "in the course of employment" and/or "in matters related to employment", the Tribunal made the following statement of principle as to when an employee is in the course of employment:

> An employee is in the course of employment when, within the period covered by the employment, he or she is carrying out:
> (1) activities which he or she might normally or reasonably do or be specifically authorized to do while so employed;
> (2) activities which fairly and reasonably may be said to be incidental to the employment or logically and naturally connected with it;
> (3) activities in furtherance of duties he or she owes to his or her employer; or
> (4) activities in furtherance of duties owed to the employer where the latter is exercising or could exercise control over what the employee does.
> An employee is still in the course of employment when he or she is carrying out intentionally or unintentionally, authorized or unauthorized, with or without the approval of his or her employer, activities which are discriminatory under the CHRA and are in some way related or associated with the employment. However, an employee is considered to have deviated from the course of his or her employment when engaged in those activities which are not related to his or her employment or are personal in nature.[15]

In granting the respondents' motion and concluding that the Tribunal was without jurisdiction, it based its decision, in large part, upon the findings as set out within the following excerpt from its reasons:

> Ms Leslie Cluff wore two hats during the entire process of planning the 1986 conference and then attending the conference. She performed her functions while at work at Agriculture Canada for planning the conference but not allowing it to interfere with her daily official work. Ms Cluff's activities at the conference were a combination of the two roles. In other words, she clearly performed two functions while at the conference — one, as the delegate of Agriculture Canada in attending sessions and even the evening events if she so decided and two, as the chairman of the conference in chairing the conference and under the name of the E.C.F.W.A. in hosting the hospitality suite. These activities were not in any way related to her job of producing radio programmes at Agriculture Canada. Ms Cluff's activities in preparing for the conference while at work for Agriculture

---

[15] *Cluff, supra*, at pp. 10-11 of unreported judgment (Can. Trib.).

Canada were allowed by her supervisor only as long as her daily duties could be satisfactorily performed. Agriculture Canada had no specification in her job description to require Ms Cluff to work for the E.C.F.W.A. nor did it require its employees to belong to the E.C.F.W.A. It is the choice of the employees to choose the professional organization which they would like to belong to in order to enhance themselves personally or in their jobs. Agriculture Canada does not keep a list of its staff who belong to the E.C.F.W.A.

More importantly, Michael Sage was not the employer of Leslie Cluff and is, therefore, not liable under section 7 and 14 of the CHRA which are the basis of these complaints.[16]

In upholding the decision of the Canadian Human Rights Tribunal in the *Cluff* case, Mr. Justice Gibson made it clear that he was in agreement with the ultimate result arrived at by the Tribunal but for different reasons. Justice Gibson was of the opinion that the Tribunal erred in applying the criteria which it laid down within the course of its reasons relating to what constitutes "in the course of employment" to the facts of the case at bar. While the judge agreed with the criteria laid down by the human rights tribunal with respect to what constitutes "in the course of employment", he held that the Tribunal erred in concluding that those criteria were conjunctive as opposed to being disjunctive.

However, even though Mr. Justice Gibson held that the Canadian Human Rights Tribunal erred in law in its decision relating to the interpretation of the criteria applicable to the concept of "in the course of employment", he none-theless concluded that the subject matter of the sexual harassment complaint did not fall within the course of Ms Cluff's employment. In this regard, Mr. Justice Gibson stated, in part:

> . . . Can what transpired after the hospitality suite can [*sic*] reasonably be inferred to have closed, what allegedly transpired in that suite, presumably behind a locked door, be said to be "not related to [the complainant's] employment" or are those activities simply on a continuum with activities that I have concluded are in the course of employment or in matters related to employment? In posing the question and concluding that I must answer it against the complainant, I am cognizant of my obligation to give the words of the Act ". . . such fair, large and liberal interpretation as will best ensure the attainment of [its] objects".

> Further, I am in no way casting aspersions on the complainant's comportment, being critical of her conduct or suggesting that she was in any sense an author of the misfortune that she alleges befell her. Perhaps someone let her down. Perhaps someone should have anticipated that she might find herself in the situation that allegedly unfolded between 2:00 a.m. and 3:00 a.m. that night, and should have taken precautions to ensure that, once the hospitality suite was closed, she would be secure in that suite that was to be her accommodation for the night. If someone failed in this respect, I conclude that it was not Agriculture Canada. At some time during the night in question, before 2:00 a.m. and at or shortly after the time the

---

[16] *Supra*, at pp. 14-15.

hospitality suite effectively closed, the complainant ceased to be in the course of her employment or engaged in matters related to employment. To conclude otherwise would place an intolerable burden of responsibility on employers who travel in the course of their employment and of those who attend conferences and the like on behalf of their employers.[17]

It is significant to note that Mr. Justice Gibson, although upholding the decision of the Canadian Human Rights Tribunal relating to the dismissal of the complaint against Agriculture Canada, nonetheless stated that he disagreed with the Tribunal's rationale in relation to the complaint as it applied to Mr. Sage:

> There is one further comment that I feel compelled to make. Just before reaching its conclusion, the Tribunal states: "more importantly, Michael Sage was not the employer of Leslie Cluff and is, therefore, not liable under sections 7 and 14 of the CHRA which are the basis of these complaints". Recognizing that what follows is not in any way essential to my decision herein, I wish to go on record as disagreeing with this conclusion.[18]

Although the comments of Mr. Justice Gibson in the above-noted passage are clearly *obiter dicta*, in the sense that by his own admission they are in no way relevant to the subject matter of the application before him, he, nonetheless, raises more questions than he answers in making this concluding statement in his reasons for judgment. It would be pure speculation to attempt to interpret specifically what Mr. Justice Gibson intended by his brief statement. However, it would be reasonable to infer that the judge would have to agree with the technical assertion that Mr. Sage was not Ms Cluff's employer and, therefore, presumably takes issue with the contention that Mr. Sage could not be held personally liable for the complaint of sexual harassment. Unfortunately, the absence of any expressly stated reason or rationale for taking this position, provides no assistance when one attempts to ascertain the basis upon which Mr. Justice Gibson presumably affixes some potential personal liability to Mr. Sage in the circumstances of the *Cluff* complaint.

3. LIABILITY OF UNIONS

A. Provisions Under the Ontario Human Rights Code

Section 6 of the Ontario *Human Rights Code* specifies the general right of every individual to equal treatment with respect to membership in a trade union:

> 6. Every person has a right to equal treatment with respect to membership in any trade union, trade or occupational association or self-governing profession without discrimination because of race, ancestry, place of origin, colour, ethnic

---

[17] *Cluff v. Canada (Department of Agriculture)*, *supra*, p. 11 of unreported judgment (F.C. T.D.).
[18] *Supra*, at p. 12.

origin, citizenship, creed, sex, sexual orientation, age, marital status, family status or handicap.

It has already been noted earlier in this chapter that s. 9 of the Ontario *Human Rights Code* is a general provision relating to potential personal liability of employees, officers and directors of a company. It is clear that s. 9, which expressly provides that "no person shall infringe or do, directly or indirectly, anything that infringes a right under this Part", would equally apply to a trade union or employee association. Under s. 46 of the *Human Rights Code*, the term "person" is defined to include:

> . . . an employment agency, an employers' organization, an unincorporated association, a trade or occupational association, a trade union, a partnership, a municipality, a board of police commissioners established under the *Police Act* . . .

Finally, s. 45 of the Ontario *Human Rights Code* makes it abundantly clear that a trade union will be held accountable for the actions or omissions of its representatives and/or members in certain situations:

> 45(1) For the purposes of this Act, except subsection 2(2), subsection 5(2), section 7 and subsection 44(1), any act or thing done or omitted to be done in the course of his or her employment by an officer, official, employee or agent of a corporation, *trade union, trade or occupational association*, unincorporated association, or employers' organization shall be deemed to be an act or thing done or omitted to be done by the corporation, *trade union, trade or occupational association*, unincorporated association or employers' organization.

(Emphasis added.)

It appears that the general principles relating to the organic theory of corporate responsibility would have equal general application to the actions of trade unions and associations through its executive, representatives and general membership. Since a trade union and association is a body which has a separate legal personality which, in many respects, is parallel to a corporation, there can be no doubt that most if not all of these general principles of the organic theory of corporate responsibility would apply to trade unions and associations.

B. Provisions Under the Canadian Human Rights Act

Section 9 of the *Canadian Human Rights Act* is the general provision relating to the right to membership in an employee organization:

> 9(1) It is a discriminatory practice for an employee organization on a prohibited ground of discrimination
> - (a) to exclude an individual from full membership in the organization;
> - (b) to expel or suspend a member of the organization; or
> - (c) to limit, segregate, classify or otherwise act in relation to an individual in a way that would deprive the individual of employment opportunities, or limit employment opportunities or otherwise adversely affect the status of the individual, where the individual is a member of the organization or where any of the obligations of the organization pursuant to a collective agreement relate to the individual.

(2) Notwithstanding subsection (1), it is not a discriminatory practice for an employee organization to exclude, expel or suspend an individual from membership in the organization because that individual has reached the normal age of retirement for individuals working in positions similar to the position of that individual.

Section 9(3) of the Act defines an employee organization to include a trade union or other organization of employees.

Section 10 of the CHRA in turn, specifically provides that:

10. It is a discriminatory practice for an employer, employee organization or organization of employers
   (a) to establish or pursue a policy or practice, or
   (b) to enter into an agreement affecting recruitment, referral, hiring, promotion, training, apprenticeship, transfer or any other matter relating to employment or prospective employment,
that deprives or tends to deprive an individual or class of individuals of any employment opportunities on a prohibited ground of discrimination.

Section 60(3) of the CHRA provides that an employee organization may be prosecuted for the following:
   (i) failing to comply with the terms of any settlement of a complaint approved and certified by the Commission under s. 48;
   (ii) obstructing a tribunal in carrying out its function under the Act;
   (iii) obstructing the investigation of a complaint;
   (iv) exacting a form of reprisal, by engaging in intimidation or discrimination against an individual who has made a complaint under the Act or given evidence in the course of a proceeding under the Act; or
   (v) had some involvement in an employer's reduction of wages for the purpose of attempting to eliminate a discriminatory practice under s. 11 of the Act, being the equal wages provision of the legislation.[19]

C. Supreme Court Decision in Renaud

On September 24, 1992, the Supreme Court of Canada issued its landmark decision in *Central Okanagan School District No. 23 v. Renaud.*[20] The *Renaud* decision represents the first time in Canadian legal history that the Supreme Court of Canada was called upon to decide whether a union could be held liable, in whole or in part, for discrimination in the workplace. In *Renaud*, the court unequivocally answered this novel question in the affirmative. Perhaps even more importantly, the court rejected the argument raised by both the employer and the union that an express provision of an enforceable collective agreement could provide a valid defence to the human rights complaint.

---

[19] See s. 60(1) of the CHRA.
[20] (1989), 90 C.L.L.C. ¶17,004, 11 C.H.R.R. D/62 (B.C.C.A.), revd 95 D.L.R. (4th) 577, [1992] 2 S.C.R. 970.

Mr. Renaud, a Seventh-Day Adventist, was a unionized custodian working regular shifts, Monday to Friday, for the respondent school board. His work schedule, which formed part of the collective agreement, included a Friday evening work shift. Since Mr. Renaud's religion prevented him from working on his sabbath, from sundown on Friday to sundown on Saturday, a number of alternatives to Mr. Renaud's working Friday nights were canvassed by him and a representative of the school board. It was agreed between Mr. Renaud and the school board representative that the creation of a Sunday to Thursday shift was the only viable solution to the problem. Since this proposed solution constituted an exception to the collective agreement, it required the consent of the union. The union refused to consent to the creation of this special shift and threatened to file a policy grievance in the event that the school board proceeded with this proposal. Mr. Renaud's employment was ultimately terminated when he failed to work his Friday evening shift as scheduled.

In granting Mr. Renaud's appeal and reversing the decision of the British Columbia Court of Appeal, Mr. Justice Sopinka, speaking for the majority of the Supreme Court of Canada, stated in part:

> . . . private arrangements, whether by contract or collective agreement, must give way to the requirements of the statute. In the case of direct discrimination which is not justified under the Act, the whole of the provision is invalid because its purpose as well as effect is to discriminate on a prohibited ground . . .
>
> On the other hand a provision such as the one in this case is neutral on its face but operates in a discriminatory fashion against the appellant. The provision is valid in its general application. What the human rights legislation requires is that the appellant be accommodated by exempting him from its provisions to the extent that it no longer discriminates against him on the basis of his religion.[21]

In addressing the duty of a union to accommodate an employee, the Supreme Court pointed out that such a duty arises only if the union is a party to the discrimination. There are two ways in which a union can become a party to the discrimination:

(a) it may cause or contribute to the discrimination in this first instance by participating in the formulation of the work rule that has the discriminatory effect on the complainant and,

(b) the union may be liable for failure to accommodate if it impedes the reasonable efforts of an employer to accommodate.

The court similarly rejected the school board's contention that the cost of defending a threatened grievance constituted "undue hardship", thereby justifying a refusal to accommodate Mr. Renaud in the circumstances.

Employers may derive some comfort from the Supreme Court of Canada's explicit recognition of the fact that the duty to accommodate is a "multi-party inquiry", involving the complainant, the employer and, if applicable, the

---

[21] *Supra*, at pp. 586-7 (S.C.C.).

union. It is not solely the duty of the employer in situations of alleged discrimination on the basis of religious belief, and other forms of discrimination, to single-handedly explore and devise alternative solutions to the problem short of constituting undue hardship.

CHAPTER 11 | *The Complaint Process*

1. HUMAN RIGHTS COMMISSION

A. Commissioners

Section 27 of the Ontario *Human Rights Code*, R.S.O. 1990, c. H.19, provides that the Ontario Human Rights Commission shall be composed of such persons, being not fewer than seven as are appointed by the Lieutenant Governor in Council. The Commission itself, consisting of a chair, a vice-chair and other commissioners, is ultimately responsible to the Minister of Citizenship for the administration of the Ontario *Human Rights Code*.

Under the *Canadian Human Rights Act*, R.S.C. 1985, c. H-6, the Canadian Human Rights Commission, consisting of not less than three or more than six members other than the chief commissioner and a deputy chief commissioner, are appointed by the Governor in Council. Both the chief commissioner and the deputy chief commissioner are full time members of the Commission and the other members may be appointed as full time or part time members of the Commission. The full time members of the Commission may be appointed for a term not exceeding seven years and each part time member may be appointed for a term not exceeding three years. Members of the Commission hold office during good behaviour but may be removed by the Governor in Council.[1]

B. Commission Staff

As of April 30, 1992, the Ontario Human Rights Commission had a total of 241 employees, seventy-seven of whom were working at its head office in central Toronto and the balance being employed at various commission offices around the province.[2] The employees of the Commission are appointed under the *Public Service Act*, R.S.O. 1990, c. P.47.[3]

Under s. 32 (1) of the *Canadian Human Rights Act* such officers and employees as are necessary for the proper conduct of the work of the Canadian

---

[1] Section 26 of the *Canadian Human Rights Act*, R.S.C. 1985, c. H-6, as amended.
[2] Ontario Human Rights Code Review Task Force, ''Achieving Equality: A Report on Human Rights Reform''(Toronto, Policy Services Branch, Ministry of Citizenship, 1992), at p. 18.
[3] Section 27(5) of the Ontario *Human Rights Code*.

Human Rights Commission are appointed in accordance with the *Public Service Employment Act*, R.S.C. 1985, c. P-33. In addition, the Commission has the authority to enter into contracts for the services of persons having technical or specialized knowledge of any matter relating to the work of the Commission, on a project-by-project basis.[4]

C. Mandate

The function of the Ontario Human Rights Commission is specifically enumerated in s. 29 of the Code and includes the following:

    (a) to forward the policy that the dignity and worth of every person be recognized and that equal rights and opportunities be provided without discrimination that is contrary to law;

    (b) to promote an understanding and acceptance of and compliance with the Ontario *Human Rights Code*;

    (c) to recommend for consideration special plans or programs in accordance with the provisions of s. 14(1) of the Code;

    (d) to develop and conduct programs of public information and education, as well as undertaking, directing and encouraging research;

    (e) to examine and review existing provincial legislation, programs and policies on an ongoing basis, in order to ensure that they are consistent with the intent of the Ontario *Human Rights Code*;

    (f) to promote, assist and encourage public, municipal or private agencies, organizations, groups or persons to engage in programs to alleviate tensions and conflicts based upon identification by a prohibited ground of discrimination;

    (g) to enforce the Ontario *Human Rights Code* and orders of boards of inquiry.[5]

The mandate of the Canadian Human Rights Commission, which is found in s. 7 of the *Canadian Human Rights Act*, includes most of the powers, duties and functions of the Ontario Human Rights Commission as enumerated above, as well as the power to issue guidelines setting out the extent to which and the manner in which, in the opinion of the Commission any provision of the legislation applies in a particular case or in a classic case as described in the guidelines.[6] Such guidelines are, until subsequently revoked or modified, binding on the Canadian Human Rights Commission, a human rights tribunal appointed under the legislation and any review tribunal constituted under s. 56(1) of the Act.[7]

---

[4] Section 32(2) of the *Canadian Human Rights Act*.
[5] See s. 29 of the Ontario *Human Rights Code*.
[6] Section 27(2) of the *Canadian Human Rights Act*.
[7] Rep. & sub. R.S.C. 1985, c. 31 (1st Supp.), s. 67.

D. Accountability

In the case of both the Ontario Human Rights Commission and the Canadian Human Rights Commission, the respective commissioners are both responsible to the Lieutenant Governor in Council in certain respects. The Ontario Human Rights Commission is also responsible to the provincial Minister of Citizenship for the administration of the legislation.

2. FILING A COMPLAINT

A. Who May Initiate a Complaint?

(i) Under the Ontario Human Rights Code

Section 32 (1) of the Ontario *Human Rights Code* provides:

> 32(1) Where a person believes that a right of the person under this Act has been infringed, the person may file with the Commission a complaint in a form approved by the Commission.

The specific wording of this section seems to suggest that a complaint has to be filed by the individual who is the victim of the discriminatory conduct in question. A logical corollary to this proposition is that an individual or entity other than the victim of the discriminatory conduct is without standing to file a complaint. Accordingly, on an objective reading of s. 32(1) of the Ontario *Human Rights Code*, public interest groups and other third parties do not have the ability to file a complaint on behalf of another individual or group of individuals.

However, under s. 32(2):

> 32(2) The Commission may initiate a complaint by itself or at the request of any person.

This subsection of the legislation indicates that a third party who, for whatever reason, wishes to ensure the initiation of a complaint with respect to discriminatory actions aimed at some other individual or group of individuals, would be required to request and/or encourage the Ontario Human Rights Commission to initiate such a complaint, as opposed to the complaint being filed directly by the third party.

(ii) Under the Canadian Human Rights Act

Section 40 of the *Canadian Human Rights Act* contains very specific provisions relating to the individuals empowered to initiate a complaint, the requirement of consent of a victim and joint or combined complaints:

> 40(1) Subject to subsections (5) and (7), any individual or group of individuals having reasonable grounds for believing that a person is engaging or has engaged in a discriminatory practice may file with the Commission a complaint in a form acceptable to the Commission.

(2) If a complaint is made by someone other than the individual who is alleged to be the victim of the discriminatory practice to which the complaint relates, the Commission may refuse to deal with the complaint unless the alleged victim consents thereto.

(3) Where the Commission has reasonable grounds for believing that a person is engaging or has engaged in a discriminatory practice, the Commission may initiate a complaint.

(4) Where complaints are filed jointly or separately by more than one individual or group alleging that a particular person is engaging or has engaged in a discriminatory practice or series of similar discriminatory practices and the Commission is satisfied that the complaints involve substantially the same issues of fact and law, it may deal with those complaints together under this Part and may request the President of the Human Rights Tribunal Panel to appoint a single Human Rights Tribunal pursuant to section 49 to inquire into those complaints.[8]

It is clear that a complaint may be directly initiated by a third party, as opposed to the victim of the discriminatory practice, under the *Canadian Human Rights Act*.

B. Time Limitations

(i) Under the Ontario Human Rights Code

Section 34(1)(d) of the Ontario *Human Rights Code* stipulates that:

34(1) Where it appears to the Commission that,

. . . . .

(d) the facts upon which the complaint is based occurred more than six months before the complaint was filed, unless the Commission is satisfied that the delay was incurred in good faith and that no substantial prejudice will result to any person affected by the delay,
the Commission may, in its discretion, decide to not deal with the complaint.

It is technically inaccurate to characterize s. 34(1)(d) as being a time limitation under the Ontario *Human Rights Code*. It is clear that a complaint filed more than six months after the fact, even in circumstances where the Commission is satisfied that the delay was not incurred in good faith and/or that substantial prejudice would result to any person affected by the delay, at best provides a basis on which the Commission may decide to exercise its discretion not to deal with the complaint. While complainants are well advised to file a complaint within six months of the event, for the purpose of avoiding any potential problem under s. 34(1)(d), failure to do so by no means makes the complaint statute barred. Furthermore, it is significant to note that the legislation does not set out any guidelines or criteria upon which the Commission ought to base its exercise of discretion whether or not to deal with a complaint that is filed more than six months after the event.

---

[8] R.S.C. 1985, c. 31 (1st Supp.), s. 62.

One Ontario board of inquiry has argued that there is no discretion to dismiss a complaint on the basis of delay in initiating proceedings:

> My own view is that while unreasonable delay might be a factor to be taken into account in refusing or fashioning a remedy . . . or in weighing the persuasive force or credibility of testimony or other evidence, delay in initiating or processing a complaint should not be considered a basis for dismissing the complaint at the outset of the proceedings before a board of inquiry unless it has given rise to a situation in which the board of inquiry is of the view that the facts relating to the incident in question cannot be established with sufficient certainty to constitute the basis of a determination that a contravention of the *Code* has occurred.[9]

The Ontario Court of Appeal in *West End Construction Ltd. v. Ontario (Ministry of Labour)*[10] held that the time-limit set out in the Ontario *Limitations Act*, R.S.O. 1990, c. L.15, did not apply to proceedings under the *Human Rights Code*. In essence, the court held that a complaint under the Ontario *Human Rights Code* cannot be characterized as an "action" within the meaning of the *Limitations Act*. Mr. Justice Finlayson speaking on behalf of the Court of Appeal in the *West End Construction* case stated, in part:

> In my opinion, the Code is neither fish nor fowl for limitation purposes. It does not create any cause of action which fits within the traditional format of the *Limitations Act*. This is demonstrated by the problems that counsel, the board of inquiry and the Divisional Court have had in attempting to bring it within an alien statutory framework.
>
> . . . . .
>
> "Action" within the meaning of the *Judicature Act* and the present *Courts of Justice Act*, 1984, S.O. 1984, c. 11, s. 1, refers to "civil proceedings" instituted in a variety of ways by a person seeking a remedy for a civil wrong, but the "action" is "commenced" as of right. It is not a request for assistance, but constitutes the unilateral implementation of a dispute resolution mechanism in accordance with prescribed rules.
>
> What occurs under the Code is more analogous to a civil proceeding than to a penal or criminal one, but it does not invoke the machinery of the civil process . . . If there is to be a limitation period, it must be fashioned to fit the Code.
>
> . . . . .
>
> The inappropriateness of the *Limitations Act* applying at all is illustrated by the order of the board under appeal. The discrimination that gave rise to the complaints of Tabar and Lee found its roots in the respondent Scott's dislike of East Indians and his refusal on behalf of West End to permit the assignment of a tuck shop lease to a person of that race or origin.
>
> . . . . .
>
> The *Limitations Act* never contemplated socio-economic and pro-active

---

[9] *Hyman v. Southam Murray Printing Ltd.* (1981), 3 C.H.R.R. D/617 (Ont. Bd. Inq.), at p. D/621.

[10] (1989), 62 D.L.R. (4th) 329, 34 O.A.C. 332 (C.A.).

legislation which permits remedies never before available to an aggrieved person and creates its own enforcement process . . . It is intended to ensure that the dignity of our citizenry is sustained and it is designed to maintain that purpose through administrative and judicial mechanisms which are quite alien to our traditional common law and statutory remedies. In short, the Code was never within the ambit of the *Limitations Act* and until the 1981 re-enactment, no limitation period applied to complaints under the Code.[11]

(ii) Under the Canadian Human Rights Act

Section 41(*e*) of the *Canadian Human Rights Act* provides:

> 41. Subject to section 40, the Commission shall deal with any complaint filed with it unless in respect of that complaint it appears to the Commission that
>
> . . . . .
>
> > (*e*) the complaint is based on acts or omissions the last of which occurred more than one year, or such longer period of time as the Commission considers appropriate in the circumstances, before receipt of the complaint.

As in the Ontario *Human Rights Code*, it is a misnomer to refer to this provision as constituting a time limitation. On the contrary, the Canadian Human Rights Commission is expressly vested with the jurisdiction to extend the otherwise applicable twelve-month time period in circumstances whereby it considers the extension to be appropriate. Furthermore, it is significant to note that the specific wording of s. 41(*e*) expressly recognizes, by implication, those discriminatory practices which are of an ongoing and continuing nature, as opposed to a single discriminatory event at a fixed point in time.

The Manitoba Court of Appeal in *Manitoba v. Manitoba (Manitoba Human Rights Commission)*[12] made the following statement in relation to the distinction between a "continuing contravention" of human rights legislation, as opposed to a separate or single contravention:

> To be a "continuing contravention", there must be a succession or repetition of separate acts of discrimination of the same character. There must be present acts of discrimination which could be considered as separate contraventions of the Act, and not merely one act of discrimination which may have continuing effects or consequences.[13]

C. Extent of Detail

(i) Under the Ontario Human Rights Code

Section 32(1) of the Ontario *Human Rights Code* provides that a complaint filed with the Commission must be in a "form approved by the Commission".

---

[11] *Supra*, at pp. 335-41.
[12] (1983), 150 D.L.R. (3d) 524, [1983] 6 W.W.R. 18 (Man. Q.B.), affd 2 D.L.R. (4th) 759, [1984] 2 W.W.R. 289 (Man. C.A.).
[13] *Supra*, at p. 764 (C.A.).

In *Dubajic v. Walbar Machine Products of Canada Ltd.*[14] the issue as to the sufficiency of the information contained in the complaint was squarely addressed by the Board of Inquiry. In that case, counsel for the respondent relied upon s. 8 of the Ontario *Statutory Powers Procedures Act*[15] which provides that any party whose "good character, propriety of conduct or competence" is in issue is to receive "reasonable information of any allegations with respect thereto". After conducting a review of the law with respect to the provision of particulars in civil litigation, Professor Gorsky stated:

> My view of section 8 of the *Act* is that it was introduced to regulate one aspect of procedural natural justice which must be followed by certain tribunals including a board of inquiry ... Whatever the scope of the information which must be furnished, its purpose is to define the issues and thereby prevent surprise by enabling the party against whom the allegations are made to prepare for the hearing ... Such material facts should include when and where the alleged acts, which raise the issues, occurred, as well as the name of such persons who are referred to in the allegations, subject to the exceptions noted above.[16]

In *Ontario (Human Rights Commission) v. Ontario (Ministry of Education)*[17] an Ontario board of inquiry, which followed the reasoning of Professor Gorsky in the *Dubajic* case, stated, in part:

> The Ontario Case law would seem to be clear that:
> 1. the complaint must contain all the "essential elements", including the identification of the complainant and the victim or class being discriminated against;
> 2. the respondent must be aware of all matters which form a "substantial part of the facts material to the issues". Evidence in support of these facts need not be divulged;
> 3. the respondent must be provided with sufficient information to allow it to prepare to meet all the allegations against it.[18]

As is the case in the civil litigation process, it is extremely difficult and somewhat arbitrary to specifically differentiate between "material facts" in support of the complaint as opposed to the evidence which support some or all of those facts.

(ii) Under the Canadian Human Rights Act

Section 40(1) of the *Canadian Human Rights Act* provides that a complaint filed with the Canadian Human Rights Commission must be "in a form acceptable to the Commission". In *Canada (Human Rights Commission) v. Bell Canada*[19] the Tribunal appointed under the *Canadian Human Rights Act*

---

[14] (1980), 1 C.H.R.R. D/228 (Ont. Bd. Inq.).
[15] R.S.O. 1990, c. S.22, as amended.
[16] *Supra*, footnote 14, at p. D/229.
[17] (1986), 9 C.H.R.R. D/4535 (Ont. Bd. Inq.).
[18] *Supra*, at p. D/712.
[19] (1981), 2 C.H.R.R. D/265 (Can. Trib.).

held that a complaint does not have to be set out in a formal document but can be initiated by way of a letter. In that case, the Commission had written to the respondent that an investigation pursuant to a complaint of discrimination on grounds of religion had failed to substantiate the allegation, but had revealed evidence of discrimination on grounds of sex. When the Commission attempted to adduce this correspondence as constituting a new complaint on grounds of sex, however, the Tribunal ruled that it was inadequate in the sense that it failed to specifically delineate very basic details in relation to the allegation including the identity of the complainant, the time period over which the alleged violation took place, the location of the alleged violation and other material details. In the course of its decision, the Tribunal held that any valid complaint must contain, at a minimum, the following items:

> (a) identification of the complainant, whether it is an individual person, a class, or the Canadian Human Rights Commission itself;
> (b) identification of the victim or the class being discriminated against as the case may be;
> (c) the time during which the violation or the act took place;
> (d) the location of the alleged violation;
> (e) the nature of the discriminatory practice;
> (f) the section and subsection of the legislation upon which the discriminatory practice is based;
> (g) an affirmation by the complainant and/or the Commission that they have reasonable grounds to believe that the conduct constituted a discriminatory practice in violation of the *Canadian Human Rights Act.*

It has been held that the criteria laid down by the Tribunal in the above-noted *Bell Canada* decision is directory in nature, as opposed to being mandatory. For example, in *Campbell v. Hudson Bay Mining & Smelting Co.*,[20] it was held that failure to comply precisely with the requirement of the criteria laid down in the *Bell Canada* decision was not fatal in that the defects in the complaint forms did not result in any prejudice to the respondent.

Finally, it is significant to note that a complaint may be amended prior to or at the hearing, on terms which are reasonable and consistent with the general principles of natural justice. A motion to amend a complaint at the hearing may well be met with the request by the opposite party for some form of an adjournment in order to properly consider and review the amendments, as well as to obtain any evidence that may be adduced at the hearing that is relevant to the amendments to the complaint.

---

[20] (1984), 7 Admin. L.R. 249, 5 C.H.R.R. D/2268 (Can. Trib.).

3. PRE-HEARING DISPOSITION OF A COMPLAINT

A. Dismissal

(i) Under the Ontario Human Rights Code

In addition to the previously noted discretion of the Ontario Human Rights Commission to decide not to deal with a complaint based upon facts which occurred more than six months prior to the filing of the complaint, section 34(1) sets out other criteria upon which the Commission may base its decision not to deal with a complaint:

> 34(1) Where it appears to the Commission that,
> (a) the complaint is one that could or should be more appropriately dealt with under an Act other than this Act;
> (b) the subject-matter of the complaint is trivial, frivolous, vexatious or made in bad faith;
> (c) the complaint is not within the jurisdiction of the Commission;
>
> . . . . .
>
> the Commission may, in its discretion, decide not to deal with the complaint.

There is very little caselaw relating to the criteria that will be considered by the Ontario Human Rights Commission in deciding whether to exercise its discretion in not dealing with a complaint on the basis that it is "trivial, frivolous, vexatious or made in bad faith". This may well be due to the fact that, on an objective reading of s. 34(1) of the Code, the decision to refrain from dealing with a complaint is an administrative decision made by the Commission at the very inception of the complaint, as opposed to a decision that is required to be made on a judicial or *quasi*-judicial basis. Once the Commission decides to deal with a complaint and, accordingly, proceeds to deal with the complaint in any respect whatsoever, including preliminary investigation, it is not then open to a respondent to challenge or attack the complaint on the basis that it is "trivial, frivolous, vexatious or made in bad faith". The only circumstances in which a respondent could legitimately raise this point is where the respondent contends that the Commission did not properly exercise its broad discretion under s. 34(1) of the Ontario *Human Rights Code* in deciding to deal with the complaint. The cases in which a respondent would have a legitimate basis on which to raise this argument are few primarily due to the difficulty in obtaining evidence to support such an allegation.

It is significant to note that the wording of s. 34(1)(b) of the Ontario *Human Rights Code* is very similar to the terminology found in Rule 25.11 of the Ontario Rules of Civil Procedure. It is suggested that, in interpreting s. 34(1)(b) of the Ontario *Human Rights Code*, one ought to consider the principles set out by Ontario courts when interpreting the express provisions of Rule 25.11 of the Ontario Rules of Civil Procedure.

Rule 25.11 of the Ontario Rules of Civil Procedure provides:

> 25.11 The court may strike out or expunge all or part of a pleading or other document, with or without leave to amend, on the ground that the pleading or other document,
> (a) may prejudice or delay the fair trial of the action;
> (b) is scandalous, frivolous or vexatious; or
> (c) is an abuse of the process of the court.

The fundamental principles articulated by Ontario courts in interpreting Rule 25.11 of the Ontario Rules of Civil Procedure include the following:

(i) allegations of fact in the impugned pleading must be taken as true or at least capable of being proved, for the purpose of any motion brought under Rule 25.11;[21]

(ii) the court on a motion under Rule 25.11 has jurisdiction to strike out a pleading or a part of a pleading that does not conform to the rules of pleading or which contains an "untenable plea". An "untenable plea" is one that is clearly impossible of success at law, that has no legal potential whatsoever or one that raises no genuine issue of law. Such a plea is "frivolous or vexatious" or "an abuse of the process of the court";[22]

(iii) a pleading should only be struck out under Rule 25.11 if it can have no effect upon the outcome of the action.[23]

In light of the above-noted principles laid down by Ontario courts in interpreting Rule 25.11 of the Ontario Rules of Civil Procedure, it is submitted that in considering whether to deal with a complaint where there is some question as to whether the complaint is "trivial, frivolous, vexatious or made in bad faith", the Ontario Human Rights Commission is bound to adhere to a procedure that is similar to the following:

(a) all allegations made within the complaint must be taken as true or at least capable of being proved;

(b) assuming all allegations in the complaint to be true or capable of being proved, the question then becomes whether there is any possibility whatsoever of a tribunal deciding that there has been a violation of any of the provisions of the Ontario *Human Rights Code*;

(c) in the event that (b) above is answered in the affirmative or, in the alternative, it cannot be definitively answered in the negative, the Commission ought to proceed to deal with the complaint unless it is

---

[21] See *Unterreiner v. Wilson* (1982), 142 D.L.R. (3d) 588, 40 O.R. (2d) 197 (H.C.J.), affd 146 D.L.R. (3d) 322, 41 O.R. (2d) 472 (C.A.).

[22] See *Panalpina Inc. v. Sharma* (1988), 29 C.P.C. (2d) 222 (Ont. S.C.).

[23] See, for example, *Wood Gundy Inc. v. Financial Trustco Capital Ltd.* (1988), 26 C.P.C. (2d) 274 (Ont. S.C.) and *Peaker v. Canada Post Corp.* (1989), 68 O.R. (2d) 8 (H.C.J.), affd (unreported, November 30, 1990, Ont. C.A.).

satisfied that the complaint is being made in bad faith (i.e., the complainant is seeking to exact some form of revenge against the respondent or is attempting to gain some advantage over the respondent in some other dispute or proceeding which is separate and distinct from the human rights complaint itself).

In the final analysis, it is safe to say that the jurisdiction of the Ontario Human Rights Commission to refrain from dealing with a complaint under s. 34(1)(b) of the Code is to be used sparingly and only in the very clearest of cases.

(ii) Under the Canadian Human Rights Act

In addition to the previously-noted discretion of the Canadian Human Rights Commission to decide not to deal with a complaint based upon acts or omissions the last of which occurred more than one year, or such longer period of time as the Commission considers to be appropriate in the circumstances, prior to the filing of the complaint. Other bases on which the Commission may refuse to deal with a complaint are specifically delineated in certain subsections of s. 40 of the Act:

> 40(2) If a complaint is made by someone other than the individual who is alleged to be the victim of the discriminatory practice to which the complaint relates, the Commission may refuse to deal with the complaint unless the alleged victim consents thereto.
>
> . . . . .
>
> (5) No complaint in relation to a discriminatory practice may be dealt with by the Commission under this Part unless the act or omission that constitutes the practice
>
> (a) occurred in Canada and the victim of the practice was at the time of the act or omission either lawfully present in Canada or, if temporarily absent from Canada, entitled to return to Canada;
>
> (b) occurred in Canada and was a discriminatory practice within the meaning of section 8, 10, 12 or 13 in respect of which no particular individual is identifiable as the victim; or
>
> (c) occurred outside Canada and the victim of the practice was at the time of the act or omission a Canadian citizen or an individual lawfully admitted to Canada for permanent residence.
>
> (6) Where a question arises under subsection (5) as to the status of an individual in relation to a complaint, the Commission shall refer the question of status to the appropriate Minister and shall not proceed with the complaint unless the question of status is resolved thereby in favour of the complainant.
>
> (7) No complaint may be dealt with by the Commission pursuant to subsection (1) that relates to the terms and conditions of a super-annuation or pension fund or plan, if the relief sought would require action to be taken that would deprive any contributor to, participant in or member of, the fund or plan of any rights acquired under the fund or plan before March 1, 1978 or of any pension or other benefits accrued under the fund or plan to that date, including
>
> (a) any rights and benefits based on a particular age of retirement; and
>
> (b) any accrued survivor's benefits.

In addition to the above-noted provisions of s. 40, the Act further stipulates certain grounds on which the Commission is not obliged to deal with a complaint. These grounds are set out in s. 41 of the Act:

> 41. Subject to section 40, the Commission shall deal with any complaint filed with it unless in respect of that complaint it appears to the Commission that,
>
> (a) the alleged victim of the discriminatory practice to which the complaint relates ought to exhaust grievance or review procedures otherwise reasonably available;
>
> (b) the complaint is one that could more appropriately be dealt with, initially or completely, according to a procedure provided for under an Act of Parliament other than this Act;
>
> (c) the complaint is beyond the jurisdiction of the Commission;
>
> (d) the complaint is trivial, frivolous, vexatious or made in bad faith.

It is significant to note that the grounds specifically enumerated in s. 41 of the *Canadian Human Rights Act* are not mandatory. In other words, the Canadian Human Rights Commission is clearly provided with a discretion to refuse to deal with a complaint that falls within any of the specific subsections of s. 41, which relate primarily to the availability of alternative remedies, the strict jurisdiction of the Commission as spelled out in s. 40 and the "trivial, frivolous, vexatious or made in bad faith" ground which is identical to s. 34(1)(b) of the Ontario *Human Rights Code*. Finally, it is clear, based on a simple reading of s. 40(5)(c) of the *Canadian Human Rights Act*, that the Commission is empowered to proceed with complaints involving discriminatory practices or conduct which may have taken place physically outside of our Canadian borders. Presumably, this specific provision is meant to provide a remedy primarily for discriminatory practices or conduct which may take place in the course of air travel, railway travel or travel by ship which begins or ends in Canada. While other potential instances of discriminatory practices may technically fall within the realm of this subsection, it would appear that its purpose is primarily to address instances of discriminatory conduct in the course of international travel.

B. Settlement

(i) Under the Ontario Human Rights Code

Section 43 of the Ontario *Human Rights Code* provides as follows:

> 43. Where a settlement of a complaint is agreed to in writing, signed by the parties and approved by the Commmission, the settlement is binding upon the parties, and a breach of the settlement is grounds for a complaint under section 32, and this part applies to the complaint in the same manner as if the breach of the settlement were an infringement of a right under this Act.

A plain reading of s. 43 of the Ontario *Human Rights Code* makes it obvious that a valid and enforceable settlement under the Code requires the approval of the Ontario Human Rights Commission. A logical corollary to this proposition is that any settlement arrived at between the parties at any point in time, which does not have the formal approval of the Human Rights Commission, is not binding and enforceable in the sense that it would preclude the Commission from proceeding with the investigation and ultimate hearing of a complaint. Accordingly, employers who are able to convince employees to sign a release at or about the time of their dismissal, in return for a severance payment, are not in a position to obtain a complete and irrevocable waiver of any complaints under the Ontario *Human Rights Code* since the Commission is not party to the negotiations and resolution of issues between employer and employee. In practice, the Commission may be of the view that such a settlement ought to be final for all purposes. However, there is nothing to preclude the Commission from conducting an investigation and proceeding with a complaint, even in circumstances whereby the employer and employee had reached what appeared to be a final agreement in relation to the termination of the individual's employment.

In *Consumers' Distributing Co. v. Ontario Human Rights Commission*[24] the complainant was represented by a lawyer in agreeing to a settlement. He subsequently contacted the Commission, advised them that he had signed the agreement under duress and requested the Commission to refrain from ratifying the agreement. Ultimately, the Commission did not ratify the agreement. The company sought judicial review of the Commission's decision to refrain from ratifying the agreement on the basis that, in the absence of direct evidence of duress, the Commission was under a statutory duty to uphold the enforcement of settlement agreements between the parties in the same manner that a court would apply general principles of common law relating to enforceability of contracts. In refusing the application, thereby rejecting the contention that the Commission was bound to ratify the agreement, the court stated, in part:

> Any settlement, even if the result of the active intervention of the Commission, would at the end of the day, have to be in consonance with what the Commission judged to promote the policy ends of the statute . . . To say the least, those policy ends are much broader in scope than would be engaged by the mere resolution of the simple issue of whether the complainant was under duress when he signed the agreement of January 18, 1985 . . .
>
> Within the purview of the Commission's duty under s. 28(f), would be a consideration of whether the agreement was procured by duress; however, a decision on that score, one way or the other, would not fulfil the Commission's obligations under s. 28(f). To merely find that a settlement, negotiated without the active intervention and participation of officers of the Commission was not a product of duress would not relieve the Commission of its duty under s. 28(f) to "take appropriate action to eliminate the source of tension or conflict". To take such appropriate action, the Commission would, indeed, have to delve further into the facts than is involved in an ascertainment of whether one agreement was procured by duress.[25]

---

[24] (1987), 36 D.L.R. (4th) 589, 19 O.A.C. 383 (Div. Ct.).
[25] *Supra*, at pp. 594-5.

(ii) Under the Canadian Human Rights Act

The *Canadian Human Rights Act* similarly provides that a settlement, at any point subsequent to the filing of a human rights complaint, must be approved by the Commission in order to be enforceable:

> 48(1) When, at any stage after the filing of a complaint and before the commencement of hearing before a Human Rights Tribunal in respect thereof, a settlement is agreed on by the parties, the terms of the settlement shall be referred to the Commission for approval or rejection.
>
> (2) If the Commission approves or rejects the terms of a settlement referred to in subsection (1), it shall so certify and notify the parties.

4. INVESTIGATION AND CONCILIATION

A. Under the Ontario Human Rights Code

Section 33 of the Ontario *Human Rights Code* is the primary section relating to the investigation of complaints by a member or employee of the Human Rights Commission. The most pertinent subsections of s. 33 are as follows:

> 33(1) Subject to section 34, the Commission shall investigate a complaint and endeavour to effect a settlement.
>
> (2) An investigation by the Commission may be made by a member or employee of the Commission who is authorized by the Commission for the purpose.
>
> (3) A person authorized to investigate a complaint may,
>
>   (a) enter any place, other than a place that is being used as a dwelling, at any reasonable time, for the purpose of investigating the complaint;
>
>   (b) request the production for inspection and examination of documents or things that are or may be relevant to the investigation;
>
>   (c) upon giving a receipt therefor, remove from a place documents produced in response to a request under clause (b) for the purpose of making copies thereof or extracts therefrom and shall promptly return them to the person who produced or furnished them; and
>
>   (d) question a person on matters that are or may be relevant to the complaint subject to the person's right to have counsel or a personal representative present during such questioning, and may exclude from the questioning any person who may be adverse in interest to the complainant.

The balance of s. 33 of the Code sets out specific provisions relating to obtaining warrants in furtherance of an investigation under the Code, penalties for obstruction in the investigation process, admissibility of copies of documents as evidence at the hearing and other such related provisions.

Section 36 of the Code stipulates that where the Commission fails to effect a settlement of the complaint and it appears to the Commission that the procedure is appropriate and the evidence warrants an inquiry, the Commission may request the Minister appoint a board of inquiry and refer to the subject matter of the complaint to the board. Where, on the other hand, the Commission decides not to request the appointment of a board of inquiry, it shall provide reasons for its decision in writing to the complainant, whereby the complainant has a right, under s. 37 of the Code, to have the decision reconsidered by the Commission within fifteen days of having received a copy of the decision.

For many years the Commission has had a backlog of claims causing long delays before claims receive attention. In an endeavour to overcome the backlog, the Commission introduced an "early settlement initiative" by which it tries to quickly settle claims without starting an investigation. According to Commission figures for 1991, 55% of claims were closed at the early settlement stage.[26]

In 1991, only 2% of cases were referred to boards of inquiry. Of the 98% of cases that were not referred to a board of inquiry, a total of 66% were settled; 20% were withdrawn; 10% were dismissed by the Commission and 4% were abandoned. The Commission advises that in 1992 approximately 3% or 4% of cases were referred to boards of inquiry.[27]

If a claim is not settled in the "early settlement initiative" it is usually many months, if not a year or more, before an investigation is begun. The chances of a case being referred to a board of inquiry are very low.[28]

The ordinary or traditional course of investigation of a human rights complaint under the Ontario *Human Rights Code* is summarized by Mary Eberts, in her article "Ontario Human Rights Commission"[29] as follows:

> . . . Firstly the respondent is asked to complete a questionnaire setting out its response to the items in the complaint. Then the parties are asked to attend a fact-finding conference (FFC) chaired by Commission staff, usually the officer in charge of the case and his or her supervisor. The allegations and answers are canvassed with a view to finding whether there is any common ground. No witnesses other than the parties are present at the FFC, and all questions and comments notionally are routed through the Chair. Thus it is very difficult to use the FFC to test the credibility of the other party, or the strength of its case. At the end of the proceedings, there will be a formal break, after which the so called conciliation phase will be embarked upon. The officers will try to discover whether a settlement is possible. Sometimes, they will play a real mediating role, going back and forth between the parties. Other times, they will be quite passive.

> During the FFC, the statements made by the parties will be recorded by Commission staff, and can form part of the record of investigation. At the start of conciliation, however, it is made clear that statements made in that phase are privileged.

> If the FFC produces no settlement, then the case enters the extended investigation phase. The officer will interview witnesses suggested by the complainant and

---

[26] Ontario Human Rights Code Review Task Force, "Achieving Equality: A Report on Human Rights Reform" (Toronto, Policy Services Branch, Ministry of Citizenship, 1992), at p. 17.

[27] *Ibid.*

[28] *Ibid.*

[29] This article is found in Judith Keene, *Human Rights in Ontario*, 2nd ed. (Scarborough, Carswell, 1992), p. 253.

respondent as well as others believed to have knowledge of the events complained of.

At the conclusion of the interviews a report is prepared, containing a summary of the evidence and analysis of investigation findings. Whereas formerly only the gist of that report was shared with the parties, now they have a copy of it, and an opportunity to make submissions in writing on it to the commissioners when they consider the case. Usually, the officer will meet once more with the parties at the end of the investigation to review the findings and attempt a settlement. If this effort is unsuccessful, the report of the case and any submissions by the parties are placed before the commissioners at their next meeting.

B. Under the Canadian Human Rights Act

The pertinent subsections of s. 43 of the *Canadian Human Rights Act* relating to the fundamental components of an investigation, are as follows:

> 43(1) The Commission may designate a person, in this Part referred to as an ''investigator'', to investigate a complaint.
>
> (2) An investigator shall investigate a complaint in a manner authorized by regulations made pursuant to subsection (4) and the Commission may authorize an investigator,
>
> > (a) subject to such limitations as the Governor in Council may prescribe in the interests of national defence or security, at any reasonable time, to enter any premises, other than a private dwelling-place or any part of any premises that is designed to be used and is being used as a permanent or temporary private dwelling-place, and carry out such inquiries as are reasonably necessary for the investigation of the complaint; and
> >
> > (b) to require any individual found at any premises entered pursuant to paragraph (a) to produce for inspection or for the purpose of obtaining copies thereof or extracts therefrom any books or other documents containing any matter relevant to the investigation of the complaint.
>
> (3) No person shall obstruct an investigator in the investigation of a complaint . . .

Section 44 of the Act then provides what is required at the conclusion of an investigation:

(a) the investigator is required to submit to the Commission a report of the findings of the investigation;[30]

(b) the Commission may refer the complainant to another procedure provided for in an Act of Parliament or direct a complainant to exhaust an existing grievance or other procedure, if, in its opinion, that is the appropriate manner in which the complainant ought to proceed;[31]

(c) may adopt the report or dismiss the complaint, depending on whether it is satisfied that the complaint has been substantiated and ought to be referred to a hearing;[32]

---

[30] Section 44(1) of the *Canadian Human Rights Act*.
[31] Section 44(2) of the CHRA.
[32] Section 44(3) (rep. & sub. R.S.C. 1985, c. 31 (1st Supp.), s. 64) of the CHRA.

Under s. 47 of the Act, the Commission may appoint a conciliator at any stage of the proceeding, whether it be at the inception of the complaint, during the investigation of the complaint or at the conclusion of the investigation, for the purpose of attempting to bring about a settlement of the complaint. The conciliator must be someone other than the individual who is appointed to conduct the investigation of the complaint.[33] Any information received by a conciliator in the course of attempting to reach a settlement of a complaint is confidential and may not be disclosed except with the consent of the person who gave the information.[34]

---

[33] Section 47(2) of the CHRA.
[34] Section 47(3) of the CHRA.

CHAPTER 12 | *The Hearing*

1. COMPOSITION OF THE TRIBUNAL

A. Under the Ontario Human Rights Code

Section 38 of the Ontario *Human Rights Code*, R.S.O. 1990, c. H.19, sets out general provisions relating to the appointment of a board of inquiry:

> 38(1) Where the Commission requests the Minister to appoint a board of inquiry, the Minister shall appoint from the panel one or more persons to form the board of inquiry and the Minister shall communicate the names of the persons forming the board to the parties to the inquiry.
>
> (2) A member of the board hearing a complaint must not have taken part in any investigation or consideration of the subject-matter of the inquiry before the hearing and shall not communicate directly or indirectly in relation to the subject-matter of the inquiry with any person or with any party or a representative of the party except upon notice to and opportunity for all parties to participate, but the board may seek legal advice from an adviser independent of the parties and in such case the nature of the advice shall be made known to the parties in order that they may make submissions as to the law.[1]

Typically, the members of the panel referred to in s. 38(1) have been professors of law who have no connection with the Ontario Human Rights Commission.[2] There was recently created an Office of the Boards of Inquiry in order to co-ordinate the individual boards of inquiry which hear human rights claims. The Commission sends cases to the Minister requiring that they be heard by a board of inquiry. The Minister then appoints upon the recommendation of the chair of this office. The office arranges for a hearing. Adjudicators are chosen to hear each human rights claim on a case-by-case basis from a list of thirty-seven persons.[3]

B. Under the Canadian Human Rights Act

Section 49 of the *Canadian Human Rights Act*, R.S.C. 1985, c. H-6, contains the pertinent provisions relating to the appointment of a human rights tribunal:

---

[1] Amended 1993, c. 27, Sched.
[2] Judith Keene, *Human Rights in Ontario*, 2nd ed. (Scarborough, Carswell, 1992), at p. 275.
[3] Ontario Human Rights Code Review Task Force, ''Achieving Equality: A Report on Human Rights Reform'' (Toronto, Policy Services Branch, Ministry of Citizenship, 1992), at p. 19.

49(1) The Commission may, at any stage after the filing of a complaint, request the President of the Human Rights Tribunal Panel to appoint a Human Rights Tribunal, in this Part referred to as a "Tribunal", to inquire into the complaint if the Commission is satisfied that, having regard to all the circumstances of the complaint, an inquiry into the complaint is warranted.

(1.1) On receipt of a request under subsection (1), the President of the Human Rights Tribunal Panel shall appoint a Tribunal to inquire into the complaint to which the request relates.

(2) A Tribunal may not be composed of more than three members.

(3) No member, officer or employee of the Commission, and no individual who has acted as investigator or conciliator in respect of the complaint in relation to which a Tribunal is appointed, is eligible to be appointed to the Tribunal.

. . . . .

(5) Subject to subsection (5.1), in selecting any individual or individuals to be appointed as a Tribunal, the President of the Human Rights Tribunal Panel shall select from among the members of the Human Rights Tribunal Panel.

(5.1) The President of the Human Rights Tribunal Panel may sit as a Tribunal or as a member of a Tribunal.

(6) Subject to subsection (7), where a Tribunal consists of more than one member, the President of the Human Rights Tribunal Panel shall designate one of the members to be the Chairman of the Tribunal.[4]

The issue as to whether boards of inquiry, appointed under provincial human rights legislation and under the *Canadian Human Rights Act*, exercise powers analogous to superior court judges, thereby violating the provisions of the Constitution, has been considered in a number of cases. To date, Canadian courts have held that these boards of inquiry do not exercise functions analogous to those assigned under s. 96 of the *Constitution Act, 1867*, to a superior court.[5] Mr. Justice La Forest of the Supreme Court of Canada, in *Scowby v. Glendinning*,[6] dissenting in the result, stated that a board of inquiry appointed pursuant to the *Saskatchewan Human Rights Code* did not exercise functions analogous to those assigned under s. 96 of the *Constitution Act, 1867*, to a superior court. The majority of the court in that decision did not address this issue.

2. DELAY

Neither the Ontario *Human Rights Code*, nor the *Canadian Human Rights Act*, contain any provisions whatsoever relating to the time period within which

---

[4] Rep. & sub. R.S.C. 1985, c. 31 (1st Supp.), s. 66(1), (2).

[5] See, for example, *Janzen v. Platy Enterprises Ltd.* (1986), 33 D.L.R. (4th) 32, [1987] 1 W.W.R. 385 (Man. C.A.), revd 59 D.L.R. (4th) 352, [1989] 1 S.C.R. 1252; *Re Wong and Manitoba Human Rights Commission* (1986), 29 D.L.R. (4th) 634, [1986] 5 W.W.R. 120 *sub nom. Human Rights Act (Man.) (Re)* (Man. Q.B.); *Commodore Business Machines Ltd. v. Olarte* (1984), 14 D.L.R. (4th) 118, 49 O.R. (2d) 17, *sub nom. Commodore Business Machines Ltd. v. Minister of Labour* (Div. Ct.).

[6] (1986), 32 D.L.R. (4th) 161, 29 C.C.C. (3d) 1 (S.C.C.).

a complaint must proceed to a hearing. Furthermore, neither piece of legislation makes any reference whatsoever to any consequence or penalty which may be invoked in the event that a tribunal is of the opinion that there has been unreasonable or inordinate delay with respect to the complaint proceeding to the hearing state. There have, however, been numerous preliminary motions brought at the commencement of proceedings in many of the various provinces and under the *Canadian Human Rights Act*, requesting that the complaint be either stayed or dismissed on the basis that there was inordinate delay in having the matter proceed to a hearing. These motions have been brought based on general principles of natural justice which apply to hearings conducted by both statutorily constituted tribunals and the courts. It is beyond the scope of this book to review all of these decisions in a comprehensive and methodical way. Rather, the authors propose to briefly make reference to a few of the leading decisions in this area in order to provide the reader with some insight and appreciation in relation to this very important procedural issue.

Motions to dismiss or stay a complaint on the basis of delay are often framed on the basis of general principles of natural justice, as well as certain fundamental provisions of the *Canadian Charter of Rights and Freedoms*. Section 7 of the Charter provides:

> 7. Everyone has the right to life, liberty and security of the person and the right not to be deprived thereof except in accordance with the principles of fundamental justice.

In addition, s. 11(*b*) of the Charter stipulates that "any person charged with an offence has the right to be tried within a reasonable time". While the courts have been reluctant to characterize a complaint under human rights legislation as an "offence", as the term is used in the context of s. 11(*b*) of the Charter, the primary issue addressed by human rights tribunals on these motions relate to whether principles of natural justice and "fundamental justice" have been violated in the circumstances by virtue of the delay and the reasons for the delay, if any, in each individual case.

In *Saskatchewan Human Rights Commission v. Kodellas*,[7] the majority of the Saskatchewan Court of Appeal reviewed a decision of Mr. Justice McClennan, a justice of the court of Queen's Bench in which the judge issued an order prohibiting the Board of Inquiry from inquiring into a complaint, the particulars of which may be summarized as follows:

    (a) two complainants alleged that Kodellas had sexually harassed them;

    (b) their complaints were filed in August, 1982 and May, 1983;

    (c) a board of inquiry was appointed in March, 1985;

---

[7] (1986), 34 D.L.R. (4th) 30, [1987] 2 W.W.R. 195 (Sask. Q.B.), vard 60 D.L.R. (4th) 143, [1989] 5 W.W.R. 1 (Sask. C.A.).

(d) the respondents brought an application for a writ of *certiorari* to quash the appointment of the Board and for an order prohibiting the human rights commission from taking any further action in relation to these complaints;

(e) the application was founded upon ss. 7 and 11(*b*) of the *Canadian Charter of Rights and Freedoms.*

A unanimous Saskatchewan Court of Appeal concluded that no stay of proceedings pursuant to the Charter of Rights should issue in respect of the corporate respondent, Tripolis Foods Limited, while upholding the order for a stay in relation to the complaints as against the personal respondent Kodellas. Each one of the three justices of the Saskatchewan Court of Appeal delivered separate judgments and two of the three judges provided similar lists of factors to be considered in determining whether there was an "unreasonable delay", which included the following:

(i) whether the delay is *prima facie* unreasonable, having regard to the time constraints inherent in such a remedial proceeding;

(ii) the reason for the delay, with reference to the conduct of the complainant, the respondent (including any acquiescence or a waiver) and the Commission (including consideration of the institutional resources available to the Commission);

(iii) prejudice or impairment to the accused or wrongdoer.

In the final analysis, the Saskatchewan Court of Appeal agreed with Mr. Justice McClellan with respect to his finding that the personal respondent's constitutional rights under s. 7 of the *Canadian Charter of Rights and Freedoms* had been violated in the circumstances and that the appropriate remedy for that infringement of the Charter of Rights was the granting of a stay of the complaint as against the personal respondent.

A recent decision of an Ontario board of inquiry in *Hancock v. Shreve*[8] had the effect of reviving the prevalence of preliminary motions to dismiss human rights complaints on the basis of delay. The pertinent facts of the *Shreve* case are:

(a) in 1986, Allan Shreve, a black individual, was refused employment by the City of Windsor as a meter attendant;

(b) Mr. Shreve filed a human rights complaint in August, 1986;

(c) the complaint was finally processed by the Ontario Human Rights Commission in 1989;

(d) a board of inquiry was appointed to hear the complaint in May, 1992.

The Board of Inquiry ruled, in rejecting the complaint, that the Commission had taken too long in its investigation. The only explanation offered by

---

[8] (1993), 93 C.L.L.C. ¶17,024, 18 C.H.R.R. D/363, *sub nom. Shreve v. Windsor (City)* (Ont. Bd. Inq.).

the Commission for the extraordinary delay was that the investigating officer "because of her workload . . . was unable to spend more concentrated time on the file".[9] The Board, however, was non-committal on whether delay alone would have resulted in the rejection of the complaint.

In this case, however, the delay was coupled with a finding of bias on the part of the commission officer which deprived the city of a fair hearing. The Board ruled:

> In combination, however, the circumstances seriously prejudice the ability of the Respondents to prepare their case in a timely fashion. This violates the principle of fairness. It causes a prejudice that cannot really be cured at the Board of Inquiry stage since one power a Board definitely lacks is that to turn back the clock.[10]

As a result of the combination of delay in conducting the investigation and bias on the part of the investigating officer, who adopted an advocacy role on the part of the complainant, the Board of Inquiry felt it appropriate to reject the complaint of Mr. Shreve. The only consolation the Board of Inquiry was able to offer Mr. Shreve was that his decision "may have some effect in reforming the process of the Commission" to the ultimate benefit of complainants and respondents.[11]

A more recent decision of an Ontario board of inquiry on the issue of delay was rendered in the case of *Koba v. Brave Beaver Press Workers (Turbo Press)*.[12] In the *Koba* case, the complainant filed her complaint on November 20, 1986, and a full six years elapsed before the matter was heard by the Board. Counsel for the respondents moved for dismissal on the grounds of excessive delay, claiming that in view of the unavailability of witnesses deemed essential by the two respondents, they were severely prejudiced and incapable of mounting a full defence. In spite of the Board of Inquiry's finding that a delay of six years appeared to be "inordinate", and raised questions as to whether it constituted an abuse of process, the Board of Inquiry, nonetheless, dismissed the motion, stating in part:

> . . . though significant or even gross delay is regrettable, the case can go forward unless prejudice or abuse of process can be shown. What criteria are to be used in determining whether prejudice or abuse of process have occurred? The test most commonly referred to is found in Hyman: dismissal of the complaint is justified
> (1) if the delay gives rise to a new situation where facts cannot be established with sufficient certainty to determine contravention of the Code;
> (2) if passage of time has made it impossible to ascertain the relevant facts.
>
> . . . . .

---

[9] *Supra*, at p. 16,228.
[10] *Supra*, at p. 16,233.
[11] *Supra*, at p. 16,234. See article by M. Norman Grosman, "Human Rights Process Dealt Severe Blow", The Employment Bulletin, Vol. 3, Issue No. 2, April 1993.
[12] (unreported, July 19, 1993, Ont. Bd. Inq.).

It is in the nature of harassment complaints that they usually occur away from the eyes of witnesses, and that therefore claim and counter-claim must be adjudged by inference and assumption. Mr. Dunlop and Ms Koba are the only ones who know what took place, and this Board must decide on the balance of probabilities who is right and who is wrong. This represents a configuration with which the public has lately become thoroughly familiar through the wide publicity the U.S. Senate confirmation hearings of a judge [now justice] Clarence Thomas and the claims of sexual harassment made by Professor Anita Hill.[13]

While it is unclear whether the nature of the complaint in the *Koba* case, a complaint of sexual harassment, significantly affected the decision of the Board of Inquiry to dismiss the motion, the case, nonetheless, stands as an authoritative decision on the subject of dismissing a human rights complaint on the basis of delay.

Perhaps the leading decision on the subject of delay in human rights complaints is the 1981 decision of an Ontario board of inquiry in *Hyman v. Southam Murray Printing Ltd.*,[14] in which the Board stated, in part:

> . . . while unreasonable delay might be a factor to be taken into account in refusing or fashioning a remedy . . . or in weighing the persuasive force or credibility of testimony or evidence, delay in initiating or processing a complaint should not be considered a basis for dismissing a complaint at the outset of the proceedings unless the Board of Inquiry is of the view that the facts relating to the incident in question cannot be established with sufficient certainty to constitute the basis of a determination that a contravention of the Code has occurred. Having been assigned, by an order of the Minister, a statutorily defined task of undertaking an inquiry . . . the Board should attempt to do so, notwithstanding the passage of considerable time, unless the passage of time has made the task impossible.[15]

3. UNBIASED TRIBUNAL

One of the fundamental principles of our Canadian legal system is the right to have a matter determined by an independent, impartial and objective tribunal. This critical requirement of natural justice has equal application to hearings conducted under human rights legislation.

Where there is a reasonable apprehension of bias in relation to the individual or individuals appointed as a tribunal in a human rights complaint, there is a legitimate legal basis on which to challenge the constitution of the tribunal. The recent decision of the Ontario Divisional Court in *Great Atlantic & Pacific Co. of Canada Ltd. v. Ontario (Human Rights Commission)*[16] provides an example of a court ordering that the appointment of the Board of Inquiry be

---

[13] *Supra*, at p. 4 of unreported judgment.
[14] (1981), 3 C.H.R.R. D/617 (Ont. Bd. Inq.).
[15] *Supra*, at p. D/621.
[16] (1993), 109 D.L.R. (4th) 214, 65 O.A.C. 227 (Div. Ct.).

struck out, in very interesting factual circumstances. The pertinent facts of the
A & P case may be summarized as follows:

(a) in November, 1985, Diane Gale filed a complaint against Miracle
Food Mart, a division of Steinbergs Incorporated, alleging sexual
discrimination against the company under the Ontario *Human Rights
Code*;

(b) in December, 1989, the Ontario Human Rights Commission filed a
complaint against the United Food and Commercial Food Workers
International Union, Local 175 and 633, alleging a violation of Ms
Gale's rights under the Code on the basis of sex discrimination;

(c) in 1991, Professor Constance Backhouse was appointed as the Board
of Inquiry to whom both complaints were referred to a hearing;

(d) in 1992, A & P, which had purchased certain assets from Steinbergs
Inc. in 1990, was added by the Board as a party respondent to the
Gale complaint;

(e) a number of preliminary motions were brought, at the outset of the
hearing, by both the union and A & P, including a motion for removal
of the Board of Inquiry on the basis that there was a reasonable
apprehension of bias on the part of the Board;

(f) Professor Backhouse ruled that there was no reasonable apprehension
of bias on her part and both A & P and the union applied to the Ontario
Divisional Court for judicial review of that decision.

It was argued by A & P and the union that there was a reasonable
apprehension of bias on the part of Professor Backhouse, having regard to the
following facts:

(i) in 1987, Professor Backhouse was one of 250 people who filed a
complaint with the Ontario Human Rights Commission alleging that
Osgoode Hall Law School had violated the provisions of the Code
by reason of systemic sex discrimination;

(ii) in addition to Professor Backhouse being a party complainant in a
human rights complaint, she had been involved as an ''advocate'' in
matters and issues involving sex discrimination prior to her appointment as a board of inquiry;

(iii) Professor Backhouse, at the time of her employment as Board of
Inquiry, was an Associate Professor at the Faculty of Law of the
University of Western Ontario for several years and during that time
she had written extensively on the subject of ''sex discrimination''.

In granting an order to quash the proceedings before the Board, thereby
effectively striking the appointment of Professor Backhouse as a board of
inquiry, the Ontario Divisional Court stated, in part:

> In our view, the unique aspect of this case is that Miss Backhouse went
> beyond the position of an advocate and descended personally, as a party, into the

very arena over which she has been appointed to preside in relation to the very same issues she has to decide.

By becoming a personal complainant before the very Commission that was prosecuting the similar case before her, she personally selected one of the parties before her as her own advocate to pursue her personal complaint about the same issue.

Counsel are in agreement that there has been no decided case in this province which deals with an allegation of systemic discrimination on the grounds of sex. Miss Backhouse is therefore in a position, in this case, should she continue as the Board, to vindicate the position she had taken as a personal complainant in a similar case. It is trite to state that simple justice requires a high degree of neutrality. We do not think that would be attained if Miss Backhouse was to continue as the Board. In our opinion, the appropriate test has not been met.[17]

It is important to note that the primary basis on which the Ontario Divisional Court granted the relief requested in the *A & P* decision, related to Professor Backhouse's historical involvement as a party complainant in a complaint of sex discrimination, as opposed to her career as a well-known advocate and legal academic on the subject of sex discrimination. There have been a number of decisions in which the appointment of a board has been challenged on the ground of reasonable apprehension of bias having regard to the personal and professional attributes of Board members, without success.[18]

4. PRE-HEARING DISCLOSURE

There are no specific provisions contained within the Ontario *Human Rights Code* or the *Canadian Human Rights Act* relating to the nature and extent of the Commission's obligation to disclose information and documentation with respect to the complaint prior to the hearing. The rules and principles that have developed in relation to this issue are the product of miscellaneous statutory provisions and general principles of natural justice set out by the courts.

In Ontario, the *Statutory Powers Procedure Act*, R.S.O. 1990, c. S.22, prescribes minimal procedural rules for the conduct of proceedings of administrative tribunals governed by the Act. In essence, virtually every proceeding by a tribunal in the exercise of a statutory power of decision conferred by or under an act of the legislature of Ontario is subject to the provisions of this Act, subject to certain exceptions that are specified in s. 3(2) of the Act. The proceedings before a board of inquiry appointed under the Ontario *Human Rights Code* are clearly subject to the provisions of the *Statutory Powers Procedure Act* ("SPPA"). The specific provisions of the Act which pertain to

---

[17] *Supra*, at p. 224.
[18] See, for example, *Rajput v. Algoma University* (unreported, 1976, Ont. Bd. Inq.).

a duty of disclosure of information and documentation prior to a hearing are as follows:

> 8. Where the good character, propriety of conduct or competence of a party is an issue in a proceeding, the party is entitled to be furnished prior to the hearing with reasonable information of any allegations with respect thereto.
>
> . . . . .
>
> 12(1) A tribunal may require any person, including a party, by summons,
>> (a) to give evidence on oath or affirmation at a hearing; and
>> (b) to produce in evidence at a hearing documents and things specified by the tribunal,
>
> relevant to the subject-matter of the proceeding and admissible at a hearing.

The above-noted sections of the SPPA are, in essence, a codification of certain general principles of natural justice that have been developed by the courts over the years in addressing issues of procedure as they relate to administrative tribunals.

A recent decision of the Ontario Divisional Court sets out certain authoritative principles in relation to the rules of disclosure in a proceeding under the Ontario *Human Rights Code*. In *Ontario Human Rights Commission v. House*,[19] the court was required to consider an application for judicial review of the decision of the Board of Inquiry to order production of witness statements and other documents relating to the investigation of complaints made pursuant to the provisions of the Ontario *Human Rights Code*. In upholding the decision of the Board of Inquiry and dismissing the application of the Ontario Human Rights Commission, the court stated, in part:

> The applicant equates proceedings under the *Human Rights Code* to the civil rather than the criminal process. It is in our view significant that in civil proceedings the "full discovery of documents and oral examination of parties and even witnesses are familiar features of the practice". The important principle enunciated by Mr. Justice Sopinka [in *R. v. Stinchcombe*[20]] is that "justice was better served when the element of surprise was eliminated from the trial and the parties were prepared to address issues *on the basis of complete information of the case to be met*" (Emphasis added.) It does not take a quantum leap to come to the conclusion that in the appropriate case, justice will be better served in proceedings under the *Human Rights Code* when there is complete information available to the respondents.
>
> *R. v. Stinchcombe* also recognized that the "fruits of the investigation" in the possession of the Crown "are not the property of the Crown for use in securing a conviction but the property of the public to be used to ensure that justice be done" (p. 331 [of S.C.R.]). We are of the opinion that this point applies with equal force to the proceedings before a Board of Inquiry and that the fruits of the investigations are not the property of the Commission.

---

[19] (1993), 67 O.A.C. 72 (Div. Ct.).
[20] (1991), 68 C.C.C. (3d) 1, [1991] 3 S.C.R. 326.

We are also of the opinion, while not necessary to our decision, that the role of Commission counsel is analogous to that of the Crown in criminal proceedings.

"It cannot be over-emphasized that the purpose of a criminal prosecution is not to obtain a conviction, it is to bring before a jury, what the Crown considers to be credible evidence relevant to what is alleged to be a crime."

R. v. Stinchcombe, p. 333.

"The tradition of Crown counsel in this country in carrying out their role as 'Ministers of Justice' and not as adversaries has generally been very high."

R. v. Stinchcombe, p. 341[21]

Prior to the decision of the Ontario Divisional Court in the *House* case, referred to above, Ontario human rights tribunals took a more limited view as to the nature and extent of disclosure by the Commission prior to a hearing. The Board of Inquiry in *Dubajic v. Walbar Machine Products of Canada Ltd.*[22] illustrates the traditionally accepted position of Ontario boards of inquiry on the subject of disclosure:

My view of section 8 of the *Act* [the *Statutory Powers Procedures Act*] is that it was introduced to regulate one aspect of procedural natural justice which must be followed by certain tribunals including a board of inquiry appointed pursuant to section 14(a)(1) of the *Code*. Whatever the scope of the information which must be furnished, its purpose is to define the issues and thereby prevent surprise by enabling the party against whom the allegations are made to prepare for the hearing. At the very least, section 8 of the *Act* in order to fulfil this purpose would require that Walbar be furnished with a written statement of the material facts on which the Commission intends to rely in support of the allegations with respect to the issues involving Walbar's good character or the propriety of its conduct. Such material facts should include when and where the alleged acts, which raised the issues, occurred, as well as the names of such persons who are referred to in the allegations, subject to the exceptions above-noted.[23]

Whether the position of human rights boards of inquiry on the subject of pre-hearing disclosure will change significantly as a result of the recent Ontario Divisional Court decision in *House* remains to be seen.

5. PROCEDURAL RULES

Both the Ontario *Human Rights Code* and the *Canadian Human Rights Act* are completely silent in relation to the procedure to be followed on hearings that are conducted by boards of inquiry. It is doubtful that this constitutes an innocent omission from the legislation. On the contrary, it would appear to be

---

[21] *Supra*, footnote 19, at pp. 76-7.
[22] (1980), 1 C.H.R.R. D/228 (Ont. Bd. Inq.).
[23] *Supra*, at p. D/229.

the intention of the legislature that, having regard to the very special nature of human rights legislation, it would logically follow that there be few restrictions placed upon the procedure to be followed by a board of inquiry. In essence, a board of inquiry has the jurisdiction to determine its own procedure subject to the general rules and principles of natural justice.

Authority for this proposition may be found in the decision of the Ontario Divisional Court in *Re Metropolitan Toronto Board of Commissioners of Police and Ontario Human Rights Commission.*[24] In that case, the court dismissed various applications for judicial review of certain decisions of a board of inquiry constituted under the Ontario *Human Rights Code*, R.S.O. 1970, c. 318. In rejecting the argument that the Board of Inquiry erred in refusing to grant an adjournment, Mr. Justice Labrosse, speaking on behalf of the court, stated:

> Finally, in respect of the adjournment granted to counsel for the board, to permit him to examine the records, this was purely a matter of discretion. The board has exclusive jurisdiction over the conduct of its procedure and the exercise of its discretion to grant the adjournment is not reviewable by this Court, provided that the board has not violated recognized principles of fairness or conducted itself in such a way as to amount to a refusal of jurisdiction, which is not the case here.[25]

6. ONUS AND BURDEN OF PROOF

The Supreme Court of Canada in *Etobicoke (Borough) v. Ontario (Human Rights Commission)*[26] made the following authoritative statement of principle in relation to both the onus and standard of proof in a human rights hearing:

> Once a complainant has established before a board of inquiry a *prima facie* case of discrimination, in this case proof of a mandatory retirement at age 60 as a condition of employment, he is entitled to relief in the absence of justification by the employer. The only justification which can avail the employer in the case at bar, is the proof, the burden of which lies upon him, that such compulsory retirement is a *bona fide* occupational qualification and requirement for the employment concerned. The proof, in my view, must be made according to the ordinary civil standard of proof, that is upon a balance of probabilities.[27]

Accordingly, since the Commission is statutorily vested with carriage of the complaint, it, together with the complainant, bears the onus of establishing a *prima facie* case of discrimination in the first instance, in which case the respondent(s) is obliged to lead evidence which contradicts, casts doubt or otherwise detracts from the *prima facie* case of discrimination or, alternatively, a defence or justification to the discriminatory conduct, failing which the complainant will ultimately succeed on the complaint.

---

[24] (1979), 105 D.L.R. (3d) 108, 27 O.R. (2d) 48 (Div. Ct.).
[25] *Supra*, at p. 113.
[26] (1982), 132 D.L.R. (3d) 14, [1982] 1 S.C.R. 202.
[27] *Supra*, at p. 19.

The Supreme Court of Canada in *Ontario (Human Rights Commission) v. Simpson-Sears Ltd.*[28] has defined a *prima facie* case under human rights legislation as follows:

> A *prima facie* case in this context is one which covers the allegations made and which, if they are believed, is complete and sufficient to justify a verdict in the complainant's favour in the absence of answer from the respondent employer.[29]

It is misleading to adopt the notion or concept of a shifting of the evidential burden in a human rights hearing. In this regard, it is quite common for there to be references to the burden of proof "shifting" to the respondent once a *prima facie* complaint of discrimination has been made by the complainant in the first instance. This erroneous notion is explained by the Supreme Court of Canada in *Snell v. Farrell*:[30]

> These references [i.e., cases that refer to the shifting of the burden] speak of the shifting of the secondary or evidential burden of proof or the burden of adducing evidence. I find it preferable to explain the process without using the term secondary or evidential burden. It is not strictly accurate to speak of the burden shifting to the defendant when what is meant is that evidence adduced by the plaintiff may result in an inference being drawn adverse to the defendant. Whether an inference is or is not drawn is a matter of weighing evidence. The defendant runs the risk of an adverse inference in the absence of evidence to the contrary. This is sometimes referred to as imposing on the defendant a provisional or tactical burden ... In my opinion, this is not a true burden of proof, and use of an additional label to describe what is an ordinary step in the fact-finding process is unwarranted.[31]

The erroneous concept of "shifting burdens" is well illustrated in the recent decision of the Ontario Court of Appeal in *Ontario (Human Rights Commission) v. London Monenco Consultants Ltd.*[32] The facts of the *London Monenco* case may be summarized as follows:

(a) the complainants were unmarried men who were employed at a remote site as an engineer and an architectural planner;

(b) the employer had a policy whereby it offered married employees company-paid return flights to their home base every three weeks, in an effort to attract married senior personnel to the remote site;

(c) the complainants were aware when they accepted employment that, being unmarried, they would not receive a travel allowance but were unaware that marital status was a prohibited ground of discrimination under s. 4(1) of the Ontario *Human Rights Code*;

---

[28] (1985), 23 D.L.R. (4th) 321, [1985] 2 S.C.R. 536.
[29] *Supra*, at p. 338.
[30] (1990), 72 D.L.R. (4th) 289, [1990] 2 S.C.R. 311.
[31] *Supra*, at p. 301.
[32] (1992), 94 D.L.R. (4th) 233, 57 O.A.C. 222 (C.A.), leave to appeal to S.C.C. refused 98 D.L.R. (4th) viii, 63 O.A.C. 398*n*.

(d) when they discovered this, they filed complaints with the Commission alleging that the company had discriminated against them in their employment with respect to relocation allowances and company-paid travel.

The Board of Inquiry in the *London Monenco* case dismissed the complaints on the basis that, even though a *prima facie* case of discrimination had been made out, discrimination on the basis of marital status was permissible in this case as it was a "reasonable and bona fide qualification because of the nature of the employment". The Ontario Divisional Court dismissed the appeal by the Human Rights Commission, thereby leading to a subsequent appeal to the Ontario Court of Appeal.

In allowing the appeal in the *London Monenco* case, Mr. Justice Robins, speaking on behalf of the Ontario Court of Appeal, made the following comments in relation to the error made by the Board of Inquiry with respect to the notion of shifting burdens:

> In this case, had the board not erred in shifting the burden of proof to the Commission, it is difficult to see how the result would have been the same. Assuming, contrary to the decision I have reached, that the discriminatory policy in question is capable of constituting a qualification within the meaning of s. 23(1)(*b*), and bearing in mind the burden of proof that should have been imposed on the respondent, the impressionistic evidence adduced in justification of the policy, on my reading of the record and the board's reasons, is insufficient to meet the objective standards set by *Etobicoke* [i.e., the SCC decision in *Etobicoke (Borough) v. Ontario (Human Rights Commission)*] and discharge the onus of establishing the respondent's entitlement to a s. 23(1)(*b*) exception.[33]

7. RULES OF EVIDENCE

Included within the exclusive jurisdiction of a board of inquiry to make its own rules relating to procedure, discussed earlier in this chapter, is the extremely broad discretion of a board of inquiry to admit into evidence both oral testimony and documentation that would not be admissible in a court of law, subject to basic rules of natural justice.

A board of inquiry appointed under the Ontario *Human Rights Code* is required to adhere to the very minimal requirements of the *Statutory Powers Procedure Act* relating to the admissibility of evidence:

> 15(1) Subject to subsections (2) and (3), a tribunal may admit as evidence at a hearing, whether or not given or proven under oath or affirmation or admissible as evidence in a court,
> (a) any oral testimony; and
> (b) any document or other thing,
> relevant to the subject-matter of the proceeding and may act on such evidence, but the tribunal may exclude anything unduly repetitious.

---

[33] *Supra*, at p. 244 (C.A.).

(2) Nothing is admissible in evidence at a hearing,
  (a) that would be inadmissible in a court by reason of any privilege under the law of evidence; or
  (b) that is inadmissible by the statute under which the proceedings arises or any other statute.

. . . . .

16. A tribunal may, in making its decision in any proceeding,
  (a) take notice of facts that may be judicially noticed; and
  (b) take notice of any generally recognized scientific or technical facts, information or opinions within its scientific or specialized knowledge.

The above-noted sections of the *Statutory Powers Procedures Act*, represent a codification of the rules of natural justice relating to the admissibility of evidence before administrative tribunals.

A. Hearsay Evidence

Hearsay evidence is admissible in hearings before boards of inquiry appointed under human rights legislation. There are numerous decisions of human rights tribunals which confirm this proposition.[34] Section 15 of the *Statutory Powers Procedures Act* allows for the admissibility of hearsay evidence, subject only to the condition that such evidence is relevant to the subject matter of the proceeding. The rationale for allowing hearsay evidence to be adduced before boards of inquiry in human rights proceedings, is succinctly stated by the Board in the case of *Bremer v. Board of School Trustees, School District No. 62*:[35]

> Boards of inquiry will frequently be required to make conclusions of fact based upon circumstantial evidence and, perhaps, with the assistance of evidence which may be inadmissible in a superior court. At the heart of a contravention of the *Code* is the determination of whether the respondent's conduct was motivated by a consideration which constitutes the absence of reasonable cause; the factual issue and motivation will in most cases not be a matter about which there exists any direct evidence.

> For these reasons this board is of the opinion that it would represent an unwarranted and potentially restrictive limitation on a board of inquiry if we were to determine that hearsay evidence subsequently contradicted will in all circumstances constitute no evidence. However, the board would hasten to add that the use of hearsay evidence must of course be approached with great caution.

Hearsay evidence is technically admissible in hearings conducted under human rights legislation but the tribunal will carefully assess such evidence for the purpose of determining what weight, if any, is to be given to the evidence.

---

[34] See, for example, *Warren v. Becket* (unreported, 1976, B.C. Bd. Inq.).
[35] (unreported, 1976, B.C. Bd. Inq.), at pp. 37-8.

B. Circumstantial Evidence

The Supreme Court of Canada in *R. v. John*[36] outlines the distinction between direct and circumstantial evidence:

"All of the evidence that has been given in this trial is what is known as circumstantial evidence. To refresh your memory as to the difference between circumstantial evidence, and what is known as direct evidence, I will give you an illustration.

"If a witness gives evidence that he saw A stab B with a knife, that is direct evidence that A stabbed B. If a witness gives evidence that he found a dagger with an unusually long blade in the possession of A and another witness testified that such a dagger could have caused B's wound, that is circumstantial evidence tending to prove that A did in fact stab B.

"The two forms of evidence are equally admissible but the superiority of direct evidence is that it contains only one source of error, namely, the unreliability of human testimony, where circumstantial evidence in addition to the unreliability of human testimony suffers from the difficulty of drawing a correct inference from the circumstantial evidence."[37]

The essence of circumstantial evidence is perhaps best stated as follows:

Each piece of evidence need not alone lead to the conclusion sought to be proved. Pieces of evidence, each by itself insufficient, may however when combined, justify the inference that the facts exist. Accordingly, the trial judge must be careful not to exclude individual pieces of evidence if there is an undertaking that the evidence tendered is part of a larger combination.[38]

Discriminatory actions are, by their very nature, actions which are often incapable of direct proof and, in many instances, witnessed only by the complainant. It is for these, and other reasons that the admissibility of circumstantial evidence in human rights proceedings is necessary. The Ontario Board of Inquiry in *Kennedy v. Mohawk College*,[39] made the following comments on the subject of circumstantial evidence in human rights hearings:

Discriminations on the ground of race or colour are frequently practiced in a very subtle manner. Overt discrimination on these grounds is not present in every discriminatory situation or occurrence. In a case where direct evidence of discrimination is absent, it becomes necessary for the board to infer discrimination from the conduct of the individual or individuals whose conduct is in issue. This is not always an easy task to carry out. The conduct alleged to be discriminatory must be carefully analyzed and scrutinized in the context of the situation in which it arises. In my view, such conduct to be found discriminatory must be consistent with the allegation of discrimination and inconsistent with any other rationale explanation. This, of course, places an onus on the person or persons whose

---

[36] (1970), 15 D.L.R. (3d) 692, 2 C.C.C. (2d) 157 (S.C.C.).
[37] *Supra*, at p. 714.
[38] Sopinka, Lederman and Bryant, *The Law of Evidence in Canada* (Markham, Butterworths, 1992), at p. 40.
[39] (unreported, 1973, Ont. Bd. Inq.).

conduct is complained of as discriminatory to explain the nature and purpose of such conduct. It should also be added that the board must view the conduct complained of in an objective manner and not from the subjective view point of the person alleging discrimination whose interpretation of the impugned conduct may well be distorted because of innate personality characteristics, such as a high degree of sensitivity or defensiveness.[40]

C. Statistical Evidence

A very specialized category of circumstantial evidence that has been adduced in a number of hearings conducted under human rights legislation, involves statistical evidence relating to the employer, its employee demographics and other such related areas. A classic example of a human rights case in which substantial and far-reaching statistical evidence supported the basis for an extraordinary remedy can be found in *Action Travail des Femmes v. C.N.R. Co.*,[41] a case decided under the *Canadian Human Rights Act*. In the *Action Travail* case, it was alleged that C.N. discriminated against women in its hiring practices. Statistical evidence suggested that women comprised 5% of the applicant pool but only 0.7% of hirees. Based on this statistical evidence, the Tribunal ordered C.N. to implement an affirmative action plan so that one out of every four hirees must be a woman until the female workforce comprises 13% of C.N. workers. The propriety of this award was ultimately upheld by the Supreme Court of Canada.

In some instances, statistical evidence is compelling largely due to the old saying that the "proof is in the pudding". Since an intention to discriminate is not a necessary element of any human rights complaint, one of the main inherent weaknesses associated with statistical surveys is thereby eliminated. In other words, statistical evidence can, in some instances, confirm that the end result of an employer's practice or policies is discriminatory, irrespective of the presence or absence of an actual intention to discriminate.

D. Similar Fact Evidence

The "similar facts" rule of evidence is defined as follows:

The so-called "similar facts rule" is an exception to the general exclusionary rule barring evidence of the bad character of a party. In exceptional circumstances, a party may adduce evidence of the bad character of the opposite party to prove or disprove a fact in issue. Similar fact evidence is admissible if it is relevant to an issue in the case other than a relevance that derives simply from showing the party as a bad person and its probative value outweighs the prejudice to the party that may arise from the admission of such evidence. Under the rule, a party may adduce expert opinion or general reputation evidence to prove the opposite party's disposition, specific incidence of misconduct on other occasions, possession of

---

[40] *Supra*, at pp. 4-5 of unreported judgment.
[41] (1987), 40 D.L.R. (4th) 193, [1987] 1 S.C.R. 1114 *sub nom. Canadian National Railway Co. v. Canada (Canadian Human Rights Commission).*

documents or past associations if such evidence is relevant to an issue in the case and the probative value of such evidence outweighs its prejudicial effect.[42]

Similar fact evidence is often resorted to in complaints involving allegations of sexual harassment. In these cases, it is quite common for the complainant to endeavour to call evidence from other individuals who had been the object of sexual harassment or subject to other such discriminatory conduct by the party respondent. For example, in *Commodore Business Machines Ltd. v. Olarte*,[43] six employees complained about sexual harassment by a foreman. The Board of Inquiry admitted the evidence of eight other employees concerning similar events occurring prior to, within and subsequent to the time period representing the subject matter of the complaint. This evidence was admitted on the basis that it was relevant to a pattern of conduct by the respondent toward female employees, thereby making the probative value of the evidence much greater than any prejudicial effect it may have had upon the respondent.

It is important to bear in mind that one of the most compelling reasons for establishing a rigid test with respect to the admissibility of similar fact evidence in criminal cases, namely the impact that it may have upon the jury, is clearly absent from human rights' proceedings. It logically follows that the rigidity of the rule at common law ought to be relaxed, to some extent at least, in relation to proceedings conducted under human rights legislation.

8. OPEN/CLOSED HEARING

A. Under the Ontario Human Rights Code

Although the Ontario *Human Rights Code* is silent with respect to whether hearings before a board of inquiry are to be open to the public, s. 9 of the *Statutory Powers Procedure Act*, which applies to the conduct of hearings before a board of inquiry, states:

> 9(1) A hearing shall be open to the public except where the tribunal is of the opinion that,
>> (a) matters involving public security may be disclosed; or
>> (b) intimate financial or personal matters or other matters may be disclosed at the hearing of such a nature, having regard to the circumstances, that the desirability of avoiding disclosure thereof in the interests of any person affected or in the public interest outweighs the desirability of adhering to the principle that hearings be open to the public,
> in which case the tribunal may hold the hearing in the absence of the public.

---

[42] Sopinka, Lederman and Bryant, *The Law of Evidence in Canada* (Markham, Butterworths, 1992), at pp. 477-8.

[43] (1984), 14 D.L.R. (4th) 118, 49 O.R. (2d) 17, *sub nom. Commodore Business Machines Ltd. v. Minister of Labour* (Div. Ct.).

B. Under the Canadian Human Rights Act

Section 52 of the *Canadian Human Rights Act* provides:

> 52. A hearing of a Tribunal shall be public, but a Tribunal may exclude members of the public during the whole or any part of a hearing if it considers that exclusion to be in the public interest.

It would appear, on a strict reading of s. 52, that a human rights tribunal appointed under the *Canadian Human Rights Act* has a much broader discretion in determining whether to conduct a hearing, in whole or in part, in camera than does a board of inquiry under the Ontario *Human Rights Code*.

9. TIME WITHIN WHICH TO RENDER DECISION

Section 41(5) of the Ontario *Human Rights Code* expressly provides that a board of inquiry shall make its finding and decision within thirty days after the conclusion of its hearing. Although the subsection does not specify what consequences, if any, flow from a board of inquiry's failure to issue its decision within thirty days after the conclusion of its hearing, an objective reading of the subsection would appear to suggest that this requirement is mandatory as opposed to being directory in nature. In addition, it is significant to note that s. 41(3) of the Ontario *Human Rights Code* provides that where a board of inquiry for any reason is unable to exercise its powers, the Commission may request the Minister to appoint a new board of inquiry in its place. Accordingly, a combined reading of s. 41(3) and (5) of the Ontario *Human Rights Code* would lead to the following conclusions:

(a) a board of inquiry must make its finding and issue its decision within thirty days after the conclusion of its hearing;

(b) the failure on the part of a board of inquiry to make its findings and issue its decision within thirty days after the conclusion of the hearing may result in the board of inquiry being without jurisdiction to issue a decision at any time subsequent to the stipulated time period;

(c) the Ontario Human Rights Commission would then have the discretion to request the appointment of a new board of inquiry in place of the former board of inquiry, on the basis that the former board of inquiry was unable to exercise its powers under the Code.

The appointment of a new board of inquiry would not, in and of itself, necessitate a re-hearing of all evidence relating to the complaint, since the Code specifically requires that oral evidence taken before a board at a hearing shall be recorded.[44] However, where the evidence of the witnesses conflict in a material or substantial way, the obvious difficulty in assessing issues of cred-

---

[44] Section 40 of the Ontario *Human Rights Code*.

ibility could well result in the evidence having to be re-heard, in whole or in part.

There is no comparable provision under the *Canadian Human Rights Act* that the tribunal render its decision within a stipulated period of time.

10. APPEALS

A. Under the Ontario Human Rights Code

Section 42 of the Ontario *Human Rights Code* provides:

> 42(1) Any party to a proceeding before a board of inquiry may appeal from a decision or order of the board to the Divisional Court in accordance with the rules of court.
>
> . . . . .
>
> (3) An appeal under this section may be made on questions of law or fact or both and the court may affirm or reverse the decision or order of the board of inquiry or direct the board to make any decision or order that the board is authorized to make under this Act and the court may substitute its opinion for that of the board.

Rule 61.04 of the Ontario Rules of Civil Procedure, R.R.O. 1990, Reg. 194, requires that a notice of appeal be served on every party to the proceeding within thirty days after the date of the order appealed from. There are other more technical and extensive provisions in Rule 61 relating to the procedure that must be followed in advancing an appeal up to and including the argument of the appeal itself.

The Ontario Divisional Court in *Emrick Plastics v. Ontario (Human Rights Commission)*[45] makes it clear that the apparently broad wording of s. 42 ought not to be interpreted by the courts as a liberal power of appeal:

> Despite this court's wide statutory power to substitute the opinion of the court for that of the board, a measure of restraint has been adopted in reviewing the factual decisions of human rights tribunals.
>
> . . . . .
>
> This court has thus expressed in different forms of words its reluctance to interfere with the factual findings of human rights tribunals. It seems to us that the common thread throughout these decisions is the common sense proposition that the trier of fact who hears and sees the witnesses, and who in this case took a view of the work place, is best equipped to sort through conflicting evidence and interpretations of medical documents.
>
> . . . . .
>
> The court's job is not to second-guess the tribunal. The court should only interfere with findings of fact made by human rights tribunal if the appellant

---

[45] (1992), 90 D.L.R. (4th) 476, 55 O.A.C. 33 (Div. Ct.).

establishes that the tribunal made a palpable and overriding error which affected its assessment of the facts. The standard of review by this court of the factual findings of human rights tribunals is the same standard of a review that applies to the factual findings of trial courts.[46]

B. Under the Canadian Human Rights Act

The *Canadian Human Rights Act* differs in two significant respects from the Ontario *Human Rights Code* with respect to the procedure for appealing a decision of a tribunal appointed under the Act. First, the right to appeal is limited to decisions of a tribunal composed of fewer than three members and does not apply to a tribunal comprised of three members. Secondly, the appeal process is internal in nature, as opposed to providing for a right to appeal to the Federal Court.

Section 55 of the Act provides:

> 55. Where a Tribunal that made a decision or order was composed of fewer than three members, the Commission, the complainant before the Tribunal or the person against whom the complaint was made may appeal the decision or order by serving a notice, in a manner and form prescribed by order of the Governor in Council, within 30 days after the decision or order appealed was pronounced, on all persons who received notice from the Tribunal under subsection 50(1).

The establishment, constitution and powers of the review tribunal are set out in s. 56 of the Act:[47]

> 56(1) Where an appeal is made pursuant to section 55, the President of the Human Rights Tribunal Panel [i.e., a panel that is established under ss. 48.1 through 48.5 of the Act] shall select three members from the Human Rights Tribunal Panel, other than the member or members of the Tribunal whose decision or order is being appealed from, to constitute a Review Tribunal to hear the appeal.
> (2) Subject to this section, a Review Tribunal shall be constituted in the same manner as, and shall have all the powers of, a Tribunal appointed pursuant to section 49, and subsection 49(4) applies in respect of members of a Review Tribunal.
> (3) An appeal lies to a Review Tribunal against a decision or order of a Tribunal on any question of law or fact or mixed law and fact.
>
> . . . . .
>
> (5) A Review Tribunal may dispose of an appeal under section 55 by dismissing it, or by allowing it and rendering the decision or making the order that, in its opinion, the Tribunal appealed against should have rendered or made.

In the case of a decision or order made by a tribunal composed of three members, the Act does not provide a right of appeal.

---

[46] *Supra*, at pp. 485-6.
[47] Section 56(1), rep. & sub. R.S.C. 1985, c. 31 (1st Supp.), s. 67.

11. JUDICIAL REVIEW

Separate and apart from the right of appeal, if any, in relation to a decision of a human rights tribunal, is the remedy of judicial review. Judicial review involves a request of the court to review an order or decision of an administrative tribunal on certain grounds, the most common of which are:

(a) the tribunal exceeded its jurisdiction in making its decision or order;

(b) the tribunal erred in the exercise of its jurisdiction;

(c) the tribunal erred in failing or refusing to exercise its jurisdiction in some significant respect;

(d) the tribunal violated one or more of the fundamental principles of natural justice in the course of the hearing;

(e) the tribunal acted upon evidence that was not properly before it, misapprehended evidence adduced at the hearing and/or made certain key findings based on a lack of evidence at the hearing.

The types of orders or relief that may be granted by a court on a successful application for judicial review include:

(i) an order in the nature of *mandamus*, which involves a formal direction that the tribunal do or proceed to do something which it had refused to do;

(ii) an order in the nature of prohibition, whereby the tribunal is judicially restrained from either proceeding with the hearing or proceeding with some form of action that is directly related to the hearing;

(iii) an order in the nature of *certiorari* which, in essence, involves a setting aside of a decision or order of the tribunal.

In Ontario, the procedure for initiating and proceeding with an application for judicial review is set out within the *Judicial Review Procedure Act*,[48] as well as Rule 68 of the Ontario Rules of Civil Procedure. In the case of an application for judicial review of a decision of a tribunal appointed under the *Canadian Human Rights Act*, the procedure is laid out in the *Federal Court Act*,[49] as well as the Federal Court Rules that have been enacted pursuant to the provisions of the *Federal Court Act*.

---

[48] R.S.O. 1990, c. J.1.
[49] R.S.C. 1985, c. F-7, as amended.

CHAPTER 13 | *Remedies*

1. STATUTORY PROVISIONS

A. Under the Ontario Human Rights Code

Section 41(1) and (2) of the Ontario *Human Rights Code*, R.S.O. 1990, c. H.19, sets out the jurisdiction of a board of inquiry with respect to the types of orders that it may make where it is found that the provisions of the Code have been violated:

> 41(1) Where the board of inquiry, after a hearing, finds that a right of the complainant under Part I has been infringed and that the infringement is a contravention of section 9 by a party to the proceeding, the board may, by order,
>
> > (a) direct the party to do anything that, in the opinion of the board, the party ought to do to achieve compliance with this Act, both in respect of the complaint and in respect of future practices; and
> >
> > (b) direct the party to make restitution, including monetary compensation, for loss arising out of the infringement, and, where the infringement has been engaged in wilfully or recklessly, monetary compensation may include an award, not exceeding $10,000, for mental anguish.
>
> (2) Where a board makes a finding under subsection (1) that a right is infringed on the ground of harassment under subsection 2(2) or subsection 5(2) or conduct under section 7, and the board finds that a person who is a party to the proceeding,
>
> > (a) knew or was in possession of knowledge from which the person ought to have known of the infringement; and
> >
> > (b) had the authority by reasonably available means to penalize or prevent the conduct and failed to use it,
>
> the board shall remain seized of the matter and upon complaint of a continuation or repetition of the infringement of the right the Commission may investigate the complaint and, subject to subsection 36(2), request the board to re-convene and if the board finds that a person who is a party to the proceeding,
>
> > (c) knew or was in possession of knowledge from which the person ought to have known of the repetition of infringement; and
> >
> > (d) had the authority by reasonably available means to penalize or prevent the continuation or repetition of the conduct and failed to use it,
>
> the board may make an order requiring the person to take whatever sanctions or steps are reasonably available to prevent any further continuation or repetition of the infringement of the right.

A review of the remedial jurisdiction of a board of inquiry, set out in s. 41(1) and (2) above, make it clear that a board of inquiry has the unfettered jurisdiction to:

(1) order a respondent to do anything that, in the board's opinion, would remedy the discriminatory act or conduct in relation to both the individual complainant and any potential future complainants;

(2) order full restitution, including loss of wages or other income from employment;

(3) order monetary compensation for mental anguish, in an amount not exceeding $10,000, where the infringement has been engaged in wilfully or recklessly;

(4) in the case of harassment in employment, in addition to the above-noted remedies, order individual respondents who were aware of and/ or had the means by which to discipline and/or prevent, employees from continuing or repeating the harassment, to take whatever sanctions or steps are reasonably available to prevent any further continuation or repetition of the infringement, present and future. In this regard, the board of inquiry continues to exercise jurisdiction by maintaining a supervisory role or function with respect to strict adherence to the terms of its order.

B. Under the Canadian Human Rights Act

The remedial jurisdiction of a tribunal appointed under the *Canadian Human Rights Act*, R.S.C. 1985, c. H-6, is set out in the following subsections of ss. 53 and 54:

53(2) If, at the conclusion of its inquiry, a Tribunal finds that the complaint to which the inquiry relates is substantiated, it may, subject to subsection (4) and section 54, make an order against the person found to be engaging or to have engaged in the discriminatory practice and include in that order any of the following terms that it considers appropriate:

(*a*) that the person cease the discriminatory practice and, in order to prevent the same or a similar practice from occurring in the future, take measures, including

(i) adoption of a special program, plan or arrangement referred to in subsection 16(1), or

(ii) the making of an application for approval and the implementing of a plan pursuant to section 17,

in consultation with the Commission on the general purposes of those measures;

(*b*) that the person make available to the victim of the discriminatory practice, on the first reasonable occasion, such rights, opportunities or privileges as, in the opinion of the Tribunal, are being or were denied the victim as a result of the practice;

(*c*) that the person compensate the victim, as the Tribunal may consider proper, for any or all of the wages that the victim was deprived of and for any expenses incurred by the victim as a result of the discriminatory practice; and (*d*) that the person compensate the victim, as the Tribunal may consider proper, for any or all additional costs of obtaining alternative goods, services, facilities or accommodation and for any expenses incurred by the victim as a result of the discriminatory practice.

(3) In addition to any order that the Tribunal may make pursuant to subsection (2), if the Tribunal finds that

(*a*) a person is engaging or has engaged in a discriminatory practice wilfully or recklessly, or

(*b*) the victim of the discriminatory practice has suffered in respect of feelings or self-respect as a result of the practice,

the Tribunal may order the person to pay such compensation to the victim, not exceeding five thousand dollars as the Tribunal may determine.

(4) If, at the conclusion of its inquiry into a complaint regarding discrimination based on a disability, the Tribunal finds that the complaint is substantiated but that the premises or facilities of the person found to be engaging or to have engaged in the discriminatory practice require adaptation to meet the needs of a person arising from such a disability, the Tribunal shall

(*a*) make such order pursuant to this section for that adaptation as it considers appropriate and as it is satisfied will not occasion costs or business inconvenience constituting undue hardship, or

(*b*) if the Tribunal considers that no such order can be made, make such recommendations as it considers appropriate,

and, in the event of such finding, the Tribunal shall not make an order unless required by this subsection.

. . . . .

54(2) No order under subsection 53(2) may contain a term

(*a*) requiring the removal of an individual from a position if that individual accepted employment in that position in good faith; or

(*b*) requiring the expulsion of an occupant from any premises or accommodation, if that occupant obtained such premises or accommodation in good faith.

While the remedial provisions of the *Canadian Human Rights Act* referred to above are more extensive than the comparable provisions of the Ontario *Human Rights Code*, it is submitted that the remedial jurisdiction of both a board of inquiry appointed under the Ontario legislation and a tribunal appointed under the federal legislation is, to a very large extent, identical. The significant differences between the two respective remedial jurisdictions include the following:

(1) the monetary limit for suffering in respect of feelings or self-respect under the CHRA is $5,000, while the OHRC imposes a ceiling of $10,000 for compensation for mental anguish;

(2) the CHRA specifically prohibits the making of an order which directly results in the removal of a third party individual from the position of employment, whereas the Ontario *Human Rights Code* is entirely silent on this jurisdictional limitation;

(3) the CHRA specifically provides for a more active and direct role played by the Commission in developing and implementing plans and programs to remedy the discriminatory act and possible future discriminatory actions, as compared to the Ontario legislation which does not expressly provide for such a direct role by the Ontario Human Rights Commission.

2. REINSTATEMENT

The remedy of reinstatement is an order which will hardly ever be made by a court within the context of a wrongful dismissal action. Although judges have, in theory, the jurisdiction to order reinstatement, which is nothing more than an order of specific performance of an employment contract, they will only exercise this jurisdiction in the most extraordinary cases. This is due to the fact that courts, almost unanimously, are of the view that it is contrary to public policy to judicially compel the continuation of the employment relationship contrary to the wishes of either party.

While reinstatement is an order that will be seriously considered by any board of inquiry in a successful complaint of discrimination which resulted in the termination of an individual's employment, there are instances in which human rights tribunals will refrain from exercising their jurisdiction to order reinstatement. An Ontario Board of Inquiry in *Obdeyn v. Walbar Machine Products of Canada Ltd.*[1] sets out authoritative principles relating to the criteria to be considered in deciding whether to order reinstatement. In that case, the complainant put forth two grounds for relief, one of which was that he had been discriminated against during the course of his employment as to terms and conditions of his employment either directly through management or indirectly through his fellow employees and then discharged for having assisted a co-worker in pursuing a human rights complaint. In upholding the complaint of retaliation and ordering relief which included the posting of standard human rights codes and brochures in prominent places within its establishment, the sending of a letter of apology, and the sum of $200 for emotional suffering, the Tribunal refrained from ordering reinstatement of the complainant. In his reasons for decision, Professor Gorsky made the following comments on the subject of reinstatement:

> ... from the evidence, I have concluded that Obdeyn suffered from poor emotional and physical health ... quite apart from the special facts of this case, Obdeyn's interpersonal relations were not good. He has had a checkered employment history with little evidence of a capacity for remaining on a job very long. From the evidence I would find that Obdeyn would be likely to follow a similar pattern at Walbar, quite apart from the breaches of the *Code* committed by Bibic, for which Walbar is responsible. Those physical and emotional problems which

---

[1] (1982), 3 C.H.R.R. D/712 (Ont. Bd. Inq.).

Obdeyn suffered from would, I conclude, even in the absence of the breaches of the *Code*, which I have found, have led to his leaving, or being discharged from his employment at Walbar, around the time he was, in fact, discharged.

He did not care for the work, showed no interest in improving his range of skills, experienced difficulty in maintaining reasonable attendance and in coming to work on time and in attending to his work when in attendance at work. Although the breaches of the *Code* directed at him no doubt aggravated an already existing emotional and physical condition, it did not, as it might have in the case of another person, significantly alter his situation. It is more likely that the greater part of the physical and emotional upset experienced by Obdeyn was not the result of the illegal discrimination directed at him. I find that the effect of the breaches of the *Code* are limited to some marginal increase in Obdeyn's emotional and physical problems. For the above reasons the remedy cannot include an order of reinstatement, as the evidence disclosed that the breaches of the *Code* found by me did not result in, or contribute to, the loss of Obdeyn's employment with Walbar.[2]

On the authority of this passage from the *Obdeyn* case, it can be said with certainty that a human rights tribunal is empowered to refrain from ordering reinstatement of the individual where it is satisfied, on a balance of probabilities, that the breach or breaches of the Code "did not result in or contribute to" the loss of the complainant's employment. What is not entirely certain from the above-noted passage, is whether Professor Gorsky was suggesting that the contributory fault of a complainant, which may include a negative or counter-productive attitude, ought to influence a board of inquiry to refrain from ordering reinstatement, separate and apart from whether the breaches of the Code resulted in the termination of the complainant's employment. Perhaps stated another way, should the principle or concept of "near cause" enter into the determination by the human rights tribunal as to whether reinstatement ought to be ordered as a remedy? Generally, the concept of "near cause" involves misconduct by an employee which, although insufficient in constituting just cause in law, nonetheless empowers the court to reduce the damages for wrongful dismissal that the individual would otherwise be entitled to but for the employee's misconduct.

Leaving aside the presence of evidence which supports some form of contributory fault on the part of the complainant, the issue arises as to what consideration, if any, ought to be given to the fact that an employer has the unqualified legal right to terminate a non-unionized employee at any time, without just cause, so long as the individual is provided with reasonable notice or compensation in lieu of notice. In other words, should this implied term of the contract of employment serve to influence or in any way dissuade a human rights tribunal from ordering reinstatement in a given case? For obvious reasons, employees are seldom provided with any form of guarantee of employ-

---

[2] *Supra*, at p. D/718.

ment for a specified time, except in cases involving a well-drafted written contract of employment.

A very recent example of reinstatement being ordered in a novel fact situation is the decision of the Ontario Divisional Court in *ONA v. Etobicoke General Hospital*.[3] In that case, the grievance of an employee based upon a clause in a collective agreement which deems all employees, absent from work for more than twenty-four months due to illness and disability, to be automatically terminated, was dismissed by the arbitrator. The arbitrator upheld the termination primarily by concluding that her dismissal came about not by virtue of her handicap but due to her absence from employment for a period of twenty-four months. The Ontario Divisional Court granted the union's application for judicial review, thereby overturning the decision of the arbitrator. The court further ordered the reinstatement of the grievor in her employment with full compensation for all losses flowing from the termination of her employment.

3. DAMAGES AND COMPENSATION

A human rights tribunal, in awarding damages and compensation to a successful complainant in a human rights hearing whose employment was terminated, is not limited by the notions of reasonable notice and the rather narrow principles of damages that are followed by the courts. One of the leading decisions on the appropriate measure of compensation in damages in a human rights complaint is the Ontario Board of Inquiry's decision in *Whitehead v. Servodyne Canada Ltd.*[4] In the *Whitehead* case, the Board of Inquiry accepted the evidence of a witness that when he was hired by the company's plant manager, he was told to learn his job from the complainant and then fire her. The Board concluded that the fact that the complainant was a woman was one of the reasons for the animosity which the plant manager, who was a personal respondent in the complaint, displayed towards her and influenced his decision to fire her.

In addressing the subject of the appropriate measure of compensation, the Board of Inquiry in *Whitehead* stated, in part:

> In recent years there has been much debate about the basis for awarding damages when an employee has been wrongfully dismissed. It has sometimes been said that an employer always has a ''right'' to dismiss an employee; the only ''wrong'' done is in not giving reasonable notice or adequate wages in lieu of that notice. I believe that such analysis is faulty. An employer has no more ''right'' to break an employment contract than has any other contracting party. Dismissal without cause and with inadequate notice of termination is a breach of

---

[3] (1993), 104 D.L.R. (4th) 379, 14 O.R. (3d) 40 (Div. Ct.).
[4] (1986), 86 C.L.L.C. ¶17,020, 15 C.C.E.L. 5 (Ont. Bd. Inq.).

the promise, express or implied in virtually every employment contract, to continue to employ and pay the employee until the contract is lawfully terminated.

While for reasons of policy, courts may not be willing to reinstate an employee wrongfully dismissed, in my view the damages should be on the same basis as reinstatement — to place the employee in the same position as if the contract had not been broken by the employers. That employees are not merely compensated for inadequate notice is supported by the fact that they often recover consequential damages for such matters as expenses incurred in seeking other employment and medical expenses, and also recover general damages for pain and suffering. These losses, especially the pain and suffering, result from the wrongful nature of the dismissal, not just from the inadequacy of notice.

. . . . .

If the employer, intending to discriminate contrary to s. 4(1), were nevertheless permitted *lawfully to dismiss* an employee simply by giving adequate notice, or compensation in lieu of notice, the employer could defeat the goals of the *Human Rights Code*. Moreover an absurd situation would exist: an employer by refusing to hire, let us say black people or women, would commit a breach of the Code, but by dismissing with sufficient notice once they become employees, would not commit a breach! Accordingly, the remedy available under the Code must not be limited to recovery for wrongful dismissal at common law.

If this reasoning is sound, then the usual measure of economic loss in contract law for wrongful dismissal — lost wages during a period of reasonable notice — is not the correct measure to compensate an aggrieved complainant under the *Human Rights Code*. While there may be circumstances where the quantum of damages for wrongful dismissal in contract coincide with the compensation for breach of s. 4(1) of the Code, such circumstances are merely fortuitous. More often the contract measure will be inadequate to compensate the complainant and also to carry out the purposes of the Code. I propose to refer to recovery for breach of the *Ontario Human Rights Code* as "statutory compensation" in order to distinguish it from common law damages in contract or tort.[5]

(Emphasis in original.)

In turning to the issue of "statutory compensation" for economic loss, the Board of Inquiry in *Whitehead* awarded the complainant compensation equal to the salary that she would have earned from the time of her termination up until the time that the company closed its operations some eighteen months subsequent to her departure. While recognizing the various contingencies that apply to the continued employment of any individual in any employment relationship, including the possibility that they would leave the company in order to take a position elsewhere, being laid off or dismissed for reasons unrelated to prohibitions in the *Human Rights Code*, the Board of Inquiry, nonetheless concluded that "in these circumstances it is reasonable, indeed highly likely, that Mrs. Whitehead would have continued to work for the respondent company until it closed its doors". In addition, the Board of Inquiry made it clear that the principles of mitigation applied to the calculation of

---

[5] *Supra*, at pp. 16,138-9.

"statutory compensation", thereby deducting from the eighteen months' salary and benefits moneys that the complainant earned over that eighteen-month time period from alternative employment. Furthermore, the complainant was awarded $2,500 in general damages for mental anguish and interest, whereby the total monetary compensation ordered to be paid by the employer exceeded $34,000.

The Ontario Court of Appeal in *Piazza v. Airport Taxicab (Malton) Assn.*[6] agreed with and judicially endorsed the reasoning adopted by the Board of Inquiry in the *Whitehead* case, with respect to the clear distinction between the remedy for wrongful dismissal at common law and the remedies available under human rights legislation.

4. MENTAL ANGUISH

The recent decision of the Ontario Divisional Court in *York Condominium No. 216 v. Dudnik*[7] appears to have significantly limited the potential class of cases in which an award of monetary compensation for mental anguish may be made, by interpreting the applicable provisions of the Ontario *Human Rights Code* in a narrow and restrictive manner.

In the *Dudnik* case, the Board of Inquiry had concluded that the respondent condominium corporations had discriminated against the complainants on the basis of age and family status by virtue of by-laws that had been enacted by the condominium corporations which purported to prohibit occupancy by children. Of the various awards made to the numerous complainants at the conclusion of the hearing, two of the complainants who had purchased condominiums in which they lived with children under the prohibited age were awarded $1,000 and their children were each awarded smaller monetary amounts on the basis that the condominium corporations in acting intentionally to enforce the "adults only" rule had acted wilfully and, by implication, provided the basis on which to make an award of monetary compensation for mental anguish under s. 41(1)(b) of the Ontario *Human Rights Code*.

In overturning the award made by the Board of Inquiry for damages for mental anguish, Mr. Justice Carruthers, speaking on behalf of the court, made the following comments in relation to the interpretation of s. 41(1)(b) of the Ontario *Human Rights Code*:

> To the extent that the Board appears to treat "wilfully" and "intentionally" as being synonymous I cannot agree. In my opinion, while the act upon which it is founded must be intentional, the infringement must be the purpose of that act in order to be wilful within the meaning of s. 40(1)(b) [i.e., the current s. 41(1)(b)]. I do not think that the circumstances of this case permit that conclusion.[8]

---

[6] (1989), 60 D.L.R. (4th) 759, 34 O.A.C. 349 (Ont. Bd. Inq.).
[7] (1991), 79 D.L.R. (4th) 161, 3 O.R. (3d) 360 (Div. Ct.).
[8] *Supra*, at p. 176.

It appears as though Mr. Justice Carruthers is suggesting that there must be clear evidence of a deliberate intention to violate the provisions of the *Human Rights Code* rather than that the respondent's conduct in question was intentional, irrespective of whether the individual understood and/or intended to violate any applicable human rights provisions. In other words, there must be evidence that the respondent acted with something tantamount to malice aforethought with a view towards violating existing human rights legislation. Assuming that this is indeed the correct interpretation to be given to the words of Mr. Justice Carruthers in the *Dudnik* case, this decision is at odds with both the spirit and intent of human rights legislation as articulated by the Supreme Court of Canada, not to mention a plain and simple reading of s. 41(1)(b) of the Ontario *Human Rights Code*.

Although the *Dudnik* case dealt specifically with the availability of an award of monetary compensation for mental anguish under the Ontario *Human Rights Code*, the decision would have equal application to the provisions of the *Canadian Human Rights Act* having regard to the similarity of the wording of the respective provisions.

In the Ontario Board of Inquiry decision in *Torres v. Royalty Kitchenware Ltd.*,[9] the Board set out a list of factors to be taken into consideration in assessing the quantum of monetary compensation to be awarded for mental anguish in a case of sexual harassment:

(i) the nature of the harassment and, more specifically, whether it was verbal and/or physical;

(ii) the degree of aggressiveness and physical contact, if any, in the harassment;

(iii) the period of time over which the harassment took place, as well as the degree of persistency over that time period;

(iv) the attributes of the victim of the harassment, including the individual's age and overall vulnerability;

(v) perhaps most important of all, the psychological impact of the harassment upon the victim.

Although these factors are specifically related to sexual harassment, similar factors ought to be taken into consideration, with necessary modifications, in virtually any case in which a human rights tribunal is considering an award of monetary compensation for mental anguish.

5. MANDATORY AND PROHIBITIVE ORDERS

The most extensive and far-reaching remedial jurisdiction of a human rights tribunal involves the non-monetary orders directing certain action to be taken and/or the discontinuation of certain practices or conduct. This particular

---

[9] (1982), 3 C.H.R.R. D/858 (Ont. Bd. Inq.).

branch of the tribunal's remedial jurisdiction is the primary mechanism by which the human rights tribunal endeavours to ensure that the discriminatory practice or conduct will not be continued or repeated in the future.

Perhaps the only limit to the types of non-monetary orders that may be made by a human rights tribunal lies in the limitation of the imagination and creativity of the members of the tribunal. They have the authority to make any order, subject to specific exceptions set out in the applicable provisions of the legislation referred to earlier, so long as the order is directed towards compensating or remedying the individual complainant and/or ensuring that the discriminatory conduct or practice not be repeated in the future. Without limiting a tribunal's broad power in this regard, there have been certain types of non-monetary orders which are more common than others and, therefore, warrant brief review.

A. Affirmative Action Programs

(i) Under the Ontario Human Rights Code

Although s. 41(1)(a) of the Code empowers the board of inquiry to direct a party respondent to "do anything that, in the opinion of the board, the party ought to do to achieve compliance with this Act, both in respect of the complaint and in respect of future practices", there has always been an issue as to whether the right to order an affirmative action program falls within the realm of this remedial jurisdiction. The argument against the authority to order affirmative action programs under s. 41(1)(a) is twofold. First, the subsection does not specifically confer upon a board of inquiry the jurisdiction to make what can be legitimately characterized as an extraordinary order in the nature of an affirmative action program. Secondly, s. 14 of the Code specifically provides for the approval of a "special program designed to relieve hardship or economic disadvantage or to assist disadvantaged persons or groups to achieve or attempt to achieve equal opportunity", on a purely voluntary basis, thereby arguably limiting the jurisdiction of the Ontario Human Rights Commission in imposing such an order contrary to the wishes of the employer.

The more compelling argument whether s. 41(1)(a) of the Code empowers a board of inquiry to make an order in the nature of affirmative action, is that the express reference to "future practices", above and beyond the specific complaint before the board, is inconsistent with the suggestion that a board of inquiry's remedial jurisdiction is somehow limited in this regard. More importantly, the absence of any express language conferring jurisdiction upon a board of inquiry to make an order in the nature of affirmative action is entirely consistent with the notion that the Ontario Legislature intended to confer an exceedingly broad remedial jurisdiction upon a board of inquiry and opted to achieve this objective by adopting very broad language in establishing that remedial jurisdiction as opposed to specifically delineating in whole or in part the types of orders that can be made by a board of inquiry.

In *Hendry v. Ontario (Liquor Control Board)*,[10] an Ontario Board of Inquiry essentially directed the parties to design an affirmative action program as opposed to specifically establishing such a program by order of the Board. The Board of Inquiry concluded that sex discrimination had been established on the evidence adduced in the course of the hearing and ordered, in part:

> That the respondent co-operate with the human rights commission and the Women's Bureau of the Ministry of Labour in designing a program to take such steps as are appropriate to reduce the imbalance between men and women employed by the respondent. And it is further ordered that the respondent provide the human rights commission with sufficient information on employment practices and statistics to permit the human rights commission to monitor the employment practices of the respondent insofar as they relate to the *Human Rights Code*, for a period of 12 months from the date of this order.[11]

(ii) Under the Canadian Human Rights Act

A tribunal appointed under the *Canadian Human Rights Act* has the remedial jurisdiction to make an order in the nature of affirmative action. Section 53(2)(*a*) of the Act specifically provides for the making of an order for the adoption of a "special program, plan or arrangement" or that the respondent make such a program, plan or arrangement, "in order to prevent the same or a similar practice from occurring in the future". Perhaps the most extraordinary example of an affirmative action order being made by a tribunal appointed under the *Canadian Human Rights Act* is found in the *Action Travail des Femmes v. C.N.R. Co.*,[12] a case that was ultimately appealed to the Supreme Court of Canada.

In the *C.N.R.* case, Action Travail des Femmes, a women's activist group, filed a complaint of discriminatory hiring and promotion practices against the railway, contrary to s. 10 of the *Canadian Human Rights Act*. It was alleged that the railway had systematically denied employment opportunities to women in certain unskilled blue-collar positions.

Statistical evidence adduced at the hearing suggested that women comprised 5% of the applicant pool but only 0.7% of hirees. Based on this and other evidence adduced at the hearing, the Human Rights Tribunal concluded that the recruitment, hiring and promotion policies at C.N. prevented and discouraged women from working in blue-collar jobs. Consequently, C.N. was ordered to undertake a special employment program designed to increase the proportion of women working in "non-traditional" occupations to 13%, which represented, at that time, the national average. Until that goal was achieved, C.N. was required to hire at least one woman in every four non-traditional jobs filled.

---

[10] (1980), 1 C.H.R.R. D/160 (Ont. Bd. Inq.).
[11] *Supra*, at p. D/166.
[12] (1987), 40 D.L.R. (4th) 193, [1987] 1 S.C.R. 1114 *sub nom. Canadian National Railway Co. v. Canada (Canadian Human Rights Commission)*.

The Supreme Court of Canada upheld the order of the Human Rights Tribunal in the *C.N.R.* case, on the basis that the affirmative action order was designed to break a continuing cycle of systemic discrimination. In arriving at this conclusion, the court held that human rights legislation is not intended to punish wrongdoing, but, rather, prevent discrimination against identifiable protected groups, in which case it ought to receive a fair, large and liberal interpretation to advance and fulfil its purposes.

B. Hiring and Promotion Orders

In addition to the remedial jurisdiction of a human rights tribunal to order reinstatement in appropriate cases, a board has the authority to direct an employer to either hire or promote a complainant in circumstances where the board is of the opinion that such an order would serve to remedy the discriminatory practice and thereby achieve compliance with the legislation. As in the case of reinstatement, a court, although vested with the jurisdiction to do so, will almost never direct the hiring or promotion of an individual, except in the most extraordinary of cases.

In *Ontario (Liquor Control Board) v. Ontario (Human Rights Commission)*,[13] the Board of Inquiry found that the Liquor Control Board discriminated against three members of a visible minority by promoting a lesser-qualified white employee to the position of director of laboratory services. The Board ordered the employer to appoint Mr. Karumanchiri, one of the complainants, to the position. The company appealed this order of the Board of Inquiry, contending that the appointment of the complainant to a position that was already occupied by an individual amounted to an excess of jurisdiction on the part of the Board. The Ontario Divisional Court disagreed with this contention, thereby upholding the order of the Board of Inquiry.

It is significant that the decision of the Ontario Divisional Court in the *Ontario (Liquor Control Board)* case referred to above would have been decided differently had the order been made by a tribunal appointed under the *Canadian Human Rights Act*. Section 54(2) of the *Canadian Human Rights Act* makes it clear that no order of a tribunal may contain a term requiring the removal of an individual from a position if that individual accepted employment in that position in good faith. Accordingly, the express provisions of the *Canadian Human Rights Act*, to some extent at least, limit the remedial jurisdiction of a tribunal under the *Canadian Human Rights Act* when making orders pertaining to the hiring or promotion of an individual.

C. Letters of Apology

Human rights tribunals have included in their orders for employment-related discrimination, from time to time, a direction that the employer submit

---

[13]   (1988), 19 C.C.E.L. 172 (Ont. Div. Ct.).

a written letter of apology to the complainant.[14] Along these same lines, there have been cases in which an employer has been directed to provide a letter of recommendation to the complainant.[15]

D. Revised Employment Records

From time to time, human rights tribunals have ordered an employer to revise its internal employment records in relation to an individual and/or a record or document submitted to a third party pertaining to the employee complainant. These types of orders may be made in cases in which an individual was disciplined or terminated in circumstances whereby an employer was motivated, at least in part, by reasons relating to a prohibited ground of discrimination under the legislation. For example, a tribunal may order an employer to revise or amend its personnel file in relation to an individual whose employment was terminated in circumstances which involved a violation of human rights legislation. This may be the case where either the individual does not wish to be reinstated or the board does not believe reinstatement to be an appropriate remedy to eliminate any potential continuing effect of the discriminatory conduct upon the individual when seeking alternative employment.

In *Cuff v. Gypsy Restaurant*,[16] an Ontario Board of Inquiry ordered the employer to send an amended version of the complainant's record of employment, stating the discriminatory reasons for dismissal, to the same government agency where the original record had been sent, which alleged termination on the basis of incompetency. The reasons given for the termination of an individual's employment may cause the person to suffer a penalty when unemployment insurance benefits are allocated. It is for this reason that it is absolutely essential that employers complete a record of employment for UIC purposes in a forthright and entirely accurate manner. Falsifying information on such a document constitutes an offence under the *Unemployment Insurance Act*, R.S.C. 1985, c. U-1.

E. Educational Programs and Practices

It is quite common for a human rights tribunal to include, as part of its order, a direction that the employer take certain steps to ensure that the employee population is educated with regard to the provisions of human rights legislation. Such action may include anything from a simple order that an employer post notices which summarize certain information relating to the

---

[14] For example, see *Hendry v. Ontario (Liquor Control Board)* (1980), 1 C.H.R.R. D/160 (Ont. Bd. Inq.).
[15] See, for example, *Pocock v. Canadian Kenworth Company (Ontario 1979)* (unreported, 1979, Ont. Bd. Inq.).
[16] (1987), 87 C.L.L.C. ¶17,015, 8 C.H.R.R. D/3972 (Ont. Bd. Inq.).

legislation to the establishment and implementation of a formal educational program in the workplace. Employers are well-advised to take such measures on their own initiative in an effort to comply with their extensive and far-reaching obligations to provide a workplace free from harassment and other forms of discriminatory practices.

An interesting example of a somewhat novel order made by a human rights tribunal with a view towards increasing education and awareness within the workplace can be found in the Ontario Board of Inquiry decision in *Dhillon v. F.W. Woolworth Co.*[17] In the *Dhillon* case, the Board concluded that the complainant had been subject to racial harassment. As part of its order, the Board of Inquiry directed the establishment and supervision of a race relations committee in the respondent's workplace:

> The respondent shall forthwith constitute an ad hoc Management-Employees Race Relation Committee (hereinafter called "the Committee") for its warehouse, consisting of an equal number of three groups: a management group, an East Indian employees' group and a non-East Indian employees' group, and the said Committee, together with an ex officio member of the Committee appointed by the human rights commission from its staff (which member of the Committee is hereafter called the "Commission Representative") shall meet together on company time at least once a month for the next four months, or more often if and when requested by the Commission Representative, with the Committee's objectives being, first, to establish effective communications on the general issue of inter-race relations within the warehouse, and second, to suggest to the management of the respondent such reasonable measures that seem appropriate and necessary from time to time to remove verbal racial harassment from within the respondent's warehouse, and the respondent shall implement such reasonable measures as are recommended by the Committee and are feasible from a practical standpoint from time to time.[18]

The Board further provided in the *Dhillon* case that it would maintain certain supervisory functions in overseeing the establishment and implementation of the committee. As well, it stipulated that the committee was to continue in existence for a minimum period of time and that the Board could reconvene the committee to address any issues relating to its establishment and role.

6. COSTS

A. Under the Ontario Human Rights Code

Section 41(4) of the Ontario *Human Rights Code* provides that the board of inquiry may award costs against the Human Rights Commission in certain instances:

> 41(4) Where, upon dismissing a complaint, the board of inquiry finds that,

---

[17] (1982), 3 C.H.R.R. D/743 (Ont. Bd. Inq.).
[18] *Supra*, at p. D/763.

(a) the complaint was trivial, frivolous, vexatious or made in bad faith; or

(b) in the particular circumstances undue hardship was caused to the person complained against,

the board of inquiry may order the Commission to pay to the person complained against such costs as are fixed by the board.

The conditions or criteria to be taken into consideration in determining whether a complaint was "trivial, frivolous, vexatious or made in bad faith" are the same as those discussed in Chapter 11.[19] As for the awarding of costs on the second ground noted within s. 41(4), being undue hardship caused to the person complained against, it would take an extraordinary fact situation to justify an award of costs to a respondent on this basis. Perhaps one example, would be the case where a respondent is subjected to extraordinary publicity and ridicule as a result of a complaint which is ultimately dismissed in circumstances where the board of inquiry is satisfied that the complainant was clearly lying under oath or otherwise fabricating evidence.

It can be legitimately argued that because s. 41(4) of the Code deals only with costs awarded against the Commission, it is beyond the jurisdiction of the board of inquiry to award costs against a respondent in the case of a successful complaint. As a practical matter, this makes sense since a complainant is not required to incur any legal costs in the investigation and ultimate hearing of a human rights complaint due to the fact that the complaint is investigated by employees of the Commission and in-house counsel of the Commission is appointed for the purpose of dealing with the complaint at the hearing stage. In most, if not all instances, the interests of the complainant and the Human Rights Commission are common. Furthermore, the Ontario Divisional Court in *Ontario (Liquor Control Board) v. Ontario (Human Rights Commission)*[20] held that as a statutory body, a board of inquiry can only have jurisdiction to award costs if such jurisdiction is expressly given to it by the Code or some other Act. Accordingly, this Ontario Divisional Court decision supports the proposition that an award of costs may only be made against the Commission.

B. Under the Canadian Human Rights Act

The *Canadian Human Rights Act* is entirely silent on the subject of costs. It is suggested that a tribunal appointed under the *Canadian Human Rights Act* would be empowered to award costs to a complainant, in a successful complaint, where the individual retained their own legal counsel to represent them at the hearing in circumstances where it was reasonable for them to have legal

---

[19] See Chapter 11, under heading 3.A. "Pre-hearing Disposition of a Complaint" by way of dismissal.

[20] (1988), 19 C.C.E.L. 172 (Ont. Div. Ct.).

representation separate and distinct from counsel representing the Canadian Human Rights Commission. Such an award of costs would simply reimburse the complainant in relation to a legitimate expense incurred by that individual in proceeding with the complaint to the hearing stage.

7. PENALTIES AND FINES

A. Under the Ontario Human Rights Code

Section 44 of the Ontario *Human Rights Code* provides that every person who contravenes:

- (a) section 9 of the Code, which prohibits direct or indirect violation of ss. 1 through 8 of the Code which set out the primary freedom from discrimination provisions of the legislation,
- (b) hinders, obstructs or interferes with a person in the execution of a warrant or otherwise impeding the investigation of a complaint under the legislation, or
- (c) violates an order of a board of inquiry,

is guilty of an offence and on conviction is liable to a fine of up to $25,000. Section 44(2) of the Code stipulates that a prosecution for an offence under s. 44(1) of the Code requires the written consent of the Attorney General's office. Accordingly, the Ontario Human Rights Commission is without jurisdiction to institute, on its own initiative, proceedings relating to the offence prescribed under s. 44(1) of the Code in the absence of express permission of the Attorney General's office.

The offence provisions prescribed in s. 44 of the Ontario *Human Rights Code* would seldom be resorted to for the singular purpose of prosecuting an individual who had discriminated against another individual. Rather, these provisions would be primarily utilized to deal with an individual who is obstructing an ongoing investigation or to take action against an individual or group of individuals who refuse to comply with the order of a board of inquiry.

B. Under the Canadian Human Rights Act

Section 60 of the *Canadian Human Rights Act* provides:

60(1) Every person is guilty of an offence who
- (a) fails to comply with the terms of any settlement of a complaint approved and certified under section 48;
- (b) obstructs a Tribunal in carrying out its functions under this Part; or
- (c) contravenes subsection 11(6) [ie no wage reduction to comply with the equal wage provision in section 11] or 43(3) [no person shall obstruct an investigator in the investigation of a complaint] or section 59 [prohibition against reprisal against a person who has made a complaint or given evidence in a hearing].

A person who is found guilty of an offence under s. 60(1) of the Act can be subject to a fine of up to $5,000. Where the person charged with an offence is an employer, an employer association or an employee organization, the maximum fine is $50,000. In addition, a prosecution under s. 60(1) of the Act requires the consent of the Attorney General of Canada and cannot be unilaterally instituted by the Canadian Human Rights Commission.

8. CIVIL CAUSE OF ACTION

In its landmark decision, the Supreme Court of Canada in *Seneca College of Applied Arts & Technology v. Bhadauria*[21] ruled that a person cannot institute a civil action that is based entirely upon a violation of human rights legislation. To put it another way, the Supreme Court of Canada in *Bhadauria* rejected the proposition that there is a common law tort of discrimination that is based on violation of a duty prescribed under existing human rights legislation.

The *Bhadauria* case involved a claim that was initiated by a qualified individual who applied, without success, for a teaching position with the college. Chief Justice Laskin, speaking on behalf of a unanimous Supreme Court of Canada, held that the Ontario *Human Rights Code* foreclosed a "civil action" based directly on a breach thereof, as well as any "common law action based on an invocation of the public policy expressed in the Code".[22] The court made it clear that the Code represents a comprehensive scheme for addressing human rights violations and any remedies sought must be acquired within the confines of the legislation. In other words, the civil courts are not an alternative route to recovery.

While the *Bhadauria* decision of the Supreme Court of Canada still stands as good law, in the sense that the Supreme Court of Canada has not revised its views as expressed within the judgment since the time of its release in 1981, certain questions remain unanswered with respect to the jurisdiction of a court to consider any allegations of discrimination. In particular, is a court precluded from determining whether an individual had been discriminated against in the context of an action for damages for wrongful dismissal, whereby the primary relief being claimed by the individual relates to the employer's failure to provide reasonable notice of termination? This issue was recently dealt with, indirectly by Mr. Justice Spence in *Alpaerts v. Obront*.[23]

In the *Alpaerts* case, a motion was brought by two defendants to strike out portions of the Statement of Claim containing allegations of sexual harassment and other mistreatment of the plaintiff, resulting in her inability to continue with her employment responsibilities. It was the position of the defendants that these allegations disclosed no reasonable cause of action and

---

[21] (1981), 124 D.L.R. (3d) 193, [1981] 2 S.C.R. 181.
[22] *Supra*, at p. 203.
[23] (1993), 46 C.C.E.L. 218 (Ont. Ct. (Gen. Div.)).

that any claim that the plaintiff had in relation to this alleged mistreatment was to be taken up under the *Human Rights Code*, on the authority of the Supreme Court of Canada in the *Bhadauria* case. In rejecting the argument of the defendants on the motion, Mr. Justice Spence stated, in part:

> With respect to the Ontario *Human Rights Code* as a barrier to the plaintiff proceeding in Court, the defendants rely on the decision in *Seneca College of Applied Arts & Technology v Bhadauria*, [124 D.L.R. (3d) 193] and on certain other cases. In *Seneca*, the Court determined that "the Code forecloses any civil action based directly upon a breach thereof" and "any common law action based on an invocation of the public policy expressed in the Code". In *Seneca*, the plaintiff had no cause of action apart from the Code, but, in the instant case, the plaintiff alleges facts which disclose a cause of action for constructive dismissal, which distinguishes *Seneca*.[24]

The above statements of Mr. Justice Spence provide a logical justification for concluding that the *Bhadauria* decision has no application to a wrongful dismissal action. Specifically, this kind of action is a claim for damages for breach of contract, in which the plaintiff alleges discriminatory actions on the part of the defendant to either increase the quantum of damages for breach of contract or to support a separate and distinct tortious claim. Moreover, had Mr. Justice Spence accepted the defendants' submissions on the motion, it would have, of necessity, resulted in the plaintiff having to commence separate proceedings with the Human Rights Commission on harassment allegations. This multiplicity of proceedings on the plaintiff's termination of employment is contrary to general principles of the administration of justice.

Finally, it is significant that in cases where an individual has filed a human rights complaint, separate and distinct from initiating a civil action for damages for wrongful dismissal, courts have, in certain cases, granted an order staying the civil proceedings pending disposition of the complaint before a human rights tribunal. For example, in *Ghosh v. Domglas Inc.*[25] Mr. Ghosh commenced an action for wrongful dismissal and subsequently lodged a complaint with the Ontario Human Rights Commission in relation to the same matter. The employer successfully applied for a stay of the civil action, pending adjudication of the human rights complaint. Madam Justice McKinlay provided the following rationale for her order:

> If proceedings before the court and under the Code were to proceed in tandem, it is conceivable that different findings of fact might be made by the board and the court; that different assessments of damages might be made with respect to similar areas of compensation; and also that awards may be made by both tribunals. Counsel for the plaintiff clearly stated that were two awards to be made, his position would be that an award by the court would be an award of damages for wrongful dismissal and any award made by the board would consti-

---

[24] *Supra*, at p. 220.
[25] (1986), 34 D.L.R. (4th) 262, 57 O.R. (2d) 710 (H.C.J.).

tute compensation for discriminatory acts and thus both would be recoverable by the plaintiff. That such a result would constitute double recovery under some heads of compensation is almost inevitable.[26]

The *Ghosh* decision was subsequently followed in the Ontario Court (General Division) in *Meiklem v. Bot Quebec Ltée.*[27] and, quite recently, in *McConnell v. Loomis Armored Car Service Ltd.*,[28] a case in which the complainant had filed a complaint with the Canadian Human Rights Commission against the defendant in the wrongful dismissal action.

---

[26] *Supra*, at p. 267.
[27] (1992), 41 C.C.E.L. 51, 5 Admin. L.R. (2d) 177 (Ont. Ct. (Gen. Div.)).
[28] (unreported, November 16, 1993, Ont. Ct. (Gen. Div.)).

CHAPTER 14

Pay Equity and Employment Equity

1. FEDERAL LEGISLATION

A. The Employment Equity Act[1]

The federal *Employment Equity Act*[2] received Royal Assent on June 27, 1986. It is a legislative scheme, affecting federal employers who employ 100 or more employees, designed to:

1. identify and eliminate discrimination in employment policies and procedures;
2. remedy the effects of past discrimination; and
3. ensure appropriate representation of what are titled "designated groups" in every affected employer's workplace.

All of these goals are designed to be achieved and monitored by a reporting system whereby employers report on a significant volume of information annually with respect to women, aboriginal persons, individuals with disabilities and persons who are, because of their race or colour, in a visible minority in Canada: the so-called designated groups.

The Act sets out its purpose in s. 2 as follows:

> 2. The purpose of this Act is to achieve equality in the work place so that no person shall be denied employment opportunities or benefits for reasons unrelated to ability and, in the fulfilment of that goal, to correct the conditions of disadvantage in employment experienced by women, aboriginal peoples, persons with disabilities and persons who are, because of their race or colour, in a visible minority in Canada by giving effect to the principle that employment equity means more than treating persons in the same way but also requires special measures and the accommodation of differences.

The Act clearly has a preventative as well as a remedial objective base. In the preventative sense, it is intended to ensure that ability is the sole motivating criteria for employers when confronted with the task of assessing employment candidates. In particular, the Act seeks to single out for protection

---

[1] This section contains excerpts from M. Norman Grosman, *Federal Employment Law in Canada* (Toronto, Carswell, 1990), ch. 7.

[2] R.S.C. 1985, c. 23 (2nd Supp.).

women, aboriginal peoples, persons with disabilities, and persons who are because of their race or colour a visible minority in Canada. In a remedial sense, the Act mandates employers to take steps to correct existing or prior conditions of disadvantage which have affected the four designated groups, and authorizes, where necessary, special measures or accommodation of differences.

According to the mandate of the legislation, employment equity exists only when all Canadians, regardless of sex, disability or racial origin, have achieved full participation in the workforce. The legislators postulate that Canadian employers, having permitted inequality to seep into the workplace over decades of both conscious and unconscious employment choices, have failed to tap the full potential of the Canadian workforce as a resource. They argue that the same workforce includes many highly competent members who, at the same time, happen to be members of a designated group. Women, aboriginal peoples, persons with disabilities, and persons who, because of their race or colour, are in a visible minority do not necessarily have less ability or fewer qualifications than individuals outside of those groups. Employment equity is a results-oriented program which seeks evidence that employment situations for the designated groups are improving, indicated primarily by their greater numerical representation in the workforce as well as by an improvement in their employment status, occupations, and salary levels and jobs for which they are available and qualified.

Employment equity is not meant to be limited to the hiring process. The natural tendency of employers is to associate the concept of the introduction of appropriate numbers of designated employees into the workplace. The Federal Employment Equity Program, rather, is intended to ensure equal treatment of designated individuals with respect not only to the hiring process, but to training, re-training, job assignment, promotions, transfers, terminations and career advancement.

The terms ''employment equity'' and ''affirmative action'' are often used interchangeably by employers and employees. They are clearly closely-related terms. Affirmative action is, however, but one type of activity which may be required to achieve employment equity. The common aspect of employment equity and affirmative action is to promote fair and equal treatment of designated groups in the workforce. The Canadian Royal Commission on Equality in Employment commented on the confusion between the two terms in this fashion:

> Ultimately, it matters little whether in Canada we call this process employment equity or affirmative action, so long as we understand that what we mean by both terms are employment practices designed to eliminate discrimination barriers and to provide in a meaningful way equitable opportunities in employment.[3]

---

[3] Report of the Commission on Equality in Employment (Ottawa, Supply and Services Canada, 1984), at p. 7.

By the same token, there is a distinction between employment equity and equal pay legislation. Equal pay is an important aspect of employment equity, but only one aspect. Equal pay legislation is aimed at ensuring that equal pay is available to men and women who perform work-related tasks of equal value within their particular occupations. Employment equity legislation is designed to reduce occupational segregation, which refers to the tendency to stereotype jobs according to sex so that some jobs become known as "women's jobs". Women represent an inordinate percentage of clerical, sales and service positions in the federal workforce. A reduction in the occupational segregation which affects women means offering women employment opportunities — which, in the past, have been largely unavailable to them — based upon ability rather than gender. Equal pay may be seen as a logical extension of employment equity designed to ensure that as women begin to break down occupational barriers and obtain new employment roles in the workforce, they will not do so only to face another form of gender discrimination in terms of pay. Rather, they may expect the same rate of pay for performing the same job or occupation as their male counterparts.

(i) Employers affected by the Act

The legislation is quite explicit in terms of who is affected by employment equity. Any person or company who employs 100 or more employees on or in connection with a federal work, undertaking or business falls within the parameters of the Act. "Federal work, undertaking or business" receives the same definition as in the *Canada Labour Code*[4] typically, this would include railways, telecommunication companies, shipping, airlines, banks and other such federally-regulated businesses.

(ii) Employees affected by the Act

The *Employment Equity Act* is limited in its application to the "designated groups" to whom it offers protection. Section 3 of the Act states:

"designated groups" means women, aboriginal peoples, persons with disabilities and persons who are, because of their race or colour, in a visible minority in Canada.

One of the fundamental issues affecting both the reliability and credibility of data collected and reported by employers under the Act is how properly to identify employees who fall within a designated group. It is, of course, contrary to human rights legislation to question individuals either at the pre-employment stage or otherwise regarding matters which might either directly or indirectly disclose the gender, existing disabilities, race or colour, or place of origin. The federal government suggests two alternative solutions to this problem:

---

[4] R.S.C. 1985, c. L-2, as amended. See discussion in Chapter 1, under heading "Areas of Federal Jurisdiction", p. 4.

1. disclose to prospective employees the existence and nature of the company's employment equity program and request self-identification from applicants as to whether or not they fall within a designated group;

2. a second opportunity for the employer to request self-identification is when the individual has become part of the employer's workforce.

Unfortunately, the voluntary nature of the self-identification mechanism virtually ensures that employer data on designated group participation in the workforce is unreliable. The degree of reliability of that data is purely a function of how successful or unsuccessful an employer is in convincing applicants or its employment population who fall within a designated group to identify themselves voluntarily.

(iii) Employer duties

Under the employment equity legislation an affected employer has the obligation to:

(a) consult with employee representatives with respect to employment equity;

(b) identify and eliminate employment practices which create barriers against people in designated groups;

(c) institute positive policies and practices to ensure persons in designated groups achieve a representative position in the employer's workforce;

(d) make reasonable accommodation for individuals in designated groups;

(e) prepare an annual plan for setting out goals in respect of employment equity with a timetable; and

(f) report employment equity data for the preceding year to the Minister of Labour on or before June 1st.

One of the chief tasks of the employee consulting team is to identify the employer's employment practices, if any, which act as or result in barriers to individuals in designated groups achieving employment. These practices thus identified, where they are not otherwise authorized by law, are then to be eliminated. Examples of such practices might include the following:

— height or weight requirements

— inflated or unnecessary educational requirements

— training programs for women for their current positions while at the same time having training programs for men for promotional purposes

— lack of developmental or bridging positions out of clerical or other "dead end" occupations

— lack of physical accommodation for disabled persons

— reliance on formal as opposed to practical training experience

The types of positive policies or practices which may be instituted as a result of employer and employee consultation, may include the following:

— establishing formal career counselling programs
— advertising employment opportunities in newspapers or journals of special interest to designated groups
— adapting work stations to accommodate the disabled
— hiring designated group recruitment officers
— providing cross-cultural training for staff
— providing language training programs
— establishing bridging positions of clerical positions
— providing on-the-job training
— providing or assisting with child care
— establishing experience equivalent standards

Employers are required to establish practices, systems and support mechanisms which are designed to accommodate differences in order that no individual experiences reduced access to employment opportunities or benefits because of his or her sex, race, colour, aboriginal background or disability. Examples of such reasonable accommodation might include:

— provision of technical equipment (i.e., brail typewriters) and social support services (i.e., train staff to assist disabled persons at work);
— company located or accessible day care facilities or contribution to the expense of such day care;
— adjustments to the work site, job duties and schedules which accommodate reasonable health, cultural and family-related needs of employees.

In this regard, employers may wish to seriously consider actively encouraging employees to come forth with their proposed accommodation requirements or perceived accommodation requirements of co-workers, along with any proposed solutions to the problem. Perhaps the most effective way of encouraging employees to work with the employer is by demonstrating a genuine sincerity, willingness and sensitivity to the unique and personal accommodation requirements of individual employees within the workforce.

The *Employment Equity Act* provides for mandatory submission of a report comprising certain specified elements of information to be represented according to a pre-set format by an affected employer. The report must be filed on or before June 1st on an annual basis. The employer, in addition to the submission of certain prescribed data with respect to its workforce, is required to prepare a plan which sets out the goals that the employer intends to achieve and implement in employment equity in the year to which the plan relates. Once again, this type of plan is to be drawn in consultation with the employee-designated representatives. The plan must also specify the timetable for the completion of the specified goals.

(iv) Employment equity planning framework

Employment & Immigration Canada has prepared a planning framework,[5] for the employer either facing the issue of employment equity for the first time or simply attempting to cope with the legislation in the most efficient manner, which provides a useful overview of many of the constituent elements of compliance with the Act. The framework is as follows:

Phase I — Organizational Readiness

Step One: Preparation

> — establish senior level commitment
> — establish mechanism for consultation with employer representatives (eg. bargaining agents)
> — identify communications resources
> — assign senior staff & resources
> — identify organizational values and attitudes, and sources of support or resistance to employment equity

Step Two: Analysis

> — collect personnel information
> — evaluate current work force information
> — review formal and informal personnel policies and practices
> — identify barriers and policies and practices to employment equity

Phase II — Management of Change

Step Three: Develop Employment Equity Plan

> — establish goals and timetables
> — design new or modified personnel systems and procedures
> — develop special measures for reasonable accommodations
> — determine monitoring and accountability of mechanisms

Step Four: Implementation

> — *assign line management responsibility and accountability*
> — *implement employment equity plan of action*
> — *support with communication strategy*

Phase III — Maintenance of Change

Step Five: Evaluation and Monitoring

> — establish feedback and problem solving mechanisms
> — carry out regular orientation and training programs for supervisors
> — follow through in management performance evaluation
> — reward achievements

---

[5] Excerpt from M. Norman Grosman, *Federal Employment Law in Canada* (Scarborough, Carswell, 1990).

— maintain and update personnel information
— make adjustments to program as required

(v) Enforcement under employment equity legislation

Nowhere within the legislation are the consequences to an employer who fails to deliver or live up to an employment equity plan spelled out. The failure to file a report is an offence punishable by a monetary fine. However, on a review of the legislation in its totality, once an employer has actually filed a report there are no other specifically prescribed sanctions for failure to set out or achieve employment equity objectives within a specified time frame or at all. However, it is significant to note that since the coming into force of the statute, the Canadian Human Rights Commission has quite clearly and boldly stepped forward to assume the role of enforcer of the provisions of the *Employment Equity Act*, in circumstances in which there is a very real question as to the jurisdiction of the Canadian Human Rights Commission to act in this capacity.[6]

2. PROVINCIAL LEGISLATION

A. The Pay Equity Act

The province of Ontario, consistent with various other provincial governments, has recently introduced pay equity legislation to ensure that women and men receive equal pay for work of equal value, regardless of whether wage differences are attributable to specific discriminatory policies or actions. Ontario's *Pay Equity Act* covers the private sector and provides for enforcement mechanisms.[7] Moreover, larger Ontario employers have had to comply with the legislation and Ontario's Pay Equity Hearings Tribunal has issued a number of decisions interpreting the legislation.

(i) The scope of pay comparisons: the "establishment"

In an attempt to recognize geographical wage discrepancies (e.g. higher secretarial salaries in Toronto), Ontario's Act limits pay comparisons to job classes maintained by an employer within each "establishment", defined as a "geographic division" of its operations. What geographic units are suitable for defining the parameters of the establishment is not specified in the Act and has not been determined by the Pay Equity Hearings Tribunal.

The Ontario *Pay Equity Act* obliges all establishments with more than ten employees to respect the principles of equal pay for male and female-dominated jobs of equal value and to start making any wage adjustments within set time

---

6 The Canadian Human Rights Commission purports to rely upon ss. 10 and 16 of the *Canadian Human Rights Act* to support its position that it has jurisdiction to ensure enforcement of the provisions of the *Employment Equity Act*.
7 R.S.O. 1990, c. P.7.

frames. All public sector establishments and private sector establishments with 100 or more employees must develop and post pay equity plans within prescribed deadlines depending on employer size.

Although not explicitly addressed in the Act, it would appear that even part-time or temporary employees count for the purposes of complying with the Act.

The Act's implementation schedule is set out below:

EMPLOYER	POSTING OF PAY EQUITY PLAN	COMMENCEMENT DATE
Public Sector	Jan. 1, 1990	Jan. 1, 1990
Private Sector with more than 500 employees	Jan. 1, 1990	Jan. 1, 1991
Private sector with 100-499 employees	Jan. 1, 1991	Jan. 1, 1992
Private sector with 50-99 employees	voluntarily by Jan. 1, 1992	Jan. 1, 1993
Private sector with 10-49 employees	voluntarily by Jan. 1, 1993	Jan. 1, 1994
Private sector with less than 10 employees	exempt	exempt

Private sector establishments with ten or more but less than 100 employees need not post a plan but must have made all wage adjustments necessary to achieve pay equity. Only if they post a pay equity plan can wage adjustments be phased in.

Any employer who has started a new establishment after January 1, 1988, must ensure pay equity is achieved from the outset.

(ii) Who is the employer?

The Act does not contain any test for determining what individuals are "employees" (as opposed, for example, to independent contractors) for the purposes of pay equity. The much more controversial issue, at least in the public sector, has been: who is the employer for the purposes of making job comparisons? Since the obligation to increase wages for a female-dominated job class depends on the availability of a male-dominated comparator job class, women in small organizations with few male employees have an interest in looking further afield to related organizations to find a comparator. For example, municipal public health nurses who feel they are underpaid have argued that they share a common employer and establishment — the municipality — with well-paid, mostly male police officers.[8]

In a decision which was upheld by the courts, the Pay Equity Hearings Tribunal confirmed that defining who is the employer must be done so as to promote pay equity. The Tribunal outlined four sets of criteria which collectively must be weighed in deciding who is the employer:

1. WHO HAS OVERALL FINANCIAL RESPONSIBILITY?

Indicia of this test include: Who has responsibility for the budget? Who bears the financial burden of compensation practices, and the burden of wage adjustments under the Act? Who is responsible for the financial adminstration of the budget? What is the shareholder investment or ownership? Who bears the responsibility of picking up the deficit or benefitting from the surplus?

2. WHO HAS RESPONSIBILITY FOR COMPENSATION PRACTICES?

The indicia for this criteria include: Who sets the overall policy for compensation practices? Who attaches the value of a job to its skill, effort, responsibility and working conditions? What is the labour relations reality, who negotiates the wages and benefits with the union or sets the wage rate in a non-unionized setting?

3. WHAT IS THE NATURE OF THE BUSINESS, THE SERVICE OR THE ENTERPRISE?

Within this test the following are helpful indicia: What is the core activity of the business, service or enterprise? Is the work in dispute integral to the organization or is it severable or dispensable? Who decides what labour is to be undertaken and attaches that responsibility to a particular job? What are the employees' perceptions of who is the employer?

4. WHAT IS MOST CONSISTENT WITH ACHIEVING THE PURPOSE OF THE PAY EQUITY ACT?

If there is more than one possible employer, it assists the Tribunal in its determination to make reference to the purposes and objectives of the *Pay Equity Act, 1987*.[9]

In subsequent Tribunal decisions which have purported to apply these tests, differing results have been reached in situations where the link between local agencies have been similar.[10]

(iii) Developing a pay equity plan

All public sector and large private sector establishments must prepare and post a pay equity plan. There are three critical steps in developing a plan.

---

[8] *Haldimand-Norfolk (Region) Commissioners of Police v. ONA* (1989), 30 C.C.E.L. 139, 36 O.A.C. 276 (H.C.J.), affd 41 O.A.C. 148 (C.A.).

[9] *Supra*, at pp. 142-3 (H.C.J.).

[10] *Metropolitan Toronto Library Board* (1989), 1 P.E.R. 112 (P.E.H.T.); *Barrie Public Library Board* (1991), 2 P.E.R. 93 (P.E.H.T.).

(a) *Defining job classes*

The conceptual framework of pay equity requires that all jobs within the establishment first be sorted into job classes which are then analyzed by sex. As a result, how the job classes are defined can determine whether pay inequities are found to exist.

For example, at one school board, elementary teachers were paid according to a grid which rewarded educational qualifications and experience. Women were predominant in the lower ends of the grid while males were clustered at the higher-paid end. When the school board proposed to treat all elementary school teachers as one job class, the women teachers' federation objected, realizing that such a broad job class might mask male-female pay differences. The Tribunal upheld the use of the pay grid as a suitable job classification scheme for pay equity, a ruling which was upheld by the courts.[11]

Once job classes are fixed, the Act designates any class with 70% or more male incumbents to be a "male job class". If a job class is 60% or more female, it is designated as a "female job class". All other job classes are designated as "gender neutral".

(b) *Valuing job classes*

One of the most sensitive steps in designing a pay equity plan is formulating a gender neutral approach to valuing the work of each job class. Section 5 of the Act states that:

> 5(1) For the purposes of this Act, the criterion to be applied in determining value of work shall be a composite of the skill, effort and responsibility normally required in the performance of the work and the conditions under which it is normally performed.

Section 5 still permits a variety of sub-criteria to identify components of skill, effort, responsibility and working conditions, and leaves open how job components are to be weighted. It does appear to exclude job valuations based on strictly economic assessments of employees' productivity or contribution to corporate output.

There are at least three possible methods of valuing jobs: ranking, grading, or points. Under ranking, each job class is ranked against others in the establishment for each of the statutory criteria: skill, effort, responsibilities and working conditions. Grading involves sorting all job classes into job "families" with comparable skill, effort, responsibilities and working conditions.

The most popular and flexible method of job evaluation is a point system. Any number of criteria can be recognized, each with distinct weights and levels. Each level in turn yields a certain number of "points". The sum of all points associated with each job may then be compared.

---

[11] *Wentworth County Board of Education* (1989), 1 P.E.R. 133 (P.E.H.T.).

The two most controversial issues which emerge in job valuation are:

(a) what sort of skills, efforts, responsibilities and working conditions should be recognized and given value?; and

(b) what relative weights should be accorded various skills, effort, responsibilities and working conditions associated with job classes?

In one recent Pay Equity Hearings Tribunal decision, the Ontario Nurses' Association was successful in challenging the job valuation system applied by a hospital. The Tribunal ruled that the evaluation system and the employee questionnaire designed to elicit information about job content failed to adequately take into account traditionally female job skills such as communicating with and caring for distressed or low functioning patients and family members.[12]

Similar problems can be encountered in weighting the criteria. Firms that have turned to a traditional job evaluation system not developed for pay equity purposes should not assume that such systems do not contain inherent bias. For example, a system which placed a lower value on the supervision of children than on supervising workers might be gender-biased. In two decisions, the Pay Equity Hearings Tribunal has ruled that management's proposed job evaluation system does not give sufficient prominence to female job skills or demands although it has not attempted to formulate any comprehensive definition of a "gender neutral" approach.[13]

(c) *Methods of job comparison*

The final step in identifying gender-based pay discrepancies is comparing the wages for similarly valued male and female job classes. Initially, the *Pay Equity Act* only permitted "job-to-job" comparisons. Under a "job-to-job" analysis, only where there is both a male job class and a female job class of similar value and the female job class is paid less does the obligation to adjust wages arise. This fails to benefit many women in establishments with few male comparators.

In legislative amendments finally passed in June, 1993,[14] Ontario retroactively approved use of an alternative method known as proportional comparison. This method already had been adopted by many employers to avoid the "equity gaps" that can occur under the "job-to-job" method. This method is suitable to larger establishments with several female and male job classes but an uneven distribution of male job classes. A line averaging all job classes is developed and all female job classes paid below the average for male job classes are then raised to the average male pay level appropriate to value of their job.

---

12 *Women's College Hospital (No. 4)* (1992), 3 P.E.R. 61 (P.E.H.T.).
13 *Supra,* and *Haldimand-Norfolk (No. 6)* (1991), 2 P.E.R. 105 (P.E.H.T.).
14 *Pay Equity Amendment Act,* S.O. 1993, c. 4, s. 2.

Pay equity advocates have called for approval of a third method known as proxy comparisons. Under the proxy comparison method, female job classes in establishments with few or no male comparators (e.g. a daycare operation) are compared to male job classes in designated "proxy" establishments (e.g. a nearby community college). The government has only sanctioned this comparison method for certain designated public sector employers,[15] presumably because it violates the basic tenet that all job comparisons be made within a particular business.

(iv) Employee participation

Under Ontario's legislation, non-union employers are under no obligation to consult with non-union employees. In unionized workplaces, by contrast, employers must negotiate a pay equity plan with its union or unions. Indeed, the legislation contemplates a separate pay equity plan for each bargaining unit plus one for non-union employees in each establishment unless agreement can be reached on a single plan.

Trade unions are entitled to negotiate each step in the pay equity planning process. In order to consider the employer's proposals or formulate their own, unions can request information on the entire workforce. Notwithstanding employer objections the Tribunal has ordered one employer to provide a union with job titles and their gender makeup, wage rates and job descriptions for all employees.[16]

(v) Implementing wage adjustments

Once pay inequities have been isolated, employers who have posted a plan must raise the wages of underpaid female job classes. Where benefits are inferior, the employer will have to improve the benefits applicable to the female job class. In one case, the employer sought to equalize vacation entitlements by paying the female job class more in lieu of vacation. The Tribunal ruled that, in the absence of evidence that the employer would suffer undue hardship, the employees were entitled to receive actual vacation.[17]

Where the annual aggregate cost of all such wage adjustments exceeds 1% of total payroll, employers are entitled to phase in raises over as many years as are needed to achieve pay equity at a maximum of 1% of payroll in each year. In scheduling pay increases, priority goes to the most under-compensated female job classes.

It is important to note that male minorities within female job classes benefit from pay increases along with their colleagues, while female members

---

[15] *Ibid.*, s. 13.
[16] *Cybermedix* (1989), 1 P.E.R. 41 (P.E.H.T.).
[17] *Lady Dunn General Hospital* (1991), 2 P.E.R. 168 (P.E.H.T.).

of neutral or male job classes receive no adjustment. Employers are not permitted to decrease the wages of any class to achieve pay equity.

(vi) Exceptions to pay equity

Ontario's legislation permits several specific exceptions to the general principle of equal pay for equal value. Pay differences based on *bona fide* seniority systems which are formally established and not inherently gender-biased are permissible. Once all wage adjustments have been made, the Act does not require a further review of pay inequities or the preparation of a further pay equity plan. It is possible that other factors such as market forces may alter relative wages after implementation of pay equity but this does not trigger further employer obligations to make wage adjustments.

Unlike employment equity, pay equity does not require ongoing employer compliance. However, it is open to employees to complain that changes in job requirements have created new pay inequities. As well, 1993 amendments allow both employers and trade unions to initiate changes to the plan where circumstances have changed making the original plan inappropriate.

(vii) Enforcement

Ontario's *Pay Equity Act* is enforced through a two-tiered system. The Pay Equity Commission's mandate is to investigate all complaints as well as promoting compliance through education and communications.

An employee or a trade union may complain about failure to post a plan, gender bias in the plan or failure to implement a plan. The deadline for complaints, other than those alleging a failure to post changes in job requirements or wages, is thirty days after posting of the plan. For smaller employers who have not posted a plan, there is no time limit for filing a complaint. Where the union has agreed to a plan, individual employees cannot file a complaint.

Complainants must file a written Request for Review Services before a Commission Review Officer will investigate. The complainant can request anonymity. If the Review Officer is unable to settle the complaint, he or she can make a compliance order. Affected employers have thirty days to appeal such an order to the independent Pay Equity Hearings Tribunal. Complainants dissatisfied with the decision of the Review Officer can also appeal.

Prior to the hearing of an appeal, the Tribunal normally holds a pre-hearing conference to review the opportunity for settlement, narrow the issues and determine the procedure at the hearing.

Given the large number of employers in Ontario which were required to comply with the legislation, there have been relatively few complaints and even fewer appeals. As of April, 1992, the Commission had reviewed 2,933 complaints but the vast majority were settled without an order or hearing. Most employers have successfully posted plans after reaching agreements with their unions without receiving employee complaints.

The complexity of the legislation may explain the low complaint rate. Few employees have sufficient knowledge of the pay equity planning process to assess the fairness of their employer's pay practices.

Whether pay equity will close the "gender gap" remains to be seen. Other governments will be carefully scrutinizing Ontario wage data in future to assess the impact of the *Pay Equity Act* in raising pay rates for traditional women's work.

B. The Employment Equity Act

Recent Ontario employment equity legislation has introduced a second generation of anti-discrimination laws. Employment equity takes a long term, more proactive and results-oriented approach to the problem of discrimination.

Under employment equity, employers have an obligation to take steps to reduce hidden barriers and improve hiring and promotion of members of the four designated groups — women, visible minorities, disabled and aboriginals — whether or not discrimination can be shown. Employment equity aims at achieving "equitable representation" of the four designated groups in all major businesses across all occupational categories and at all levels of firms' hierarchies. In the long term, the governments which have passed employment equity laws hope to reduce the unemployment rates and raise incomes of designated group members.

Employers must set and strive to meet numerical targets for increased participation of designated groups in non-traditional occupations and in management. In Ontario, failure to comply will lead to enforcement action and compliance orders by the Employment Equity Tribunal.

(i) Application of the legislation

The Ontario *Employment Equity Act, 1993*,[18] which was passed but not proclaimed in force at the date of writing, will apply to a much larger number of employers. Public and "broader public sector" employers with more than ten employees must comply, although the Bill provides for less onerous obligations for organizations with between ten and fifty employees. "Broader public sector" entities are the same as those which have been named in the Ontario *Pay Equity Act*.[19] Generally, they include municipalities, hospitals, school boards, universities and many other public institutions funded by the provincial government.

What is more remarkable is the broad coverage of the private sector. All private sector employers with more than fifty staff must also implement employment equity.

---

[18] S.O. 1993, c. 35.
[19] R.S.O. 1990, c. P.7, Appendix.

The deadlines for implementation range from one to three years after an effective date to be set by the government but expected to be sometime in 1994. Deadlines depend on employer size and whether the employer is private or public sector. Table 1 below outlines the timetable for compliance.

TABLE 1

Employer Type	Number of Employees	Deadline (months from Effective date of Legislation)
Ontario Public Service	n/a	12
Broader Public Sector	10 or more	18
Private Sector	500 or more	18
Private Sector	between 100 and 500	24
Private Sector	50 or more but less than 100	36

(ii) Identifying designated group members

The legislation is intended to benefit four disadvantaged groups: women, visible minorities, disabled and aboriginals. While membership in the first-mentioned group is easy enough to determine, membership in the latter three may be a matter of degree.

Employers must rely solely on voluntary self-identification by employees and job applicants. Given the sensitivity of such identification both to designated and non-designated group workers, some underreporting is likely. Indeed, one study suggests that self-identification may lead to underreporting of more than 50%.[20]

Ontario has published a draft regulation prescribing the wording of the questionnaire to be used in surveying the workforce in order to assist employees in determining whether they belong to a designated group.[21]

This draft regulation offers little assistance in cataloguing borderline cases of individuals in disadvantaged groups such as persons of mixed race or persons with mild epilepsy. Such discretionary decisions are left to the worker. Even where an employee fails to respond to a survey or clearly misidentifies him or herself, the employer apparently has no right to correct the response.

---

[20] A study conducted on the federal civil service found $2\frac{1}{2}$ times more disabled than had self-identified themselves and $1\frac{1}{2}$ times more visible minorities: see "A Matter of Fairness, Report of the Special Committee on the Review of the Employment Equity Act" (Ottawa, Queen's Printer, May 1992).

[21] Consultation Draft Regulation for Bill 79 — The *Employment Equity Act, 1993*, found in CCH Canadian Pay Equity Compliance Guide (1993), 27,501. See section 6.

Information collected for employment equity purposes is subject to strict confidentiality.[22] While it is important under employment equity to survey job applicants for membership in designated groups, employers must be careful not to allow employment equity data to be used for any discriminatory purposes. The best practice is to carefully explain to all survey participants the purpose of employment equity generally as well as the limited use for the data and its confidentiality. Accurate profiling of the workforce and overall employee cooperation are usually facilitated by a strong communications plan. Indeed, the Ontario draft employment equity regulation requires the employer to develop a communications strategy to explain employment equity to employees.[23]

(iii) Who is an employee / employer?

The Ontario *Employment Equity Act* gives an extended meaning to the definition of an "employee" for the purposes of employment equity. The Act includes permanent, seasonal and persons employed for a term in excess of three months as employees. As well, commission sales representatives, dependent contractors and others to be designated by regulation are deemed employees.[24] The definition of employer includes trustees, receivers and any person who "regularly engages the services of others on such other basis as may be prescribed by the regulations".[25]

Employees or unions can apply to the Ontario Employment Equity Tribunal for a declaration that two or more employers constitute a single employer for the purposes of complying with employment equity.[26] It is important to note that businesses which have structured their relationships in an attempt to avoid creating an "employment" relationship (e.g. "freelance" writers) may still be "employees" who count for the purpose of deciding whether employment equity rules apply.

It is likely that Ontario's Employment Equity Tribunal will treat as an employee anyone who is subject to the hiring and promotion policies and decisions of the alleged employer. Moreover, the Tribunal can be expected to take an inclusive approach to maximize the number of employers and employees covered by the legislation. The legislation obliges new employer entities or employers with a growing workforce to comply with the legislation once they surpass the applicable threshold of employer size.

---

[22] See *Employment Equity Act*, footnote 18.
[23] *Ibid.*, footnote 21, section 40.
[24] *Ibid.*, section 3.
[25] *Ibid.*, section 3.
[26] *Ibid.*, section 28.1.

(iv) Analyzing the workforce

The keystone of the draft Ontario legislation is the obligation on employers to formulate "goals and timetables" for improving representation of designated group members. The Ontario government has stressed that goals and timetables can be distinguished from quotas in two respects: first, they are set internally by each employer organization rather than being imposed by government. Secondly, failure to achieve objectives does not necessarily lead to sanctions. However, employers will bear a heavy onus of showing "all reasonable efforts" were made to achieve goals.

Goals and timetables constitute the quantitative output of the employment equity planning process. Before they can be set, employers must first develop a framework for identifying occupational groups and levels within their workforce and survey staff to see how the designated groups are currently represented. Information gathered from the survey must then be compared with data on the availability of designated group members for the various types of jobs. In some types of entry level or unskilled jobs, the Ontario regulations will require comparisons with working-age populations of the designated groups rather than the pool of experienced or qualified candidates. Each step in this process raises important issues. Ontario has tabled a draft regulation requiring employers to analyze their workforce according to census geographical regions and occupational groups. Employers with over 500 employees must also divide employees into four salary ranges.[27]

Employers will also have to consider whether they should aggregate employees at various locations. It may be appropriate to combine several business establishments in the same municipality but segregate workplaces in different regions for employment equity planning purposes. The theory of employment equity is that the particular business establishment's workforce should reflect the makeup of the labour pool or community in the geographical area from which the establishment draws employees. By way of illustration, it may be appropriate to measure head office representation against the provincial or even national available labour pools if they draw from these labour markets.[28] On the other hand, manual labourers may only be recruited locally, suggesting that representation of designated groups should only be compared with local census data.

Although many employers outside major cities may only be able to attract job applicants within the immediate vicinity, they currently can only compare their workforce with regional data since Statistics Canada only breaks down workforce information below the regional level in major cities, known as Census Metropolitan Area ("CMAs").

---

[27] *Ibid.*, sections 21, 22 and 47.
[28] See, *ibid.*, sections 21, 22 and 24.

Again because Statistics Canada census data is currently the only comparator available, employers must adopt the Standard Occupational Categories ("SOCs") defined for census purposes when surveying and classifying their workforce by occupation.

In occupational groups or managerial levels where designated group members are under-represented, numerical targets for improving representation with time-frames must be set — the "goals and timetables".

(v) Setting goals and timetables

Employers must first select the population measure they wish to use as the comparator for goal-setting purposes. Options range from the percent representation of the designated group in the population at large, in the working-age population, in the population actually working or seeking work, or the population having the necessary education or experience to qualify for specific positions at the employer firm.

The federal legislation does not dictate which population measure should be adopted for goal-setting purposes. Ontario's draft regulation states on the one hand that the goals and timetables must aim at representation of the designated groups proportional to their presence in the working-age population, but permit the employer to take into account the availability of designated group workers with the necessary qualifications to fill the employer's positions.[29]

Once an employer has selected a long term goal, for example, to increase women engineers on staff to the same proportion found in the profession in the province, further analysis is required to establish feasible time-frames. Since job incumbents cannot be dismissed to speed the attainment of equitable representation, progress must be achieved through new hiring and promotions. Employers will have to start tracking quits, terminations, promotions and new job openings in order to assess how fast designated group participation can be improved. Firms with low turnover or those laying off workers will obviously have less scope for rapid change than expanding firms or firms with high turnover. In addition, employers must consider the impact of lay-off plans on designated group representation.

Interim hiring and promotion targets should be set somewhat higher than the longer term representation goal to serve as short term guideposts to equitable representation. By way of illustration, if the long term goal of a firm of consulting engineers is to employ 30% women engineers, when only 10% of engineers are currently women, the hiring target might be 50% to ensure progress is made. Ontario's legislation draft regulation calls for the formulation of explicit hiring and promotion targets which constitute "reasonable prog-

---

[29] *Ibid.*, sections 23 and 24.

ress'' towards equitable representation,[30] without going on to impose specific minimum standards.

Unless the employer fails to comply with the legislation, employment equity does not prescribe rigid quotas and proportionality in all job classes but rather relies on employers to set progressive goals which must take into account opportunities for hiring and advancement within the firm, as well as the makeup of the workforce and surrounding community. Employers are bound to review goals and timetables periodically to take into account the changing composition of the labour force.[31]

(vi) Eliminating barriers, positive measures, supportive measures and accommodation

Both federal and Ontario employment equity laws oblige employers to review current hiring, training and promotion practices with a view to eliminating hidden biases against designated groups or, where necessary, extending special measures to recruit or promote designated group members. These steps will assist the employer in meeting its goals and timetables.

Examples of hidden barriers are inflated or unnecessary educational prerequisites for a position or unjustified height and weight requirements. The former might tend to screen out groups such as aboriginals with less education. The latter can often exclude women and members of some racial minorities.

Larger employers can take an analytical approach to identify barriers to participation. By reviewing resignation rates and promotion patterns, hidden biases may become apparent. To illustrate, if visible minority members are twice as likely as others to quit a particular department or plant, this may be symptomatic of discriminatory management practices or an offensive work environment. If predominantly female secretarial and clerical workers are never promoted to supervisory positions, an in-house training programme might help raise female representation in management.

Experts point to recruitment practices as the single biggest hurdle to equalizing opportunities for designated group members. A careful employment practices review starts with scrutiny of the job description and minimum qualifications to ensure that unbiased language is used and that mandatory job qualifications are really necessary. The text of the job advertisement or posting should also be reviewed. For example, where a degree is not essential, the ad should read ''X degree an asset'' rather than ''X degree required''.

The employer should also consider the best means of reaching designated group candidates. Word-of-mouth hiring can be an invisible barrier to recruit-

---

[30] *Ibid.*, section 23.
[31] See *Employment Equity Act*, R.S.C. 1985, c. 23 (2nd Supp.), s. 5, requiring a plan for each year and Ontario Draft regulation, section 29, mandating a review and revision of the plan every three years.

ing from these groups. If the firm prefers promoting from within, all staff should have equal access to the job posting. Outside advertising might include buying space in designated group publications or posting in the offices of designated group associations.

Interviewers may also need coaching in cross-cultural sensitivity. By way of illustration, some visible minorities avoid eye contact or seem overly reticent by Canadian standards yet may still be perfectly competent for the position.

Positive measures are crucial to achieving goals and timetables. They entail workplace changes and additional resources targeted at under-represented groups. Possible positive measures could include advertising job openings in designated group publications, supplying management training to designated group members or providing on-site daycare.

Employment equity also imposes a related duty on employers to offer "accommodation" and "supportive measures" for the needs of designated group members. Accommodation becomes necessary where a workplace rule which does not appear to discriminate against a designated group nonetheless places a disproportionately heavy burden on a designated group. By way of illustration, regular shift rotations which ensures that workers share an unpopular shift may need to be relaxed to accommodate a wheelchair-bound worker who has limited access to transportation. Ontario's draft regulation contains detailed directives for the specific types of accommodation which must be extended to persons with disabilities.[32]

"Supportive measures" refer to special steps taken to assist members of designated groups in succeeding in the workplace. One example would be a mentor programme which matched senior executives with junior employees from designated groups. Another example would be a workplace anti-harassment education programme.

Under Ontario's employment equity legislation, the employer plan must state specific deadlines for implementing barrier elimination, positive measures, accommodation and supportive measures. As with goals and timetables, no specific deadlines are imposed by law and employers must only make "reasonable progress" towards a barrier-free workplace.[33]

(vii) Enforcement

The Ontario *Employment Equity Act* ensures compliance through a variety of mechanisms. Enforcement is entrusted to an independent Employment Equity Commission and unresolved complaints are referred to the separate Employment Equity Tribunal. For the moment, it would appear that both agencies will remain separate from the Ontario Human Rights Commission.

---

[32] Draft regulation, *ibid.*, footnote 21, section 20.
[33] *Ibid.*, section 20.

The first enforcement mechanism is to require affected employers to file an initial report on the makeup of their workforce and progress reports every three years with the Employment Equity Commission along with a certificate of compliance signed by the chief executive officer.[34] Broader public sector employers with fifty or more employees and private sector employers with 100 or more employees must also file a summary of the contents of the plan, including measures called for in it, in a form to be designated by regulation.

Secondly, the Commission will be authorized to conduct ''spot audits'' to ensure that employers are living up to their plans.[35] Thirdly, any concerned person will be able to file a complaint with the Commission about an employer's failure to prepare an employment equity plan, to take steps required by its employment equity plan or to achieve its goals and timetables.[36] If goals and timetables have not been met, the onus will be on the employer to show it used ''all reasonable efforts'' to comply.

In addition, failure by any employer doing business with the Ontario government to abide by the legislation will be deemed a fundamental breach of contract entitling the government to terminate the contract.[37]

Employment Equity Commission-initiated investigations which have not been settled and privately-initiated complaints will be adjudicated by the Employment Equity Tribunal.

The passage of Ontario's *Employment Equity Act* will not change the mandate of the Human Rights Commission. Boards of Inquiry under the *Human Rights Code* retain full jurisdiction to hear complaints about practices which are dealt with in an employer's employment equity plan and even to order additional remedial action beyond the steps contemplated by the employment equity plan. However, the Act does clarify that measures taken towards complying with employment equity which favour designated groups do not constitute ''reverse discrimination'' against other groups under the *Human Rights Code.*

---

[34] *Ibid.*, sections 45, 46, 47 and 48.
[35] *Ibid.*, see *Employment Equity Act, 1993*, S.O. 1993, c. 35.
[36] *Ibid.*, Draft regulation, section 26.
[37] *Ibid.*, section 49.

Table of Schedules

Table of Schedules

Schedule (i)

HUMAN RIGHTS CODE

R.S.O. 1990, c. H.19

Amended 1993, c. 27, Sch.; deemed in force December 31, 1991
Amended 1993, c. 35, s. 56; to come into force on proclamation

PART I
FREEDOM FROM DISCRIMINATION

PART II
INTERPRETATION AND APPLICATION

PART III
THE ONTARIO HUMAN RIGHTS COMMISSION

HUMAN RIGHTS CODE

PART I
FREEDOM FROM DISCRIMINATION

1. Services.—Every person has a right to equal treatment with respect to services, goods and facilities, without discrimination because of race, ancestry, place of origin, colour, ethnic origin, citizenship, creed, sex, sexual orientation, age, marital status, family status or handicap. 1981, c. 53, s. 1; 1986, c. 64, s. 18(1).

2. (1) **Accommodation.**—Every person has a right to equal treatment with respect to the occupancy of accommodation, without discrimination because of race, ancestry, place of origin, colour, ethnic origin, citizenship, creed, sex, sexual orientation, age, marital status, family status, handicap or the receipt of public assistance. 1981, c. 53, s. 2(1); 1986, c. 64, s. 18(2).

(2) **Harassment in accommodation.**—Every person who occupies accommodation has a right to freedom from harassment by the landlord or agent of the landlord or by an occupant of the same building because of race,

ancestry, place of origin, colour, ethnic origin, citizenship, creed, age, marital status, family status, handicap or the receipt of public assistance. 1981, c. 53, s. 2(2).

3. Contracts.—Every person having legal capacity has a right to contract on equal terms without discrimination because of race, ancestry, place of origin, colour, ethnic origin, citizenship, creed, sex, sexual orientation, age, marital status, family status or handicap. 1981, c. 53, s. 3; 1986, c. 64, s. 18(3).

4. (1) **Accommodation of person under eighteen.**—Every sixteen or seventeen year old person who has withdrawn from parental control has a right to equal treatment with respect to occupancy of and contracting for accommodation without discrimination because the person is less than eighteen years old.

(2) **Idem.**—A contract for accommodation entered into by a sixteen or seventeen year old person who has withdrawn from parental control is enforceable against that person as if the person were eighteen years old. 1986, c. 64, s. 18(4).

5. (1) **Employment.**—Every person has a right to equal treatment with respect to employment without discrimination because of race, ancestry, place of origin, colour, ethnic origin, citizenship, creed, sex, sexual orientation, age, record of offences, marital status, family status or handicap. 1981, c. 53, s. 4(1); 1986, c. 64, s. 18(5).

(2) **Harassment in employment.**—Every person who is an employee has a right to freedom from harassment in the workplace by the employer or agent of the employer or by another employee because of race, ancestry, place of origin, colour, ethnic origin, citizenship, creed, age, record of offences, marital status, family status or handicap. 1981, c. 53, s. 4(2).

6. Vocational associations.—Every person has a right to equal treatment with respect to membership in any trade union, trade or occupational association or self-governing profession without discrimination because of race, ancestry, place of origin, colour, ethnic origin, citizenship, creed, sex, sexual orientation, age, marital status, family status or handicap. 1981, c. 53, s. 5; 1986, c. 64, s. 18(6).

7. (1) **Harassment because of sex in accommodation.**—Every person who occupies accommodation has a right to freedom from harassment because of sex by the landlord or agent of the landlord or by an occupant of the same building.

(2) **Harassment because of sex in workplaces.**—Every person who is an employee has a right to freedom from harassment in the workplace because of sex by his or her employer or agent of the employer or by another employee.

(3) **Sexual solicitation by a person in position to confer benefit, etc.**—Every person has a right to be free from,

    (a)   a sexual solicitation or advance made by a person in a position to confer, grant or deny a benefit or advancement to the person where the person making the solicitation or advance knows or ought reasonably to know that it is unwelcome; or

    (b)   a reprisal or a threat of reprisal for the rejection of a sexual solicitation or advance where the reprisal is made or threatened by a person in a position to confer, grant or deny a benefit or advancement to the person. 1981, c. 53, s. 6.

8. Reprisals.—Every person has a right to claim and enforce his or her rights under this Act, to institute and participate in proceedings under this Act and to refuse to infringe a right of another person under this Act, without reprisal or threat of reprisal for so doing. 1981, c. 53, s. 7.

9. Infringement prohibited.—No person shall infringe or do, directly or indirectly, anything that infringes a right under this Part. 1981, c. 53, s. 8.

PART II
INTERPRETATION AND APPLICATION

10. (1) Definitions.—In Part I and in this Part,

"age" means an age that is eighteen years or more, except in subsection 5(1) where "age" means an age that is eighteen years or more and less than sixty-five years; ("âge")

"because of handicap" means for the reason that the person has or has had, or is believed to have or have had,

    (a)   any degree of physical disability, infirmity, malformation or disfigurement that is caused by bodily injury, birth defect or illness and, without limiting the generality of the foregoing, including diabetes mellitus, epilepsy, any degree of paralysis, amputation, lack of physical co-ordination, blindness or visual impediment, deafness or hearing impediment, muteness or speech impediment, or physical reliance on a guide dog or on a wheelchair or other remedial appliance or device,

    (b)   a condition of mental retardation or impairment,

    (c)   a learning disability, or a dysfunction in one or more of the processes involved in understanding or using symbols or spoken language,

    (d)   a mental disorder, or

    (e)   an injury or disability for which benefits were claimed or received under the *Workers' Compensation Act*; (''à cause d'un handicap'')

''equal'' means subject to all requirements, qualifications and considerations that are not a prohibited ground of discrimination; (''égal'')

''family status'' means the status of being in a parent and child relationship; (''état familial'')

''group insurance'' means insurance whereby the lives or well-being or the lives and well-being of a number of persons are insured severally under a single contract between an insurer and an association or an employer or other person; (''assurance-groupe'')

''harassment'' means engaging in a course of vexatious comment or conduct that is known or ought reasonably to be known to be unwelcome; (''harcèlement'')

''marital status'' means the status of being married, single, widowed, divorced or separated and includes the status of living with a person of the opposite sex in a conjugal relationship outside marriage; (''état matrimonial'')

''record of offences'' means a conviction for,

    (a)   an offence in respect of which a pardon has been granted under the *Criminal Records Act* (Canada) and has not been revoked, or

    (b)   an offence in respect of any provincial enactment; (''casier judiciaire'')

''services'' does not include a levy, fee, tax or periodic payment imposed by law; (''services'')

''spouse'' means the person to whom a person of the opposite sex is married or with whom the person is living in a conjugal relationship outside marriage. (''conjoint'') 1981, c. 53, s. 9; 1984, c. 58, s. 39.

    (2) **Pregnancy.**—The right to equal treatment without discrimination because of sex includes the right to equal treatment without discrimination because a woman is or may become pregnant. 1986, c. 64, s. 18(7).

    11. (1) **Constructive discrimination.**—A right of a person under Part I is infringed where a requirement, qualification or factor exists that is not discrimination on a prohibited ground but that results in the exclusion, restriction or preference of a group of persons who are identified by a prohibited ground of discrimination and of whom the person is a member, except where,

    (a)   the requirement, qualification or factor is reasonable and *bona fide* in the circumstances; or

    (b)   it is declared in this Act, other than in section 17, that to discriminate because of such ground is not an infringement of a right.

(2) **Idem.**—The Commission, a board of inquiry or a court shall not find that a requirement, qualification or factor is reasonable and *bona fide* in the circumstances unless it is satisfied that the needs of the group of which the person is a member cannot be accommodated without undue hardship on the person responsible for accommodating those needs, considering the cost, outside sources of funding, if any, and health and safety requirements, if any.

(3) **Idem.**—The Commission, a board of inquiry or a court shall consider any standards prescribed by the regulations for assessing what is undue hardship. 1986, c. 64, s. 18(8).

12. Discrimination because of association.—A right under Part I is infringed where the discrimination is because of relationship, association or dealings with a person or persons identified by a prohibited ground of discrimination. 1981, c. 53, s. 11.

13. (1) **Announced intention to discriminate.**—A right under Part I is infringed by a person who publishes or displays before the public or causes the publication or display before the public of any notice, sign, symbol, emblem, or other similar representation that indicates the intention of the person to infringe a right under Part I or that is intended by the person to incite the infringement of a right under Part I.

(2) **Opinion.**—Subsection (1) shall not interfere with freedom of expression of opinion. 1981, c. 53, s. 12.

14. (1) **Special programs.**—A right under Part I is not infringed by the implementation of a special program designed to relieve hardship or economic disadvantage or to assist disadvantaged persons or groups to achieve or attempt to achieve equal opportunity or that is likely to contribute to the elimination of the infringement of rights under Part I.

(2) **Review by Commission.**—The Commission may,

(a) upon its own initiative;

(b) upon application by a person seeking to implement a special program under the protection of subsection (1); or

(c) upon a complaint in respect of which the protection of subsection (1) is claimed,

inquire into the special program and, in the discretion of the Commission, may by order declare,

(d) that the special program, as defined in the order, does not satisfy the requirements of subsection (1); or

(e) that the special program as defined in the order, with such modifications, if any, as the Commission considers advisable, satisfies the requirements of subsection (1).

(3) **Reconsideration.**—A person aggrieved by the making of an order under subsection (2) may request the Commission to reconsider its order and section 37, with necessary modifications, applies.

(4) **Effect of order.**—Subsection (1) does not apply to a special program where an order is made under clause (2)(d) or where an order is made under clause (2)(e) with modifications of the special program that are not implemented.

(5) **Subs. (2) does not apply to Crown.**—Subsection (2) does not apply to a special program implemented by the Crown or an agency of the Crown. 1981, c. 53, s. 13.

NOTE: Section 14.1 as enacted by 1993, c. 35, s. 56, *part* (to come into force on proclamation) reads as follows:

14.1 (1) Components of employment equity plans.—*A right under Part I is not infringed because positive measures or numerical goals that are contained in an employment equity plan under the Employment Equity Act, 1993 are restricted to members of the designated groups identified under section 4 of that Act.*

(2) Definitions.—*In this section,*

"numerical goal" means a goal with respect to the composition of an employer's workforce that is determined in accordance with the Employment Equity Act, 1993; ("objectif quantitatif")

"positive measure" means a positive measure established under the Employment Equity Act, 1993. ("mesure corrective")

15. Age sixty-five or over.—A right under Part I to non-discrimination because of age is not infringed where an age of sixty-five years or over is a requirement, qualification or consideration for preferential treatment. 1981, c. 53, s. 14.

16. (1) Canadian Citizenship.—A right under Part I to non-discrimination because of citizenship is not infringed where Canadian citizenship is a requirement, qualification or consideration imposed or authorized by law.

(2) **Idem.**—A right under Part I to non-discrimination because of citizenship is not infringed where Canadian citizenship or lawful admission to Canada for permanent residence is a requirement, qualification or consideration adopted for the purpose of fostering and developing participation in cultural, educational, trade union or athletic activities by Canadian citizens or persons lawfully admitted to Canada for permanent residence.

(3) **Idem.**—A right under Part I to non-discrimination because of citizenship is not infringed where Canadian citizenship or domicile in Canada with the intention to obtain Canadian citizenship is a requirement, qualification or consideration adopted by an organization or enterprise for the holder of chief or senior executive positions. 1981, c. 53, s. 15.

17. (1) **Handicap.**—A right of a person under this Act is not infringed for the reason only that the person is incapable of performing or fulfilling the essential duties or requirements attending the exercise of the right because of handicap. 1986, c. 64, s. 18(9).

(2) **Accommodation.**—The Commission, a board of inquiry or a court shall not find a person incapable unless it is satisfied that the needs of the person cannot be accommodated without undue hardship on the person responsible for accommodating those needs, considering the cost, outside sources of funding, if any, and health and safety requirements, if any.

(3) **Idem.**—The Commission, a board of inquiry or a court shall consider any standards prescribed by the regulations for assessing what is undue hardship. 1986, c. 64, s. 18(10).

(4) **Powers of Commission.**—Where, after the investigation of a complaint, the Commission determines that the evidence does not warrant the appointment of a board of inquiry because of the application of subsection (1), the Commission may nevertheless use its best endeavours to effect a settlement as to the duties or requirements. 1981, c. 53, s. 16(2); 1986, c. 64, s. 18(11).

18. Special interest organizations.—The rights under Part I to equal treatment with respect to services and facilities, with or without accommodation, are not infringed where membership or participation in a religious, philanthropic, educational, fraternal or social institution or organization that is primarily engaged in serving the interests of persons identified by a prohibited ground of discrimination is restricted to persons who are similarly identified. 1981, c. 53, s. 17.

19. (1) **Separate school rights preserved.**—This Act shall not be construed to adversely affect any right or privilege respecting separate schools enjoyed by separate school boards or their supporters under the *Constitution Act, 1867* and the *Education Act*.

(2) **Duties of teachers.**—This Act does not apply to affect the application of the *Education Act* with respect to the duties of teachers. 1981, c. 53, s. 18.

20. (1) **Restriction of facilities by sex.**—The right under section 1 to equal treatment with respect to services and facilities without discrimination because of sex is not infringed where the use of the services or facilities is restricted to persons of the same sex on the ground of public decency. 1981, c. 53, s. 19(1).

(2) **Minimum drinking age.**—The right under section 1 to equal treatment with respect to services, goods and facilities without discrimination because of age is not infringed by the provisions of the *Liquor Licence Act* and the regulations under it relating to providing for and enforcing a minimum drinking age of nineteen years. 1990, c. 15, s. 65.

(3) **Recreational clubs.**—The right under section 1 to equal treatment with respect to services and facilities is not infringed where a recreational club restricts or qualifies access to its services or facilities or gives preferences with respect to membership dues and other fees because of age, sex, marital status or family status. 1981, c. 53, s. 19(3).

21. (1) **Shared accommodation.**—The right under section 2 to equal treatment with respect to the occupancy of residential accommodation without discrimination is not infringed by discrimination where the residential accommodation is in a dwelling in which the owner or his or her family reside if the occupant or occupants of the residential accommodation are required to share a bathroom or kitchen facility with the owner or family of the owner.

(2) **Restrictions on accommodation, sex.**—The right under section 2 to equal treatment with respect to the occupancy of residential accommodation without discrimination because of sex is not infringed by discrimination on that ground where the occupancy of all the residential accommodation in the building, other than the accommodation, if any, of the owner or family of the owner, is restricted to persons who are of the same sex. 1981, c. 53, s. 20(1, 2).

22. Restrictions for insurance contracts, etc.—The right under sections 1 and 3 to equal treatment with respect to services and to contract on equal terms, without discrimination because of age, sex, marital status, family status or handicap, is not infringed where a contract of automobile, life, accident or sickness or disability insurance or a contract of group insurance between an insurer and an association or person other than an employer, or a life annuity, differentiates or makes a distinction, exclusion or preference on reasonable and *bona fide* grounds because of age, sex, marital status, family status or handicap. 1981, c. 53, s. 21.

23. (1) **Discriminatory employment advertising.**—The right under section 5 to equal treatment with respect to employment is infringed where an invitation to apply for employment or an advertisement in connection with employment is published or displayed that directly or indirectly classifies or indicates qualifications by a prohibited ground of discrimination.

(2) **Application for employment.**—The right under section 5 to equal treatment with respect to employment is infringed where a form of application for employment is used or a written or oral inquiry is made of an applicant that directly or indirectly classifies or indicates qualifications by a prohibited ground of discrimination.

(3) **Questions at interview.**—Nothing in subsection (2) precludes the asking of questions at a personal employment interview concerning a prohibited ground of discrimination where discrimination on such ground is permitted under this Act.

(4) **Employment agencies.**—The right under section 5 to equal treatment with respect to employment is infringed where an employment agency discriminates against a person because of a prohibited ground of discrimination in receiving, classifying, disposing of or otherwise acting upon applications for its services or in referring an applicant or applicants to an employer or agent of an employer. 1981, c. 53, s. 22.

24. (1) **Special employment.**—The right under section 5 to equal treatment with respect to employment is not infringed where,

(a)   a religious, philanthropic, educational, fraternal or social institution or organization that is primarily engaged in serving the interests of persons identified by their race, ancestry, place of origin, colour, ethnic origin, creed, sex, age, marital status or handicap employs only, or gives preference in employment to, persons similarly identified if the qualification is a reasonable and *bona fide* qualification because of the nature of the employment;

(b)   the discrimination in employment is for reasons of age, sex, record of offences or marital status if the age, sex, record of offences or marital status of the applicant is a reasonable and *bona fide* qualification because of the nature of the employment;

(c)   an individual person refuses to employ another for reasons of any prohibited ground of discrimination in section 5, where the primary duty of the employment is attending to the medical or personal needs of the person or of an ill child or an aged, infirm or ill spouse or other relative of the person; or

(d)   an employer grants or withholds employment or advancement in employment to a person who is the spouse, child or parent of the employer or an employee. 1981, c. 53, s. 23.

(2) **Reasonable accommodation.**—The Commission, a board of inquiry or a court shall not find that a qualification under clause (1)(b) is reasonable and *bona fide* unless it is satisfied that the circumstances of the person cannot be accommodated without undue hardship on the person responsible for

accommodating those circumstances considering the cost, outside sources of funding, if any, and health and safety requirements, if any.

(3) **Idem.**—The Commission, a board of inquiry or a court shall consider any standards prescribed by the regulations for assessing what is undue hardship. 1986, c. 64, s. 18(15).

NOTE: Section 24.1 as enacted by 1993, c. 35, s. 56, *part* (to come into force on proclamation) reads as follows:

*24.1 (1) **Undue hardship where employment equity plan exists.**—If a complaint is made against an employer that has an employment equity plan under the Employment Equity Act, 1993, the Commission, a board of inquiry or a court may consider the cost of implementing the employment equity plan in any assessment of undue hardship that it makes under subsection 11(2), 17(2) or 24(2) with respect to the complaint.*

*(2) **Same.**—Despite subsection (1), the Commission, a board of inquiry, or a court shall consider the cost of implementing an employment equity plan in any assessment of undue hardship that it makes under subsection 11(2), 17(2) or 24(2) with respect to the complaint if, on or before the day that the complaint is filed with the Commission,*

  (a)   the Employment Equity Tribunal has determined that the plan complies with Part III of the Employment Equity Act, 1993; or

  (b)   the Employment Equity Commission has determined that the plan complies with Part III of that Act.

25. (1) **Employment conditional on membership in pension plan.**—The right under section 5 to equal treatment with respect to employment is infringed where employment is denied or made conditional because a term or condition of employment requires enrolment in an employee benefit, pension or superannuation plan or fund or a contract of group insurance between an insurer and an employer, that makes a distinction, preference or exclusion on a prohibited ground of discrimination.

(2) **Pension or disability plan.**—The right under section 5 to equal treatment with respect to employment without discrimination because of age, sex, marital status or family status is not infringed by an employee superannuation or pension plan or fund or a contract of group insurance between an insurer and an employer that complies with the *Employment Standards Act* and the regulations thereunder.

(3) **Employee disability and pension plans: handicap.**—The right under section 5 to equal treatment with respect to employment without discrimination because of handicap is not infringed,

  (a)   where a reasonable and *bona fide* distinction, exclusion or preference is made in an employee disability or life insurance plan or benefit because of a pre-existing handicap that substantially increases the risk;

(b)   where a reasonable and *bona fide* distinction, exclusion or preference is made on the ground of a pre-existing handicap in respect of an employee-pay-all or participant-pay-all benefit in an employee benefit, pension or superannuation plan or fund or a contract of group insurance between an insurer and an employer or in respect of a plan, fund or policy that is offered by an employer to employees if they are fewer than twenty-five in number.

(4) **Compensation.**—An employer shall pay to an employee who is excluded because of a handicap from an employee benefit, pension or superannuation plan or fund or a contract of group insurance between an insurer and the employer compensation equivalent to the contribution that the employer would make thereto on behalf of an employee who does not have a handicap. 1981, c. 53, s. 24.

26. (1) **Discrimination in employment under government contracts.**—It shall be deemed to be a condition of every contract entered into by or on behalf of the Crown or any agency thereof and of every subcontract entered into in the performance thereof that no right under section 5 will be infringed in the course of performing the contract.

(2) **Idem: government grants and loans.**—It shall be deemed to be a condition of every grant, contribution, loan or guarantee made by or on behalf of the Crown or any agency thereof that no right under section 5 will be infringed in the course of carrying out the purposes for which the grant, contribution, loan or guarantee was made.

(3) **Sanction.**—Where an infringement of a right under section 5 is found by a board of inquiry upon a complaint and constitutes a breach of a condition under this section, the breach of condition is sufficient grounds for cancellation of the contract, grant, contribution, loan or guarantee and refusal to enter into any further contract with or make any further grant, contribution, loan or guarantee to the same person. 1981, c. 53, s. 25.

PART III
THE ONTARIO HUMAN RIGHTS COMMISSION

27. (1) **Commission continued.**—The Ontario Human Rights Commission is continued under the name Ontario Human Rights Commission in English and Commission ontarienne des droits de la personne in French and shall be composed of such persons, being not fewer than seven, as are appointed by the Lieutenant Governor in Council. 1981, c. 53, s. 26(1), *revised*.

(2) **Responsible to Minister.**—The Commission is responsible to the Minister for the administration of this Act.

(3) **Chair.**—The Lieutenant Governor in Council shall designate a member of the Commission as chair, and a member as vice-chair.

(4) **Remuneration.**—The Lieutenant Governor in Council may fix the remuneration and allowance for expenses of the chair, vice-chair and members of the Commission.

(5) **Employees.**—The employees of the Commission shall be appointed under the *Public Service Act.*

(6) **Divisions.**—The Commission may authorize any function of the Commission to be performed by a division of the Commission composed of at least three members of the Commission. 1981, c. 53, s. 26(2-6).

28. (1) **Race relations division.**—The Lieutenant Governor in Council shall designate at least three members of the Commission to constitute a race relations division of the Commission and shall designate one member of the race relations division as Commissioner for Race Relations.

(2) **Functions.**—It is the function of the race relations division of the Commission to perform any of the functions of the Commission under clause 29(f), (g) or (h) relating to race, ancestry, place of origin, colour, ethnic origin or creed that are referred to it by the Commission and any other function referred to it by the Commission. 1981, c. 53, s. 27.

29. Function of Commission.—It is the function of the Commission,
- (a) to forward the policy that the dignity and worth of every person be recognized and that equal rights and opportunities be provided without discrimination that is contrary to law;
- (b) to promote an understanding and acceptance of and compliance with this Act;
- (c) to recommend for consideration a special plan or program designed to meet the requirements of subsection 14(1), subject to the right of a person aggrieved by the implementation of the plan or program to request the Commission to reconsider its recommendation and section 37 applies with necessary modifications;
- (d) to develop and conduct programs of public information and education and undertake, direct and encourage research designed to eliminate discriminatory practices that infringe rights under this Act;
- (e) to examine and review any statute or regulation, and any program or policy made by or under a statute and make recommendations on any provision, program or policy, that in its opinion is inconsistent with the intent of this Act;

(f) to inquire into incidents of and conditions leading or tending to lead to tension or conflict based upon identification by a prohibited ground of discrimination and take appropriate action to eliminate the source of tension or conflict;

(g) to initiate investigations into problems based upon identification by a prohibited ground of discrimination that may arise in a community, and encourage and co-ordinate plans, programs and activities to reduce or prevent such problems;

(h) to promote, assist and encourage public, municipal or private agencies, organizations, groups or persons to engage in programs to alleviate tensions and conflicts based upon identification by a prohibited ground of discrimination;

(i) to enforce this Act and orders of boards of inquiry; and

(j) to perform the functions assigned to it by this or any other Act. 1981, c. 53, s. 28.

30. (1) **Evidence obtained in course of investigation.**—No person who is a member of the Commission shall be required to give testimony in a civil suit or any proceeding as to information obtained in the course of an investigation under this Act.

(2) **Idem.**—No person who is employed in the administration of this Act shall be required to give testimony in a civil suit or any proceeding other than a proceeding under this Act as to information obtained in the course of an investigation under this Act. 1981, c. 53, s. 29.

31. (1) **Annual report.**—The Commission shall make a report to the Minister not later than the 30th day of June in each year upon the affairs of the Commission during the year ending on the 31st day of March of that year.

(2) **Idem.**—The Minister shall submit the report to the Lieutenant Governor in Council who shall cause the report to be laid before the Assembly if it is in session, or, if not, at the next session. 1981, c. 53, s. 30.

PART IV
ENFORCEMENT

32. (1) **Complaints.**—Where a person believes that a right of the person under this Act has been infringed, the person may file with the Commission a complaint in a form approved by the Commission.

(2) **Idem.**—The Commission may initiate a complaint by itself or at the request of any person.

(3) **Combining of complaints.**—Where two or more complaints,

(a) bring into question a practice of infringement engaged in by the same person; or

(b) have questions of law or fact in common,

the Commission may combine the complaints and deal with them in the same proceeding. 1981, c. 53, s. 31.

33. (1) **Investigation of complaints.**—Subject to section 34, the Commission shall investigate a complaint and endeavour to effect a settlement.

(2) **Investigation.**—An investigation by the Commission may be made by a member or employee of the Commission who is authorized by the Commission for the purpose.

(3) **Powers on investigation.**—A person authorized to investigate a complaint may,

(a) enter any place, other than a place that is being used as a dwelling, at any reasonable time, for the purpose of investigating the complaint;

(b) request the production for inspection and examination of documents or things that are or may be relevant to the investigation;

(c) upon giving a receipt therefor, remove from a place documents produced in response to a request under clause (b) for the purpose of making copies thereof or extracts therefrom and shall promptly return them to the person who produced or furnished them; and

(d) question a person on matters that are or may be relevant to the complaint subject to the person's right to have counsel or a personal representative present during such questioning, and may exclude from the questioning any person who may be adverse in interest to the complainant.

(4) **Entry into dwellings.**—A person investigating a complaint shall not enter a place that is being used as a dwelling without the consent of the occupier except under the authority of a warrant issued under subsection (8).

(5) **Denial of entry.**—Subject to subsection (4), if a person who is or may be a party to a complaint denies entry to any place, or instructs the person investigating to leave the place, or impedes or prevents an investigation therein, the Commission may request the Minister to appoint a board of inquiry or may authorize an employee or member to apply to a justice of the peace for a warrant to enter under subsection (8).

(6) **Refusal to produce.**—If a person refuses to comply with a request for production of documents or things, the Commission may request the Minister to appoint a board of inquiry, or may authorize an employee or member to apply to a justice of the peace for a search warrant under subsection (7). 1981, c. 53, s. 32(1-6).

(7) **Warrant for search.**—Where a justice of the peace is satisfied on evidence upon oath or affirmation that there are in a place documents that there is reasonable ground to believe will afford evidence relevant to the complaint, he or she may issue a warrant in the prescribed form authorizing a person named in the warrant to search a place for any such documents, and to remove them for the purposes of making copies thereof or extracts therefrom, and the documents shall be returned promptly to the place from which they were removed.

(8) **Warrant for entry.**—Where a justice of the peace is satisfied by evidence upon oath or affirmation that there is reasonable ground to believe it is necessary that a place being used as a dwelling or to which entry has been denied be entered to investigate a complaint, he or she may issue a warrant in the prescribed form authorizing such entry by a person named in the warrant. 1981, c. 53, s. 32(7, 8), *revised.*

(9) **Execution of warrant.**—A warrant issued under subsection (7) or (8) shall be executed at reasonable times as specified in the warrant.

(10) **Expiration of warrant.**—Every warrant shall name a date on which it expires, which shall be a date not later than fifteen days after it is issued.

(11) **Obstruction.**—No person shall hinder, obstruct or interfere with a person in the execution of a warrant or otherwise impede an investigation under this Act.

(12) **Idem.**—Subsection (11) is not contravened by a refusal to comply with a request for the production of documents or things made under clause (3)(b).

(13) **Admissibility of copies.**—Copies of, or extracts from, documents removed from premises under clause (3)(c) or subsection (7) certified as being true copies of the originals by the person who made them, are admissible in evidence to the same extent as, and have the same evidentiary value as, the documents of which they are copies or extracts. 1981, c. 53, s. 32(9-13).

34. (1) **Decision to not deal with complaint.**—Where it appears to the Commission that,

    (a)   the complaint is one that could or should be more appropriately dealt with under an Act other than this Act;

    (b)   the subject-matter of the complaint is trivial, frivolous, vexatious or made in bad faith;

    (c)   the complaint is not within the jurisdiction of the Commission; or

    (d)   the facts upon which the complaint is based occurred more than six months before the complaint was filed, unless the Commission is satisfied that the delay was incurred in good faith and no substantial prejudice will result to any person affected by the delay, the Commission may, in its discretion, decide to not deal with the complaint.

(2) **Notice of decision and reasons.**—Where the Commission decides to not deal with a complaint, it shall advise the complainant in writing of the decision and the reasons therefor and of the procedure under section 37 for having the decision reconsidered. 1981, c. 53, s. 33.

35. (1) **Panel of members for boards of inquiry.**—The Minister shall appoint a panel of persons to act as members of boards of inquiry.

(2) **Remuneration.**—The members of boards of inquiry shall be paid such allowances and expenses as are fixed by the Lieutenant Governor in Council. 1981, c. 53, s. 34.

36. (1) **Referred to board of inquiry.**—Where the Commission fails to effect a settlement of the complaint and it appears to the Commission that the procedure is appropriate and the evidence warrants an inquiry, the Commission may request the Minister to appoint a board of inquiry and refer the subject-matter of the complaint to the board.

(2) **Notice of decision not to appoint inquiry.**—Where the Commission decides to not request the Minister to appoint a board of inquiry, it shall advise the complainant and the person complained against in writing of the decision and the reasons therefor and inform the complainant of the procedure under section 37 for having the decision reconsidered. 1981, c. 53, s. 35.

37. (1) **Reconsideration.**—Within a period of fifteen days of the date of mailing the decision and reasons therefor mentioned in subsection 34(2) or subsection 36(2), or such longer period as the Commission may for special reasons allow, a complainant may request the Commission to reconsider its decision by filing an application for reconsideration containing a concise statement of the material facts upon which the application is based.

(2) **Notice of application.**—Upon receipt of an application for reconsideration the Commission shall as soon as is practicable notify the person complained against of the application and afford the person an opportunity to make written submissions with respect thereto within such time as the Commission specifies.

(3) **Decision.**—Every decision of the Commission on reconsideration together with the reasons therefor shall be recorded in writing and promptly communicated to the complainant and the person complained against and the decision shall be final. 1981, c. 53, s. 36.

38. (1) **Appointment of board.**—Where the Commission requests the Minister to appoint a board of inquiry, the Minister shall appoint from the panel one or more persons to form the board of inquiry and the Minister shall communicate the names of the persons forming the board to the parties to the inquiry. 1981, c. 53, s. 37(1).

(2) **Members at hearing not to have taken part in investigation, etc.**—A member of the board hearing a complaint must not have taken part in any investigation or consideration of the subject-matter of the inquiry before the hearing and shall not communicate directly or indirectly in relation to the subject-matter of the inquiry with any person or with any party or a representative of the party except upon notice to and opportunity for all parties to participate, but the board may seek legal advice from an adviser independent of the parties and in such case the nature of the advice shall be made known to the parties in order that they may make submissions as to the law. 1981, c. 53, s. 37(2); 1993, c. 27, Sch.

39. (1) **Hearing.**—The board of inquiry shall hold a hearing,

(a) to determine whether a right of the complainant under this Act has been infringed;

(b) to determine who infringed the right; and

(c) to decide upon an appropriate order under section 41,

and the hearing shall be commenced within thirty days after the date on which the members were appointed.

(2) **Parties.**—The parties to a proceeding before a board of inquiry are,

(a) the Commission, which shall have the carriage of the complaint;

(b) the complainant;

(c) any person who the Commission alleges has infringed the right;

(d) any person appearing to the board of inquiry to have infringed the right;

(e) where the complaint is of alleged conduct constituting harassment under subsection 2(2) or subsection 5(2) or of alleged conduct under section 7, any person who, in the opinion of the board, knew or was in possession of facts from which the person ought reasonably to have known of the conduct and who had authority to penalize or prevent the conduct.

(3) **Adding parties.**—A party may be added by the board of inquiry under clause (2)(d) or clause (2)(e) at any stage of the proceeding upon such terms as the board considers proper.

(4) **Adjournment on production.**—Where a board exercises its power under clause 12(1)(b) of the *Statutory Powers Procedure Act* to issue a summons requiring the production in evidence of documents or things, it may, upon the production of the documents or things before it, adjourn the proceedings to permit the parties to examine the documents or things.

(5) **Adjournment for view.**—The board may, where it appears to be in the interests of justice, direct that the board and the parties and their counsel or representatives shall have a view of any place or thing, and may adjourn the proceedings for that purpose. 1981, c. 53, s. 38.

40. Recording of evidence.—The oral evidence taken before a board at a hearing shall be recorded, and copies of a transcript thereof shall be furnished upon request upon the same terms as in the Ontario Court (General Division). 1981, c. 53, s. 39, *revised.*

41. (1) Orders of boards of inquiry.—Where the board of inquiry, after a hearing, finds that a right of the complainant under Part I has been infringed and that the infringement is a contravention of section 9 by a party to the proceeding, the board may, by order,

(a)   direct the party to do anything that, in the opinion of the board, the party ought to do to achieve compliance with this Act, both in respect of the complaint and in respect of future practices; and

(b)   direct the party to make restitution, including monetary compensation, for loss arising out of the infringement, and, where the infringement has been engaged in wilfully or recklessly, monetary compensation may include an award, not exceeding $10,000, for mental anguish. 1981, c. 53, s. 40(1).

(2) **Order to prevent harassment.**—Where a board makes a finding under subsection (1) that a right is infringed on the ground of harassment under subsection 2(2) or subsection 5(2) or conduct under section 7, and the board finds that a person who is a party to the proceeding,

(a)   knew or was in possession of knowledge from which the person ought to have known of the infringement; and

(b)   had the authority by reasonably available means to penalize or prevent the conduct and failed to use it,

the board shall remain seized of the matter and upon complaint of a continuation or repetition of the infringement of the right the Commission may investigate the complaint and, subject to subsection 36(2), request the board to re-convene and if the board finds that a person who is a party to the proceeding,

(c)   knew or was in possession of knowledge from which the person ought to have known of the repetition of infringement; and

(d)   had the authority by reasonably available means to penalize or prevent the continuation or repetition of the conduct and failed to use it,

the board may make an order requiring the person to take whatever sanctions or steps are reasonably available to prevent any further continuation or repetition of the infringement of the right.

(3) **Reappointment of board.**—Where a board of inquiry for any reason is unable to exercise its powers under this section or section 39, the Commission may request the Minister to appoint a new board of inquiry in its place.

(4) **Costs.**—Where, upon dismissing a complaint, the board of inquiry finds that,

    (a)   the complaint was trivial, frivolous, vexatious or made in bad faith; or

    (b)   in the particular circumstances undue hardship was caused to the person complained against,

the board of inquiry may order the Commission to pay to the person complained against such costs as are fixed by the board.

(5) **Decision within 30 days.**—The board of inquiry shall make its finding and decision within thirty days after the conclusion of its hearing. 1981, c. 53, s. 40(4-7).

NOTE: Section 41.1 as enacted by 1993, c. 35, s. 56, *part* (to come into force on proclamation) reads as follows:

41.1 (1) Orders re employment equity plans.—Despite any provision of this Act, the Commission or a board of inquiry shall not, by order, amend an employment equity plan under the Employment Equity Act, 1993.

(2) Orders where plan exists.—If a board of inquiry finds that a right of a complainant under Part I has been infringed by an employer that has an employment equity plan under the Employment Equity Act, 1993, the board may make an order that has the effect of imposing requirements on the employer that are in addition to those contained in the employment equity plan.

(3) Order not part of plan.—An order under subsection (2) shall not be interpreted as forming part of the employment equity plan.

42. (1) **Appeal from decision of board of inquiry.**—Any party to a proceeding before a board of inquiry may appeal from a decision or order of the board to the Divisional Court in accordance with the rules of court.

(2) **Record to be filed in court.**—Where notice of an appeal is served under this section, the board of inquiry shall forthwith file in the Divisional Court the record of the proceedings before it in which the decision or order appealed from was made and the record, together with a transcript of the oral evidence taken before the board if it is not part of the record of the board, shall constitute the record in the appeal.

(3) **Powers of court.**—An appeal under this section may be made on questions of law or fact or both and the court may affirm or reverse the decision or order of the board of inquiry or direct the board to make any decision or

order that the board is authorized to make under this Act and the court may substitute its opinion for that of the board. 1981, c. 53, s. 41.

43. Settlements.—Where a settlement of a complaint is agreed to in writing, signed by the parties and approved by the Commission, the settlement is binding upon the parties, and a breach of the settlement is grounds for a complaint under section 32, and this Part applies to the complaint in the same manner as if the breach of the settlement were an infringement of a right under this Act. 1981, c. 53, s. 42.

44. (1) **Penalty.**—Every person who contravenes section 9, subsection 33(11), or an order of a board of inquiry, is guilty of an offence and on conviction is liable to a fine of not more than $25,000.

(2) **Consent to prosecution.**—No prosecution for an offence under this Act shall be instituted except with the consent in writing of the Attorney General. 1981, c. 53, s. 43.

45. (1) **Acts of officers, etc.**—For the purposes of this Act, except subsection 2(2), subsection 5(2), section 7 and subsection 44(1), any act or thing done or omitted to be done in the course of his or her employment by an officer, official, employee or agent of a corporation, trade union, trade or occupational association, unincorporated association or employers' organization shall be deemed to be an act or thing done or omitted to be done by the corporation, trade union, trade or occupational association, unincorporated association or employers' organization.

(2) **Opinion re authority or acquiescence.**—At the request of a corporation, trade union, trade or occupational association, unincorporated association or employers' organization, a board of inquiry in its decision shall make known whether or not, in its opinion, an act or thing done or omitted to be done by an officer, official, employee or agent was done or omitted to be done with or without the authority or acquiescence of the corporation, trade union, trade or occupational association, unincorporated association or employers' organization, and the opinion does not affect the application of subsection (1). 1981, c. 53, s. 44.

PART V
GENERAL

46. Definitions.—In this Act,

"Commission" means the Ontario Human Rights Commission; ("Commission")

"Minister" means the member of the Executive Council to whom the powers and duties of the Minister under this Act are assigned by the Lieutenant Governor in Council; ("ministre")

"person" in addition to the extended meaning given it by the *Interpretation Act*, includes an employment agency, an employers' organization, an unincorporated association, a trade or occupational association, a trade union, a partnership, a municipality, a board of police commissioners established under the *Police Act*, being chapter 381 of the Revised Statutes of Ontario, 1980, and a police services board established under the *Police Services Act*. ("personne") 1981, c. 53, s. 45.

47. (1) **Act binds Crown.**—This Act binds the Crown and every agency of the Crown.

(2) **Act has primacy over other Acts.**—Where a provision in an Act or regulation purports to require or authorize conduct that is a contravention of Part I, this Act applies and prevails unless the Act or regulation specifically provides that it is to apply despite this Act. 1981, c. 53, s. 46(1, 2).

48. Regulations.—The Lieutenant Governor in Council may make regulations,
   (a)   prescribing standards for assessing what is undue hardship for the purposes of section 11, 17 or 24;
   (b)   prescribing forms and notices and providing for their use. 1981, c. 53, s. 47; 1986, c. 64, s. 18(17).

Schedule (ii)

CANADIAN HUMAN RIGHTS ACT

R.S.C. 1985, c. H-6

Amended R.S.C. 1985, c. 31 (1st Supp.), ss. 62 to 68; proclaimed in force
October 15, 1985
Amended R.S.C. 1985, c. 32 (2nd Supp.), Sch.; in force January 1, 1987
Amended 1992, c. 22, s. 13; in force July 24, 1992
Amended 1993, c. 28, Sch. III; to come into force April 1, 1999 or earlier
by order of the Governor in Council

SHORT TITLE

1. Short title.—This Act may be cited as the *Canadian Human Rights Act.* 1976-77, c. 33, s. 1.

PURPOSE OF ACT

2. Purpose.—The purpose of this Act is to extend the laws in Canada to give effect, within the purview of matters coming within the legislative authority of Parliament, to the principle that every individual should have an equal opportunity with other individuals to make for himself or herself the life that he or she is able and wishes to have, consistent with his or her duties and obligations as a member of society, without being hindered in or prevented from doing so by discriminatory practices based on race, national or ethnic origin, colour, religion, age, sex, marital status, family status, disability or conviction for an offence for which a pardon has been granted. 1976-77, c. 33, s. 2; 1980-81-82-83, c. 143, ss. 1, 28.

PART I

PROSCRIBED DISCRIMINATION

General

3.(1) **Proscribed grounds of discrimination.**—For all purposes of this Act, race, national or ethnic origin, colour, religion, age, sex, marital status, family status, disability and conviction for which a pardon has been granted are prohibited grounds of discrimination.

(2) **Idem.**—Where the ground of discrimination is pregnancy or child-birth, the discrimination shall be deemed to be on the ground of sex. 1976-77, c. 33, s. 3; 1980-81-82-83, c. 143, s. 2.

4. Orders in respect of discriminatory practices.—A discriminatory practice, as described in sections 5 to 14, may be the subject of a complaint under Part III and anyone found to be engaging or to have engaged in a discriminatory practice may be made subject to an order as provided in sections 53 and 54. 1976-77, c. 33, s. 4; 1980-81-82-83, c. 143, s. 2.

Discriminatory Practices

5. Denial of good, service, facility or accommodation.—It is a discriminatory practice in the provision of goods, services, facilities or accommodation customarily available to the general public
(*a*)   to deny, or to deny access to, any such good, service, facility or accommodation to any individual, or
(*b*)   to differentiate adversely in relation to any individual,
on a prohibited ground of discrimination. 1976-77, c. 33, s. 5.

6. Denial of commercial premises or residential accommodation.—It is a discriminatory practice in the provision of commercial premises or residential accommodation
(*a*)   to deny occupancy of such premises or accommodation to any individual, or
(*b*)   to differentiate adversely in relation to any individual,
on a prohibited ground of discrimination. 1976-77, c. 33, s. 6.

7. Employment.—It is a discriminatory practice, directly or indirectly,
(*a*)   to refuse to employ or continue to employ any individual, or
(*b*)   in the course of employment, to differentiate adversely in relation to an employee,
on a prohibited ground of discrimination. 1976-77, c. 33, s. 7.

8. Employment applications advertisements.—It is a discriminatory practice
(*a*)   to use or circulate any form of application for employment, or
(*b*)   in connection with employment or prospective employment, to publish any advertisement or to make any written or oral inquiry
that expresses or implies any limitation, specification or preference based on a prohibited ground of discrimination. 1976-77, c. 33, s. 8.

9.(1) Employee organizations.—It is a discriminatory practice for an employee organization on a prohibited ground of discrimination
(*a*)   to exclude an individual from full membership in the organization;
(*b*)   to expel or suspend a member of the organization; or
(*c*)   to limit, segregate, classify or otherwise act in relation to an individual in a way that would deprive the individual of employment

opportunities, or limit employment opportunities or otherwise adversely affect the status of the individual, where the individual is a member of the organization or where any of the obligations of the organization pursuant to a collective agreement relate to the individual.

(2) **Exception.**—Notwithstanding subsection (1), it is not a discriminatory practice for an employee organization to exclude, expel or suspend an individual from membership in the organization because that individual has reached the normal age of retirement for individuals working in positions similar to the position of that individual.

(3) **Definition of "employee organization".**—For the purposes of this section and sections 10 and 60, "employee organization" includes a trade union or other organization of employees or local thereof, the purposes of which include the negotiation, on behalf of employees, of the terms and conditions of employment with employers. 1976-77, c. 33, s. 9; 1980-81-82-83, c. 143, s. 4.

10. Discriminatory policy or practice.—It is a discriminatory practice for an employer, employee organization or organization of employers
  (*a*) to establish or pursue a policy or practice, or
  (*b*) to enter into an agreement affecting recruitment, referral, hiring, promotion, training, apprenticeship, transfer or any other matter relating to employment or prospective employment,
that deprives or tends to deprive an individual or class of individuals of any employment opportunities on a prohibited ground of discrimination. 1976-77, c. 33, s. 10; 1980-81-82-83, c. 143, s. 5.

11.(1) **Equal wages.**—It is a discriminatory practice for an employer to establish or maintain differences in wages between male and female employees employed in the same establishment who are performing work of equal value.

(2) **Assessment of value of work.**—In assessing the value of work performed by employees employed in the same establishment, the criterion to be applied is the composite of the skill, effort and responsibility required in the performance of the work and the conditions under which the work is performed.

(3) **Separate establishments.**—Separate establishments established or maintained by an employer solely or principally for the purposes of establishing or maintaining differences in wages between male and female employees shall be deemed for the purposes of this section to be the same establishment.

(4) **Different wages based on prescribed reasonable factors.**—Notwithstanding subsection (1), it is not a discriminatory practice to pay to male and female employees different wages if the difference is based

on a factor prescribed by guidelines, issued by the Canadian Human Rights Commission pursuant to subsection 27(2), to be a reasonable factor that justifies the difference.

(5) **Idem.**—For greater certainty, sex does not constitute a reasonable factor justifying a difference in wages.

(6) **No reduction of wages.**—An employer shall not reduce wages in order to eliminate a discriminatory practice described in this section.

(7) **Definition of "wages".**—For the purposes of this section, "wages" means any form of remuneration payable for work performed by an individual and includes
- (*a*)   salaries, commissions, vacation pay, dismissal wages and bonuses;
- (*b*)   reasonable value for board, rent, housing and lodging;
- (*c*)   payments in kind;
- (*d*)   employer contributions to pension funds or plans, long-term disability plans and all forms of health insurance plans; and
- (*e*)   any other advantage received directly or indirectly from the individual's employer. 1976-77, c. 33, s. 11.

12. Publication of discriminatory notices, etc.—It is a discriminatory practice to publish or display before the public or to cause to be published or displayed before the public any notice, sign, symbol, emblem or other representation that
- (*a*)   expresses or implies discrimination or an intention to discriminate, or
- (*b*)   incites or is calculated to incite others to discriminate

if the discrimination expressed or implied, intended to be expressed or implied or incited or calculated to be incited would otherwise, if engaged in, be a discriminatory practice described in any of sections 5 to 11 or in section 14. 1976-77, c. 33, s. 12; 1980-81-82-83, c. 143, s. 6.

13.(1) **Hate messages.**—It is a discriminatory practice for a person or a group of persons acting in concert to communicate telephonically or to cause to be so communicated, repeatedly, in whole or in part by means of the facilities of a telecommunication undertaking within the legislative authority of Parliament, any matter that is likely to expose a person or persons to hatred or contempt by reason of the fact that that person or those persons are identifiable on the basis of a prohibited ground of discrimination.

(2) **Exception.**—Subsection (1) does not apply in respect of any matter that is communicated in whole or in part by means of the facilities of a broadcasting undertaking.

(3) **Interpretation.**—For the purposes of this section, no owner or operator of a telecommunication undertaking communicates or causes to be com-

municated any matter described in subsection (1) by reason only that the facilities of a telecommunication undertaking owned or operated by that person are used by other persons for the transmission of that matter. 1976-77, c. 33, s. 13.

14.(1) **Harassment.**—It is a discriminatory practice,

(a) in the provision of goods, services, facilities or accommodation customarily available to the general public,

(b) in the provision of commercial premises or residential accommodation, or

(c) in matters related to employment,

to harass an individual on a prohibited ground of discrimination.

(2) **Sexual harassment.**—Without limiting the generality of subsection (1), sexual harassment shall, for the purposes of that subsection, be deemed to be harassment on a prohibited ground of discrimination. 1980-81-82-83, c. 143, s. 7.

15. Exceptions.—It is not a discriminatory practice if

(a) any refusal, exclusion, expulsion, suspension, limitation, specification or preference in relation to any employment is established by an employer to be based on a *bona fide* occupational requirement;

(b) employment of an individual is refused or terminated because that individual has not reached the minimum age, or has reached the maximum age, that applies to that employment by law or under regulations, which may be made by the Governor in Council for the purposes of this paragraph;

(c) an individual's employment is terminated because that individual has reached the normal age of retirement for employees working in positions similar to the position of that individual;

(d) the terms and conditions of any pension fund or plan established by an employer provide for the compulsory vesting or locking-in of pension contributions at a fixed or determinable age in accordance with sections 17 and 18 of the *Pension Benefits Standards Act, 1985*;

(e) an individual is discriminated against on a prohibited ground of discrimination in a manner that is prescribed by guidelines, issued by the Canadian Human Rights Commission pursuant to subsection 27(2), to be reasonable;

(f) an employer grants a female employee special leave or benefits in connection with pregnancy or child-birth or grants employees special leave or benefits to assist them in the care of their children; or

(g) in the circumstances described in section 5 or 6, an individual is denied any goods, services, facilities or accommodation or access thereto or occupancy of any commercial premises or residential accommodation or is a victim of any adverse differentiation and there is *bona fide* justification for that denial or differentiation. 1976-77, c. 33, s. 14; 1980-81-82-83, c. 143, s. 7; R.S.C. 1985, c. 32 (2nd Supp.), Sch.

16.(1) **Special programs.**—It is not a discriminatory practice for a person to adopt or carry out a special program, plan or arrangement designed to prevent disadvantages that are likely to be suffered by, or to eliminate or reduce disadvantages that are suffered by, any group of individuals when those disadvantages would be or are based on or related to the race, national or ethnic origin, colour, religion, age, sex, marital status, family status or disability of members of that group, by improving opportunities respecting goods, services, facilities, accommodation or employment in relation to that group.

(2) **Advice and assistance.**—The Canadian Human Rights Commission may

- (*a*) make general recommendations concerning desirable objectives for special programs, plans or arrangements referred to in subsection (1); and
- (*b*) on application, give such advice and assistance with respect to the adoption or carrying out of a special program, plan or arrangement referred to in subsection (1) as will serve to aid in the achievement of the objectives the program, plan or arrangement was designed to achieve. 1976-77, c. 33, s. 15; 1980-81-82-83, c. 143, s. 8.

17.(1) **Plans to meet the needs of disabled persons.**— A person who proposes to implement a plan for adapting any services, facilities, premises, equipment or operations to meet the needs of persons arising from a disability may apply to the Canadian Human Rights Commission for approval of the plan.

(2) **Approval of plan.**—The Commission may, by written notice to a person making an application pursuant to subsection (1), approve the plan if the Commission is satisfied that the plan is appropriate for meeting the needs of persons arising from a disability.

(3) **Effect of approval of accommodation plan.**—Where any services, facilities, premises, equipment or operations are adapted in accordance with a plan approved under subsection (2), matters for which the plan provides do not constitute any basis for a complaint under Part III regarding discrimination based on any disability in respect of which the plan was approved.

(4) **Notice when application not granted.**—When the Commission decides not to grant an application made pursuant to subsection (1), it shall

send a written notice of its decision to the applicant setting out the reasons for its decision. 1980-81-82-83, c. 143, s. 9.

18.(1) **Rescinding approval of plan.**—If the Canadian Human Rights Commission is satisfied that, by reason of any change in circumstances, a plan approved under subsection 17(2) has ceased to be appropriate for meeting the needs of persons arising from a disability, the Commission may, by written notice to the person who proposes to carry out or maintains the adaptation contemplated by the plan or any part thereof, rescind its approval of the plan to the extent required by the change in circumstances.

(2) **Effect where approval rescinded.**—To the extent to which approval of a plan is rescinded under subsection (1), subsection 17(3) does not apply to the plan if the discriminatory practice to which the complaint relates is subsequent to the rescission of the approval.

(3) **Statement of reasons for rescinding approval.**—Where the Commission rescinds approval of a plan pursuant to subsection (1), it shall include in the notice referred to therein a statement of its reasons therefor. 1980-81-82-83, c. 143, s. 9.

19.(1) **Opportunity to make representations.**—Before making its decision on an application or rescinding approval of a plan pursuant to section 17 or 18, the Canadian Human Rights Commission shall afford each person directly concerned with the matter an opportunity to make representations with respect thereto.

(2) **Restriction on deeming plan inappropriate.**—For the purposes of sections 17 and 18, a plan shall not, by reason only that it does not conform to any standards prescribed pursuant to section 24, be deemed to be inappropriate for meeting the needs of persons arising from disability. 1980-81-82-83, c. 143, s. 9.

20. Certain provisions not discriminatory.—A provision of a pension or insurance fund or plan that preserves rights acquired prior to March 1, 1978 or that preserves pension or other benefits accrued prior to that time does not constitute the basis for a complaint under Part III that an employer is engaging or has engaged in a discriminatory practice. 1976-77, c. 33, s. 16.

21. Funds and plans.—The establishment of separate pension funds or plans for different groups of employees does not constitute the basis for a complaint under Part III that an employer is engaging or has engaged in a discriminatory practice if the employees are not grouped in those funds or plans according to a prohibited ground of discrimination. 1976-77, c. 33, s. 17.

22. Regulations.—The Governor in Council may, by regulation, prescribe the provisions of any pension or insurance fund or plan, in addition to those provisions described in sections 20 and 21, that do not constitute the basis for a complaint under Part III that an employer is engaging or has engaged in a discriminatory practice. 1976-77, c. 33, s. 18.

23. Regulations.—The Governor in Council may make regulations respecting the terms and conditions to be included in or applicable to any contract, licence or grant made or granted by Her Majesty in right of Canada providing for
- (*a*)   the prohibition of discriminatory practices described in sections 5 to 14; and
- (*b*)   the resolution, by the procedure set out in Part III, of complaints of discriminatory practices contrary to such terms and conditions. 1976-77, c. 33, s. 19; 1980-81-82-83, c. 143, s. 10.

24.(1) **Accessibility standards.**—The Governor in Council may, for the benefit of persons having any disability, make regulations prescribing standards of accessibility to services, facilities or premises.

(2) **Effect of meeting accessibility standards.**—Where standards prescribed pursuant to subsection (1) are met in providing access to any services, facilities or premises, a matter of access thereto does not constitute any basis for a complaint under Part III regarding discrimination based on any disability in respect of which the standards are prescribed.

(3) **Publication of proposed regulations.**—Subject to subsection (4), a copy of each regulation that the Governor in Council proposes to make pursuant to this section shall be published in the *Canada Gazette* and a reasonable opportunity shall be afforded to interested persons to make representations with respect thereto.

(4) **Exception.**—Subsection (3) does not apply in respect of a proposed regulation that had been published pursuant to that subsection, whether or not it has been amended as a result of representations made pursuant to that subsection.

(5) **Discriminatory practice not constituted by variance from standards.**—Nothing shall, by virtue only of its being at variance with any standards prescribed pursuant to subsection (1), be deemed to constitute a discriminatory practice. 1980-81-82-83, c. 143, s. 11.

25. Definitions—In this Act,

"conviction for which a pardon has been granted" means a conviction of an individual for an offence in respect of which a pardon has been granted by any authority under law and, if granted or issued under the *Criminal Records Act*, has not been revoked or ceased to have effect;

"disability" means any previous or existing mental or physical disability and includes disfigurement and previous or existing dependence on alcohol or a drug. 1976-77, c. 33, s. 20; 1980-81-82-83, c. 143, s. 12; 1992, c. 22, s. 13.

PART II

CANADIAN HUMAN RIGHTS COMMISSION

26.(1) **Commission established.**—A commission is hereby established to be known as the Canadian Human Rights Commission, in this Part and Part III referred to as the "Commission", consisting of a Chief Commissioner, a Deputy Chief Commissioner and not less than three or more than six other members, to be appointed by the Governor in Council.

(2) **Members.**—The Chief Commissioner and Deputy Chief Commissioner are full-time members of the Commission and the other members may be appointed as full-time or part-time members of the Commission.

(3) **Term of appointment.**—Each full-time member of the Commission may be appointed for a term not exceeding seven years and each part-time member may be appointed for a term not exceeding three years.

(4) **Tenure.**—Each member of the Commission holds office during good behaviour but may be removed by the Governor in Council on address of the Senate and House of Commons.

(5) **Re-appointment.**—A member of the Commission is eligible to be re-appointed in the same or another capacity. 1976-77, c. 33, s. 21.

Powers, Duties and Functions

27.(1) **Powers, duties and functions.**—In addition to its duties under Part III with respect to complaints regarding discriminatory practices, the Commission is generally responsible for the administration of this Part and Parts I and III and

    (*a*)   shall develop and conduct information programs to foster public understanding of this Act and of the role and activities of the Commission thereunder and to foster public recognition of the principle described in section 2;

    (*b*)   shall undertake or sponsor research programs relating to its duties and functions under this Act and respecting the principle described in section 2;

(c)   shall maintain close liaison with similar bodies or authorities in the provinces in order to foster common policies and practices and to avoid conflicts respecting the handling of complaints in cases of overlapping jurisdiction;

(d)   shall perform duties and functions to be performed by it pursuant to any agreement entered into under subsection 28(2);

(e)   may consider such recommendations, suggestions and requests concerning human rights and freedoms as it receives from any source and, where deemed by the Commission to be appropriate, include in a report referred to in section 61 reference to and comment on any such recommendation, suggestion or request;

(f)   shall carry out or cause to be carried out such studies concerning human rights and freedoms as may be referred to it by the Minister of Justice and include in a report referred to in section 61 a report setting out the results of each such study together with such recommendations in relation thereto as it considers appropriate;

(g)   may review any regulations, rules, orders, by-laws and other instruments made pursuant to an Act of Parliament and, where deemed by the Commission to be appropriate, include in a report referred to in section 61 reference to and comment on any provision thereof that in its opinion is inconsistent with the principle described in section 2; and

(h)   shall, so far as is practical and consistent with the application of Part III, endeavour by persuasion, publicity or any other means that it considers appropriate to discourage and reduce discriminatory practice referred to in sections 5 to 14.

(2) **Guidelines.**—The Commission may, on application or on its own initiative, by order, issue a guideline setting out the extent to which and the manner in which, in the opinion of the Commission, any provision of this Act applies in a particular case or in a class of cases described in the guideline.

(3) **Guideline binding.**—A guideline issued under subsection (2) is, until it is subsequently revoked or modified, binding on the Commission, any Human Rights Tribunal appointed pursuant to subsection 49(1) and any Review Tribunal constituted pursuant to subsection 56(1) with respect to the resolution of any complaint under Part III regarding a case falling within the description contained in the guideline.

(4) **Publication or communication.**—Each guideline issued under subsection (2) that relates to the manner in which a provision of this Act applies in a class of cases shall be published in Part II of the *Canada Gazette*, and each guideline that applies in a particular case shall be communicated to the persons directly affected thereby in such manner as the Commission deems appropriate. 1976-77, c. 33, s. 22; 1977-78, c. 22, s. 5; 1980-81-82-83, c. 143, s. 13.

28.(1) **Assignment of duties.**—On the recommendation of the Commission, the Governor in Council may, by order, assign to persons or classes of persons specified in the order who are engaged in the performance of the duties and functions of the Department of Labour of the Government of Canada such of the duties and functions of the Commission in relation to discriminatory practices in employment outside the public service of Canada as are specified in the order.

(2) **Interdelegation.**—Subject to the approval of the Governor in Council, the Commission may enter into agreements with similar bodies or authorities in the provinces providing for the performance by the Commission on behalf of those bodies or authorities of duties or functions specified in the agreements or for the performance by those bodies or authorities on behalf of the Commission of duties or functions so specified. 1976-77, c. 33, s. 22.

29. Regulations.—The Governor in Council, on the recommendation of the Commission, may make regulations authorizing the Commission to exercise such powers and perform such duties and functions, in addition to those prescribed by this Act, as are necessary to carry out the provisions of this Part and Parts I and III. 1976-77, c. 33, s. 23.

Remuneration

30.(1) **Salaries and remuneration.**—Each full-time member of the Commission shall be paid a salary to be fixed by the Governor in Council and each part-time member of the Commission may be paid such remuneration, as is prescribed by by-law of the Commission, for attendance at meetings of the Commission, or of any division or committee of the Commission, that the member is requested by the Chief Commissioner to attend.

(2) **Additional remuneration.**—A part-time member of the Commission may, for any period during which that member, with the approval of the Chief Commissioner, performs any duties and functions additional to the normal duties and functions of that member on behalf of the Commission, be paid such additional remuneration as is prescribed by by-law of the Commission.

(3) **Travel expenses.**—Each member of the Commission is entitled to be paid such travel and living expenses incurred by the member in the performance of duties and functions under this Act as are prescribed by by-law of the Commission. 1976-77, c. 33, s. 24.

Officers and Staff

31.(1) **Chief Commissioner.**—The Chief Commissioner is the chief executive officer of the Commission and has supervision over and direction of the Commission and its staff and shall preside at meetings of the Commission.

(2) **Absence or incapacity.**—In the event of the absence or incapacity of the Chief Commissioner, or if that office is vacant, the Deputy Chief Commissioner has all the powers and may perform all the duties and functions of the Chief Commissioner.

(3) **Idem.**—In the event of the absence or incapacity of the Chief Commissioner and the Deputy Chief Commissioner, or if those offices are vacant, the full-time member with the most seniority has all the powers and may perform all the duties and functions of the Chief Commissioner. 1976-77, c. 33, s. 25.

32.(1) **Staff.**—Such officers and employees as are necessary for the proper conduct of the work of the Commission shall be appointed in accordance with the *Public Service Employment Act.*

(2) **Contractual assistance.**—The Commission may, for specific projects, enter into contracts for the services of persons having technical or specialized knowledge of any matter relating to the work of the Commission to advise and assist the Commission in the exercise of its powers or the performance of its duties and functions under this Act, and those persons may be paid such remuneration and expenses as may be prescribed by by-law of the Commission. 1976-77, c. 33, s. 26.

33.(1) **Compliance with security requirements.**—Every member of the Commission and every person employed by the Commission who is required to receive or obtain information relating to any investigation under this Act shall, with respect to access to and the use of such information, comply with any security requirements applicable to, and take any oath of secrecy required to be taken by, individuals who normally have access to and use of such information.

(2) **Disclosure.**—Every member of the Commission and every person employed by the Commission shall take every reasonable precaution to avoid disclosing any matter the disclosure of which
- (*a*) might be injurious to international relations, national defence or security or federal-provincial relations;
- (*b*) would disclose a confidence of the Queen's Privy Council for Canada;
- (*c*) would be likely to disclose information obtained or prepared by any investigative body of the Government of Canada
   - (i) in relation to national security,
   - (ii) in the course of investigations pertaining to the detection or suppression of crime generally, or
   - (iii) in the course of investigations pertaining to particular offences against any Act of Parliament;

(*d*) might, in respect of any individual under sentence for an offence against any Act of Parliament,

    (i) lead to a serious disruption of that individual's institutional, parole or mandatory supervision program,

    (ii) reveal information originally obtained on a promise of confidentiality, express or implied, or

    (iii) result in physical or other harm to that individual or any other person;

(*e*) might impede the functioning of a court of law, or a quasi-judicial board, commission or other tribunal or any inquiry established under the *Inquiries Act*; or

(*f*) might disclose legal opinions or advice provided to a government department or body or privileged communications between lawyer and client in a matter of government business. 1976-77, c. 33, s. 27.

34.(1) **Head office.**—The head office of the Commission shall be in the National Capital Region described in the schedule to the *National Capital Act*.

(2) **Other offices.**—The Commission may establish such regional or branch offices, not exceeding twelve, as it considers necessary to carry out its powers, duties and functions under this Act.

(3) **Meetings.**—The Commission may meet for the conduct of its affairs at such times and in such places as the Chief Commissioner considers necessary or desirable. 1976-77, c. 33, s. 28.

35. Majority is a decision of the Commission.—A decision of the majority of the members present at a meeting of the Commission, if the members present constitute a quorum, is a decision of the Commission. 1976-77, c. 33, s. 28.

36.(1) **Establishment of divisions.**—For the purposes of the affairs of the Commission, the Chief Commissioner may establish divisions of the Commission and all or any of the powers, duties and functions of the Commission, except the making of by-laws, may, as directed by the Commission, be exercised or performed by all or any of those divisions.

(2) **Designation of presiding officer.**—Where a division of the Commission has been established pursuant to subsection (1), the Chief Commissioner may designate one of the members of the division to act as the presiding officer of the division. 1976-77, c. 33, s. 28.

37.(1) **By-laws.**—The Commission may make by-laws for the conduct of its affairs and, without limiting the generality of the foregoing, may make by-laws

(a) respecting the calling of meetings of the Commission or any division thereof and the fixing of quorums for the purposes of those meetings;

(b) respecting the conduct of business at meetings of the Commission or any division thereof;

(c) respecting the establishment of committees of the Commission, the delegation of powers, duties and functions to those committees and the fixing of quorums for meetings thereof;

(d) respecting the procedure to be followed in dealing with complaints under Part III that have arisen in the Yukon Territory or the Northwest Territories;

NOTE: The above clause (d) as re-enacted by 1993, c. 28, Sch. III (to come into force April 1, 1999 or earlier by order of the Governor in Council) reads as follows:

(d) *respecting the procedure to be followed in dealing with complaints under Part III that have arisen in the Yukon Territory, the Northwest Territory or Nunavut:*

(e) prescribing the rates of remuneration to be paid to part-time members, members of a Human Rights Tribunal and any person engaged pursuant to subsection 32(2); and

(f) prescribing reasonable rates of travel and living expenses to be paid to members of the Commission, members of a Human Rights Tribunal and any person engaged pursuant to subsection 32(2).

(2) **Treasury Board approval.**—No by-law made under paragraph (1)(e) or (f) has effect unless it is approved by the Treasury Board. 1976-77, c. 33, s. 29.

38. Superannuation, etc.—The full-time members of the Commission are deemed to be persons employed in the Public Service for the purposes of the *Public Service Superannuation Act* and to be employed in the public service of Canada for the purposes of the *Government Employees Compensation Act* and any regulations made under section 9 of the *Aeronautics Act.* 1976-77, c. 33, s. 30.

PART III

DISCRIMINATORY PRACTICES AND GENERAL PROVISIONS

39. Definition of "discriminatory practices".—For the purposes of this Part, a "discriminatory practice" means any practice that is a discriminatory practice within the meaning of sections 5 to 14. 1976-77, c. 33, s. 31; 1980-81-82-83, c. 143, s. 14.

40.(1) **Complaints.**—Subject to subsections (5) and (7), any individual or group of individuals having reasonable grounds for believing that a person is engaging or has engaged in a discriminatory practice may file with the Commission a complaint in a form acceptable to the Commission.

(2) **Consent of victim.**—If a complaint is made by someone other than the individual who is alleged to be the victim of the discriminatory practice to which the complaint relates, the Commission may refuse to deal with the complaint unless the alleged victim consents thereto.

(3) **Investigation commenced by Commission.**—Where the Commission has reasonable grounds for believing that a person is engaging or has engaged in a discriminatory practice, the Commission may initiate a complaint. 1976-77, c. 33, s. 32(1-3).

(4) **Complaints may be dealt with together.**—Where complaints are filed jointly or separately by more than one individual or group alleging that a particular person is engaging or has engaged in a discriminatory practice or a series of similar discriminatory practices and the Commission is satisfied that the complaints involve substantially the same issues of fact and law, it may deal with those complaints together under this Part and may request the President of the Human Rights Tribunal Panel to appoint a single Human Rights Tribunal pursuant to section 49 to inquire into those complaints. R.S.C. 1985, c. 31 (1st Supp.), s. 62.

(5) **No complaints to be considered in certain cases.**—No complaint in relation to a discriminatory practice may be dealt with by the Commission under this Part unless the act or omission that constitutes the practice

    (*a*)   occurred in Canada and the victim of the practice was at the time of the act or omission either lawfully present in Canada or, if temporarily absent from Canada, entitled to return to Canada;

    (*b*)   occurred in Canada and was a discriminatory practice within the meaning of section 8, 10, 12 or 13 in respect of which no particular individual is identifiable as the victim; or

    (*c*)   occurred outside Canada and the victim of the practice was at the time of the act or omission a Canadian citizen or an individual lawfully admitted to Canada for permanent residence. 1976-77, c. 33, s. 32(5); 1980-81-82-83, c. 143, s. 15.

(6) **Determination of status.**—Where a question arises under subsection (5) as to the status of an individual in relation to a complaint, the Commission shall refer the question of status to the appropriate Minister and shall not proceed with the complaint unless the question of status is resolved thereby in favour of the complainant.

(7) **No complaints to be dealt with in certain cases.**—No complaint may be dealt with by the Commission pursuant to subsection (1) that relates

to the terms and conditions of a superannuation or pension fund or plan, if the relief sought would require action to be taken that would deprive any contributor to, participant in or member of, the fund or plan of any rights acquired under the fund or plan before March 1, 1978 or of any pension or other benefits accrued under the fund or plan to that date, including

(*a*)   any rights and benefits based on a particular age of retirement; and

(*b*)   any accrued survivor's benefits. 1976-77, c. 33, s. 32(6, 7).

41. Commission to deal with complaint.—Subject to section 40, the Commission shall deal with any complaint filed with it unless in respect of that complaint it appears to the Commission that

(*a*)   the alleged victim of the discriminatory practice to which the complaint relates ought to exhaust grievance or review procedures otherwise reasonably available;

(*b*)   the complaint is one that could more appropriately be dealt with, initially or completely, according to a procedure provided for under an Act of Parliament other than this Act;

(*c*)   the complaint is beyond the jurisdiction of the Commission;

(*d*)   the complaint is trivial, frivolous, vexatious or made in bad faith; or

(*e*)   the complaint is based on acts or omissions the last of which occurred more than one year, or such longer period of time as the Commission considers appropriate in the circumstances, before receipt of the complaint. 1976-77, c. 33, s. 33.

42.(1) **Notice.**—Subject to subsection (2), when the Commission decides not to deal with a complaint, it shall send a written notice of its decision to the complainant setting out the reason for its decision.

(2) **Attributing fault for delay.**—Before deciding that a complaint will not be dealt with because a procedure referred to in paragraph 41(*a*) has not been exhausted, the Commission shall satisfy itself that the failure to exhaust the procedure was attributable to the complainant and not to another. 1976-77, c. 33, s. 34.

Investigation

43.(1) **Designation of investigator.**—The Commission may designate a person, in this Part referred to as an "investigator", to investigate a complaint. 1976-77, c. 33, s. 35(1).

(2) **Manner of investigation.**—An investigator shall investigate a complaint in a manner authorized by regulations made pursuant to subsection (4).

(2.1) **Power to enter.**—Subject to such limitations as the Governor in Council may prescribe in the interests of national defence or security, an investigator with a warrant issued under subsection (2.2) may, at any reasonable time, enter and search any premises in order to carry out such inquiries as are reasonably necessary for the investigation of a complaint.

(2.2) **Authority to issue warrant.**— Where on *ex parte* application a judge of the Federal Court is satisfied by information on oath that there are reasonable grounds to believe that there is in any premises any evidence relevant to the investigation of a complaint, the judge may issue a warrant under the judge's hand authorizing the investigator named therein to enter and search those premises for any such evidence subject to such conditions as may be specified in the warrant.

(2.3) **Use of force.**—In executing a warrant issued under subsection (2.2), the investigator named therein shall not use force unless the investigator is accompanied by a peace officer and the use of force has been specifically authorized in the warrant.

(2.4) **Production of books.**—An investigator may require any individual found in any premises entered pursuant to this section to produce for inspection or for the purpose of obtaining copies thereof or extracts therefrom any books or other documents containing any matter relevant to the investigation being conducted by the investigator. R.S.C. 1985, c. 31 (1st Supp.), s. 63(1).

(3) **Obstruction.**—No person shall obstruct an investigator in the investigation of a complaint. 1976-77, c. 33, s. 35(3).

(4) **Regulations.**—The Governor in Council may make regulations
(*a*)　prescribing procedures to be followed by investigators;
(*b*)　authorizing the manner in which complaints are to be investigated pursuant to this Part; and
(*c*)　prescribing limitations for the purpose of subsection (2.1). 1976-77, c. 33, s. 35(4); R.S.C. 1985, c. 31 (1st Supp.), s. 63(2).

44.(1) **Report.**—An investigator shall, as soon as possible after the conclusion of an investigation, submit to the Commission a report of the findings of the investigation.

(2) **Action on receipt of report.**—If, on receipt of a report referred to in subsection (1), the Commission is satisfied
(*a*)　that the complainant ought to exhaust grievance or review procedures otherwise reasonably available, or
(*b*)　that the complaint could more appropriately be dealt with, initially or completely, by means of a procedure provided for under an Act of Parliament other than this Act,
it shall refer the complainant to the appropriate authority. 1976-77, c. 33, s. 36(1, 2).

(3) **Idem.**—On receipt of a report referred to in subsection (1), the Commission

(a) may request the President of the Human Rights Tribunal Panel to appoint a Human Rights Tribunal in accordance with section 49 to inquire into the complaint to which the report relates if the Commission is satisfied

(i) that, having regard to all the circumstances of the complaint, an inquiry into the complaint is warranted, and

(ii) that the complaint to which the report relates should not be referred pursuant to subsection (2) or dismissed on any ground mentioned in paragraphs 41(c) to (e); or

(b) shall dismiss the complaint to which the report relates if it is satisfied

(i) that, having regard to all the circumstances of the complaint, an inquiry into the complaint is not warranted, or

(ii) that the complaint should be dismissed on any ground mentioned in paragraphs 41(c) to (e). R.S.C. 1985, c. 31 (1st Supp.), s. 64.

(4) **Notice.**—After receipt of a report referred to in subsection (1), the Commission

(a) shall notify in writing the complainant and the person against whom the complaint was made of its action under subsection (2) or (3); and

(b) may, in such manner as it sees fit, notify any other person whom it considers necessary to notify of its action under subsection (2) or (3). 1976-77, c. 33, s. 36(4).

45.(1) **Definition of "Review Committee".**—In this section and section 46, "Review Committee" has the meaning assigned to that expression by the *Canadian Security Intelligence Service Act*.

(2) **Complaint involving security considerations.**—When, at any stage after the filing of a complaint and before the commencement of a hearing before a Human Rights Tribunal in respect thereof, the Commission receives written notice from a minister of the Crown that the practice to which the complaint relates was based on considerations relating to the security of Canada, the Commission may

(a) dismiss the complaint; or

(b) refer the matter to the Review Committee.

(3) **Notice.**—After receipt of a notice mentioned in subsection (2), the Commission

(a) shall notify in writing the complainant and the person against whom the complaint was made of its action under paragraph (2)(a) or (b); and (*b*) may, in such manner as it sees fit, notify any other person whom it considers necessary to notify of its action under paragraph 2(*a*) or (*b*).

(4) **Stay of procedures.**—Where the Commission has referred the matter to the Review Committee pursuant to paragraph (2)(*b*), it shall not deal with the complaint until the Review Committee has, pursuant to subsection 46(1), provided it with a report in relation to the matter.

(5) **Application of the *Canadian Security Intelligence Service Act*.**—Where a matter is referred to the Review Committee pursuant to paragraph (2)(*b*), subsections 39(2) and (3) and sections 43, 44 and 47 to 51 of the *Canadian Security Intelligence Service Act* apply, with such modifications as the circumstances require, to the matter as if the referral were a complaint made pursuant to section 42 of that Act except that a reference in any of those provisions to ''deputy head'' shall be read as a reference to the minister referred to in subsection (2).

(6) **Statement to be sent to person affected.**—The Review Committee shall, as soon as practicable after a matter in relation to a complaint is referred to it pursuant to paragraph (2)(*b*), send to the complainant a statement summarizing such information available to it as will enable the complainant to be as fully informed as possible of the circumstances giving rise to the referral. 1984, c. 21, s. 73.

46.(1) **Report.**—On completion of its investigation under section 45, the Review Committee shall, not later than forty-five days after the matter is referred to it pursuant to paragraph 45(2)(*b*), provide the Commission, the minister referred to in subsection 45(2) and the complainant with a report containing the findings of the Committee.

(2) **Action on receipt of report.**—After considering a report provided pursuant to subsection (1), the Commission
   (*a*) may dismiss the complaint or, where it does not do so, shall proceed to deal with the complaint pursuant to this Part; and
   (*b*) shall notify, in writing, the complainant and the person against whom the complaint was made of its action under paragraph (*a*) and may, in such manner as it sees fit, notify any other person whom it considers necessary to notify of that action. 1984, c. 21, s. 73.

Conciliator

47.(1) **Appointment of conciliator.**—Subject to subsection (2), the Commission may, on the filing of a complaint, or if the complaint has not been
   (*a*) settled in the course of investigation by an investigator,
   (*b*) referred or dismissed under subsection 44(2) or (3) or paragraph 45(2)(*a*) or 46(2)(*a*), or

(c) settled after receipt by the parties of the notice referred to in subsection 44(4),

appoint a person, in this Part referred to as a "conciliator", for the purpose of attempting to bring about a settlement of the complaint.

(2) **Eligibility.**—A person is not eligible to act as a conciliator in respect of a complaint if that person has already acted as an investigator in respect of that complaint.

(3) **Confidentiality.**—Any information received by a conciliator in the course of attempting to reach a settlement of a complaint is confidential and may not be disclosed except with the consent of the person who gave the information. 1976-77, c. 33, s. 37; 1984, c. 21, s. 74.

Settlement

48.(1) **Referral of a settlement to Commission.**—When, at any stage after the filing of a complaint and before the commencement of a hearing before a Human Rights Tribunal in respect thereof, a settlement is agreed on by the parties, the terms of the settlement shall be referred to the Commission for approval or rejection.

(2) **Certificate.**—If the Commission approves or rejects the terms of a settlement referred to in subsection (1), it shall so certify and notify the parties. 1976-77, c. 33, s. 38.

Human Rights Tribunal Panel

48.1 Human Rights Tribunal Panel.—There is hereby established a panel to be known as the Human Rights Tribunal Panel consisting of a President and such other members as may be appointed by the Governor in Council.

48.2 Term of office.—The President of the Human Rights Tribunal Panel shall be appointed to hold office during good behaviour for a term of three years and each of the other members of the Panel shall be appointed to be a member of the Panel during good behaviour for a term not exceeding five years, but may be removed by the Governor in Council for cause.

48.3 Absence or incapacity.—In the event of the absence or incapacity of the President of the Human Rights Tribunal Panel, or if there is no President, the Governor in Council may authorize a member of the Panel to act as President and a member so authorized, while so acting has all the powers and may perform all the duties of the President.

48.4 Re-appointment.—A President of the Human Rights Tribunal Panel as well as any member of the Panel whose term has expired is eligible for re-appointment in the same or any other capacity.

48.5 Remuneration of President.—The President of the Human Rights Tribunal Panel shall be paid remuneration and expenses for the performance of duties as President at the same rate as is prescribed by by-law of the Commission for a member of a Tribunal acting in the capacity of a Chairman thereof. R.S.C. 1985, c. 31 (1st Supp.), s. 65.

Human Rights Tribunal

49.(1) Human Rights Tribunal.—The Commission may, at any stage after the filing of a complaint, request the President of the Human Rights Tribunal Panel to appoint a Human Rights Tribunal, in this part referred to as a "Tribunal", to inquire into the complaint if the Commission is satisfied that, having regard to all the circumstances of the complaint, an inquiry into the complaint is warranted.

(1.1) **President to appoint Tribunal.**—On receipt of a request under subsection (1), the President of the Human Rights Tribunal Panel shall appoint a Tribunal to inquire into the complaint to which the request relates. R.S.C. 1985, c. 31 (1st Supp.), s. 66(1).

(2) **Membership.**—A Tribunal may not be composed of more than three members.

(3) **Eligibility.**—No member, officer or employee of the Commission, and no individual who has acted as investigator or conciliator in respect of the complaint in relation to which a Tribunal is appointed, is eligible to be appointed to the Tribunal.

(4) **Remuneration.**—A member of a Tribunal is entitled to be paid such remuneration and expenses for the performance of duties as a member of the Tribunal as may be prescribed by by-law of the Commission. 1976-77, c. 33, s. 39(2-4).

(5) **Selection from Panel.**—Subject to subsection (5.1), in selecting any individual or individuals to be appointed as a Tribunal, the President of the Human Rights Tribunal Panel shall select from among the members of the Human Rights Tribunal Panel.

(5.1) **President may appoint himself.**—The President of the Human Rights Tribunal Panel may sit as a Tribunal or as a member of a Tribunal.

(6) **Chairman.**—Subject to subsection (7), where a Tribunal consists of more than one member, the President of the Human Rights Tribunal Panel shall designate one of the members to be the Chairman of the Tribunal.

(7) **Idem.**—Where the President of the Human Rights Tribunal Panel is a member of a Tribunal consisting of more than one member, the President shall be Chairman of the Tribunal. R.S.C. 1985, c. 31 (1st Supp.), s. 66(2).

50.(1) **Duties.**—A Tribunal shall, after due notice to the Commission, the complainant, the person against whom the complaint was made and, at the discretion of the Tribunal, any other interested party, inquire into the complaint in respect of which it was appointed and shall give all parties to whom notice has been given a full and ample opportunity, in person or through counsel, to appear before the Tribunal, present evidence and make representations to it.

(2) **Powers.**—In relation to a hearing under this Part, a Tribunal may

(*a*)   in the same manner and to the same extent as a superior court of record, summon and enforce the attendance of witnesses and compel them to give oral or written evidence on oath and to produce such documents and things as the Tribunal deems requisite to the full hearing and consideration of the complaint;

(*b*)   administer oaths; and

(*c*)   receive and accept such evidence and other information, whether on oath or by affidavit or otherwise, as the Tribunal sees fit, whether or not that evidence or information is or would be admissible in a court of law.

(3) **Limitation in relation to evidence.**—Notwithstanding paragraph (2)(*c*), a tribunal may not admit or accept as evidence anything that would be inadmissible in a court by reason of any privilege under the law of evidence.

(4) **Conciliator not competent or compellable.**—Notwithstanding paragraph (2)(*a*), a conciliator appointed to settle a complaint is not a competent or compellable witness at a hearing of a Tribunal appointed to inquire into the complaint.

(5) **Witness fees.**—Any person summoned to attend a hearing pursuant to this section is entitled in the discretion of the Tribunal to receive the like fees and allowances for so doing as if summoned to attend before the Federal Court. 1976-77, c. 33, s. 40.

51. Duty of Commission on appearing.—The Commission, in appearing before a Tribunal, presenting evidence and making representations to it, shall adopt such position as, in its opinion, is in the public interest having regard to the nature of the complaint being inquired into. 1976-77, c. 33, s. 40.

52. Hearing in public.—A hearing of a Tribunal shall be public, but a Tribunal may exclude members of the public during the whole or any part of a hearing if it considers that exclusion to be in the public interest. 1976-77, c. 33, s. 40.

53.(1) **Complaint dismissed.**—If, at the conclusion of its inquiry, a Tribunal finds that the complaint to which the inquiry relates is not substantiated, it shall dismiss the complaint.

(2) **Order.**—If, at the conclusion of its inquiry, a Tribunal finds that the complaint to which the inquiry relates is substantiated, it may, subject to subsection (4) and section 54, make an order against the person found to be engaging or to have engaged in the discriminatory practice and include in that order any of the following terms that it considers appropriate

(*a*) that the person cease the discriminatory practice and, in order to prevent the same or a similar practice from occurring in the future, take measures, including

(i) adoption of a special program, plan or arrangement referred to in subsection 16(1), or

(ii) the making of an application for approval and the implementing of a plan pursuant to section 17,

in consultation with the Commission on the general purposes of those measures;

(*b*) that the person make available to the victim of the discriminatory practice, on the first reasonable occasion, such rights, opportunities or privileges as, in the opinion of the Tribunal, are being or were denied the victim as a result of the practice;

(*c*) that the person compensate the victim, as the Tribunal may consider proper, for any or all of the wages that the victim was deprived of and for any expenses incurred by the victim as a result of the discriminatory practice; and

(*d*) that the person compensate the victim, as the Tribunal may consider proper, for any or all additional cost of obtaining alternative goods, services, facilities or accommodation and for any expenses incurred by the victim as a result of the discriminatory practice.

(3) **Special compensation.**—In addition to any order that the Tribunal may make pursuant to subsection (2), if the Tribunal finds that

(*a*) a person is engaging or has engaged in a discriminatory practice wilfully or recklessly, or

(*b*) the victim of the discriminatory practice has suffered in respect of feelings or self-respect as a result of the practice,

the Tribunal may order the person to pay such compensation to the victim, not exceeding five thousand dollars, as the Tribunal may determine.

(4) **Order or recommendation to be made to avoid undue hardship.**—If, at the conclusion of its inquiry into a complaint regarding discrimination based on a disability, the Tribunal finds that the complaint is substantiated but that the premises or facilities of the person found to be engaging or to have engaged in the discriminatory practice require adaptation to meet the needs of a person arising from such a disability, the Tribunal shall

(*a*) make such order pursuant to this section for that adaptation as it considers appropriate and as it is satisfied will not occasion costs or business inconvenience constituting undue hardship, or (*b*)   if the Tribunal considers that no such order can be made, make such recommendations as it considers appropriate,

and, in the event of such finding, the Tribunal shall not make an order unless required by this subsection. 1976-77, c. 33, s. 41; 1980-81-82-83, c. 143, s. 20.

54.(1) **Limitation of order.**—Where a Tribunal finds that a complaint related to a discriminatory practice described in section 13 is substantiated, it may make only an order referred to in paragraph 53(2)(*a*).

(2) **Idem.**—No order under subsection 53(2) may contain a term

(*a*)   requiring the removal of an individual from a position if that individual accepted employment in that position in good faith; or

(*b*)   requiring the expulsion of an occupant from any premises or accommodation, if that occupant obtained such premises or accommodation in good faith. 1976-77, c. 33, s. 42.

55. Appeals.—Where a Tribunal that made a decision or order was composed of fewer than three members, the Commission, the complainant before the Tribunal or the person against whom the complaint was made may appeal the decision or order by serving a notice, in a manner and form prescribed by order of the Governor in Council, within thirty days after the decision or order appealed was pronounced, on all persons who received notice from the Tribunal under subsection 50(1). 1976-77, c. 33, s. 42.1(1).

56.(1) **Establishment of Review Tribunal.**—Where an appeal is made pursuant to section 55, the President of the Human Rights Tribunal Panel shall select three members from the Human Rights Tribunal Panel, other than the member or members of the Tribunal whose decision or order is being appealed from, to constitute a Review Tribunal to hear the appeal. R.S.C. 1985, c. 31 (1st Supp.), s. 67.

(2) **Constitution and powers.**—Subject to this section, a Review Tribunal shall be constituted in the same manner as, and shall have all the powers of, a Tribunal appointed pursuant to section 49, and subsection 49(4) applies in respect of members of a Review Tribunal.

(3) **Grounds for appeal.**—An appeal lies to a Review Tribunal against a decision or order of a Tribunal on any question of law or fact or mixed law and fact.

(4) **Hearing of appeal.**—A Review Tribunal shall hear an appeal on the basis of the record of the Tribunal whose decision or order is appealed and of submissions of interested parties but the Review Tribunal may, if in its opinion it is essential in the interests of justice to do so, admit additional evidence or testimony.

(5) **Disposition of appeal.**—A Review Tribunal may dispose of an appeal under section 55 by dismissing it, or by allowing it and rendering the decision or making the order that, in its opinion, the Tribunal appealed against should have rendered or made. 1976-77, c. 33, s. 42.1(3-6).

57. Enforcement of order.—Any order of a Tribunal under subsection 53(2) or (3) or any order of a Review Tribunal under subsection 56(5) may, for the purpose of enforcement, be made an order of the Federal Court by following the usual practice and procedure or, in lieu thereof, by the Commission filing in the Registry of the Court a copy of the order certified to be a true copy, and thereupon that order becomes an order of the Court. 1976-77, c. 33, s. 43.

58.(1) **Application respecting disclosure of information.**—Where any investigator or Tribunal requires the disclosure of any information and a minister of the Crown or any other person interested objects to its disclosure, the Commission may apply to the Federal Court for a determination of the matter.

(2) **Certificate.**—Where the Commission applies to the Federal Court pursuant to subsection (1) and the minister of the Crown or other person interested objects to the disclosure in accordance with sections 37 to 39 of the *Canada Evidence Act*, the matter shall be determined in accordance with the terms of those sections.

(3) **No certificate.**—Where the Commission applies to the Federal Court pursuant to subsection (1) but the minister of the Crown or other person interested does not within ninety days thereafter object to the disclosure in accordance with sections 37 to 39 of the *Canada Evidence Act*, the Court may take such action as it deems appropriate. 1976-77, c. 33, s. 44; 1980-81-82-83, c. 111, s. 5, c. 143, s. 21.

59. Intimidation or discrimination.—No person shall threaten, intimidate or discriminate against an individual because that individual had made a complaint or given evidence or assisted in any way in respect of the initiation or prosecution of a complaint or other proceeding under this Part, or because that individual proposes to do so. 1976-77, c. 33, s. 45.

Offences and Punishment

60.(1) **Offence.**—Every person is guilty of an offence who
(a) fails to comply with the terms of any settlement of a complaint approved and certified under section 48;
(b) obstructs a Tribunal in carrying out its functions under this Part; or
(c) contravenes subsection 11(6) or 43(3) or section 59.

(2) **Punishment.**—A person who is guilty of an offence under subsection (1) is liable on summary conviction

(*a*)   if the accused is an employer, an employer association or an employee organization, to a fine not exceeding fifty thousand dollars; or

(*b*)   in any other case, to a fine not exceeding five thousand dollars.

(3) **Prosecution of employer association or employee organization.**—A prosecution for an offence under this section may be brought against an employer association or employee organization and in the name of that association or organization and for the purpose of the prosecution that association or organization shall be deemed to be a person and any act or thing done or omitted by an officer or agent of that association or organization within the scope of that officer's or agent's authority to act on behalf of the association or organization shall be deemed to be an act or thing done or omitted by the association or organization.

(4) **Consent of Attorney General.**—A prosecution for an offence under this section may not be instituted except by or with the consent of the Attorney General of Canada.

(5) **Definition of "employer association".**—For the purposes of this section, "employer association" means any organization of employers the purposes of which include the negotiation, on behalf of employers, of the terms and conditions of employment of employees. 1976-77, c. 33, s. 46.

Reports

61.(1) **Annual report.**—The Commission shall, within three months after December 31 in each year, transmit to the Minister of Justice a report on the activities of the Commission under this Part and Part II for that year including references to and comments on any matter referred to in paragraph 27(1)(*e*) or (*g*) that it considers appropriate.

(2) **Special reports.**—The Commission may, at any time, transmit to the Minister of Justice a special report referring to and commenting on any matter within the scope of its powers, duties and functions where, in its opinion, the matter is of such urgency or importance that a report thereon should not be deferred until the time provided for transmission of its next annual report under subsection (1).

(3) **Tabling reports.**—The Minister shall cause any report transmitted to the Minister pursuant to this section to be laid before each House of Parliament on any of the first fifteen days on which that House is sitting after the day the Minister receives it. 1976-77, c. 33, s. 47; 1980-81-82-83, c. 143, s. 22.

Application

62.(1) **Limitation.**—This Part and Parts I and II do not apply to or in respect of any superannuation or pension fund or plan established by an Act of Parliament enacted before March 1, 1978.

(2) **Review of Acts referred to in subsection (1).**—The Commission shall keep under review those Acts of Parliament enacted before March 1, 1978 by which any superannuation or pension fund or plan is established and, where the Commission deems it to be appropriate, it may include in a report mentioned in section 61 reference to and comment on any provision of any of those Acts that in its opinion is inconsistent with the principle described in section 2. 1976-77, c. 33, s. 48.

63. Application in the Territories.—Where a complaint under this Part relates to an act or omission that occurred in the Yukon Territory or the Northwest Territories, it may not be dealt with under this Part unless the act or omission could be the subject of a complaint under this Part had it occurred in a province. 1976-77, c. 33, s. 48.

NOTE: The above section 63 as re-enacted by 1993, c. 28, Sch. III (to come into force April 1, 1999 or earlier by order of the Governor in Council) reads as follows:

63. Application in the territories.—Where a complaint under this Part relates to an act or omission that occurred in the Yukon Territory, the Northwest Territories or Nunavut, it may not be dealt with under this Part unless the act or omission could be the subject of a complaint under this Part had it occurred in a province.

64. Canadian Forces and Royal Canadian Mounted Police.—For the purposes of this Part and Parts I and II, members of the Canadian Forces and the Royal Canadian Mounted Police are deemed to be employed by the Crown. 1976-77, c. 33, s. 48.

65.(1) **Acts of employees, etc.**—Subject to subsection (2), any act or omission committed by an officer, a director, an employee or an agent of any person, association or organization in the course of the employment of the officer, director, employee or agent shall, for the purposes of this Act, be deemed to be an act or omission committed by that person, association or organization.

(2) **Exculpation.**—An act or omission shall not, by virtue of subsection (1), be deemed to be an act or omission committed by a person, association or organization if it is established that the person, association or organization did

not consent to the commission of the act or omission and exercised all due diligence to prevent the act or omission from being committed and, subsequently, to mitigate or avoid the effect thereof. 1980-81-82-83, c. 143, s. 23.

PART IV

APPLICATION

66.(1) **Binding on Her Majesty.**—This Act is binding on Her Majesty in right of Canada, except in matters respecting the Government of the Yukon Territory or the Northwest Territories.

NOTE: The above subsection (1) as re-enacted by 1993, c. 28, Sch. III (to come into force April 1, 1999 or earlier by order of the Governor in Council) reads as follows:

*66.(1) **Binding on Her Majesty.**—This Act is binding on Her Majesty in right of Canada, except in matters respecting the Government of the Yukon Territory, the Northwest Territories or Nunavut.*

(2) **Commencement.**—The exception referred to in subsection (1) shall come into operation in respect of the Government of the Yukon Territory on a day to be fixed by proclamation.

(3) **Idem.**—The exception referred to in subsection (1) shall come into operation in respect of the Government of the Northwest Territories on a day to be fixed by proclamation. 1976-77, c. 33, s. 63; 1980-81-82-83, c. 143, ss. 24, 29.

NOTE: The following subsection (4) as enacted by 1993, c. 28, Sch. III (to come into force April 1, 1999 or earlier by order of the Governor in Council) reads as follows:

*(4) **Idem.**—The exception referred to in subsection (1) shall come into operation in respect of the Government of Nunavut on a day to be fixed by order of the Governor in Council.*

67. Saving.—Nothing in this Act affects any provision of the *Indian Act* or any provision made under or pursuant to that Act. 1976-77, c. 33, s. 63.

Schedule (iii)

SOR/80-68

CANADIAN HUMAN RIGHTS BENEFIT REGULATIONS

Amended SOR/82-783
Amended SOR/83-615
Amended SOR/85-512

Short Title

1. These Regulations may be cited as the *Canadian Human Rights Benefit Regulations.*

Interpretation

2.(1) In these Regulations,

"Act" means the *Canadian Human Rights Act*;

"actuarial basis" means the basis of the assumptions and methods used by a Fellow of the Canadian Institute of Actuaries to establish the costs of benefits under a benefit plan, taking into consideration the contingencies of human life, such as death, accident, sickness or disease;

"benefit", in respect of a benefit plan, includes

    (*a*) an aggregate amount or an annual, a monthly or other periodic amount or the accrual of such amounts to which an employee or his beneficiary, survivor, spouse, child or dependant is or may become entitled under the plan on superannuation, retirement, termination of employment, disability, accident, sickness or death,

    (*b*) any amount to which one of the persons referred to in paragraph (*a*) is or may become entitled under the plan for medical, hospital, nursing, drug or dental expenses or other similar expenses, and

    (*c*) any amount to which one of the persons referred to in paragraph (*a*) is or may become entitled under the plan on superannuation, retirement or termination of employment or to which any person is or may become entitled under the plan on the death of another person;

"benefit plan" means an insurance plan or a pension plan, whether or not the terms and conditions thereof have been set out in writing;

319

"child", in relation to an employee under a benefit plan, has the meaning given that term under the plan, and includes a natural child, stepchild or adopted child;

"dependant", in relation to an employee under a benefit plan, has the meaning given that term under the plan;

"disability income insurance plan" or "disability income benefit plan" means a plan, fund or arrangement provided, furnished or offered to an employee that provides, in accordance with the terms of the plan, fund or arrangement, benefits to the employee for loss of income because of sickness, accident or disability;

"health insurance plan" or "health benefit plan" means a plan, fund or arrangement provided, furnished or offered to or in respect of an employee that provides, in accordance with the terms of the plan, fund or arrangement, benefits

(a)   to the employee or the spouse, child or dependant of the employee, or

(b)   in the case of a deceased employee, to the spouse, child or dependant of the employee,

for medical, hospital, nursing, drug or dental expenses or other similar expenses;

"insurance plan" means a disability income insurance plan, a health insurance plan or a life insurance plan;

"life insurance plan" means a plan, fund or arrangement, provided, furnished or offered to an employee that provides, in accordance with the terms of the plan, fund or arrangement, benefits

(a)   on the death of the employee, to a beneficiary, survivor or dependant of the employee, or

(b)   on the death of the spouse, a child or a dependant of the employee, to the employee,

payable either in a lump sum or by periodic payments;

"normal age of retirement", in respect of any employment or position of a person, means the maximum age applicable to that employment or position referred to in paragraph 14(b) of the Act or the age applicable to that employment or position referred to in paragraph 14(c) of the Act, as the case may be;

"normal pensionable age" under a pension plan, means the earliest date specified in the plan on which an employee can retire from his employment and receive all the benefits provided by the plan to which he would otherwise be entitled under the terms of the plan, without adjustment by reason of early retirement, whether such date is the day on which the employee has attained a given age or on which the employee has completed a given period of employment;

"pension plan" means a superannuation, retirement or pension plan, fund or arrangement provided, furnished or offered to an employee that provides, in accordance with the terms of the plan, fund or arrangement, to or in respect of the employee on the superannuation, retirement or termination of employment of the employee, benefits that are determined by reference to

(a) contributions made by the employee or his employer, or both, or

(b) contributions referred to in paragraph (a) and the investment income, gains, losses and expenses in respect of those contributions,

and includes

(c) a defined benefit pension plan under which the benefits are determined by reference to

    (i) a percentage of the salary, wages or other remuneration of the employee in addition to the length of employment of the employee or a specified period of employment, or

    (ii) the length of employment of the employee or a specified period of employment,

(d) a money purchase pension plan under which the benefits are determined by reference to

    (i) the accumulated amount of the contributions paid by or to the credit of the employee and the investment income, gains, losses and expenses in respect of those contributions, or

    (ii) the accumulated amount of the benefits purchased by each contribution paid by or to the credit of the employee,

(e) a profit-sharing pension plan under which contributions by an employer are determined by reference to the profits earned from his business and the benefits are determined by reference to

    (i) the accumulated amount of the contributions paid by or to the credit of the employee and the investment income, gains, losses and expenses in respect of those contributions, or

    (ii) the accumulated amount of the benefits purchased by each contribution paid by or to the credit of the employee, and,

(f) a composite pension plan the terms and conditions of which are any combination of the terms and conditions of a defined benefit pension plan, a money purchase pension plan and a profit-sharing pension plan or any two of those plans;

"spouse", in relation to an employee under a benefit plan, has the meaning given that term under the plan, and includes the person who is the common-law spouse of the employee within the meaning given that expression under the plan, if

(a) for at least the minimum period determined in accordance with subsection (2),
(i) that person had been residing continuously with the employee who was a member of the opposite sex, whom by law that person was prohibited from marrying by reason of a previous marriage either of the employee or of himself, and
(ii) the employee and that person had been publicly represented as husband and wife, or

(b) for at least the minimum period determined in accordance with subsection (3), that person had been residing continuously with the employee who was a member of the opposite sex and throughout that period the employee and that person had been publicly represented as husband and wife and at the time of the applicable event that causes a benefit to be paid under the terms of the plan neither that person nor the employee was married to any other person;

"voluntary employee contribution" means a contribution made voluntarily by an employee to or under a benefit plan, except a contribution the payment of which, under the terms of the plan, imposes on an employer an obligation to make a concurrent additional contribution to or under the plan.

(2) For the purposes of paragraph (a) of the definition "spouse" in subsection (1), the minimum period in respect of a benefit plan is the period, not exceeding three years immediately before the application event that causes a benefit to be paid under the terms of the plan, that is specified under the terms of the plan.

(3) For the purposes of paragraph (b) of the definition "spouse" in subsection (1), the minimum period in respect of a benefit plan is the period, not exceeding one year immediately before the applicable event that causes a benefit to be paid under the terms of the plan, that is specified under the terms of the plan.

Participation in Benefit Plans

3. The following provisions of a benefit plan do not constitute the basis for a complaint under Part III of the Act that an employer is engaging or has engaged in a discriminatory practice:
(a) in the case of any pension plan, provisions that result in
(i) where employees do not make contributions to the plan, an employee not being required or permitted to participate in the plan until the employee has attained the age of not more than twenty-five years,
(ii) where employees make contributions to the plan, an employee not being required to participate in the plan until the employee has attained the age of not more than twenty-five years,

    (iii) an employee being excluded from participation in the plan because the provisions of the plan permit participation therein only in the case of an employee who would be eligible to receive pension benefits under the plan if he was to retire at the normal age of retirement and the provisions do not permit an employee who participates therein to continue to accrue benefits after he has reached the normal age of retirement, or

    (iv) an employee being unable to accrue benefits under the plan in respect of his periods of service prior to the time he became a member of the plan because he did not satisfy the requirements in respect of health in order to accrue such benefits;

(b) in the case of any disability income insurance plan, provisions that result in an employee being excluded from participation in the plan because the employee has attained the age at which a member of the plan would not be eligible to receive benefits under the plan or has attained that age less the length of the waiting period following the commencement of a disability that must pass before benefits may become payable thereunder, if that age is not less than 65 or the normal pensionable age under the pension plan of which the employee is a member, whichever occurs first;

(c) in the case of any disability income insurance plan or health insurance plan that contains provisions that result in an employee of an employer employing less than 25 employees being excluded from participation in the plan because the employer does not satisfy the requirements in respect of health in order to participate therein, provisions under which the employer pays to the excluded employee an amount equal to the contribution that is made by the employer in respect of an employee who is able to participate in that plan;

(d) in the case of any voluntary employee-pay-all insurance plan or any insurance plan that has a voluntary employee contribution feature, provisions that result in an employee being excluded from participation in the plan or in the voluntary employee contribution feature, as the case may be, because he does not satisfy the requirements in respect of health in order to participate therein;

(e) provisions of any benefit plan that result in an employee being excluded from participation in the plan

    (i) because the employee chose not to participate in the plan when he was first eligible to do so and he did not satisfy the requirements in respect of health in order to participate in the plan on subsequently seeking to participate therein, or

    (ii) until the first day on which the employee is actively at work after he has satisfied all other requirements for participation therein; and (*f*)   the provisions of any benefit plan relating to participation therein that do not differentiate between employees on any ground of discrimination referred to in section 3 of the Act otherwise than in the manner referred to in paragraphs (*a*) to (*e*). SOR/82-783, s. 1.

Benefit Provisions

4. The following provisions of a pension plan do not constitute the basis for a complaint under Part III of the Act that an employer is engaging or has engaged in a discriminatory practice:

(*a*)   provisions that result in eligibility for various benefits under the plan being subject to the attainment by a person of specified ages;

(*b*)   provisions that result in differentiation being made between employees in the amounts of the monthly or other periodic benefits payable under the plan to or in respect of the employees,

    (i) because of age, where such differentiation is determined on an actuarial basis, or because of an adjustment that recognizes the availability of benefits payable under the *Canada Pension Plan*, the *Old Age Security Act* or a provincial pension plan as defined in section 3 of the *Canada Pension Plan*, where the adjustment is permitted under and is made in accordance with the *Pension Benefits Standards Act* and any regulations thereunder,

    (ii) because of marital status, where

        (A)   benefits are payable periodically to the surviving spouse of a deceased employee, or

        (B)   an increase in benefits is payable to a former employee because the employee has a dependent spouse, or

    (iii) because of family status, where benefits are payable periodically to or in respect of a surviving child of a deceased employee;

(*c*)   provisions that result in differentiation being made between employees

    (i) because of marital status, where a lump sum benefit is payable under the plan to the surviving spouse of a deceased employee, or

    (ii) because of family status, where a lump sum benefit is payable under the plan to or in respect of a surviving child of a deceased employee;

(*d*)   in the case of any voluntary employee-pay-all pension plan or any pension plan that has a voluntary employee contribution feature, provisions of such a plan respecting voluntary employee contributions that result in differentiation being made between employees in the amounts of the benefits provided under the plan or in respect of the employees because of sex, where such differentiation is determined on an actuarial basis;

(e)   provisions that result in differentiation being made between employees when benefits payable under the plan to or in respect of the employees are converted under an option contained therein, in the amounts of those benefits because of sex, where such differentiation is determined on an actuarial basis;

(e.1)   provisions that result in an employee being unable to exercise an option under the plan to convert the benefits payable thereunder to or in respect of that employee to benefits of another type or of an amount other than the amount of the benefits payable under the plan because that employee did not satisfy the requirements in respect of health in order to exercise that option; and

(f)   provisions that result in no differentiation being made between employees in the amounts of the benefits payable under the plan to or in respect of the employees on any ground of discrimination referred to in section 3 of the Act, other than the differentiation referred to in paragraphs (a) to (e), or the differentiation that results from the provisions of a benefit plan referred to in section 3. SOR/ 82-783, s. 2; SOR/85-512, s. 1(2, 4).

5. The following provisions of an insurance plan do not constitute the basis for a complaint under Part III of the Act that an employer is engaging or has engaged in a discriminatory practice:

(a)   in the case of any voluntary employee-pay-all life insurance plan or any life insurance plan that has a voluntary employee contribution feature, provisions respecting voluntary employee contributions that result in differentiation being made between employees in the amounts of the benefits payable under the plan to or in respect of the employees because of age, where such differentiation is determined on an actuarial basis;

(b)   in the case of any disability income insurance plan, provisions that result in differentiation being made between employees because the benefits payable under the plan to an employee cease when the employee has attained the age of not less than 65, or the normal pensionable age under the pension plan of which the employee is a member, whichever occurs first;

(c)   in the case of any disability income insurance plan or health insurance plan, provisions that result in differentiation being made between employees because, during a period not exceeding one year after the date when an employee first became insured under the plan, the benefits under the plan are not payable to the employee in respect of conditions arising from an injury, accident or sickness that commenced prior to that date and in respect of which the employee had received medical care, treatment or services, drug therapy or medicine prescribed by a qualified medical practitioner during a period not exceeding one year prior to that date;

(*d*) in the case of any life insurance plan, provisions that result in differentiation being made between employees because the rate or the amount of the benefits payable under the plan to or in respect of a member of the plan who satisfies certain requirements as to health exceeds the maximum rate or amount of benefits payable under the plan to or in respect of every member of the plan, whether or not a member satisfies those requirements as to health, where

   (i) the rates of contributions of the employees or the employer, or both, to the plan in respect of benefits up to or equal to the maximum rate or amount payable to or in respect of every member of the plan, have been determined on an actuarial basis with regard to those benefits, and

   (ii) the rates of contributions of the employees or the employer, or both, to the plan in excess of the contributions referred to in subparagraph (i), in respect of benefits, in excess of the maximum rate or amount, referred to in that subparagraph, payable to or in respect of a member of the plan who satisfies certain requirements as to health, have been determined on an actuarial basis with regard to the benefits in excess of that maximum;

(*e*) in the case of any life insurance plan, provisions that result in differentiation being made between employees

   (i) because of marital status, where

      (A) benefits are payable on the death of an employee, in a lump sum or periodically, to the surviving spouse of the employee, or

      (B) benefits are payable to an employee, in a lump sum or periodically, on the death of his spouse or,

   (ii) because of family status, where benefits are payable on the death of an employee, in a lump sum or periodically, to or in respect of a surviving child or dependant of the employee or where benefits are payable to an employee, in a lump sum or periodically, on the death of this child or dependant;

(*f*) in the case of any health insurance plan, provisions that result in differentiation being made between employees,

   (i) because of marital status in order to provide benefits for the spouse of an employee,

   (ii) because of family status, where benefits are provided under the plan to or in respect of a child or dependant of the employee, or

(iii) where benefits under the plan are reduced on attainment of a certain age in respect of certain medical, hospital, nursing, drug or dental expenses or other similar expenses when equivalent or greater benefits become payable by the health insurance plan of a province under which an employee or his survivor, spouse, child or dependant, as the case may be, is insured; and

(g) provisions that result in no differentiation being made between employees in the amounts of the benefits payable under the plan to or in respect of the employees on any ground of discrimination referred to in section 3 of the Act, other than the differentiation referred to in paragraphs (a) to (f), or the differentiation that results from the provisions of a benefit plan referred to in sections 3 and 6. SOR/82-783, s. 3; SOR/83-615, s. 1; SOR/85-512, s. 2(2, 4).

6. [*Revoked* SOR/85-512, s. 3.]

Contributions

7. The following provisions of a pension plan do not constitute the basis for a complaint under Part III of the Act that an employer is engaging or has engaged in a discriminatory practice:

(a) provisions that result in differentiation being made between employees in the rates of contribution of the employer to the plan, where such differentiation is made on an actuarial basis because of age or sex, or both, in order to provide equal benefits under the plan to the employees;

(b) in the case of any defined benefit pension plan, provisions that result in differentiation being made between employees in the rates of contribution of the employer to the plan, where such differentiation is made on an actuarial basis because of age, sex, marital status or family status in order to provide an increase in benefits under the plan to a former employee in respect of his dependent spouse or to pay benefits under the plan to the surviving spouse of a deceased employee or to or in respect of a surviving child of a deceased employee;

(c) in the case of any money purchase pension plan or profit-sharing pension plan, provisions that result in differentiation being made between employees in the rates of contribution of employees to the plan, where such differentiation is made on an actuarial basis because of age in order to provide equal benefits under the plan to the employees;

(d) provisions that result in differentiation being made between employees in the rates of voluntary contributions of an employee to the plan, where such differentiation is made on an actuarial basis because of age, sex, marital status or family status; and

(e)   provisions that result in no differentiation being made between employees in the rates of contribution under the plan or any ground of discrimination referred to in section 3 of the Act, other than the differentiation referred to in paragraphs (a) to (d) and sections 9 and 10, or the differentiation that results from the provisions of a benefit plan referred to in section 3. SOR/85-512, s. 4.

8. The following provisions of an insurance plan do not constitute the basis for a complaint under Part III of the Act that an employer is engaging or has engaged in a discriminatory practice:

(a)   provisions that result in differentiation being made between employees in the rates of contribution of the employer to the plan, where such differentiation is made on an actuarial basis because of age, disability or sex in order to provide equal benefits under the plan to the employees;

(b)   in the case of any life insurance plan, provisions that result in differentiation being made between employees in the rates of contribution of employees or the employer, or both, to the plan, where such differentiation is made on an actuarial basis because of the marital status in the case of employee contributions, or because of age, disability, sex, marital status or family status in the case of employer contributions, in order to pay benefits under the plan to the surviving spouse of a deceased employee or to or in respect of a surviving child or dependant of a deceased employee;

(c)   in the case of any life insurance plan or health insurance plan, provisions that result in differentiation being made between employees in the rates of contribution of employees or the employer to the plan, where such differentiation is made on an actuarial basis because of marital status or family status in order to pay benefits under the plan on the death of or for the health care of the spouse, children or dependants of an employee;

(d)   provisions that result in differentiation being made between employees in the rates of contribution of employees or the employer, or both, to the plan, where such differentiation is made because of the circumstances described in paragraph 5(b), (c) or (d), as the case may be, or because of a difference in the contributions required of employees of that employer under health insurance plans of different provinces;

(e)   in the case of any voluntary employee-pay-all insurance plan or any insurance plan that has a voluntary employee contribution feature, provisions respecting voluntary employee contributions that result in differentiation being made between employees in the rates of contribution of employees to the plan, where such differentiation is determined on an actuarial basis because of age, sex, marital status or family status; and

(*f*)   provisions that result in no differentiation being made between employees in the rates of contribution under the plan on any ground of discrimination referred to in section 3 of the Act, other than the differentiation referred to in paragraphs (*a*) to (*e*) and sections 9 and 10, or the differentiation that results from the provisions of a benefit plan referred to in section 3. SOR/82-783, s. 4; SOR/85-512, s. 5.

9. The provisions of any benefit plan respecting leave of absence that result in differentiation being made between employees in the rates of contribution

(*a*)   [*Revoked* SOR/85-512, s. 6.]

(*b*)   of an employer or employees, or both, to the plan, where such differentiation consists of a reduction in the contributions required of an employee who is absent on a maternity leave of absence or on a leave of absence due to sickness, injury or disability and an increase in the contributions of the employer to the plan by reason of such reduction,

do not constitute the basis of a complaint under Part III of the Act that an employer is engaging or has engaged in a discriminatory practice.

10. The provisions of any benefit plan that result in differentiation being made between employees in the rates of contribution of an employer to the plan because an employee has exercised an option not to participate in the whole or a portion of the plan do not constitute the basis of a complaint under Part III of the Act that an employer is engaging or has engaged in a discriminatory practice.

Schedule (iv)

SOR/86-1082

EQUAL WAGES GUIDELINES, 1986

Short Title

1. These Guidelines may be cited as the *Equal Wages Guidelines, 1986.*

Interpretation

2. In these Guidelines, ''Act'' means the *Canadian Human Rights Act.* (*Loi*)

Assessment of Value

Skill

3. For the purposes of subsection 11(2) of the Act, intellectual and physical qualifications acquired by experience, training, education or natural ability shall be considered in assessing the skill required in the performance of work.

4. The methods by which employees acquire the qualifications referred to in section 3 shall not be considered in assessing the skill of different employees.

Effort

5. For the purposes of subsection 11(2) of the Act, intellectual and physical effort shall be considered in assessing the effort required in the performance of work.

6. For the purpose of section 5, intellectual and physical effort may be compared.

Responsibility

7. For the purposes of subsection 11(2) of the Act, the extent of responsibility by the employee for technical, financial and human resources shall be considered in assessing the responsibility required in the performance of work.

Working Conditions

8.(1) For the purposes of subsection 11(2) of the Act, the physical and psychological work environments, including noise, temperature, isolation, physical danger, health hazards and stress, shall be considered in assessing the conditions under which the work is performed.

(2) For the purposes of subsection 11(2) of the Act, the requirement to work overtime or to work shifts is not to be considered in assessing working conditions where a wage, in excess of the basic wage, is paid for that overtime or shift work.

Method of Assessment of Value

9. Where an employer relies on a system in assessing the value of work performed by employees employed in the same establishment, that system shall be used in the investigation of any complaint alleging a difference in wages, if that system

    (*a*)   operates without any sexual bias;

    (*b*)   is capable of measuring the relative value of work of all jobs in the establishment; and

    (*c*)   assesses the skill, effort and responsibility and the working conditions determined in accordance with sections 3 to 8.

Employees of an Establishment

10. For the purpose of section 11 of the Act, employees of an establishment include, notwithstanding any collective agreement applicable to any employees of the establishment, all employees of the employer subject to a common personnel and wage policy, whether or not such policy is administered centrally.

Complaints by Individuals

11.(1) Where a complaint alleging a difference in wages is filed by or on behalf of an individual who is a member of an identifiable occupational group, the composition of the group according to sex is a factor in determining whether the practice complained of is discriminatory on the ground of sex.

(2) In the case of a complaint by an individual, where at least two other employees of the establishment perform work of equal value, the weighted average wage paid to those employees shall be used to calculate the adjustment to the complainant's wages.

Complaints of Groups

12. Where a complaint alleging different wages is filed by or on behalf of an identifiable occupational group, the group must be predominantly of one sex and the group to which the comparison is made must be predominantly of the other sex.

13. For the purpose of section 12, an occupational group is composed predominantly of one sex where the number of members of that sex constituted, for the year immediately preceding the day on which the complaint is filed, at least

(*a*) 70 per cent of the occupational group, if the group has less than 100 members;

(*b*) 60 per cent of the occupational group, if the group has from 100 to 500 members; and

(*c*) 55 per cent of the occupational group, if the group has more than 500 members.

14. Where a comparison is made between the occupational group that filed a complaint alleging a difference in wages and other occupational groups, those other groups are deemed to be one group.

15.(1) Where a complaint alleging a difference in wages between an occupational group and any other occupational group is filed and a direct comparison of the value of the work performed and the wages received by employees of the occupational groups cannot be made, for the purposes of section 11 of the Act, the work performed and the wages received by the employees of each occupational group may be compared indirectly.

(2) For the purposes of comparing wages received by employees of the occupational groups referred to in subsection (1), the wage curve of the other occupational group referred to in that subsection shall be used to establish the difference in wages, if any, between the employees of the occupational group on behalf of which the complaint is made and the other occupational group.

Reasonable Factors

16. For the purpose of subsection 11(3) of the Act, a difference in wages between male and female employees performing work of equal value in an establishment is justified by

(*a*) different performance ratings, where employees are subject to a formal system of performance appraisal that has been brought to their attention;

(*b*) seniority, where a system of remuneration that applies to the employees provides that they receive periodic increases in wages based on their length of service with the employer;

(*c*) a re-evaluation and downgrading of the position of an employee, where the wages of that employee are temporarily fixed, or the increases in the wages of that employee are temporarily curtailed, until the wages appropriate to the downgraded position are equivalent to or higher than the wages of that employee;

(*d*) a rehabilitation assignment, where an employer pays to an employee wages that are higher than justified by the value of the work performed by that employee during recuperation of limited duration from an injury or illness;

(e) a demotion procedure, where the employer, without decreasing the employee's wages, reassigns an employee to a position at a lower level as a result of the unsatisfactory work performance of the employee caused by factors beyond the employee's control, such as the increasing complexity of the job or the impaired health or partial disability of the employee, or as a result of an internal labour force surplus that necessitates the reassignment;

(f) a procedure of gradually reducing wages for any of the reasons set out in paragraph (e);

(g) a temporary training position, where, for the purposes of an employee development program that is equally available to male and female employees and leads to the career advancement of the employees who take part in the program, an employee temporarily assigned to the position receives wages at a different level than an employee working in such a position on a permanent basis;

(h) the existence of an internal labour shortage in a particular job classification;

(i) a reclassification of a position to a lower level, where the incumbent continues to receive wages on the scale established for the former higher classification; and

(j) regional rates of wages, where the wage scale that applies to the employees provides for different rates of wages for the same job depending on the defined geographic area of the workplace.

17. For the purpose of justifying a difference in wages on the basis of a factor set out in section 16, an employer is required to establish that the factor is applied consistently and equitably in calculating and paying the wages of all male and female employees employed in an establishment who are performing work of equal value.

18. In addition to the requirement of section 17, for the purpose of justifying a difference in wages on the basis of paragraph 16(h), an employer is required to establish that similar differences exist between the group of employees in the job classification affected by the shortage and another group of employees predominantly of the same sex as the group affected by the shortage, who are performing work of equal value.

19. In addition to the requirement of section 17, for the purpose of justifying a difference in wages on the basis of paragraph 16(i), an employer is required to establish that (*a*)   since the reclassification, no new employee has received wages on the scale established for the former classification; and

(*b*)   there is a difference between the incumbents receiving wages on the scale established for the former classification and another group of employees, predominantly of the same sex as the first group, who are performing work of equal value.

Schedule (v)

HUMAN RIGHTS: EMPLOYMENT APPLICATION FORMS AND INTERVIEWS*

Employment Applications: Forms, Interviews

The *Human Rights Code, 1981*, promotes equal employment opportunity regardless of race, ancestry, place of origin, colour, ethnic origin, citizenship, creed, sex, sexual orientation, age, record of offences, marital status, family status or handicap.

The *Code* prohibits the use of an employment application form or a "written or oral inquiry . . . that directly or indirectly classifies or indicates qualifications by a prohibited ground of discrimination": section 22(2).

Human rights legislation is based upon the principle that employment decisions should be based on criteria relating to the applicant's ability to do the job in question rather than on factors that are unrelated to job performance. Also covered by the *Code* are recruitment and employment practices that are not openly or intentionally discriminatory, but are discriminatory in their effect.

The *Code* recognizes the legitimate right of employers to obtain the most qualified and suitable candidate for a particular job. Employers are advised to ask only those questions on application forms that relate to job requirements, and not questions that contravene the *Code* or may constitute evidence of unlawful discrimination in the event that a complaint is filed. For example, instead of asking for an applicant's age or date of birth, in contravention of the *Code*, it is permissible to ask whether the applicant is between 18 and 65 years of age. Instead of asking whether an applicant has, or plans to have, children, it is advisable to ask if the applicant is free to travel or relocate.

This booklet, and the sample application form included, are intended to illustrate the types of questions that are appropriate or inappropriate on employment application forms and at personal employment interviews in typical circumstances. It does not purport to be exhaustive; if you have further questions, you should contact your local Commission office, listed below. Reference may also be had to the *Human Rights Code*, particularly sections 4, 13, 16, 22, 23, 24 and 25.

---

* Toronto: Ontario Human Rights Commission, 1991.

Application Forms

It is not appropriate to include on application forms any questions that relate directly or indirectly to the following prohibited grounds of discrimination.

race, ancestry, place of origin, colour, ethnic origin, citizenship, creed, sex, sexual orientation, record of offences, marital status, family status or handicap.

(The terms "disability" and "person with a disability" are used throughout this document instead of "handicap" or "handicapped person". Although the term "handicap" is used in the *Code*, many people with disabilities prefer the term "disability".)

	Permissible Questions	**Prohibited Questions**
Race Colour	• None.	• Inquiries which elicit information about physical characteristics such as colour of eyes, hair, height, weight, or requests for photographs.
Creed	• None.	• Inquiries as to religious affiliation, churches attended, religious holidays, customs observed, willingness to work on a specific day which may conflict with requirements of a particular faith (eg., Saturday or Sunday). • Requests for character references that would indicate religious affiliation.

	Permissible Questions	**Prohibited Questions**
Citizenship Place of Origin Ethnic Origin	• Are you legally entitled to work in Canada?	• Inquiries about Canadian citizenship, landed immigrant status, permanent residency, naturalization, requests for Social Insurance Number. (A S.I.N. may contain information about an applicant's place of origin or citizenship status. A S.I.N. may be requested following a conditional offer of employment). • Inquiries as to memberships in organizations which are identified by a prohibited ground (eg., Anglo-Canadian Association). • Inquiries as to the name and location of schools attended.
Sex	• None.	• Categories on application forms or inquiries such as maiden or birth name; Mr., Mrs., Miss, Ms.; relationship with person to be notified in case of emergency or insurance beneficiary.

	Permissible Questions	**Prohibited Questions**
Sexual Orientation.	● None.	● Categories on application forms or inquiries such as married, divorced, common-law relationship, single, separated; information about spouse (eg., is spouse willing to transfer); relationship with person to be notified in case of emergency or insurance beneficiary.
Marital Status	● None.	● Categories on application forms such as married, divorced, common-law relationship, single, separated; maiden or birth name; Mr., Mrs., Miss, Ms.; information about spouse (eg., is spouse willing to transfer); second income, relationship with person to be notified in case of emergency or insurance beneficiary.
Family Status	● None.	● Categories on application forms such as married, divorced, common-law relationship, single,

Permissible Questions	**Prohibited Questions**
	separated; maiden or birth name; Mr., Mrs., Miss, Ms.; children or dependants; child care arrangements; information about spouse (eg., is spouse willing to transfer); second income; relationship with person to be notified in case of emergency or insurance beneficiary.
Record of Offences	• Have you ever been convicted of a criminal offence for which a pardon has not been granted?	• Inquiries as to whether an applicant has ever been convicted of any offence; has ever spent time in jail; has ever been convicted under a provincial statute (eg., *Highway Traffic Act*) or been convicted of an offence for which a pardon has been granted.
Age	• Are you 18 years of age or older and less than 65 years of age?	• Questions as to age, date of birth or requests for birth or baptismal records, or other documents such as driver's licence, or educational transcripts which indicate age.

	Permissible Questions	**Prohibited Questions**
Disability	• None.	• Inquiries about health, handicaps, illnesses, mental disorders, physical or intellectual limitations, developmental handicaps or intellectual impairment, medical history, learning disability, injuries or Workers' Compensation claims, medication, membership in medical or patient associations (eg., Alcoholics Anonymous).
		• Inquiries as to whether accommodation of disability-related needs is required, and as to the nature of such accommodation.
		• Requirements that applicants undergo pre-employment medical examinations.
		• Indication of eligibility for, or possession of, a valid driver's licence.

Driver's Licence

• Requests for a copy of a driver's licence on an application form are not appropriate for two reasons; it may screen out applicants with disabilities without consideration of whether the individual may be accommodated and it allows use of the licence to determine age.

- If operating a vehicle is an essential job duty, and if individual accommodation is not possible (eg., truck, bus or taxi driver or chauffeur) the requirement for a valid driver's licence may be referred to in an advertisement.

- If disability is an issue and accommodation may be possible (see Commission "Guidelines for Assessing Accommodation Requirements for Persons With Disabilities"), this should be discussed at the interview stage. A request for a driver's licence number or a copy of the licence can be made following a conditional offer of employment.

Employment Interviews

At the interview stage of the employment process, the employer may expand the scope of job-related questions if necessary to determine, for example, the applicant's qualifications or his/her ability to perform the essential duties. Inquiries in relation to the "Exceptions", outlined below, are also appropriate at the interview stage. Examples of permissible interview questions follow:

	Permissible Questions	Prohibited Questions
Race **Colour** **Ancestry** **Place of Origin** **Ethnic Origin**	• Inquiries by a service organization working with a particular community as to membership in the group served, if such membership can be justified as required to do the particular job.	• All inquiries which do not fall into the "Special Interest Organizations" on page 9.
Creed	• Inquiries by a denominational school as to religious membership, if the job involves communicating religious values to students.	• All inquiries which do not fall in to the "Special Interest Organizations" on page 9.

	Permissible Questions	**Prohibited Questions**
Citizenship	• Inquiries as to citizenship, if required by law for a particular job. • Inquiries as to citizenship or permanent resident status, where required to foster participation in cultural, educational, trade union or athletic activities by citizens or permanent residents. • Inquiries as to citizenship or domicile with intention to obtain citizenship, when the job is a senior executive position.	• All other inquiries concerning the applicant's citizenship.
Sex	• Inquiries as to gender, if it is a reasonable and genuine requirement for a particular job, such as where employment is in a shelter for battered women.	• All other inquiries concerning the applicant's sex.
Record of Offences	• Inquiries to determine if an applicant is bondable, if this is a reasonable and genuine qualification of the job.	• All other questions except those with respect to unpardoned Criminal Code convictions.

	Permissible Questions	**Prohibited Questions**
	• Inquiries to determine if an applicant has a record of convictions under the *Highway Traffic Act*, if driving is an essential job duty (eg., bus driver).	
Disability (Handicap)	• Inquiries directly related to the applicant's ability to perform the essential duties of the job and the nature of any accommodation which may be required.	• All other inquiries concerning the applicant's handicap or disability.
Age	• Inquiries as to age if the employer serves a particular age group and/or if age requirements are reasonable to qualify for employment.	• All other inquiries as to age.
Marital Status	• Inquiries as to marital status if the employer serves a particular group (identified by marital status) eg. single women) and/or if marital status is a reasonable requirement for employment.	• All other inquiries as to marital status.

Exceptions

The *Code* sets out a number of special exceptions to the rule prohibiting discrimination in employment. The exceptions are made primarily on the basis of equity considerations, such as the need to allow programs to serve the needs of particular communities, or on the basis of other special circumstances.

For assistance in determining whether an exception applies, contact the nearest office of the Human Rights Commission. You may also wish to obtain copies of two publications: "Exceptions to the Equality Rights Provisions of the *Ontario Human Rights Code* which Relate to the Workplace" and "Guidelines on Special Programs".

Included above under "Permissible Questions" are examples of inquiries based on the exceptions which may be made at the interview stage.

For greater clarity, the exceptions are outlined in detail below:

Special Programs (*Code*, Section 13)

Employers may implement special programs designed to relieve hardship or economic disadvantage or to assist disadvantaged groups to achieve equal opportunity: section 15. Inquiries as to membership in a group experiencing hardship or disadvantage would be permissible.

Special Interest Organizations (*Code*, Section 23)

A religious, philanthropic, education, fraternal or social institution or organization that is primarily engaged in serving the interests of persons identified by race, ancestry, place of origin, colour, ethnic origin, creed, sex, age, marital status or handicap, is allowed to give preference in employment to persons similarly identified, if the qualification is a reasonable and genuine one because of the nature of the employment: section 23(1)(a). Inquiries about such affiliation may be made at the employment interview stage.

Special Employment (*Code*, Section 23)

In some instances, because of the nature of the employment, age, sex, record of offences or marital status may be a reasonable and genuine qualification for the particular job: section 23(1)(b). In such instances, inquiries with regard to the particular qualification may be made at the employment interview stage.

Private Medical/Personal Attendants (*Code*, Section 23)

A person may refuse to employ a medical or personal attendant for him/herself or a family member on a prohibited ground of discrimination: section 23(1)(c). Inquiries as to a prohibited ground of discrimination would be permitted in this situation.

Nepotism or Anti-Nepotism Policies (*Code*, Section 23)

An employer may grant or withhold employment or advancement in employment to a person who is a spouse, child or parent of the employer or an employee: section 23(1)(d). Inquiries which would solicit information as to whether an applicant for employment is a spouse, child or parent of a current employee would be permissible.

Questions after a conditional offer of employment

In order to avoid a misapprehension of discrimination, it is appropriate in some circumstances to defer asking for particular information until after making an offer of employment conditional on a satisfactory response.

This is because the information or documentation may include particulars in relation to a prohibited ground of discrimination.

For example:

- a driver's licence will contain information on date of birth
- a work authorization issued by Immigration Canada will contain information regarding date of arrival in Canada
- a social insurance number card (S.I.N.) may contain information regarding date of arrival in Canada
- an education transcript often includes date of birth, or information regarding place of origin

Requests for medical examinations or health information necessary for pension, disability, superannuation, life insurance and benefit plans should also be made after acceptance of a conditional offer of employment.

APPLICATION FOR EMPLOYMENT

Position being applied for	Date available to begin work

PERSONAL DATA

Last name	Given name(s)

Address	Street	Apt. No.	Home Telephone Number
City	Province	Postal Code	Business Telephone Number

Are you legally eligible to work in Canada?	☐ Yes	☐ No

Are you 18 years and more and less than 65 years of age?	☐ Yes	☐ No

Are you willing to relocate in Ontario?	Preferred Location	
☐ Yes ☐ No		

To determine your qualification for employment, please provide below and on the reverse, information related to your academic and other achievements including volunteer work, as well as employment history. Additional information may be attached on a separate sheet.

EDUCATION

SECONDARY SCHOOL ■	BUSINESS, TRADE OR SECONDARY SCHOOL ■	
Highest grade or level completed	Name of course	Lenth of course
Type of certificate or diploma obtained	License, certificate or diploma awarded? ☐ Yes ☐ No	

COMMUNITY COLLEGE ■	UNIVERSITY ■		
Name of Program Length of Program	Length of course	Degree awarded ☐ Yes ☐ No	☐ Pass ☐ Honours
Diploma received ☐ Yes ☐ No	Major subject		
Other courses, workshops, seminars	Licenses, Certificates, Degrees		

Work related skills

Describe any of your work related skills, experience, or training that relate to the position being applied for.

EMPLOYMENT

Name and Address of present/last employer	Present/Last job title	
	Period of employment From To	Present/Last salary
	Name of Supervisor	Telephone
Type of Business	Reason for leaving	

Functions/Responsibilities

Name and Address of former employer	Present/Last job title	
	Period of employment From To	Present/Last salary
	Name of Supervisor	Telephone
Type of Business	Reason for leaving	

Functions/Responsibilities

Name and Address of former employer	Present/Last job title	
	Period of employment From To	Present/Last salary
	Name of Supervisor	Telephone
Type of Business	Reason for leaving	

Functions/Responsibilities

For employment references we may approach:

Your present/last employer?	☐ Yes	☐ No
Your former employer(s)?	☐ Yes	☐ No

List references if different than above on a separate sheet.

Personal interests and activities (civic, athletic etc.)

I hereby declare that the foregoing information is true and complete to my knowledge. I understand that a false statement may disqualify me from employment, or cause my dismissal.	Have you attached an additional sheet? ☐ Yes ☐ No _____ _____ Signature Date

Schedule (vi)

POLICY ON EMPLOYMENT-RELATED MEDICAL INFORMATION*

This policy is intended to help applicants, workers and employers to understand their rights and responsibilities regarding employment-related medical information.

In the past employers often screened out applicants with disabilities based on medical information requested on application forms or obtained through pre-employment medical examinations. The Commission believes that such questions, asked as part of the applicant screening process, violate subsection 22.-(2) of the *Code*, which states:

22.-(2) The right under section 4 to equal treatment with respect to employment is infringed where a form of application for employment is used or a written or oral inquiry is made of an applicant that directly or indirectly classifies or indicates qualifications by a prohibited ground of discrimination.

Pursuant to subsection 22.-(2), any assessment to verify or decide an individual's ability to do the job, including a medical examination, should only take place after a conditional offer of employment is made, preferably in writing. This allows the applicant with a disability the right to be considered exclusively on his or her merits during the selection process.

The prohibition contained in subsection 22.-(1) is qualified by subsection 22.-(3), which states:

22.-(3) Nothing in subsection (2) precludes the asking of questions at a personal employment interview concerning a prohibited ground of discrimination where discrimination on such grounds is permitted under this Act.

That section allows an employer to ask, at a personal interview, whether an applicant has any disability-related needs that would require accommodation to enable him or her to do the essential duties of the job. The duty to provide such accommodation is discussed in greater detail below.

It is not unusual for an employer to ask about, or for a worker to volunteer information about, his or her specific medical condition. While not expressly prohibited by the *Code*, an employer or supervisor may be placed in a vulnerable position if he or she

---

* Ontario Human Rights Commission (Toronto, 1991).

directly receives any information about the particular medical condition of an applicant or worker. Any subsequent employment-related decision may be perceived to be based on this information and a human rights complaint may result. It is the view of the Commission that to protect the employer as well as the applicant or worker, such information should remain exclusively with the examining physician and away from a worker's personnel file.

Duty to Accommodate

In some circumstances, the nature or degree of a person's disability may prevent that individual from performing the essential duties of a job. Subsection 16.-(1) provides that the right to equal treatment in respect of employment is not infringed where an individual is treated differently because he or she is incapable of performing or fulfilling the essential duties of the position because of handicap.

Subsection 16.-(1a) states, however, that an employee shall not be found incapable of performing the essential duties of a job unless it can be shown that it would cause undue hardship to fit his or her needs.

To avail themselves of the defence in section 16, employers must establish that they are unable to fit the needs of the individual without undue hardship, considering the cost of accommodation and any health and safety concerns.*

The duty to provide accommodation extends to all facets of the employment process: hiring, employment testing, on-the-job training, working conditions, transfer, promotions, etc.

To help in determining whether an individual can do the essential duties of a particular position, it is recommended that employers conduct a "Physical Demands Analysis. Such an analysis is used to define what is physically needed to perform the essential duties of each job in the workplace. Detailed job descriptions allow an employer to identify the skills and qualifications that are required for a job, and the physical requirements necessary to do the essential duties of that job. To help in this task, physical demands analysis checklists are available through the Centre for Disability and Work at the Ontario Ministry of Labour.

* Please refer to the Commission's *Guidelines for Assessing Accommodation Requirements for Persons With Disabilities* to receive a detailed explanation of these standards.

Schedule (vii)

POLICY STATEMENT ON HEIGHT AND WEIGHT REQUIREMENTS*

Height and weight requirements are sometimes used to screen or evaluate applicants in various employment settings. The policy of the Commission with regard to such practices is set out below, and applies to all height and weight requirements in the context of employment.

Section 10 of the *Ontario Human Rights Code*, prohibits employers from imposing a requirement or qualification on potential employees that results in the exclusion, restriction or preference of a group of persons who are identified by a prohibited ground of discrimination unless the requirement is reasonable and bona fide in the circumstances. In other words, employers cannot impose requirements which have the effect of excluding members of those groups covered by the *Code*, unless it can be shown that the requirements are reasonable and bona fide in the circumstances.

The Commission is of the opinion that height and weight requirements, which on their face appear to be neutral criteria, may contravene section 10 of the *Code*.

Such standards are, in most instances, based upon the average height and weight of white anglo-saxon males and tend to exclude women and members of other racial and ethnic groups who on the average are physically smaller than the average white anglo-saxon male. The establishment of two separate sets of requirements for men and women, while reducing the discriminatory impact on women, would still tend to exclude individuals from minority groups such as Asians who are on average smaller than non-Asians.

There also appears to be little evidence to demonstrate that height and weight requirements constitute bona fide occupational requirements. This view is supported by decisions of human rights tribunals in Ontario, other Canadian provinces, and the United States, as well as empirical research which indicates that physical stature alone is not determinative of an individual's ability to perform the essential duties of jobs which require significant physical exertion. Accordingly, such requirements would in all likelihood not be covered by the exception provided in section 10 for reasonable and bona fide requirements.

In any event, it should be noted that section 10 of the *Code* incorporates a duty to ''accommodate'' persons

---

* Ontario Human Rights Commission (Toronto, 1989).

adversely affected into the analysis of whether requirements are reasonable and bona fide. In the instance of height and weight standards, accommodation would be required for women and members of any ethnic or racial group who are adversely affected unless the particular employer were able to demonstrate that such accommodation would cause undue hardship. In assessing undue hardship, consideration will be given to the cost, any outside sources of funding and any health and safety requirement.

The Commission would urge all Ontario employers to abandon the use of uniform height and weight requirements in hiring employees unless they can demonstrate their lack of adverse effect on women or members of minority ethnic or racial groups.

In the event that such requirements are maintained on the basis of their demonstrated necessity, accommodation of women and members of minority groups will be required short of undue hardship.

Schedule (viii)

POLICY STATEMENT ON RACIAL SLURS AND HARASSMENT AND RACIAL JOKES*

INTRODUCTION

Racial slurs, jokes and harassment are a form of discrimination and tend to emphasize or define a relationship in which the parties are viewed as unequal simply on the basis of their race. They constitute an unacceptable form of behaviour which is contrary to Ontario's public policy — to recognize the dignity and worth of every person and to provide for equal rights and opportunities without discrimination.

This policy sets out the Commission's interpretation of the provisions of the Human Rights Code, 1981 relating to racial slurs, jokes and harassment. For the purpose of this document, and in the interest of brevity, the term "race" should be read to include all of the race-related grounds i.e. race, ancestry, place of origin, colour, ethnic origin, citizenship and creed.

The Human Rights Code, (*Code*) is more than a statement of principles and goals. It is the law of the province of Ontario. A violation of the *Code* is an infraction of the law.

HARASSMENT

The *Code* provides that all employees have a right to freedom from harassment in the workplace by the employer, employer's agent, or by another employee because of, among other grounds, race, ancestry, place of origin, colour, ethnic origin, citizenship and creed.

Similarly, every person who occupies accommodation has a right to freedom from harassment by the landlord or agent of the landlord or by an occupant of the same building (s. 2(2)).

It is also the view of the Commission that, while there are no express provisions dealing with harassment in the area of services, goods and facilities, harassment in such situations would constitute a violation of section 1 of the *Code*. Section 1 provides for a right to equal treatment with respect to services, goods and facilities.

The comments below apply to harassment which occurs in all three of these areas i.e. employment, accommodation, as well as services, goods and facilities.

---

* Ontario Human Rights Commission (Toronto, 1991). Prepared with the assistance of the Race Relations Directorate.

(i) Harassment — General Principles

Harassment is defined in s. 9(1)(f) of the *Code* to mean "engaging in a course of vexatious comment or conduct that is known or ought reasonably to be known to be unwelcome."

The reference to comment or conduct "that is known or ought reasonably to be known to be unwelcome" imports an objective element into the definition of harassment. This factor acknowledges that in some situations it should be anticipated that the racially motivated conduct or comments would be offensive or unwelcome and there is no requirement that the behaviour be objected to before a violation of the *Code* is found. This element of the definition also recognizes that in many instances, it would be unreasonable to require an individual, who may be in a vulnerable position, to object to the offensive treatment before being able to claim a right to be free from such treatment. Therefore, if a person engages in a course of activity or comment which refers to or emphasizes the race or other race-related characteristics of an individual, and it could reasonably be anticipated that such comment or conduct would be unwelcome, then that person may be considered to have engaged in harassment, contrary to the provisions of the *Code*.

It should be noted that in order for the harassment provisions of the *Code* to apply, the activity at issue need not expressly refer to a person's race, place or origin, creed, etc. but need only be motivated by those considerations. For example, in circumstances where an individual is consistently treated in a less favourable manner, e.g. is repeatedly made the brunt of practical jokes or ridicule, an inference may be drawn from the particular circumstances that the treatment was racially motivated although the practical jokes or ridicule may not have contained any reference to race.

Each situation will be assessed on its own merits. However, racial epithets, comments ridiculing individuals because of race-related physical characteristics, religious dress, etc. or singling an individual out for humiliating or demeaning "teasing" or jokes related to race or to any of the race-related grounds, would in most instances be viewed as conduct or comments which "ought reasonably to be known to be unwelcome."

Conduct or comments which are motivated by consideration of a person's membership in one of the race-related groups and which may not, on their face, be considered offensive on an objective basis, may still be "unwelcome" from the perspective of a particular individual. If the individual clearly indicates that this is the case, then a repetition of a similar type of activity will, in most instances, constitute a violation of the *Code*.

It should be noted that the jurisprudence in the area of "harassment" is in its early stages of development. It is the view of the Commission that some circumstances which may not clearly come within the harassment provisions may nevertheless be covered under the *Code* under the general equality rights provisions. These circumstances and accompanying issues are discussed more fully in the next section.

EQUALITY RIGHTS — POISONED ENVIRONMENT

The *Code* provides a right to equal treatment in the areas of services, goods, facilities, accommodation, contracts, employment and membership in a vocational association (Sections 1-5). It is the position of the Commission that offensive or threatening comments or conduct may, in some instances, have the effect of "poisoning" the environment for persons affected. As a result, those individuals are subjected to terms and conditions of employment, tenancy, services etc. that are quite different from those experienced by individuals who are not subjected to the same type of comments or treatment. In such instances, the right to equal treatment may have been violated.

Again, every situation will be judged on its merits. However, an example of a situation which could be viewed as a violation of the *Code* by creating a "poisoned environment" would be one in which a supervisor or a landlord says to a person who is a member of a racial minority, "I don't know why you people don't go back to where you came from, because you sure don't belong here." Even though the statement may be made only once, the person at which it is directed, or those persons that are included in the group identified, will quite validly have concerns regarding their long term prospects in that workplace or rental unit. Other employees or tenants who are not members of that racial group will not experience the same concern and anxiety.

Similarly, persons who encounter comments, signs, caricatures, or cartoons displayed in a service environment such as a store, restaurant etc. or a work or tenancy situation which depict members of their race, religious group etc., in a demeaning manner may be subjected to a "poisoned environment" in violation of the *Code*. This is also the case with graffiti of a similar nature when the service provider, employer, or landlord is aware of it, but does nothing to have it removed. Depending on the particular circumstances it may be the case that those persons are humiliated or experience feelings of anger and resentment that others in that setting do not have imposed upon them because of their race.

It should also be noted that individuals who are not the specific targets of a discriminatory comment or action or who are not members of the targeted group may also have a right to bring a complaint in circumstances such as those described above.

Such a right has been upheld in other jurisdictions and is based on the following principle: regardless of whether an individual has been targeted as the object of discriminatory treatment, if exposure to such treatment has a negative impact upon the "sensibilities" of an individual, that individual's rights have been violated. Similarly, in a situation dealing with discriminatory rental practices aimed at members of visible minorities, it has been held that a caucasian tenant had the right to bring a complaint on the basis that that tenant had been injured by the loss of important benefits from inter-racial associations.

The application of these principles is discussed in more detail below.

COMMENTS OR ACTIONS NOT DIRECTED TOWARD A PARTICULAR INDIVIDUAL

As indicated above, in the Commission's view, the equality provisions of the *Code* may be breached by racial slurs or actions which are not directed toward a particular individual but nonetheless adversely affect the environment for that individual. Examples include the following:

- demeaning racial remarks, jokes or innuendos about an employee, client or customer, or tenant told to other employees, tenants, clients or customers
  - may impair the right of those persons who are the subject of the comments to be viewed as equals and create a "them/us" barrier.
- racial remarks, jokes or innuendos made about other racial groups in the presence of an employee, tenant or client

- may create an apprehension on the part of members of other racial minorities that they are also targeted when they are not present.
- the displaying of racist, derogatory or offensive pictures, graffiti or materials
  - is humiliating and also impairs the right of those persons who are members of the targeted racial group to be viewed as equals.
- racial remarks, jokes or innuendos about an employee, client, or tenant or about the racial group of which they are a member, which are stated to or in the presence of a non-racial minority person
  - may cause discomfort on the part of the non-racial minority person and may have the effect of creating an environment where the opportunity for beneficial inter-racial interaction is lost or impaired.

In the above or similar situations, the conduct at issue must be objectively evaluated. It must be of such a nature and degree so as to amount to a denial of equality through the creation of a poisoned environment.

THE LIABILITY OF PRINCIPALS FOR THE ACTIONS OF THEIR AGENTS

An employer may be liable for acts of harassment carried out by its employees through the "organic theory of corporate responsibility". This theory provides that where an employee is in a position of authority (i.e. part of the "directing mind") in the organization, the employer will be held responsible for the actions of that employee. To put it in more direct terms, the acts of supervisors, managers, etc. are considered to be the acts of the employer.

The employer's liability as described in the preceding paragraph is to be distinguished from vicarious liability. The *Code* (s. 44(1)) provides that anything done or omitted to be done by an officer, official, employee or agent of a corporation, trade union, trade or occupational association, unincorporated association or employers' organization in the course of his or her employment shall be deemed to be an act or thing done or omitted to be done by the corporation, trade union, trade or occupational association, unincorporated association or employers' organization. This means that those bodies will be held responsible for breaches of the *Code* committed by their employees or agents, as though they had committed the breaches themselves. This principle applies not only to employers, but also to providers of accommodation and providers of service.

Although the doctrine of vicarious liability does not apply to harassment as defined in s. 9(1)(f) of the *Code*, it does apply to breaches of the equality rights provisions. In this regard, please refer to the "Equality Rights — Poisoned Environment" section of this paper.

It should also be noted that pursuant to s. 38(2) of the *Code*, a board of inquiry that is hearing a complaint of harassment can add as a party to the hearing, any person who knew or should have known of the harassment from the information or facts in his or her possession and who failed to prevent the harassment or penalize the harasser although it was within his or her authority to do so. Subsection 40(4) then enables the board of inquiry to remain seized of the matter. This means that in the event the harassment continues, the board can reconvene. Persons who believe that such circumstances exist should bring them to the attention of the Commission. If, following an investigation, the Commission finds that in its view, the evidence supports the allegation that the harassment has continued, the Commission will request that the Minister reconvene the board of inquiry to hear the matter. If the board then finds that a party who knew, or should have known about the harassment failed to exercise his or her authority to prevent or penalize the repetition of the harassment, the board can order that person to take whatever steps are reasonable to prevent any further continuation of the harassment.

It is very important, therefore, that employers, including those whose business it is to provide accommodation or services, have policies in place making it clear that activity which results in a poisoned environment is prohibited in the context of the workplace, whether directed at employees, clients, customers, or tenants and will be met with strict discipline if it occurs. Similarly, it is important that managers and supervisors be instructed to ensure that all staff are aware of the policy and to deal with any such incidents which come to their attention quickly and effectively.

RIGHT TO FILE A COMPLAINT

When a person believes that he or she has been discriminated against or harassed in any of the areas and on any of the grounds covered by the *Code*, he or she may bring a complaint to the Ontario Human Rights Commission. A complaint may be filed by contacting the nearest office of the Commission.

The Commission also has the authority to initiate a complaint. It has been the practice of the Commission to do this only when no individual complaint is available.

As stated throughout this document, each situation will be assessed on its merits by the Commission following an investigation and after receiving submissions from all the parties. In deciding what action to take, the Commission will take into consideration the context within which the comment or action took place, the history and relationship of the parties as well as the actions, if any, taken to remedy the incident.

COLLECTIVE AGREEMENTS AND COMPANY POLICIES

An increasing number of collective agreements include clauses relating to discrimination and harassment. In addition to the rights available under the *Code*, a person may have rights which he or she may pursue under a collective agreement. Similarly, a number of companies have implemented policies in this regard which may afford a remedy to a person who has been harassed or otherwise discriminated against. However, parties cannot contract out of the *Code* and neither a collective agreement nor a company policy can preclude a person from pursuing his or her rights under the *Code*.

CONCLUSION

People have the right to live and work in an environment free of demeaning comments and actions based on race, ancestry, place of origin, colour, ethnic origin, citizenship and creed. This type of activity is a destructive practice which affects everyone. Even when meant as a joke, it is derogatory and humiliating in its effect.

Schedule (ix)

GUIDELINES FOR ASSESSING ACCOMMODATION REQUIREMENTS FOR PERSONS WITH DISABILITIES* UNDER THE ONTARIO *HUMAN RIGHTS CODE*, 1981, AS AMENDED**

INTRODUCTION

A. The Ontario *Human Rights Code*, 1981, (referred to as "the *Code*") states that it is public policy in Ontario to recognize the inherent dignity and worth of every person and to provide for equal rights and opportunities without discrimination. The provisions of the *Code* are aimed at creating a climate of understanding and mutual respect for the dignity and worth of each person so that each person feels a part of the community and feels able to contribute to the community.

B. It is the intention of the *Code* to guarantee to members of groups protected under the *Code* equal treatments in the provision of goods, services and facilities, occupancy of accommodation, contracts, employment, and membership in associations. They are also protected from discrimination which results from requirements, qualifications, or factors which may appear neutral but which have the effect of placing at a disadvantage members of those groups covered by the *Code*. i.e. those identified by their race, colour, creed, sex, age, handicap, etc. For example, a requirement that a person must work on Saturdays can result in discrimination if he or she practices a religion which observes the Sabbath on Saturdays.

C. However, a reasonable requirement, qualification or factor may be used even if it is discriminatory as long as it can be shown that the needs of the group or individual affected by the requirement cannot be accommodated without undue hardship. The special needs of every group protected by the *Code* must be accommodated unless such accommodation would create undue hardship.

D. This is the first phase of guidelines on accommodation to be issued by the Commission, and these guidelines

---

* The terms "diability" and "person with a disability" are used throughout this document instead of "handicap" or "handicapped person." Although the term "handicap" is used in the *Code*, many people with disabilities prefer the term "disability".

* * Ontario Human Rights Commission (Toronto).

will deal only with the protected ground of "handicap". Subsequent guidelines will cover accommodation of the other groups protected under the *Code*.

E. The provisions of the *Human Rights Code* which deal with reasonable requirements, accommodation and undue hardship can be found in Appendix "A".

F. The *Code* requires accommodation from providers of services, goods, facilities and housing, employers, trade unions, trade or occupational associations, and self-governing professions. In these guidelines, the term "person [or enterprises] responsible for accommodation" will be used to refer to all of these entities, and it includes individuals, partnerships, corporations, companies, joint ventures, and organizations. The term "person [or individual] with a disability" is used to refer to the individual for whom accommodation is to be made.

Purpose of the Guidelines

G. The purpose of these guidelines is to state the Commission's interpretation of what is meant by accommodation of the needs of persons with disabilities and what will constitute undue hardship in the context of disability complaints. It is hoped that the guidelines will help persons with disabilities, persons responsible for accommodation, and the general public to understand and apply the concepts of accommodation and undue hardship.

H. The Commission's goal is to promote a discrimination-free environment through the encouragement of voluntary compliance with the *Code* and these guidelines. Where complaints are filed, Commission staff will apply the guidelines in their investigations. In this context and for purposes of board of inquiry and court proceedings, the terms "person with a disability" and "person responsible for accommodation" (and their equivalents described in paragraph F, on page 1) are intended to signify "complainant" and "respondent", respectively.

Process of Developing the Guidelines

I. These guidelines were developed through a process of extensive consultation and revision. More than 30 briefs were received from interested groups and individuals in response to advertisements which were placed in newspapers throughout Ontario and in response to letters which were sent to particular organizations. A committee of ten members, including a Commissioner, Commission staff, and an outside consultant, reviewed the submissions and several drafts of proposed guidelines, and then invited all groups which had submitted briefs to attend consultation meetings. Groups that were interested in attending received a copy of the draft guidelines, and meetings were held with those groups before the final version was adopted.

Background

J. It is recognized that many of the barriers to the equal participation of persons with disabilities in our society exist because of inadvertence or lack of awareness of special needs, and not because people have deliberately sought to discriminate against persons with a disability. The removal of these barriers has now become a responsibility to be shared by everyone. The *Code* requires these changes in order to give meaning to the rights to equality and freedom from discrimination guaranteed to disabled persons in Part I of the *Code*. Historically, persons with disabilities have borne virtually all of the costs, both financial and personal, of their special needs. Accommodation can be understood as a means of removing the barriers which prevent persons with disabilities from enjoying equality of opportunity in a way which is sensitive to their individual circumstances so that we all may benefit from their active participation in the community.

K. For persons with disabilities, the *Code* guarantees equal treatment if the person is capable of performing or fulfilling the essential duties that accompany the exercise of his or her rights. This requirement recognizes that, in some circumstances, the nature or degree of a person's disability may preclude him or her from being able to perform the essential duties. However, a person cannot be found incapable of performing those essential duties unless an effort has been made to accommodate his or her needs. Accommodation of a person's individual needs is required by the *Code* unless such accommodation would cause undue hardship for the person (or organization or company) responsible for making it.

L. The first step in the accommodation is to determine what is "essential" and what is not. The person must be accommodated with respect to non-essential duties if necessary by having those duties re-assigned or by the person responsible for accommodation using an alternate method for having those duties fulfilled. Then, if the person cannot perform the essential duties, accommodation is to be explored that will enable the person to perform those essential duties.

M. Accommodation of needs includes, for example, making buildings and transportation accessible, making print information available in alternative formats such as tape, or braille, translating auditory information into visual or tactile modes for persons with a hearing impairment, adapting equipment or providing special devices or supports so that the person with a disability will be able to function independently, and altering the ways in which tasks are accomplished in order to allow for a person's disability. Generally, accommodation means people with disabilities will have choices about pursuing their individual goals and purposes in life, including the situations in which they work, live, travel, eat, shop, play, and are entertained.

N. The essence of accommodating people who have disabilities is individualization. That is, each person with a disability must be considered individually in order to determine what changes can be made to a situation, including the physical environment, to accommodate his or her needs. There is no formula for accommodation to alleviate the barriers which confront people with disabilities. Each person's needs are unique and must be considered afresh when a barrier is encountered. A technical solution may meet one person's requirements but not another's. It is also the case that many accommodations will benefit large numbers of persons with disabilities.

O. Those responsible for accommodation ought to consult with persons with disabilities to determine what they need and how it can best be provided. The voluntary assumption of responsibility for making accommodations and a willingness to explore creative solutions will go a long way towards accomplishing equality. Voluntary compliance also may avoid future complaints under the *Code*, including the time and expense involved in defending those complaints.

P. Where a person responsible for accommodation has adopted a plan for accommodation in good faith, and it is being phased in with an established and acceptable time frame, such a plan will be taken into account in the consideration of any complaints against that person. However, complaints will still be considered on an individual basis and there may be requirements of interim accommodation where it would not cause undue hardship (see page 16, paragraph C).

Structure of the Guidelines

Q. There are four parts to these guidelines. The first part sets out the scope of the requirement of accommodation. The second part describes the standards for undue hardship, which involve cost and health and safety requirements. This part includes a list of factors to be considered in interpreting the terms used in the cost standard, and the matters which are to be taken into account in assessing health and safety risk. The third part sets out requirements for further action where application of the standards in part two has resulted in a potential finding of undue hardship. The final part deals with requirements relating to evidence and proof of undue hardship. The commentary which accompanies each part is lettered in a manner which corresponds to the sections.

STANDARDS FOR ACCOMMODATION

1. Requirement of Accommodation

THE NEEDS OF PERSONS WITH DISABILITIES MUST BE ACCOMMODATED IN A MANNER WHICH MOST RESPECTS THEIR DIGNITY, IF TO DO SO DOES NOT CREATE UNDUE HARDSHIP.

2. Respecting the Dignity of Persons with Disabilities

THE PHRASE "RESPECTS THEIR DIGNITY" MEANS TO ACT IN A MANNER WHICH RECOGNIZES THE PRIVACY, CONFIDENTIALITY, COMFORT, AUTONOMY, AND SELF-ESTEEM OF PERSONS

WITH DISABILITIES, WHICH MAXI-
MIZES THEIR INTEGRATION AND
WHICH PROMOTES THEIR FULL PAR-
TICIPATION IN SOCIETY.

Commentary

A. The purpose of this part is to clarify that the scope of the obligation to
accommodate encompasses the concept of dignity. Dignity includes consideration of the means as well as the
goals of accommodation and participation. Accommodation is a matter of
degree, rather than an all-or-nothing
proposition. Different ways of accommodating the needs of persons with a
disability can be drawn along a continuum from those means which are
most respectful of privacy, autonomy,
integration and other human values,
to those which are least respectful of
those values. Perhaps the most common example of an accommodation
which demonstrates little respect for
the dignity of a person with a disability is a wheelchair entrance over the
loading dock or through the garbage
room.

B. There is also a continuum with
respect to how the accommodation
may be accomplished. At one end of
this continuum would be full accommodation (i.e., that which would most
respect the person's dignity) that
could be done immediately. Next
would be phased-in full accommodation, followed by full accommodation
accomplished through a reserve fund.
Alternative accommodation (i.e., that
which would be less respectful of the
person's dignity) that could be
accomplished immediately would be

next on the continuum, followed by
phased-in and reserve fund alternative
accommodations, respectively.
Interim accommodation which is
most respectful of dignity could be
placed anywhere on the continuum in
addition to alternatives to immediate,
full accommodation. The concepts of
phasing-in, reserve fund, and alternatives are described more fully in
Sections 5 and 6.

C. It is well established in human
rights law that equality may sometimes require unequal or different
treatment. In some circumstances, the
best way to ensure the dignity of persons with disabilities may be to provide separate or specialized services.
However, the guidelines require generally that employment, housing, services and facilities be built or adapted
to accommodate individuals with disabilities in the conventional system.
Segregated treatment in the provision
of services, employment, or housing
is an example of an attempt to accommodate individual needs which may
not be acceptable unless integrated
treatment would pose undue hardship
as described in the following pages.

STANDARDS FOR ASSESS-
ING UNDUE HARDSHIP

A. The *Code* prescribes three factors
which are to be considered in assessing whether a requested accommodation would cause undue hardship.
These are cost, outside sources of
funding, if any, and health and safety
requirements, if any. In the following
discussion, outside sources of funding

are incorporated as part of the cost standard.

B. The person responsible for accommodation will want to know whose needs must be accommodated in order to determine the extent of its obligation. The cost standard states that it is the needs of the individual person with a disability and/or the group of which that person is a member. This recognizes that there are two types of situations in which the requirement to accommodate may arise. One situation is where a person with a disability is a member of a group against which discrimination is alleged and that person requests an accommodation which would also accommodate the needs of the whole group (section 10(2) of the *Code*). The other situation is where an individual requires accommodation for his or her own needs (section 16(1a) of the *Code*). In instances where accommodation of the needs of the group would cause undue hardship, but the needs of an individual with a disability could still be accommodated without undue hardship, the individual accommodation must be made.

C. The standard requires that the current abilities of a person with a disability and the situation's current risks are to be taken into account, rather than abilities or risks which may arise in the future. Where the person has a condition which may cause deterioration of ability over time, the unpredictable nature and extent of future disability cannot be used as a basis for assessing needs in the present. For example, a person who has multiple sclerosis may experience increased

fatigue as a symptom of his or her condition, but it will not be possible to predict with accuracy when, for how long, or in what ways the fatigue will affect a person. Or a person may not have that symptom at all, but may show other effects of the illness. These unpredictable future possibilities cannot be used to assess needs for accommodation in the present.

D. The *Code* and the guidelines notably exclude other factors from consideration by specifically designating cost and health or safety factors as determinants of undue hardship. For example, there is no provision for "business inconvenience" or "undue interference" with the enterprise responsible for accommodation in determining undue hardship. The term "business inconvenience" was removed from the *Code* during the legislative debates on amendments to the *Code*. If there are demonstrable costs attributable to decreased productivity, efficiency or effectiveness, they can be taken into account in assessing undue hardship under the cost standard, providing that they are quantifiable and demonstrably related to the proposed accommodation.

E. Another element which cannot be considered in assessing undue hardship is customer preference, or other third party preferences. It is well established in human rights case law that third party preferences do not constitute a justification for discriminatory acts, and the same rule applies here.

F. A term of a collective agreement or other contractual arrangement cannot act as a bar to providing the kinds of accommodation an employee with a disability might require. It has been held in previous legal cases that the terms of a collective agreement cannot be used to justify discrimination which is prohibited by the *Human Rights Code*. It is a joint responsibility of the employer and the union to work out a solution with respect to any accommodation involving a conflict with the collective agreement, but if a solution cannot be reached, the employer must make the accommodation in spite of the agreement. If the union takes the position that the collective agreement prevails, and attempts to thwart efforts to accommodate the employee, then the union may be added as a respondent to a complaint filed with the Commission.

G. These standards reflect the expectation that significant changes will be required in employment situations (including collective agreements), transportation systems, buildings (except private residences), rental accommodation, services, restaurants, shopping centres, stores, and other places and activities from which persons with a disability are currently excluded by barriers to equal participation. The *Code* requires these changes in order to give meaning to the rights to equality and freedom from discrimination guaranteed to persons with disabilities in Part 1 of the *Code*.

3. Cost
(1) Standard
UNDUE HARDSHIP WILL BE SHOWN TO EXIST IF THE FINANCIAL COSTS THAT ARE DEMONSTRABLY ATTRIBUTABLE TO THE ACCOMMODATION OF THE NEEDS OF THE INDIVIDUAL WITH A DISABILITY, AND/OR THE GROUP OF WHICH THE PERSON WITH A DISABILITY IS A MEMBER, WOULD ALTER THE ESSENTIAL NATURE OR WOULD SUBSTANTIALLY AFFECT THE VIABILITY OF THE ENTERPRISE RESPONSIBLE FOR ACCOMMODATION.

Commentary
A. Costs will amount to undue hardship if they are:
1. quantifiable;
2. shown to be related to the accommodation; and
3. (a) so substantial that they would alter the essential nature of the enterprise, or
(b) so significant that they would substantially affect the viability of the enterprise.

B. There are circumstances under which the undue hardship provisions of the *Code* (sections 10, 16 and 23) could require a person responsible for accommodation to undertake significant expenditures to accommodate persons with disabilities. This applies whether one person would benefit from the accommodation, or large numbers of people would benefit. The test of altering the essential nature of the enterprise or substantially affecting its viability will apply whether the benefit is to an individual or to a group. Paragraph B on page 7 offers a further explanation of the situations in which individual and group needs are to be accommodated.

C. The types of costs which will be taken into account in determining the effect on the person responsible for accommodation are listed below, in subsection (2), and will be discussed further there. The elements to be considered in applying the second part of the requirement, i.e., whether the costs would alter the essential nature or substantially affect the viability of the enterprise, are listed below in subsection (3), and will be discussed further there.

(2) Types of Financial Costs

FINANCIAL COSTS OF THE ACCOMMODATION INCLUDE:

(A) CAPITAL AND OPERATING COSTS;

(B) THE COST OF ADDITIONAL STAFF TIME, BEYOND WHAT CAN BE ACCOMPLISHED THROUGH RESTRUCTURING EXISTING RESOURCES AND JOB DESCRIPTIONS, IN ORDER TO PROVIDE APPROPRIATE ASSISTANCE TO THE PERSON WITH A DISABILITY; AND

(C) ANY OTHER QUANTIFIABLE AND DEMONSTRABLY RELATED COSTS.

Commentary

D. All projected costs which can be quantified and shown to be related to the proposed accommodation will be taken into account. However, mere speculation, for example, about monetary losses which may follow the accommodation of the person with a disability will not generally be persuasive.

E. Where substantial capital expenditures are anticipated, for example, in making physical alterations to a building, work site, vehicle or equipment, it is advisable for the person responsible for accommodation to obtain a proposal and estimate from experts in barrier-free design and construction. This is one step that might be followed by the Commission when investigating a complaint.

F. Creative design solutions can often avoid expensive capital outlays. This may involve very specifically tailoring the design to the individual's functional capabilities rather than installing a device or feature which may not even be appropriate. Where undue hardship is claimed, cost estimates will be carefully examined to ensure that they are not excessive in relation to the stated objective, and to determine whether a less expensive alternative exists which could accomplish the accommodation while still fully respecting the dignity of the person with a disability.

G. Increased insurance costs or sickness benefits would be included as operating costs where they were quantified (i.e., actual higher rates, not hypothetical) and shown not to be contrary to the principles enunciated in the *Code* with respect to insurance coverage. Increased liability insurance costs are unlikely to arise, but where the increased liability is quantifiable and provable, and where efforts to obtain other forms of coverage have been unsuccessful, it can be included.

H. Examples of costs of additional staff time (paragraph (2)(b) above) might be the cost of an assistant or a personal attendant to assist the person with a disability to do his or her job or to use the service or facility being provided.

(3) Altering the Nature or Affecting the Viability of the Enterprise

FOR THE PURPOSES OF DETERMINING WHETHER A FINANCIAL COST WOULD ALTER THE ESSENTIAL NATURE OR SUBSTANTIALLY AFFECT THE VIABILITY OF THE ENTERPRISE, CONSIDERATION WILL BE GIVEN TO:

(A) THE ABILITY OF THE PERSON RESPONSIBLE FOR ACCOMMODATION TO RECOVER THE COSTS OF ACCOMMODATION IN THE NORMAL COURSE OF BUSINESS;

(B) THE AVAILABILITY OF ANY GRANTS, SUBSIDIES OR LOANS FROM THE FEDERAL, PROVINCIAL OR MUNICIPAL GOVERNMENT OR FROM NON-GOVERNMENT SOURCES WHICH COULD OFFSET THE COSTS OF ACCOMMODATION;

(C) THE ABILITY OF THE PERSON RESPONSIBLE FOR ACCOMMODATION TO DISTRIBUTE THE COSTS OF ACCOMMODATION THROUGHOUT THE WHOLE OPERATION;

(D) THE ABILITY OF THE PERSON RESPONSIBLE FOR ACCOMMODATION TO AMORTIZE OR DEPRECIATE CAPITAL COSTS ASSOCIATED WITH THE ACCOMMODATION ACCORDING TO GENERALLY ACCEPTED ACCOUNTING PRINICIPLES;

(E) THE ABILITY OF THE PERSON RESPONSIBLE FOR ACCOMMODATION TO DEDUCT FROM THE COSTS OF ACCOMMODATION ANY SAVINGS THAT MAY BE AVAILABLE AS A RESULT OF THE ACCOMMODATION, INCLUDING:

(I) TAX DEDUCTIONS AND OTHER GOVERNMENT BENEFITS;

(II) AN IMPROVEMENT IN PRODUCTIVITY, EFFICIENCY OR EFFECTIVENESS;

(III) ANY INCREASE IN THE RESALE VALUE OF PROPERTY, WHERE IT IS REASONABLY FORESEEABLE THAT THE PROPERTY MIGHT BE SOLD;

(IV) ANY INCREASE IN CLIENTELE, POTENTIAL LABOUR POOL, OR TENANTS; AND

(F) THE AVAILABILITY OF THE WORKERS' COMPENSATION BOARD'S "SECOND INJURY AND ENHANCEMENT FUND".

Commentary

I. It is expected that the person responsible for accommodation would take steps to recover the costs of accommodation through reasonable changes to its business practices or by availing itself of grants or subsidies which would offset the expense of making an accommodation. If the person responsible for accommodation believes that such measures will not be effective in avoiding undue hardship, it will have to demonstrate that such steps to recover costs are inadequate in the circumstances, or impossible, or will not yield the needed resources. In other words, the person responsible for accommodation would be required to establish that the costs which remain after steps are taken to recover costs will alter the essential nature or substantially affect the viability of the enterprise.

J. The Office for Disabled Persons will be able to provide information about available grants and subsidies and how to make application for such assistance with accommodation.

K. It is also required that costs of accommodation be distributed as widely as possible within the enterprise responsible for accommodation so that no single department, employee, or subsidiary of a large enterprise is burdened with the cost of an accommodation. Subparagraph 3(c), above, establishes that the appropriate basis for evaluating the effect of the cost is the company as a whole, not the branch or unit in which the person with a disability works or to which the person has made application.

L. In the case of government, the term ''whole operation'' in clause 3(3)(c) refers to the programs and services offered or funded by the government. For example, there may be accommodations which require substantial expenditure and if implemented immediately would alter the essential nature or substantially affect the viability of government programs in total or in part. In such instances, it may be necessary to implement the required accommodation incrementally (see page 16, Section 5).

M. In most cases it is unlikely that the test for undue hardship will be met solely by demonstrating that the program, ministry or agency responsible for providing the accommodation does not have adequate funds to provide it.

N. Spreading the financing of accommodation over time could be accomplished through taking out loans, issuing shares or bonds, or other methods. Amortization or depreciation is another means of spreading cost that a person responsible for accommodation will be expected to use to reduce the financial burden, where possible.

O. Tax deductions or other government benefits flowing from the accommodation will also be taken into account as offsetting the cost of accommodation. The person responsible for accommodation is expected to consider whether accommodation of the needs of a person with a disability may improve productivity, efficiency or effectiveness, expand the business, or improve the value of the business or property. For example, an accommodation which affects a significant number of people with disabilities, such as wheelchair access, could open up a new market for a storekeeper or provider of a service.

P. Finally, the effects of the second injury and enhancement fund of the Workers' Compensation Board must be considered. In the event of an injury to a worker, where that injury is caused by the workers' disability, a claim may be made against this fund even if the employer did not have knowledge of the employee's pre-existing condition. The workers' compensation rates for the employee will not be increased as a result of making claims on the fund. Since 90% of employees in the province of Ontario are under the protection of the Board, and the fund is available to most employees covered, there will be few instances where increased liability insurance premiums for risk of injury to a person due to a pre-existing condition or disability will be a factor in creating undue hardship.

Q. After all of these costs, benefits, deductions, and other factors have been considered, the next step is to determine whether the remaining cost will alter the essential nature of the enterprise responsible for making the accommodation or substantially affect its viability. The person responsible for accommodation would need to show how it would be altered or its viability affected. It will not be acceptable for the person responsible for accommodation to merely state, without evidence to support the statement, that the company operates on low margins and would go out of business if required to undertake the required accommodation.

R. Larger enterprises and government may be in a better position to set an example or provide leadership in accommodating persons with disabilities. Accommodations will likely be more easily absorbed by larger enterprises. According to 1988 statistics, fewer than 5% of businesses in Ontario employ more than 100 people, but they account for 65% of all paid employment in the province. Thus, a few large employers have the opportunities and the means to provide employment for greater numbers of persons with disabilities by accommodating their needs.

S. A topic which has generated considerable controversy is the accessibility of heritage buildings. A general exemption from accessibility requirements for heritage properties is not included in the guidelines because it would result in very broad exclusions as more and more buildings gain protection because of their heritage status. In a situation involving a heritage property, it is recognized that the cost of making the proposed accommodation may be increased by the necessity to preserve the defining historic design features. However, aesthetic features in and of themselves are not to be included in the assessment.

T. The test of altering the essential nature or substantially affecting the viability of the enterprise allows the preservation of the defining features of a heritage property to be taken into account as a justifiable factor in assessing undue hardship.

4. Health or Safety Risk
(1) Standard
UNDUE HARDSHIP WILL BE SHOWN TO EXIST WHERE A PERSON RESPONSIBLE FOR ACCOMMODATION IS SUBJECT TO OR HAS ESTABLISHED A BONA FIDE HEALTH OR SAFETY REQUIREMENT AND THE PERSON HAS ATTEMPTED TO MAXIMIZE THE HEALTH AND SAFETY PROTECTION THROUGH ALTERNATE MEANS WHICH ARE CONSISTENT WITH THE ACCOMMODATION REQUIRED, BUT THE DEGREE OF RISK WHICH REMAINS AFTER THE ACCOMMODATION HAS BEEN MADE OUTWEIGHS THE BENEFITS OF ENHANCING EQUALITY FOR DISABLED PERSONS.

THE HEALTH OR SAFETY REQUIREMENT MAY BE INFORMAL OR IT MAY BE A REQUIREMENT ESTABLISHED BY LAW.

Commentary
A. The guidelines cover the situation where the proposed accommodation creates a potential conflict with a health or safety requirement. This requirement may be one which is contained in a law or regulation, or it may

be a rule, practice or procedure which the person responsible for accommodation has established on its own or in conjunction with other businesses or services engaged in similar kinds of activity. Where the effect of such a requirement is to exclude a person with a disability from the workplace or service, it may be necessary to modify or waive the health or safety requirement. Whether this will create undue hardship or not depends upon whether the remaining degree of risk outweighs the benefit of enhancing equality for persons with disabilities.

B. Section 46(2) of the *Code* requires that, in the event of a conflict between the *Code* and other provincial legislation, the *Code* requirements prevail. Therefore, in some instances, persons responsible for accommodation may be obliged to modify or waive health and safety requirements in order to accommodate a person with a disability.

C. An example of such a situation would be where all individuals on a construction site are required to wear safety boots but an individual's disability necessitates his or her use of special orthopaedic shoes or assistive devices which preclude that individual from wearing safety boots. The obligation of the person responsible for accommodation is first to attempt to provide appropriate safety footwear for the person. If that is not possible, there should be an enquiry into whether some other method of achieving adequate safety for the person's feet can be used. If that, too, fails, then the standard would have to

be modified or waived if the individual is willing to accept the risk.

D. When a situation arises where it appears that a proposed accommodation conflicts with another requirement or law, the person responsible for accommodation should approach the Commission about resolving the issue with the appropriate authorities.

E. The text in Section 4(1) states that the risk created by modifying or waiving the health and safety requirement is to be weighed against the right to equality of the person with a disability. Where the risk is so significant as to outweigh the benefits of equality, it will be considered to create undue hardship. The factors to be considered in weighing the risk are listed below in subsection (2) and will be discussed further there.

F. The phrase ''benefits of enhancing equality'' is intended to include consideration of benefits from the accommodation which may accrue to a person's co-workers, family, friends, fellow students, or the general public by the accommodation being made.

(2) Factors Relevant to Health and Safety Risk

IN DETERMINING WHETHER AN OBLIGATION TO MODIFY OR WAIVE A HEALTH OR SAFETY REQUIREMENT, WHETHER ESTABLISHED BY LAW OR NOT, CREATES A SIGNIFICANT RISK TO ANY PERSON, CONSIDERATION WILL BE GIVEN TO:

(A) THE WILLINGNESS OF A PERSON WITH A DISABILITY TO ASSUME THE RISK IN CIRCUMSTANCES WHERE THE

RISK IS TO HIS OR HER OWN HEALTH OR SAFETY;

(B) WHETHER THE MODIFICATION OR WAIVING OF THE REQUIREMENT IS REASONABLY LIKELY TO RESULT IN A SERIOUS RISK TO THE HEALTH OR SAFETY OF INDIVIDUALS OTHER THAN THE PERSON WITH A DISABILITY;

(C) THE OTHER TYPES OF RISKS WHICH THE PERSON RESPONSIBLE FOR ACCOMMODATION IS ASSUMING WITHIN ITS ENTERPRISE; AND

(D) THE TYPES OF RISKS TOLERATED WITHIN SOCIETY AS A WHOLE, REFLECTED IN LEGISLATED STANDARDS SUCH AS LICENCING STANDARDS, OR IN SIMILAR TYPES OF ENTERPRISES.

THE RISK TO BE ASSUMED UNDER PARAGRAPH (A) AND THE RISK TO BE EVALUATED IN PARAGRAPH (B) IS THE RISK REMAINING AFTER ALL ACCOMMODATIONS HAVE BEEN MADE TO REDUCE THE RISK.

Commentary

G. Where a person responsible for accommodation believes that accommodation of an individual's needs may involve the modification or waiver of a health or safety requirement and that such a modification or waiver could place the individual with a disability at risk, the person responsible for accommodation is obliged to explain the potential risk to the individual with a disability and to allow the person to decide if he or she will assume that risk. This obligation applies only to the situation where the potential risk is to that person's health or safety alone. If the individual with

a disability agrees to take the risk, the person responsible for accommodation cannot refuse to employ, serve, or provide housing or shelter to the individual unless the increased risk results in a quantifiable cost which amounts to undue hardship under section 3 (see page 8).

H. A term of a collective agreement relating to health or safety will not preclude an appropriate remedy under the *Code*. Such a term would be subject to the analysis set out above. If the health or safety requirements has the effect of excluding persons with disabilities, modification or waiver of the health or safety requirement will be necessary unless undue hardship can be demonstrated. Occupational Health and Safety Committees, which include representatives of both management and labour, could be helpful in working out individual accommodations for injured workers.

I. Where modification or waiver of a health or safety requirement is believed to result in a risk to the health or safety of others, it must be determined whether the risk is serious. Subsection (3) gives further guidance in evaluating the seriousness of the risk in this instance.

J. When assessing the seriousness of the risk posed by the obligation to modify or waive a health or safety requirement, consideration must be given to the other types of risks which are assumed within an enterprise. For example, some jobs require considerable physical exertion or stamina, e.g., driving buses, fighting fires, or doing public work. The fitness levels of persons doing these jobs may not be monitored very closely, or at all, after a person has been hired, even though the lack of fitness results in greatly reduced abilities to perform the strenuous tasks involved in the job. Potential employees may be denied employment on the basis of existing disabilities and conditions, yet these same or similar limitations are often developed by existing employees with little or no effect on their ability to satisfactorily perform their duties, and with no impact on their careers.

K. Many sources of risk exist in the workplace, aside from those risks that may result from accommodating an employee with a disability. All employees assume everyday risks that may be inherent in a work site, or in working conditions, or which may be caused by a co-worker's fatigue, temporary inattentiveness, hangover, or stress. Employers have recognized that not all employees are 100% productive every day by providing counselling programs or other means of coping with financial problems, emotional difficulties, or addiction to alcohol or other substances. Risks from these situations are factored into the level of safety that we all accept in our lives every day.

L. A potential risk that is created by accommodation should be assessed in the light of those other, more common, sources of risk in the workplace. An example of this is an employee who has a condition which makes him or her especially susceptible to respiratory illnesses. This employee requests a promotion to a different section of the plant. The employer refuses the promotion on the grounds that the processes involved in that section pose an increased risk to this employee because of his or her disability. Yet the employer permits smoking everywhere on its premises, including the area where the employee is now working.

M. Other types of risks which are present in similar enterprises or in society as a whole should be considered. While maximizing safety is always desirable, as a society we constantly balance the degree of safety to be achieved against competing benefits. For example, we balance the risks of injury in sports against the economic and entertainment benefits. We balance the risks involved in permitting higher speed limits against the benefits of increasing the efficient flow of traffic. We balance the risks involved in driving affordable cars against the costs that would be involved in making them even safer.

N. The seriousness of the risk is to be determined on the assumption that suitable precautions have been taken to reduce the risk. For example, a person's ability to drive a car is to be evaluated when wearing his or her eyeglasses. If an individual with a physical disability has applied for a position as a shipper and has asked for a rolling platform to be provided to allow him or her to safely reach boxes, the risks of the situation are to be considered on the assumption that the platform has been put in place. The ability of a pharmacist with a hearing impairment to take prescription orders over the telephone safely and reliably must be assessed assuming that he or she is using a hearing aid and a hearing aid-compatible telephone.

O. It should be noted that the issue of cost of the accommodation is to be considered separately from the issue of risk.

(3) Seriousness of Risk

IN DETERMINING THE SERIOUSNESS OF RISK, THE FOLLOWING FOUR FACTORS WILL BE CONSIDERED:

(A) THE NATURE OF THE RISK: WHAT COULD HAPPEN THAT WOULD BE HARMFUL?

(B) THE SEVERITY OF THE RISK: HOW SERIOUS WOULD THE HARM BE IF IT OCCURRED?

(C) THE PROBABILITY OF THE RISK: HOW LIKELY IS IT THAT THE POTENTIAL HARM WILL ACTUALLY OCCUR? IS IT A REAL RISK, OR MERELY HYPOTHETICAL OR SPECULATIVE? COULD IT OCCUR FREQUENTLY?

(D) THE SCOPE OF THE RISK: WHO WILL BE AFFECTED BY THE EVENT IF IT OCCURS?

Commentary

Q. The four factors listed will be considered together to determine the seriousness of the risk. If the potential harm is minor and not very likely to occur, the risk should not be considered serious. Where there is a risk to public safety, consideration will be given to the increased numbers of people potentially affected, as part of factor (D), while the likelihood that the harmful event may occur would be considered under paragraph (C).

R. The fact that a person has a disability, in itself, is not sufficient to establish that there is a risk. This raises the issue of the nature and quality of evidence that will be required to prove the nature, severity, probability and scope of the risk. Guidelines regarding evidence generally for proof of undue hardship are given on page 18, under the heading "Demonstrating Undue Hardship". However, additional guidance specific to proof of risk will be provided here.

S. There must be an objective basis for identifying and assessing the risk. Impressionistic evidence will not be acceptable. Objective evidence would include existing scientific information, empirical data, expert opinions (including medical opinions) based on facts and data, and detailed information about the nature of the job, service, or activity to be undertaken by the person with a disability. As well, evidence about the conditions of the job, service or activity, and about the effect of the conditions on the person with a disability or the group of which the person is a member would be considered.

RESPECTING THE DIGNITY OF PERSONS WITH DISABILITIES

5. Phasing In or Reserve Fund

WHERE THE COSTS OR RISKS OF AN ACCOMMODATION WHICH WOULD MOST FULLY RESPECT THE DIGNITY OF THE PERSON WITH A DISABILITY, OR

THE DIGNITY OF THE GROUP OF WHICH THE PERSON IS A MEMBER, WOULD CONSTITUTE UNDUE HARDSHIP IF REQUIRED IMMEDIATELY ACCORDING TO THE STANDARDS IN SECTIONS 3 AND 4, THE ACCOMMODATION WILL BE REQUIRED IF IT CAN BE ACCOM-PLISHED WITHOUT UNDUE HARDSHIP BY SUCH MEANS AS:

(A) PHASING IT IN OVER A REASONA-BLE PERIOD OF TIME, OR

(B) ESTABLISHING A RESERVE FUND INTO WHICH PERIODIC PAYMENTS WOULD BE MADE ACCORDING TO SPECIFIED CONDITIONS, AND OUT OF WHICH PAYMENTS WOULD BE MADE TO ACCOMPLISH THE ACCOMMODA-TION.

Commentary

A. Some accommodations will be very important but will be difficult to accomplish in a short period of time. For example, a small community may be able to show that to make its community centre or transportation system accessible at once would cause undue hardship. Or a small employer may not find it possible to make its entrance and washroom facilities accessible immediately without undue hardship. In these situations, undue hardship may be avoided by phasing in the accessible features gradually, or by establishing a reserve fund to pay for the work.

B. Some accommodations will benefit large numbers of persons with disabilities, yet the cost may prevent them from being accomplished. One approach which may reduce the hardship is to spread the cost over several years by phasing in the accommodation gradually. For example, a commuter railroad might be required to make accessible a certain number of stations per year.

C. Where an accommodation is being phased in over an extended time period, it may still be possible to make interim accommodation for an individual. If both the short-term and long-term accommodation can ultimately be accomplished without undue hardship, both accommodations may be required. This would also apply in the situation where a person responsible for accommodation has adopted, in good faith, a plan for phased-in accommodation.

D. A second method of reducing the impact of the cost of an accommodation is to establish a reserve fund into which payments are to be made by a person responsible for accommodation, under specified conditions. One of the obvious conditions should be that the reserve fund is to be used only to pay for accommodation costs in future. This may be accomplished by requiring that the fund be set up as a trust. Other conditions related to timing, amounts of expenditures, nature of the accommodation, etc., could be included in a settlement agreement or an order of a board of inquiry or court, as appropriate. This would be similar to phasing in an accommodation over a period of time, as it is anticipated that the accommodation would gradually be accomplished by expenditures out of the reserve fund or would eventually be accomplished once enough funds had been set aside.

E. A reserve fund should not be considered as an alternative to a loan where the accommodation could be made immediately and the cost paid back over time. Rather, the reserve fund is to be used in circumstances where it would create undue hardship for the person responsible for accommodation to obtain a loan and accomplish the accommodation immediately. The reserve fund is one of several financing options to be considered in assessing the feasibility of an accommodation. If a reserve fund is to be established, provision should be made in the agreement or order for considering future changes in circumstances.

F. Both phasing in and the establishment of a reserve fund are to be considered only after the person responsible for accommodation has demonstrated that an accommodation could not be accomplished immediately in accordance with Sections 3 and 4. Phasing in is to be preferred to the establishment of a reserve fund wherever possible.

G. There may be circumstances in which risk to health or safety, which results in undue hardship, could be reduced to an acceptable level over time, such as by adding equipment or other safety features to the work site, or changing the job descriptions to accommodate an individual with a disability. Development of a new technology may take some time to make a reduction in risk possible. In principle, therefore, a person responsible for accommodation could be required to phase in an accommodation that would lessen health or safety risk over time.

6. Alternative Means

IF THE ACCOMMODATION WHICH MOST RESPECTS THE DIGNITY OF A PERSON WITH A DISABILITY HAS BEEN FOUND TO CAUSE UNDUE HARDSHIP ACCORDING TO SECTIONS 3, 4, AND 5, ALTERNATIVE MEANS OF ACCOMMODATING THE PERSON'S NEEDS MUST BE CONSIDERED, AND THE ACCOMMODATION WHICH WOULD BE MOST COMPATIBLE WITH RESPECTING THE DIGNITY OF THE PERSON WITH A DISABILITY WITHOUT CAUSING UNDUE HARDSHIP IS TO BE IMPLEMENTED.

Commentary

H. Where it can be demonstrated that the costs or risks of an accommodation which would maximize the individual's dignity would cause undue hardship according to the criteria set out in Sections 3, 4, and 5, it is required that alternatives be considered. These alternatives may fall short of providing maximum dignity, but if the cost or risks of some of them would not cause undue hardship, then that alternative should be chosen which most respects the dignity of the person to be accommodated.

I. Before it is determined that full accommodation, i.e. the accommodation which would maximize dignity, should be abandoned in favour of a less desirable alternative, the options described in Section 5, on page 16, must be considered.

DEMONSTRATING UNDUE HARDSHIP

7. THE ONUS OF PROVING UNDUE HARDSHIP IS ON THE PERSON RESPONSIBLE FOR ACCOMMODATION.

8. A PERSON WHO REQUESTS ACCOMMODATION HAS A RESPONSIBILITY TO COMMUNICATE HIS OR HER NEEDS IN SUFFICIENT DETAIL AND TO CO-OPERATE IN CONSULTATIONS TO ENABLE THE PERSON RESPONSIBLE FOR ACCOMMODATION TO RESPOND TO THE REQUEST.

9. THERE MUST BE OBJECTIVE EVIDENCE FOR DETERMINING FINANCIAL COSTS, EFFECTS OF PROJECTED COSTS ON THE ENTERPRISE RESPONSIBLE FOR ACCOMMODATION, AND FOR DETERMINING THE SERIOUSNESS OF THE HEALTH OR SAFETY RISK, AS DETAILED IN PRECEDING SECTIONS. OBJECTIVE EVIDENCE INCLUDES, BUT IS NOT LIMITED TO, ITEMS SUCH AS FULL FINANCIAL STATEMENTS AND BUDGETS, SCIENTIFIC DATA, INFORMATION AND DATA RESULTING FROM EMPIRICAL STUDIES, EXPERT OPINION, DETAILED INFORMATION ABOUT THE ACTIVITY AND THE REQUESTED ACCOMMODATION, INFORMATION ABOUT THE CONDITIONS SURROUNDING THE ACTIVITY AND THEIR EFFECTS ON THE PERSON WITH A DISABILITY, AND SIMILAR KINDS OF INFORMATION.

Commentary

A. The person who is responsible for making the accommodation is required to prove that the accommodation causes undue hardship within the meaning of the standards set out in Sections 3, 4, 5 and 6. It is not up to the person with a disability to prove that the requested accommodation can be accomplished without undue hardship.

B. However, the person with a disability does have the responsibility to make his or her needs known in order that the person responsible for accommodation may be in a position to properly assess and know how to make the requested accommodation. The person with a disability is obliged to answer questions which are within his or her knowledge and ability to answer with regard to the particular circumstances or equipment required in the specific situation. The person with a disability may not have the technical expertise to determine what accommodation is necessary to meet his or her needs. In that situation, the person responsible for accommodation may have to obtain expert opinions or advice.

C. The guideline is not intended to require the person with a disability to disclose private or confidential matters. For example, if a person needs a flexible schedule in order to accommodate daily psychiatric appointments, he or she should not be required to reveal to his or her supervisor the nature of the appointments as long as acceptable evidence of the need can be provided. It may be possible to have the person submit a medical certificate saying that he or she requires the flexible schedule for medical reasons, without specifying further details. The certificate could be provided to the company's health department rather than directly to the supervisor to further protect confidentiality.

D. The nature of the evidence required to prove undue hardship is objective. The person responsible for accommodation must provide facts, figures, and scientific data or opinion to support its claim that the proposed accommodation causes undue hardship. Impressionistic evidence or arguments based upon stereotypes will not be sufficient. In other words, the Commission will expect more than a plain statement that the cost or risk posed by an accommodation is too high. Objective evidence will have to be provided to support the opinion.

E. Making decisions regarding accommodation will often require special expertise or special knowledge. Individuals with disabilities and persons responsible for accommodation are encouraged to seek assistance when assessing the type of accommodation required and what the costs and risks of such accommodation will be. Assistance may be gained from experts in barrier-free design, job restructuring, adapted work environments, and from groups which are concerned with the accommodation of persons with disabilities, such as the Handicapped Employment Program of the provincial Ministry of Labour, the Barrier Free Design Centre, private practitioners, and other organizations, as well as the Commission.

APPENDIX

Constructive
discrimination

10.—(1) A right of a person under Part I is infringed where a requirement, qualification or factor exists that is not discrimination on a prohibited ground but that results in the exclusion, restriction or preference of a group of persons who are identified by a prohibited ground of discrimination and of whom the person is a member, except where,

(a) the requirement, qualification or factor is reasonable and *bona fide* in the circumstances; or

(b) it is declared in this Act, other than in section 16, that to discriminate because of such ground is not an infringement of a right.

Idem

(2) The Commission, a board of inquiry or a court shall not find that a requirement, qualification or factor is reasonable and *bona fide* in the circumstances unless it is satisfied that the needs of the group of which the person is a member cannot be accommodated without undue hardship on the person responsible for accommodating those needs, considering the cost, outside sources of funding, if any, and health and safety requirements, if any.

Idem

(3) The Commission, a board of inquiry or a court shall consider any standards prescribed by the regulations for assessing what is undue hardship. 1986, c. 64, s. 18(8).

Handicap

16.—(1) A right of a person under this Act is not infringed for the reason only that the person is incapable of performing or fulfilling the essential duties of requirements attending the exercise of the right because of handicap. 1986, c. 64, s. 18(9).

Reasonable
accommodation

(1a) The Commission, a board of inquiry or a court shall not find a person incapable unless it is satisfied that the needs of the person cannot be accommodated without undue hardship on the person responsible for accommodating those needs, considering the cost, outside sources of funding, if any, and health and safety requirements, if any.

Idem

(1b) The Commission, a board of inquiry or a court shall consider any standards prescribed by the regulations for assessing what is undue hardship. 1986, c. 64, s. 18(10).

Powers of
Commission

(2) Where, after the investigation of a complaint, the Commission determines that the evidence does not warrant the appointment of a board of inquiry because of the application of subsection (1), the Commission may nonetheless use its best endeavours to effect a settlement as to the duties or requirements. 1981, c. 53, s. 16(2); 1986, c. 64, s. 18(11).

Special
employment

23.—(1) The right under section 4 to equal treatment with respect to employment is not infringed where,

    (a) a religious, philanthropic, educational, fraternal or social institution or organization that is primarily engaged in serving the interests of persons identified by their race, ancestry, place of origin, colour, ethnic origin, creed, sex, age, marital status or handicap employs only, or gives preference in employment to, persons similarly identified if the qualification is a reasonable and *bona fide* qualification because of the nature of the employment;

    (b) the discrimination in employment is for reasons of age, sex, record of offences or marital status if the age, sex, record of offences or marital status of the applicant is a reasonable and *bona fide* qualification because of the nature of the employment;

    (c) an individual person refuses to employ another for reasons of any prohibited ground of discrimination in section 4, where the primary duty of the employment is attending to the medical or personal needs of the person or of an ill child or an aged, infirm or ill spouse or other relative of the person; or

    (d) an employer grants or withholds employment or advancement in employment to a person who is the spouse, child or parent of the employer or an employee. 1981, c. 53, s. 23.

Reasonable
accommodation

(2) The Commission, a board of inquiry or a court shall not find that a qualification under clause (1)(b) is reasonable and *bona fide* unless it is satisfied that the circumstances of the person cannot be accommodated without undue hardship on the person responsible for accommodating those circumstances considering the cost, outside sources of funding, if any, and health and safety requirements, if any.

Idem

(3) The Commission, a board of inquiry or a court shall consider any standards prescribed by the regulations for assessing what is undue hardship. 1986, c. 64, s. 18(15).

Schedule (x)

EXCEPTIONS TO THE EQUALITY RIGHTS PROVISIONS OF THE ONTARIO HUMAN RIGHTS CODE IN THE WORKPLACE*

Guidelines for the Interpretation and Application of Subsections 23(1) and (2)

1. INTRODUCTION

Section 4 of the Ontario *Human Rights Code (Code)* provides to every person the right to equal treatment with respect to employment without discrimination because of race, ancestry, place of origin, colour, ethnic origin, citizenship, creed, sex, sexual orientation, age, record of offences, marital status, family status or handicap.

Section 23 of the *Code* provides an exception to the rights set out in section 4, in particular circumstances. In some instances, persons can be dealt with differently within an employment situation, because of their age, sex, marital status, etc. without thereby violating the *Code*. It is important to note that section 23 does not provide exceptions on all the grounds referred to in section 4.

While each circumstance must be judged on its own merits, it is the intention that these guidelines will be of assistance in determining whether a particular employment practice or decision which treats individuals or groups differently on the basis of what are usually prohibited grounds is based on a bona fide occupational qualification (BFOQ). **These guidelines are to be applied in a restrictive manner, since exceptions to the *Code's* provisions must be narrowly construed.**

It is important to note that the Commission examines very carefully an employer's claim that its practices involving differential treatment are protected by section 23, to ensure that such claims are well founded.

The provisions of subsections 23(1) and (2) are set out below.

23.—(1) The right under Section 4 to equal treatment with respect to employment is not infringed where,

---

* Ontario Human Rights Commission (Toronto, 1989).

383

(a) a religious, philanthropic, education, fraternal or social institution or organization that is primarily engaged in serving the interests of persons identified by their race, ancestry, place of origin, colour, ethnic origin, creed, sex, age, marital status or handicap employs only, or gives preference in employment to, persons similarly identified if the qualification is a reasonable and bona fide qualification because of the nature of the employment;

(b) the discrimination in employment is for reasons of age, sex, record of offences or marital status if the age, sex, record of offences or marital status of the applicant is a reasonable and bona fide qualification because of the nature of the employment.

(c) an individual person refuses to employ another for reasons of any prohibited ground of discrimination in section 4, where the primary duty of the employment is attending to the medical or personal needs of the person or of an ill child or an aged, infirm or ill spouse or other relative of the person; or

(d) an employer grants or withholds employment or advancement in employment to a person who is the spouse, child or parent of the employer or an employee.

(2) The Commission, a board of inquiry or a court shall not find that a qualification under clause (1)(b) is reasonable and bona fide unless it is satisfied that the circumstances of the person cannot be accommodated without undue hardship on the person responsible for accommodating those circumstances considering the cost, outside sources of funding, if any, and health and safety requirements, if any.

Clause 23(1)(a)

The exceptions provided in clause 23(1)(a) apply only to special interest organizations, i.e. religious, philanthropic, educational, fraternal or social institutions or organizations. They apply only in instances where the exception is reasonable and bona fide because of the nature of the employment. Any employer that does not fall into the category of a special interest organization can be considered only under clause 23(1)(b) (discussed below).

With respect to the types of institutions and organizations to which this subsection applies, it is helpful to consider the dictionary definitions of these terms.

Religious: relating to adherence to a particular system of faith and worship (e.g. a church or religious order).* *

---

* * Oxford English Dictionary.

Philanthropic: relating to an act of practical benevolence (e.g. Ontario Hae-mophiliac Society). This includes many organizations that are registered as charities under the *Income Tax Act.*

Educational: relating to instruction received at school or college as well as more comprehensive training whether it be moral, religious, vocational, intel-lectual or physical (e.g. a Hebrew school.).* * *

Fraternal: relating or belonging to an organization of persons formed for mutual aid or benefit, but not for profit (e.g. a fraternity or sorority).* * *

Social: relating to an interdependent co-operative or to an agreement to co-operate for social benefits (e.g. a cultural club focusing on a particular ethnic group).**

It should be noted that organizations which include, albeit as only a part of their function, a forum in which business or professional contacts are made or enhanced might not be viewed as coming within the exception contained in clause 23(1)(a).

Clause 23(1)(b)

Clause 23(1)(b) allows discrimination on the basis of age, sex, record of offences or marital status in circumstances in which such discriminatory treat-ment is reasonable and bona fide because of the nature of the employment. This exception recognizes that certain workplace circumstances warrant hiring limitations that would otherwise be prohibited under Section 4 of the *Code*. This clause includes a provision requiring the employer to accommodate job applicants who are not members of the preferred group. This requirement is discussed below.

2. DEFINITION OF BONA FIDE OCCUPATIONAL QUALIFICATION

Organizations and institutions seeking a defence under clauses 23(1)(a) or (b) must demonstrate the legitimacy of a discriminatory qualification for employ-ment. It is unlikely, for example, that a Filipino social club could deny employ-ment as a cook to a non-Filipino who was an expert in preparing Filipino cuisine. However, a Hebrew school could restrict the hiring of teachers whose duties involve promulgation of the faith to members of the Jewish faith in order to maintain the essential character of that faith.

---

* * * Black's Law Dictionary.

Clauses 23(1)(a) and (b) apply in circumstances where a specific characteristic is necessary for the satisfactory performance of a job, and, as such, is a bona fide occupational qualification.

The Supreme Court of Canada has provided a clear definition of a "bona fide occupational qualification and requirement" in the case of the *Ontario Human Rights Commission et al v. The Borough of Etobicoke* (1982), 3 C.H.R.R. D/781 (S.C.C.).

The Court stated:

> "To be a bona fide occupational qualification and requirement, a limitation . . . must be imposed honestly, in good faith and in the sincerely held belief that such limitation is imposed in the interests of the adequate performance of the work involved with all reasonable dispatch, safety and economy, and not for ulterior or extraneous reasons aimed at objectives which could defeat the purposes of the Code. In addition, it must be related in an objective sense to the performance of the employment concerned, in that it is reasonably necessary to assure the efficient and economical performance of the job without endangering the employee, his fellow employees and the general public."

Therefore, the employer must sincerely believe that an exclusion is necessary and must demonstrate that a direct relationship exists between a particular requirement and the satisfactory performance of the job.

Since the fundamental purpose of the *Code* is to ensure equality of opportunity for, and equal treatment of all members of society, a defence under section 23 will be valid only in cases where in all the circumstances the job functions require that the successful applicant be a member of the specified group.

3. DUTY OF ACCOMMODATION

In order for a hiring restriction to be found to be reasonable and bona fide, the employer is required to accommodate a job applicant who does not meet the qualifications unless such accommodation would cause undue hardship. This requirement applies only to employers relying on an exception provided under clause 23(1)(b).

An employer who wishes to exclude members of one sex from a position on the ground of public decency, for example, must demonstrate that accommodation of members of the excluded group would cause undue hardship.

Areas in which accommodation can be made include:

(a) Modification of the job or the terms and conditions of employment;

  e.g. where an applicant's record of offences relates to a crime involving theft, the job in question could be modified so as to remove any duties that involve handling money. An example is the position of stock clerk in a supermarket which has involved relieving the cashier from time to time. The responsibility to relieve the cashier could be reassigned to someone else to enable the applicant to be hired.

(b) Adjustments to the work environment.

e.g. closing the men's washroom for a short period to enable a female cleaner to clean the facility.

The responsibility of demonstrating undue hardship rests with the employer which must show that the accommodation would alter the essential nature of or substantially affect the viability of the business. In assessing undue hardship, consideration is given to the cost, any outside sources of funding and any health and safety requirements.

4. **PRACTICES WHICH ARE NOT BASED ON A BONA FIDE OCCUPATIONAL REQUIREMENT:**

The following are a number of instances that may serve as examples of employment practices which are not likely to meet the test set out above. This list is in no way exhaustive, and is supplied only to assist in applying the Commission's policy regarding BFOQ's.

Practices that are unlikely to be based on BFOQ's are those which:

(a) rely upon the ability of members of the excluded groups to perform incidental duties rather than essential components of the job in question;

(b) impose a requirement based on co-worker or customer preference unrelated to capacity to perform the job;

(c) are discriminatory even though they are in a collective agreement;

(d) rely upon stereotypical assumptions in order to determine an individual's capacity to perform the job duties. i.e., no position should be exempted based on physical characteristics attributed to one sex or another, such as relative physical strength or capacity for endurance.

(e) require that the job be performed only in a certain way where reasonable alternative ways may exist.

(f) involve the types of role-modelling where the particular application of role-modelling theory is based on traditional or stereotypical conceptions of the appropriate roles of males and females, and where the role-modelling has the effect of reinforcing such stereotypes among the clientele.

5. Clause 23(1)(a)

EXAMPLES OF BONA FIDE OCCUPATIONAL REQUIREMENTS

As mentioned above, distinctions made under clause 23(1)(a) are only available to those organizations which fall within the categories cited and which are engaged in serving the interests of persons who are similarly identified.

Each case is assessed on its individual merits. The following examples of how the exception provisions are interpreted by the Commission are illustrative only.

(a) Race, Ancestry, Place of Origin, Colour, Ethnic Origin

It could be reasonable for a cultural and community centre serving members of a racial or ethnic group to hire a person who shares the same characteristics of race, ancestry, place of origin, colour or ethnic origin as the clientele to develop and implement programs designed to promote and foster cultural retention among its members.

(b) Creed

Inculcation of the faith in students is often an important duty of teachers in religious schools. Where promotion of a particular faith is central to a teachers' function, it may be reasonable to require that any incumbent be a member of and practice that faith.

However, where an employee's essential duties do not involve teaching or counselling, it is difficult to justify a requirement that he or she be a member of a particular religion.

(c) Sex

Sex may be a BFOQ in certain types of employment such as a counsellor in a rape crisis centre, where sex-role identification is a necessary component of treatment and recovery.

(d) Age

It may be legitimate to limit hiring to older persons where the duties involve the counselling of retirees who are members of a senior citizens' social club.

(e) Handicap

To prefer a blind applicant for the position of senior executive of an organization serving the blind may be legitimate in order to enhance group identification and role-modelling for the clientele.

6. Clause 23(1)(b)
EXAMPLES OF BONA FIDE OCCUPATIONAL REQUIREMENTS

(a) Age

It may be legitimate to recruit young persons for the position of counsellor in a facility serving a clientele of homeless youths.

(b) Sex

There may be instances in which the demands of public decency or the need for sex-role identification will be sufficiently compelling to warrant an exception. Examples are nurses' aides or orderlies providing intimate personal care for chronically ill persons who request same-sex care and female counsellors in shelters for battered women.

(c) Record of Offences

Public safety considerations may allow an employer to exclude individuals with a serious record of offences under the *Highway Traffic Act* from employment as bus drivers.

Whether "record of offences" is a bona fide occupational qualification will depend on a variety of factors including job duties; the length of time since the individual's conviction; the nature of the offences; what he or she has been doing since the offence was committed; and whether rehabilitation was undertaken and was successful.

Clause 23(1)(c)

This exception applies in those limited circumstances involving the hiring of a person who will provide personal and medical care to the employer or to members of the employer's immediate family. While the employee may perform other duties, personal or medical care must be the primary function. For example, it would be acceptable to hire a same-sex practical nurse to tend a sick spouse.

Clause 23(1)(d)

This provision enables an employer to establish either a nepotism or an anti-nepotism policy with respect to the hiring or promotion of employees. (Nepotism refers to a policy of preferential treatment for the spouses, children and parents of existing employees; an anti-nepotism policy prohibits the hiring of such relatives.) It is important to note that this exception does not allow for the dismissal of employees once they are hired, and that it also refers to advancement in employment.

Moreover, the range of the section is narrow, applying only to spouses, parents or children of the employer or employee. For example, an employer setting an anti-nepotism policy could prohibit the hiring of an employee's spouse. An example of a nepotism policy is an employer's policy to give preference in summer employment to the children of employees.

Please note

These guidelines contain the Commission's interpretation of section 23 of the *Code*. They are subject to interpretation by boards of inquiry and the courts, and should be read in conjunction with the specific provisions of the *Code*. Any questions about BFOQs that employers may have should be directed to their legal counsel or to the staff of the Ontario Human Rights Commission.

GUIDELINES ON SPECIAL PROGRAMS*

PREAMBLE

As the Commission's enforcement initiatives focus increasingly on systemic discrimination and special program remedies, employers, landlords and service providers may choose to proactively adopt measures to address systemic barriers which may exist within their operations. To assist them in these efforts to promote greater equality, the Commission has developed the following Guidelines on Special Programs.

INTRODUCTION

Ontario is a society of ever-expanding diversity, composed of women and men of different racial and ethnic origins, cultures, religious beliefs, abilities and a host of other differences.

In our province it is, therefore, imperative that we value all people in their diversity and ensure that each person has the opportunity to fully participate in our society. It is only in this way that we can create an environment of true equality.

The *Human Rights Code, 1981,* reflects Ontario's commitment to equality for all members of society. Historically, the concept of equality has been interpreted to mean that all persons should receive the same or similar treatment. Over time, however, we have come to recognize that the provision of the same or similar treatment to all persons or groups does not always yield an equal result or equality in its fullest sense. The notion of similar treatment ignores diversity and the special needs of disadvantaged groups.

Often the hardship or economic disadvantage experienced by particular groups can be remedied only through the provision of treatment that is responsive to the particular needs of that group. Programs which incorporate such treatment are referred to in the *Code* as "special programs". Such programs have also been called "affirmative action" programs or "equity" programs (e.g. employment equity, service equity). These guidelines are intended to encourage the adoption of special programs by clarifying the scope and application of section 13, the role of the Commission with respect to special programs and general criteria for assessing a pro-

---

* Ontario Human Rights Commission (Toronto, 1991).

posed special program. The groups for whom these programs are developed are generally referred to as "target" or "designated" groups. In this document, we will refer to these groups as "designated" groups.

Section 13 of the *Code* expressly allows for the adoption of special programs which are designed to relieve hardship or economic disadvantage; to achieve or attempt to achieve equal opportunity. Section 13 also allows for special programs that are likely to contribute to eliminating the infringement of rights of those who experience discrimination.

For example, when an employer imposes a strict height requirement for everyone who enters employment, the result can be fewer women and members of certain minority groups entering the organization because, on average, they are shorter than the applied standard. This results in a form of discrimination referred to in the *Code* as "constructive" discrimination. Constructive discrimination may result in restricted access to, or complete exclusion from, equality of opportunity or equality of result.

Some groups have experienced longstanding, direct and intentional discrimination which has created formidable and continuing disadvantage. An organization with a history of failing to hire racial minorities may experience difficulty in recruiting members of this group despite an existing policy to invest the same effort in their recruitment as the recruitment of other groups. Such factors as persistent negative attitudes held by existing employees towards racial minority employees, and the perception on the part of prospective racial minority candidates that the work environment is hostile to them, will serve to hinder the company's attempts to remedy under-representation of this group in its workforce.

When one or both of these forms of discrimination pervades a system such as an employment or service delivery system, "systemic discrimination" may be said to exist. Where systemic discrimination has occurred or continues to occur, efforts to provide the same or similar treatment to members of a particular group may not result in equality for that group. In the interests of true equality different forms of treatment may be required.

For this reason, a special program may also be considered the appropriate remedy to a complaint of systemic discrimination. Special programs may, therefore, be recommended by Commission staff and form part of the settlements in such cases. Moreover, boards of inquiry under the *Human Rights Code, 1981*, may order a special program as the remedy to a finding of discrimination.

In addition, section 28(c) gives the Ontario Human Rights Commission an active mandate to facilitate and encourage the implementation of special programs that comply with section 13. The Commission, therefore, supports and encourages service providers, landlords, contractors, employers and trade unions or vocational associations to voluntarily adopt special programs.

HOW THE CODE DEFINES A SPECIAL PROGRAM

Section 13(1) of the *Code* defines a special program as a program which is:

1) designed to relieve hardship or economic disadvantage;
2) designed to assist disadvantaged persons or groups to achieve or attempt to achieve equal opportunity; or
3) likely to contribute to the elimination of the infringement of rights under Part I of the *Code.*

Section 13, therefore, recognizes the necessity and legitimacy of programs which take proactive steps to eliminate both the causes and results of disadvantage, regardless of how this disadvantage has arisen. As well, section 13(1) expressly states that equality rights under Part I of the *Code* are not infringed by the implementation of a special program. In light of this provision, the common objection to special programs as "reverse discrimination" is not supported by the *Code.*

STANDARDS FOR SPECIAL PROGRAMS

This section describes the standards for special programs and how they will be applied by the Commission in reviewing special programs. The ideal special program conforms to all of these standards.

Commission staff will apply these standards when constructing settlements involving special program remedies. The Commission will also consider these standards when conducting inquiries into special programs pursuant to section 13(2) of the *Code* (see the following Section entitled "The Commission's Authority to Inquiry Into Special Programs"), and when reviewing for approval those settlements which include special program remedies.

The more closely a program approximates the standards articulated in these guidelines, the more likely the program provider will have a successful section 13(1) defense to a complaint against that program. However, the Commission recognizes that not all special programs will meet these standards. In such circumstances, the Commission will be flexible in determining whether a program constitutes a special program that would be protected by section 13(1). Each case coming before the Commission will be considered on its own merits. The following standards should be considered when implementing a special program. A special program should:

1. Be designed to assist disadvantaged persons or groups

A special program should be designed to assist disadvantaged persons or groups with respect to employment, accommodation, contracts, membership in unions or vocational associations, the provision of services, goods and facilities or some other sphere of activity.

Examples of such assistance could include the provision of special training opportunities, job coaching or mentor programs for designated group members. Targeting non-traditional jobs or training positions for designated group members may also constitute examples of assistive treatment within a special program.

2. Identify Designated Group(s)

The program should clearly define the designated persons or groups that it purports to assist.

The designated groups may include (but are not limited to) persons or groups identified by a prohibited ground of discrimination under the *Code* (race, ancestry, place of origin, colour, ethnic origin, citizenship, creed, sex, sexual orientation, age, marital status, family status, handicap, record of offences or receipt of public assistance).

Note: **Advertising** opportunities for which members of these designated groups will be given preference or exclusive consideration may be an important facet of a special program. While section 22(1) of the *Code* prohibits employment-related advertisements which directly or indirectly classify persons by their membership in specific protected groups, such advertisements are permitted by the Commission in the context of legitimate special programs directed at members of these groups.

3. Provide a Rationale

The program should be based on clearly articulated reasons why the designated groups are considered to be experiencing hardship or disadvantage, and explain how the proposed measures will relieve this hardship or disadvantage. Evidence of hardship or disadvantage should be objective and where possible, quantifiable, as opposed to impressionistic in nature. For example, in order to show disadvantage in the form of under-representation of a designated group, statistics may be necessary.

Note: **Date collection** documenting the type and extent of disadvantage experienced by designated group members will often form the foundation for establishing the need for a special program. Ongoing data collection will also provide a means of assessing the results of program initiatives and a tool with which to assess the need for further special measures.

In employment equity programs, internal work force data and applicant data may be collected and compared with external data on designated group availability in order to demonstrate underutilization of particular groups.

In instances where requesting information concerning protected grounds may otherwise constitute a violation of the *Code*, such data collection is clearly permitted in the context of a legitimate special program.

Program providers are encouraged to clearly inform participants in a special program of the purpose for which this information will be used. If participants are confident that this data will be utilized for special program objectives only, they are more likely to be comfortable in providing the requested information.

The *Code* does not specify any requirements with respect to the structure or format that such data collection should take. There are three standard formats for identifying the representation of designated group members within, or served by, an organization: self-identification surveys, identification by a designate of the organization, and identification by a designate of the organization with confirmation by each identified person. Each method presents its own advantages and disadvantages with respect to associated cost to the organization, rate of return, accuracy of result and preservation of the privacy of the individual. The decision as to which format a particular organization chooses should be made with a view to selecting the method that best suits the program goals and organizational culture.

The privacy and dignity of the individual should be of major concern in the collection of data. Those organizations which are subject to freedom of information and privacy legislation may wish to ensure that the identification method they chose complies with section 41 of the *Freedom of Information and Privacy Act.* Organizations that are not subject to privacy legislation should also attempt to collect data in a manner that respects the dignity and privacy of each individual.

Organizations subject to data collection requirements of contract compliance programs should note that these requirements are not in conflict with the *Code.*

It should also be noted that data collected in the context of a special program must be used for special program purposes only. For this reason, storage and access of data should be carefully controlled.

4. Follow a Plan

The program provider should prepare a plan outlining how the special program will be implemented, including terms and conditions of the program; duration of the program; special measures to be implemented; and goals, timetables and anticipated results. Goals, timetables and anticipated results should be expressed in objective and, where possible, quantifiable terms in order to demonstrate how the program is designed to address the existing hardship or economic disadvantage of the designated group or persons. Additionally, accountability for program results should be specified at the appropriate levels within the organization. If for example, the plan includes goals and objectives regarding hiring, and hiring is the responsibility of line managers, those managers should be made accountable within the plan to meet hiring objectives.

5. Include a Monitoring and Evaluation Mechanism

The program should include a mechanism to monitor and evaluate the progress towards the desired results.

Such a mechanism is important to evaluate the effectiveness of the program, to facilitate accountability within the organization and to communicate program results to the organization and/or its client groups.

Tracking of applicants through the system and data collection concerning the changing composition of client groups are examples of ongoing data collection which may be necessary components of such a mechanism. As in the case of data collection for the purpose of targeting designated groups, data collection for monitoring and evaluation purposes is also permitted by the *Code* in the context of a legitimate special program.

6. Include Consultation
Appropriate steps should be taken prior to implementation to identify and consult with all persons and groups who may be affected by the proposed special program, including labour unions or employee associations, tenant associations, service-users and designated group members themselves, or their representatives.

THE COMMISSION'S AUTHORITY TO INQUIRE INTO SPECIAL PROGRAMS

Section 13(2) authorizes the Commission to inquire into a special program upon its own initiative or upon an application of a person seeking to implement a special program under the protection of section 13(1). In either case, the Commission may inquire into the program to ensure that the program satisfies the requirements of section 13 of the *Code* (as set out in the above section "Standards for Special Programs").

Special programs are not immune to complaints of discrimination. Upon a complaint with respect to a proposed special program, the Commission may also inquire into that program to determine whether it qualifies as a special program pursuant to section 13 of the *Code*.

COMMISSION ORDERS IN RESPECT OF SPECIAL PROGRAMS

Following inquiry into a special program, the Commission may, at its discretion, declare by order that:

1) the special program does not satisfy the requirements of section 13(1); or

2) the special program, with or without modifications, satisfies the requirements of section 13(1).

No person is obliged to seek an order from the Commission prior to implementing a special program, nor is the Commission obligated to issue an order in response to an application. In fact, the Commission encourages service providers, landlords, contractors, employers and trade unions or vocational associations to review their own operations in light of these guidelines, with a view to voluntarily undertaking initiatives aimed at promoting greater equality in our society.

The circumstances in which the Commission will consider a request to issue an order respecting a special program are generally limited to situations where the parties involved are in dispute about whether the special program complies with section 13, and the dispute cannot be resolved in any other way.

COMPLAINTS OF DISCRIMINATION IN THE ABSENCE OF A PRIOR ORDER

Where there is no prior order from the Commission declaring that a particular program does **not** satisfy the requirements of section 13(1), the program provider may invoke section 13(1) as a defence to a complaint of discrimination involving that program. If the Commission concludes after investigating the matter that the special program does, in fact, constitute a special program with or without modifications as defined in section 13(1), it may so declare by order, and/or decide not to request the appointment of a board of inquiry, pursuant to section 35(2).

If, however, the Commission determines that the special program does not meet the requirements of section 13(1), the Commission has the authority under section 13(2)(d) to order that the program does not qualify as a special program and/or request the

appointment of a board of inquiry under section 35(1) to determine whether a right has been infringed.

Again, it should be noted that orders made by the Commission are entirely discretionary. The Commission may, for example, decide to send a complaint to a board of inquiry without having issued an order in respect of that program.

COMPLAINTS OF DISCRIMINATION WHERE A PRIOR ORDER EXISTS

An order of the Commission declaring that a special program satisfies the requirements of section 13(1) does not preclude the filing of a complaint of discrimination. However, such an order issued pursuant to section 13(2)(e) provides a defence to the complaint, as long as the terms and conditions of the order are satisfied.

On the other hand, an order of the Commission pursuant to section 13(2)(d) declaring that a special program does **not** satisfy the requirements of section 13(1), deprives the program provider of the opportunity to invoke a section 13(1) defence to a complaint at a board of inquiry.

SPECIAL PROGRAMS IMPLEMENTED BY THE CROWN

In accordance with section 13(5) of the *Code*, the Commission has no authority to inquire into a special program implemented by the Ontario Government or by an Ontario Government agency **for the purpose of issuing orders under section 13(2)**. However, the Crown programs must comply with the provisions of section 13(1) and are not immune to individual or Commission-initiated complaints of discrimination. Such complaints would be handled in accordance with regular complaint procedures.

In deciding whether to request the appointment of a board of inquiry in respect of a complaint concerning a special program of the government or a government agency, the Commission will assess the alleged special program in accordance with the criteria set out above. Should the complaint proceed to a board of inquiry, the board has the authority to make a decision as to whether the program constitutes a special program consistent with section 13(1).

APPLICATIONS FOR AN ORDER IN RESPECT OF A SPECIAL PROGRAM

Applications for orders in respect of special programs should be submitted to the Director, Systemic Investigation, of the Ontario Human Rights Commission. Applications should indicate:

1) the reason(s) an order is being sought, relative to these guidelines, and

2) how the program in question meets the standards set out in these guidelines, (or how it does not meet these standards, in instances where the applicant is requesting an order pursuant to section 13(2)(d) that declares the program does not satisfy the requirements of section 13(1)).

RECONSIDERATION OF AN ORDER

Any person who is aggrieved by the making of an order pursuant to subsection 13(2), is entitled to ask the Commission to reconsider its order.

Inquiries regarding these guidelines may be directed to:

Systemic Investigation Unit
Ontario Human Rights Commission
400 University, 11th floor
Toronto, Ontario
M7A 2R9

EXTRACT FROM HUMAN RIGHTS CODE (1981)

SECTION 13

(1) A right under Part I is not infringed by the implementation of a special program designed to relieve hardship or economic disadvantage or to assist disadvantaged persons or groups to achieve or attempt to achieve equal opportunity or that is likely to contribute to the elimination of

the infringement of rights under Part I.

(2) The Commission may,

    (a) upon its own initiative;

    (b) upon application by a person seeking to implement a special program under the protection of subsection (1); or

    (c) upon a complaint in respect of which the protection of subsection (1) is claimed

inquire into the special program and, in the discretion of the Commission, may by order declare,

    (d) that the special program, as defined in the order, does not satisfy the requirements of subsection (1); or

    (e) that the special program as defined in the order, which such modifications, if any, as the Commission considers advisable, satisfied the requirements of subsection (1).

(3) A person aggrieved by the making of an order under subsection (2) may request the Commission to reconsider its order and section 36, with necessary modifications, applies.

(4) Subsection (1) does not apply to a special program where an order is made under clause (2)(d) or where an order is made under clause (2)(e) with modifications of the special program that are not implemented.

(5) Subsection (2) does not apply to a special program implemented by the Crown or an agency of the Crown. 1981, c. 53, s. 13.

Schedule (xii)

POLICY STATEMENT ON DRUGS AND ALCOHOL TESTING*

DRUG OR ALCOHOL DEPENDENCY AS A DISABILITY

Subsection 4.—(1) of the Ontario *Human Rights Code* (the *Code*) prohibits discrimination in employment on several grounds including "handicap".

The *Code* adopts an expansive definition of the term "handicap". Included are numerous physical and mental disabilities. The following examples represent ways in which the use of legal and illicit drugs or alcohol may fall within the *Code's* definition of "handicap":

1. Where an individual's use of drugs or alcohol has reached the stage that it constitutes an addiction or dependency.

2. Where an individual is perceived as having an addiction or dependency due to drug or alcohol use.

   Such a perception could be held by an employer without in fact being true. For example, an employer may interpret a positive test of a casual drug user to mean that the individual has a drug addiction or dependency. If the employer were to take action as a result of this inaccurate perception, the individual's right to equal treatment under the *Code* may have been infringed.

TESTING FOR DRUG AND ALCOHOL USE AS PART OF AN EMPLOYMENT-RELATED MEDICAL EXAMINATION

Since the testing for alcohol or drug use would constitute a medical examination, the Commission's policy on *Employment-Related Medical Information*** would be applicable. The main features of that policy are as follows:

1. Employment-related medical examinations or inquiries, conducted as part of the applicant screening process, are prohibited under subsection 22.–(2) of the *Code*.

2. Medical examinations should only be administered after a conditional offer of employment has been made, preferably in writing.

---

* Ontario Human Rights Commission (Toronto, 1991).
** A copy of the Ontario Human Rights Commission Policy on *Employee-Related Medical Information* is available through any of the Commission offices.

401

3. Any employment-related medical examinations or inquiries are to be limited to determining the individual's ability to perform the essential duties of a job. If the applicant or employee requires accommodation in order to enable him or her to perform the essential duties, the employer is required to provide such accommodation unless to do so would cause undue hardship.

It is essential that drug testing, when performed, be done by qualified professionals and the results be analyzed in a competent laboratory. Further, it is the responsibility of the employer to ensure that the samples taken are properly labelled and protected at all times.

In order to protect the confidentiality of testing results, all health assessment information should remain exclusively with the examining physician and away from the worker's personnel file.

Procedures also should be instituted for the physician to review the testing results with the employee concerned.

If workers will be required to undergo drug and alcohol testing during the course of their employment — on the grounds that such testing, at the time that it is administered, would indicate actual impairment of ability to perform or fulfil the essential duties or requirements of the job, as opposed to merely detecting the presence of substances in the system — the employer should notify them of this requirement at the beginning of their employment.

In order to discern the necessity for testing, the following questions should be considered by employers, where applicable:

1. Is there an objective basis for believing that job performance would be adversely affected by the disability of drug or alcohol dependency?

2. In respect of a specific employee, is there an objective basis for believing that unscheduled or recurring absences from work or habitual lateness to work are related to alcoholism or drug addiction/dependency?

3. Is there an objective basis to believe that the degree, nature, scope and probability of risk caused by this addiction or dependency will adversely affect the safety of co-workers or members of the public?

DUTY TO ACCOMMODATE

Although the emphasis in the *Human Rights Code* is on ensuring that persons with disabilities are not treated in a discriminatory manner because of their disability, it is recognized that in some circumstances the nature and/or degree of a person's disability may preclude that individual from performing the essential duties of a job. Consequently, subsection 16.–(1) states that the right to equal treatment in respect of employment is not infringed where an individual is treated differently because he or she is incapable of performing or fulfilling the essential duties of the position because of handicap.

Subsection 16.–(1a) provides, however , that such a worker shall not be found incapable of performing the essential duties of a job unless it can be demonstrated that no appropriate accommodation exists, or that it would cause undue hardship to accommodate the worker's needs, taking into account the cost of the accommodation and health and safety concerns.*

This means that if a worker's drug or alcohol addiction/dependency is interfering with that worker's ability to perform the essential duties of the job, the employer must provide the supports necessary to enable that worker to undertake a rehabilitation program unless he or she can show that such accommodation is not possible, e.g. the worker is refusing to undertake such treatment. The employer will also be relieved of the duty to accommodate the needs of the alcohol or drug addicted/dependent worker if the employer can show either that:

— the cost of the accommodation would affect the essence of viability of the enterprises or,

— notwithstanding accommodation efforts, health or safety risks to other workers or members of the public are still of such a serious degree that they outweigh the benefits of providing equal treatment to the worker with an addiction or dependency.

When considering how best to address the needs of workers with a drug or alcohol addiction/dependency, employers are encouraged to consider the establishment of an employee assistance program. Such a program can assist not only individuals with a drug or alcohol addiction/dependency, but can also help workers deal with the stresses which may lead to such an addiction or dependency.

These Guidelines contain the Commission's interpretation of the *Code* provisions as they related to testing for drug and alcohol use. They are subject to interpretation by boards of inquiry and the courts, and should be read in conjunction with the specific provisions of the *Code*. Any questions regarding this policy or the *Code* generally should be directed to staff of the Ontario Human Rights Commission.

---

* Please refer to the Commission's *Guidelines for Assessing Accommodation Requirements for persons with Disabilities* for a detailed explanation of these standards. A copy of the guidelines is available through any of the Commission offices.

Index

ACCOMMODATION. *See* DUTY TO ACCOMMODATE

ADVERTISING
Canadian Human Rights Act provisions, 45
discrimination grounds, 43
Ontario Human Rights Code provisions, 43-5

AFFIRMATIVE ACTION
Canadian Human Rights Act provisions, 38
criticisms of, 40
employment equity and, 246
importance of, 39
Ontario Human Rights Code provisions, 37

AGE DISCRIMINATION
coerced early retirement, 88-90
mandatory retirement —
    bona fide occupational requirement exception, 85
    Charter consideration, 83
    historical development of, 83
    statutory provisions re, 82
    written vs. unwritten policy re, 86
maximum hiring age —
    age stereotyping, 87
    U.S. case, 86

AIDS DISCRIMINATION. *See* HIV-AIDS

ANCESTRY DISCRIMINATION
definition of ancestry, 73-4
English language proficiency requirement as, 75
ethnic group, definition of, 74
height and weight requirements, 74-5
place of origin, definition of, 74

FAMILY STATUS DISCRIMINATION — *continued*
Ontario Human Rights Code definition, 95
sexual orientation vs., 94

HEARING
appeals —
    Canadian Human Rights Act, under, 222
    Ontario Human Rights Code, under, 221
decision, time limitation on rendering, 220
delay, motions to dismiss for —
    Charter arguments, 205-6
    prejudice due to unavailabilty of witnesses,
    207-8
    unreasonable delay, meaning of, 206
evidence, rules of —
    circumstantial evidence, 217
    hearsay evidence, 216
    similar fact evidence, 218-19
    statistical evidence, 217
    Statutory Powers Procedure Act provisions, 215-16
judicial review, 223
onus and burden of proof —
    basic principles re, 213
    "shifting burdens" concept, 214
open/closed hearing
    Canadian Human Rights Act, under, 220
    Ontario Human Rights Code, under, 219
pre-hearing disclosure —
    expanded principles of, 211
    Statutory Powers Procedure Act provisions re, 210-11
    traditional principles of, 212
procedural rules, 212-13
tribunal composition —
    Canadian Human Rights Act, under, 203-4
    Ontario Human Rights Code, under, 203
unbiased tribunal requirement, 208-210

HEIGHT AND WEIGHT REQUIREMENTS, 74-5

HIRING AGE, MAXIMUM. *See* AGE DISCRIMINATION

HIRING POLICIES
C.N.R. case, 54